D1561740

The
MEN *and the* VISION *of the*
SOUTHERN
COMMERCIAL
CONVENTIONS, *1845–1871*

The MEN and the VISION of the SOUTHERN COMMERCIAL CONVENTIONS, 1845–1871

VICKI
VAUGHN
JOHNSON

UNIVERSITY OF MISSOURI PRESS
COLUMBIA AND LONDON

Copyright © 1992 by
The Curators of the University of Missouri
University of Missouri Press, Columbia, Missouri 65201
Printed and bound in the United States of America
All rights reserved
5   4   3   2   1   96   95   94   93   92

Library of Congress Cataloging-in-Publication Data

Johnson, Vicki Vaughn, 1948–
    The men and the vision of the southern commercial conventions,
    1845–1871 / Vicki Vaughn Johnson.
        p.   cm.
    Based on the author's dissertation.
    Includes bibliographical references and index.
    ISBN 0–8262–0855–X (alk. paper)
    1. Southern States—Commerce—History—19th century. 2. Southern
Commercial Convention—History. I. Title.
HF3153.J57   1992
338.975'006—dc20   92–26398
                                                                              CIP

∞™ This paper meets the requirements of the
American National Standard for Permanence of Paper
for Printed Library Materials, Z39.48, 1984.

Designer: Rhonda Miller
Typesetter: Connell-Zeko Type & Graphics
Printer and Binder: Thomson-Shore, Inc.
Typeface: Goudy Old Style

To David

CONTENTS

ACKNOWLEDGMENTS

There are many individuals and institutions whose assistance made this book possible. I thank the staffs at the Southern Historical Collection at Chapel Hill, the Perkins Library at Duke University, the North Carolina Department of Archives and History at Raleigh, and the Manuscript Division of the Library of Congress for their assistance. Elaine C. Everly of the Military Archives Division, National Archives and Records Service, was kind enough to arrange for photocopies of manuscripts from the Amnesty Papers, and the history department of the University of Missouri at Columbia generously provided scholarship funds to defray the expense. I am grateful to Ralph A. Wooster for allowing me access to his records at Beaumont, Texas, on southern officeholders. Others shared data on individuals involved in the convention movement that had been compiled as part of their own work: William McKinley Cash, Frank Mitchell Lowrey, Johanna Nicol Shields, and David N. Young. The late Lewis Atherton guided me in evaluating the ranking order of public offices in the nineteenth-century South. Mark J. Cedeck, Curator of the John W. Barriger III National Railroad Library at the St. Louis Mercantile Library Association, led me to information and sources on nineteenth-century railroad enterprise in the Southwest. Ronald Jackson of the Collection Management Division, Library of Congress, assisted in locating and making available to me critical materials needed for this study. Libraries across the country assisted in locating records of the convention proceedings.

My thanks go to those colleagues who read this manuscript as it evolved, from whose comments and suggestions this study profited. Noble E. Cunningham, Jr., served as second reader when the work began as a dissertation and helped me see what it might eventually become. Harold D. Woodman read a chapter of the manuscript, and his comments led me to new considerations of the issue of continuity in the South. David Roediger heroically read the entire manuscript, and his suggestions were always interesting and much appreciated. I am grateful as well to the careful reading by those designated by the University of Missouri Press, and their suggestions led to what I hope they will see as improvements. Beverly Jarrett of the University of Missouri Press provided encouragement for me and gave the project personal attention and considerable effort. My editors, Jane Lago and Tim Fox, were exceedingly patient with me, and their guidance was most useful and welcome. Most of all, this book could not have been completed were it not for the willingness of Thomas B. Alexander to assist. As my longtime teacher and friend, he guided me in producing the dissertation that formed the basis of the work, and he worked with me once again in the preparation of the book manuscript. Deliberating with me too many hours to count, reading each chapter, he challenged me every step of the way, kept me excited about the project, and taught me history. Whatever errors this book contains are mine alone, but Tom Alexander is in large part responsible for whatever value this book has for its readers.

I owe special thanks to my circle of family and close friends for their support throughout the years of this project. Elise Pritchett Alexander, a very special friend, graciously shared her time and her home with me again and again, and she adopted me in her heart into her family. My sisters and my mother and stepfather remained enthusiastic, and my daughter, Jennifer Louise Johnson, was willing to adapt the life of a busy teenager to the schedule of a determined writer. My husband, David B. Johnson, encouraged me to commit to writing the book, read the many drafts of each chapter, and kept me believing that what I was engaged in was worthwhile.

The
MEN *and the* VISION *of the*
SOUTHERN
COMMERCIAL
CONVENTIONS, *1845–1871*

INTRODUCTION

The years between 1845 and 1871 taxed the strength of the American nation. Sectional disputes escalated into hostilities and then devastating warfare. The resulting peace brought its own tensions as leaders North and South sought a workable solution to the challenge of reconstituting the Union. Major changes took place and moved the nation into a world different in profound ways from that which had existed before Fort Sumter, before Antietam, and before Appomattox. The institution of slavery was banished from American soil, the horrors of bloodletting within the national family left a trail of bitterness and despair, and the federal government successfully flexed its power beyond limits established by decades of compromises. As the loser in the contest, the South could no longer presume the right to shape its society on its own terms. Southerners who had envisioned expanding prosperity during the flush years of the 1850s faced a very different reality in 1865. Agriculturalists whose wealth had been created by a slave society found themselves grappling with challenges in an economic arena that had substantially more in common with the antebellum North than with the Old South. Yet, other conditions remained unchanged. King Cotton had not been dethroned, there was no rush on the part of native southern whites to revolutionize the social underpinnings of their region, and many of the same men who played leadership roles in antebellum society found themselves sought after once again to guide the South in whatever the future held in store.

This book focuses on a group of southern men of this era who shared much in common. Most were middle-aged during the tumultuous twenty-six years between 1845 and 1871, and many attained a fair measure of material success in their personal lives and were honored with distinction in their public lives. They had similar backgrounds in training and religion, and they interacted with each other on many levels and in many contexts. For their society and time, their pattern of activities and achievements might serve to define a Southern Elite. These men chose to be members of the commercial convention movement, in which forum they outlined shared hopes and dreams for the South. It is that membership that determined their inclusion in this collective biography.

The commercial convention movement provided a touchstone of continuity within an era of profound change. As it evolved from small meetings intent on expanding levels of direct trade between the South and Europe into large assemblies that delved into most aspects of southern economic life, the movement constituted a southwide regional assembly of unmatched size and endurance. Originating in Direct Trade Conventions, held between 1837 and 1839 on the Atlantic seaboard, the convention movement spread during the 1840s to the western borders of the South with a series of conventions in support of improved internal transportation facilities. By 1852 the meetings had developed into a formal organization, the Southern Commercial Convention, which met annually until 1859, visiting nine of the South's cities and towns in eight different states and crisscrossing the region from Baltimore to New Orleans and from Savannah to Memphis. Its forums addressed a wide range of economic issues, in addition to voicing growing unrest at perceived sectional threats. After the defeat of the Confederacy, organizers reassembled the convention movement between 1869 and 1871 in an effort to pull the South out of its postwar economic plight. Sessions met chiefly in border-South cities and even ventured across the border once at Cincinnati. In all, beginning with the earliest Direct Trade Conventions and ending with the last convention in 1871, there were twenty-two separate sessions, involving thousands of delegates. In this book I examine the sixteen major sessions held between 1845 and 1871, as they were the meetings most regional in representativeness and most extensive in terms of subject matter discussed.

The history of this institution presents a rare vantage point from which to observe change and constancy in the lives and thoughts of those whose world spanned the transition from slave South to reconstructed South. The convention movement provided leaders with a nonpartisan arena, and yet it was an arena very public and well covered by regional and national press. In fact, the conventions were one of the few places for leaders from all southern states to meet together, on the public record, outside of the halls of Congress. The publicity of the conventions worked to the advantage of disunionists on the eve of the war, and to the advantage of reconcilers after the war. Before the Civil War the convention institution, speaking largely through the press, served to air southern voices to both fellow southerners and to the North. After the war, when the conventions included delegates from northern as well as southern states, they enabled men of influence from both sections to meet each other face-to-face and to openly discuss their future together.

The focus of my study is both the convention debates and the 5,716 southerners who attended the sessions. I present a quantitatively measured collective biography of the participants and a biography within that biography of the movement's activists. As southern collective biographies go, this is one of the largest groups ever studied. Furthermore, it is one of the few groups under study whose association bridged from the prewar into the postwar era.[1] The historical significance of this particular group lies, of course, in its size and its longevity, but the group's significance is immeasurably enhanced by the level of distinction of its members.

What the systematic analysis of the background characteristics of the delegates reveals is an overall continuing activism on the part of men who satisfy social science requisites for an elite. As would be expected by their participation in the movement, these delegates were men of wealth above the average levels of the general population. What is remarkable is the degree of their wealth. Even when they are compared with other prominent groups of southerners, such as members of the Confederate Congress or members of state secession bodies, their extraordinary distinction in wealth and slaveowning is beyond expectations. Similarities hold in other characteristics as well, particularly in those indicating power. Time after time, the commercial conventions attracted southerners of note: men who held important national political offices, men who played leading roles in their state governments, men who were selected as decision makers for the Confederacy. These men were not private though affluent members of their society, but rather they were prominent actors in public life. Such men participated in the convention movement at every stage of its history. They attended the conventions as delegates, they took an active part in the movement's organization, and they voiced their opinions in the conventions' debates.

The presence of such southern leaders and men of distinction speaks well for the reputation enjoyed by the conventions among those who, in this and in other areas of activity, sought to improve both the contemporary circumstances of southern life and the more distant prospects for their home region. The conventions, therefore, take on additional meaning. They served as vehicles for long-range planning, not just short-term results. Debates at the conventions focused primarily on ways to secure a future of economic prosperity for the South. Their purpose was to set the course bearings for a long journey forward in time, a journey that would last presumably beyond the lifetimes of the individuals engaged in debate.

As the characteristics of this group are described and as its members' viewpoints presented at the conventions are examined, several major historical issues can be addressed. One such issue is the extent of persistence of leadership between the Old South and the New. Those who have seen much continuity in power structures during this transition have pointed to the way antebellum white-male elites continued to play influential roles after the war. Included among this school are Wilbur J. Cash, Thomas B. Alexander, Jonathan M. Wiener, Dwight B. Billings, and others; opposed is, most notably, C. Vann Woodward.[2] This book supports the argument in favor of continuity on both an institutional level and a personal level. On an institutional level, the very survival of the convention mechanism, with few changes in its form or its function, over a span of so many years, speaks to the persistence of the institution. On an individual level, persistence is evident in two ways: in the way the movement drew men who had served as prewar delegates back into its association after the Civil War, and in the way the institution repeatedly attracted a similar type of delegate body throughout the entire lifetime of the movement.

What is evident, too, is a persistence of outlook. The most consistent underlying conviction voiced in the debates was optimism about the potential for southern economic growth. This optimism is understandable enough before the Civil War if the picture of prosperity presented by Gavin Wright, Robert W. Fogel, Stanley L. Engerman, and others is correct.[3] Cotton prices and slave values climbed after 1850. While delegates were quick to point out areas of underdevelopment, they did not do so in a context of alarm. Antebellum convention delegates sought ways to increase the South's prosperity by improving her commercial sectors, but they did not claim to do so in order to save the region from advancing ruin. Taken to its most extreme, this faith in southern potential formed an integral part of the disunionist arguments posed in sessions held after 1856. Nor was this optimism quashed by defeat of the Confederacy, for delegates at the postwar conventions evidenced a similar conviction about a better future along with a belief in their ability to pull themselves out of a war-imposed debacle. Admitting the need for outside help from the federal government and northern investors, they nonetheless exhibited faith in their own power to contribute to the South's regeneration, and thus to the national betterment.

This enduring faith in southern opportunity was grounded literally in the soil. Delegates to prewar and postwar conventions looked to agricultural production as the basis of southern wealth. In their eyes, the energy of native southerners, combined with the richness of the soil, could produce export crops sufficient to sustain prosperity before 1861 and revive prosperity after 1865. This agrarian emphasis would be expected if the majority of the delegates were themselves involved in agriculture. Such, however, does not seem to have been the case. The majority of the delegates for whom occupation could be determined were not engaged directly in planting or farming. This is not to dismiss the planter element, however, as it was quite visible. The sessions held between 1854 and 1856 were actually mergers of the Southern Commercial Convention and the Planters' Conventions. Even though planters seem to have been in the minority among convention delegates, the antebellum sessions supported the predominance of a plantation economy and defended slavery consistently. For that reason it may well be argued that the commercial conventions present strong evidence of antebellum planter hegemony.[4] Clearly, as planters and nonplanters alike, these participants in the convention movement saw their own interests and those of the region as a whole tied directly to an agricultural economy. Meeting together as men interested in commercial development, they sought ways to expand the marketing strengths of the South in an effort to insure maximum rewards from the natural bounties found therein.

The commercial convention movement was a creation of the urban South: that was its locale and that was home to most of its members. The movement's allegiance to commercial agriculture, then, tells us much about the urban South and its leaders. There was a mutuality of interests between the planters in the audience and the urban professionals and commercialists in attendance, and their combined definition of a strong southern economy remained basically unchanged from 1845 through 1871. Recent scholarship on the urban South traces the antebellum roots of the cities of the New South and emphasizes the way agricultural demands shaped southern urbanization. Several historians have found that the role of the urban business class was critical in determining how cities developed in the face of changing conditions, and that business organizations provided an institutional base for successful community revitalization after 1865. The history of the commercial convention movement shows that southern business organizations played a prominent part in antebellum economic policy making, and that there existed a discernable business interest group in the South long before 1865.[5]

What of support for economic diversification? The conventions did not ideologically oppose industrialization. Delegates listened with interest to reports of success in manufacturing ventures from leaders of industry such as William Gregg. They did not go so far as to endorse protective tariffs, but most conventions included Committees on Manufacturing and Mining, and their reports in support of home industry were endorsed by the delegate bodies. The Charleston convention of 1854 approved a recommendation balancing things this way: "That whilst agriculture is, and properly should be, the predominant pursuit of the people . . . [their] interests would be very greatly promoted by the employment of capital in other pursuits, and especially in manufactures and mining."[6] The general convention attitude toward manufacturing can be described as friendly, though not committed.

Persistence of type of participant and constancy of priorities—these are the major findings of this study of the commercial conventions. Little evidence can be found to label this movement revolutionary. It was a movement of the establishment on behalf of an expanded, slightly modified status quo. Those who assembled at sessions held before 1860 did not challenge slavery, did not advocate vast industrialization to replace staple-crop production, and did not seek to northernize their homeland but instead glorified its distinctiveness. Those who revived the movement during Reconstruction recognized the changes that had occurred and sought ways to move toward renewed prosperity in what was still an agriculture-based economy. They seemed anxious about securing a stable labor supply and hoped to attract immigrants into the region, but they did not reject outright the notion that the former slave population could fulfill that need. They realized that the South had to modernize its transportation facilities and that it did not have the capital resources to do so alone. They presented themselves to northerners as men willing to shoulder the job of restoring the South within the reality of a Union that had a pervasive general interest in such a restoration. While the road to prosperity seemed to many to lead to secession before 1860, it led to reconciliation after 1869. Whether the postwar delegates were acting to lull the Republicans into a more liberal southern strategy or to convince northern businessmen that the real issue of importance to the South was economics, not politics, these delegates voiced a desire to get on with the business of rebuilding.

The message of the commercial convention movement was not the call for a New South creed, promulgating widespread industrialization, urban growth, and diversified agriculture. But neither was it the voice of an antibourgeois opposition to change. The agenda of the conventions remained focused on material prosperity within an agrarian economy, before and after the Civil War. Commercial convention debates show little evidence of conflict between planters and commercialists or industrialists. Participants seem instead to have been accommodationists, men willing to modify the status quo in ways designed to enhance, not challenge, the primacy of staple-crop agriculture. That the agricultural economy the commercial conventions sought to enrich was a staple-crop agriculture is critical to understanding the delegates' endorsement of features associated with modernism, such as railroads, government activism on the side of business, and various improvements to the infrastructure designed to enhance interchange between producers and consumers. The lawyers, commercialists, and agriculturalists who participated in the commercial conventions sought these improvements on behalf of an economy dependent upon market access. Indeed, the very changes they endorsed tended to broaden the reach of commercial agriculture into the southern interior.[7]

Among the most interesting evidence presented by the conventions is the revelation of a perception on the part of prominent men of the extent to which the South's economy had become enmeshed in the modern world. In the debates at the commercial conventions and in the personal economic ties of participants in these debates, it is apparent that many southerners had an orientation to the same marketplace relationships understood by northern commercialists. What separated them in the years before 1860 was the fact that the South's agriculture incorporated a slave labor system. That difference was fundamental, and it was one fully endorsed by the antebellum commercial conventions. As the convention movement leaders balanced the needs of their economy to reach out to the world marketplace against the need to defend its slavery base, the latter outweighed the former. Thus, despite rhetoric and support for the very economic policies that would have otherwise placed them firmly beside other American entrepreneurs of their time, the activists of the immediate prewar conventions came to be numbered among the most vocal contingent moving the South toward a separate political destiny. After the war, due in part to the fact that most had been committed to a defense of slavery, those southerners who came back to the commercial convention movement brought uncertainty about how to proceed in establishing an economic relationship between former slaveholder and former slave.[8]

Many of these themes have been discussed by other historians who have studied the antebellum commercial conventions. The story of the conventions held before the Civil War is far from new to students of southern history. In fact, the most extensive work to date on the conventions was written within the early decades of the life of the modern historical profession. As early as 1904, William W. Davis, a student of the Dunning school, became the first to relate the history of the convention movement. There followed an expanded discussion of the conventions by Robert Royal Russel in 1924 and two major studies of the antebellum conventions by John G. Van Deusen in 1926 and by Herbert Wender in 1930. The analysis of each historian fits their common perspective of economic determinism in explaining the development of the secession movement. These historians saw the conventions as vehicles for expressing both a plea for southern economic regeneration and a warning of southern decline as compared to northern prosperity. They saw the primary success of the movement in its effort to make inquiry into the needs of the southern economy, and they agreed that the convention movement reinforced parallel efforts to consolidate public opinion in favor of secession. Van Deusen and Wender acknowledged the conventions' loyalty to the South's cotton economy, and they condemned that tie as a fatal weakness of the convention movement. There have been more limited studies of particular conventions written since these publications, but these two works, especially that by Wender, have remained the standard sources cited about the antebellum convention series.[9]

The antebellum commercial convention movement has been granted a place of note in the history of the Old South by some of its best-known students. Major interpretations by such prominent historians in the fields of economic history, political history, and intellectual history as Ulrich B. Phillips, Avery O. Craven, David M. Potter, Charles S. Sydnor, Clement Eaton, Eugene D. Genovese, Harold D. Woodman, Carl N. Degler, Richard N. Current, and John McCardell have included discussions of the convention movement. These writers concentrated on the subject matter discussed at the various sessions without systematically assessing the men involved in the movement, and they disagreed as to the significance of the movement within the broader story of antebellum southern history. Phillips, Craven, and Potter stressed the way commercial conventions spurred on a disruptive sectionalism. Sydnor, Eaton, and Genovese, all citing Wender on the conventions, criticized the movement for not recognizing the economic weaknesses of the South's slave economy. In more positive interpretations, Woodman, Degler, and Fred Bateman and Thomas Weiss cited the conventions as general supporters of manufacturing and as disseminators of information about the attractiveness of manufacturing as an investment. Current, in tracing the ways southerners elected to "northernize" themselves, saw the commercial conventions as evidence that many saw economic diversification as a way to preserve the South. Conversely, McCardell saw the delegates' belief in the South's solidarity as an agricultural region and their pride in its distinctiveness from the industrializing North as the major impact of commercial conventions on the southern nationalist movement.[10]

Students of the 1850s' public debate over reopening the African slave trade have pointed out that the commercial conventions publicized that issue. Ronald T. Takaki analyzed the way politicians used those conventions held after 1856 to create support for the broader proslavery argument. Laurence Shore saw the convention debates over reopening the slave trade as the "ruling elite's desperate search for agreement on a 'true policy' for the South that would foster belief in the strength and fairness of the political economy of slavery." Economist Gavin Wright quoted from the commercial convention debates to underline his contention that most southerners opposed reopening the trade from an economic standpoint.[11] As these writers have documented, the debate over reopening the African slave trade became a dominant part of the late antebellum commercial conventions. That aspect of the story of the conventions, as the succeeding chapters will show, further reflects how southern anxieties over the future of slavery came to smother consideration of most other matters in the final years before the Civil War.

In contrast to how much attention has been paid to the antebellum conventions, very little has been written about the postwar commercial conventions. None of the previous works on the commercial conventions takes the history of the movement beyond 1859. The most extensive discussion of the 1869–1871 series to date is that by E. Merton Coulter in his 1947 study of the South during Reconstruction, and it is but a brief description of the reemergence of the movement.[12] This lack of attention to the persistence of such an enduring antebellum institution is surprising, given the amount of scholarship focusing on the degree of linkage between Old South and New. My book includes an effort to fill the historical gap by presenting the story of the postwar segment of the commercial convention movement.

Previous works on the conventions have presented the participants only by generalizations. I also make generalizations, but they are more firmly grounded in biographical research on the delegates than those of any presentation published to date. In Part One, I clarify what type of southerner was drawn to the movement by presenting a quantitatively measured description of twenty-five biographical attributes for two groups: the entire pool of 5,716 convention delegates, and the more select group of 596 leaders within the movement. While information could not be obtained on all attributes for every delegate, the amount of data available allows for well-substantiated summaries about the two groups. What emerges is a computer-assisted portrait of a Southern Elite, hand-colored by the real-life stories of many of the individuals involved.

The distinctiveness of the men who created the convention movement and of those who continued to find it useful lends special interest to the ideas revealed at its sessions. Parts Two and Three of this book use primarily convention debates as windows on the minds of southern leadership, supplemented by other records of their attitudes. The primary focus is on the degree to which the goals in the leadership's definition of what made up a "good society" remained intact, along with their continuing attraction to the same core list of means to achieve those goals. The chapters on antebellum conventions explore evidence of an escalation of defensiveness against what were perceived as increasing attacks on slavery. Those chapters on the postwar conventions reveal how seemingly anxious southerners at these sessions were to rejoin the Union and how they defined the new relationship between the sections to be an economic partnership based on mutual interests. While the convention sessions eschewed party politics, their public pronouncements were nevertheless of interest to all parties, and I suggest ways in which the conventions may have influenced regional and national political developments.

Members of the commercial convention association spoke as individuals, yet they also perceived themselves to be representing others. Whether it was as broad a constituency as their home state or county, or as specific a one as their business association, each roster identified the delegates with some group or community. It is not my intention to argue that their opinions as made public on the floors of any of the commercial conventions served as statements for the South as a whole. Nonetheless, the public recognition given to these southerners outside the halls of the conventions lent a significance to their actions inside the confines of the convention that would not otherwise be as historically noteworthy. After all, it was not the commercial convention association that legislated slave codes, or ironed out congressional compromises on territorial expansion, or kept alive the Fugitive Slave Act. It was not the meetings of the commercial conventions that voted to secede, and it was not the duty of the commercial convention to wage warfare. Nor was it at the commercial convention that hearings were held by the Joint Committee on Reconstruction. Yet the men of the commercial conventions played a role in all of these events, and more, and they associated with those who made other equally important decisions. Leaders at the conventions took on many public responsibilities, and they chose to join this particular public forum, where they placed their opinions on the record for others to reflect upon. Whether those doing the reflecting were actually seated in the audience at the convention or were hearing or reading about it secondhand, the message went out. In an effort to understand better how these men and their perceptions might have influenced the history of the years of their lives, this book holds a mirror to the commercial convention messenger, and a microphone to the message.

I.

*THE
CONVENTION INSTITUTION
AND THE
CONVENTION DELEGATES*

1
A Durable Institution

The scene was the southwest gateway city of Memphis, Tennessee, November 12, 1845. Inside the Methodist Episcopal Church, a convention of 566 men representing nine southern states, two neighboring states of Illinois and Indiana, the territory of Iowa, and Texas assembled at eleven that morning to greet their eminent president, Senator John C. Calhoun of South Carolina. His opening address extolled the resources of their homeland, cited their opportunities to expand access to the marketplace, and hinted at the not-too-distant day when national interests would span from Atlantic to Pacific. In closing, Calhoun set forth his own aspiration for the convention: "May the results of your deliberations be such as to accomplish not only the objects for which you have convened but to strengthen the bonds of our Union, and to render us the greatest and most prosperous community the world ever beheld."[1]

Among those hundreds of delegates were sixteen who would return twenty-four years later to another commercial convention in Memphis, but one held under very different circumstances. The bonds of the Union had broken, war had brought defeat to the effort at southern nationhood, and in many ways the lives of southerners had changed. Yet, as 882 delegates greeted each other on that spring morning in May, 1869, their mood was optimistic. In the chair as temporary president sat former governor Robert M. Patton of Alabama.[2] Once again, just as their predecessors had done two decades earlier, the men of the commercial convention set about the business of charting a course to prosperity. Their dreams of a South anchored in its agrarian roots yet taking full advantage of modern access to a world marketplace were the same.

To assemble under the auspices of a commercial convention was a familiar experience, one that drew together more than six thousand like-minded southerners over a period of some thirty-five years. The convention was an institution that appealed to the nullification generation and bridged the eras of Old and New South. Its sessions served as forums for debate and as opportunities for men of the South to meet together in search of remedies for what they perceived as impediments to full prosperity. Between 1837 and 1872 there were a total of twenty-two conventions of varying size, ranging from small gatherings of less than one hundred delegates to the largest of more than nine hundred. A closer investigation of the history of the conventions provides an insight into the transition of the movement from its start as an operation of limited scope and intent to its development into one of the broadest public forums and most enduring institutions of the South during its time.

The earliest precursors of the formal body, the Southern Commercial Convention that would emerge in 1852, were a series of conventions held in cities along the Atlantic seaboard during the late 1830s. Merchants in the Southeast had become concerned about the stability of their trade relations with both northern importers and European markets in the wake of the uncertainties created by the Panic of 1837. William Dearing of Athens, Georgia, a merchant and president of the Georgia Railroad, thought that a meeting of fellow commercialists within the southeastern area should be called to consider both the problems and the opportunities at hand. Accordingly, he issued a circular calling for those concerned about the problem to meet at Augusta, Georgia, in October, 1837. His message was that a crisis had developed for the South because northern importers had usurped the role of the southern merchant. Those who met in Augusta adjourned with a call to convene there again the following April; the second convention likewise issued a call for a third session, which was held in October, 1838. The April session was chaired by Arthur P. Hayne of Charleston, later to serve South Carolina briefly in the United States Senate. His account of the session, written as a letter to Henry W. DeSaussure and published in the *Columbus Enquirer*, called for joint efforts by planters and merchants to unite in bringing back direct trade to southern ports. The October convention passed resolutions in favor of formation of trade associations and in support of expanded legislative support to banks in order to provide capital needed for successful trade initiatives. Up the coast in Norfolk, Virginia, citizens held a similar convention in November, 1838. One last Direct Trade Convention met in Charleston, South Carolina, during April, 1839.[3]

As limited in scope and regional draw as they were, these efforts represent the starting point for the commercial convention movement within the South. Debates focused on the South's commercial life, as they would continue to do throughout the history of the convention movement. While they lamented the South's slow progress compared to northern commercial development, proponents of these meetings expressed confidence in the ability of the South to succeed. Their confidence was grounded in two perceptions: their belief in the power of cotton as a source of capital, and their faith in the abundance of the South's natural resources. They spoke to merchants, and they spoke to planters who, in their eyes, could provide the investment resource to make "Direct Trade" a reality. Together, this declaration of native southern confidence and the appeal to southerners as both producers and investors were to remain a part of the basic tenets of the movement throughout its history.[4]

The second step in the evolution of the commercial convention movement took place within the Mississippi River valley. The Panic of 1837 that prompted agitation for direct trade along the Atlantic seaboard had served to dampen optimism inspired by tremendous population growth rates in the Southwest. Prompted by tightened credit and limited involvement of the various state governments in furnishing financial aid to transportation projects, southwesterners hoped to channel western trade into southern markets. At the urging of an entrepreneur seeking investment support to build a plank road into the western Indian territory, citizens of Memphis called for a transportation improvement convention to be held in November, 1845. What resulted was the convention that attracted some very prominent southerners, most notably John C. Calhoun, who agreed to participate in the convention at the urging of his friend James Gadsden. Calhoun risked criticism at home for his support of western internal improvements, but he hoped to secure western support for congressional tariff reform in exchange for his involvement. As the name selected by its organizers implies, this South-Western Convention represented an effort to join the West and South in a united front to further economic goals of each region. This session spurred similar meetings between 1847 and 1851 in Chicago, St. Louis, a second gathering in Memphis, and New Orleans; at each session boosters made a case for selection of their city to become a major trading terminus.[5]

The conventions in this second phase focused primarily on improving internal transportation facilities. Their resolutions supported limited government assistance to river and harbor improvements and indirect aid to railroad development. These sessions were an important step in the evolution of the convention movement both for their broadened subject matter and because of the presence of a particular delegate at the 1845 Memphis convention. J. D. B. De Bow traveled to the Memphis convention of 1845 as a delegate from South Carolina and was selected to serve as one of the secretaries of the convention. Following his trip to Memphis, De Bow moved to New Orleans in November of 1845, and from there he launched the effort to establish an ongoing body, a Southern Commercial Convention. While he practiced law and published his *Review*, De Bow promoted the convention movement through lectures in New Orleans.[6]

Six years later, it was from the Crescent City that a call went out for a large southern convention. In the interim, several small conventions for railroad promotion had met in Louisiana and Mississippi, and from one of these, a convention held in New Orleans in June of 1851, De Bow and his fellow committee members called the people of the South and West to assemble in six months' time for a major convention. Not surprisingly, De Bow published this proposal in his *Review*. Southerners responded, and a crowd of over six hundred delegates assembled for a railroad convention in New Orleans in January, 1852. The delegates agreed on the need to expand southern railroad mileage, and they vied with each other to have the convention endorse their individual railroad companies and routes. De Bow took advantage of the occasion to speak in favor of a permanent organization to promote southern commerce. The delegates did not formalize that recommendation, but reports of the session printed in his *Review* included his suggestion.[7]

Whether to initiate an ongoing session was left to the delegates at the next major convention, to be held in Baltimore in December of 1852. The Baltimore meeting was arranged by that city's board of trade, and De Bow printed a notice of the upcoming session in his *Review*. When the convention met that December, local civic boosters rhapsodized about the advantages of the port of Baltimore. Even so, the delegates kept their eyes focused on the broader subject of southern commercial development, and they concluded their convention with a call to reassemble the following year in Memphis.[8]

Thus began the institution known as the Southern Commercial Convention. Between the years 1852 and 1859, it convened at least once during each year. The 1853 session at Memphis was followed by an 1854 Charleston convention, an 1855 session at New Orleans, two meetings during 1856, first at Richmond and then at Savannah, one session in 1857 at Knoxville, an 1858 meeting at Montgomery, and a final session at Vicksburg in 1859. De Bow remained ever faithful to the movement, and he continued to carry complete coverage of each session in his *Review*. This opportunity for exchanging viewpoints drew thousands of delegates as the movement crossed and recrossed the South.[9]

The Southern Commercial Convention survived the Civil War. Like the antebellum series before it, the postwar movement emerged from a time of economic disorder to serve the needs of those who sought to find some direction for southern economic growth. The resurrected convention movement began like the Direct Trade Conventions back in the 1830s. Citizens in an Atlantic seaboard port, this time Norfolk, Virginia, sought to strengthen ties for direct trade with Europe. Their hope was to establish a steamship line between Norfolk and Liverpool, and the would-be organizers included William Mahone, Virginia railroad developer, and William Lamb, local president of the board of trade. They needed $300,000 for the venture, and they invited prospective investors to a meeting at Norfolk in October, 1868, where they hoped to secure at least $30,000 in pledges. Mahone urged them to act immediately: "If there are to be found any good results from the late struggle it is that we are now standing on a new field and the whole products of the country are seeking new centers of trade." According to the *New York Times*, they raised one-half of their goal.[10] In the process, they reintroduced a familiar institution.

The postwar Southern Commercial Convention movement was tied to its antebellum antecedent by more than economic circumstance. Organizers of the postwar sessions included many with personal experience in the antebellum movement. In all, more than one hundred who had attended at least one session prior to 1860 would become reinvolved in the convention movement after the war. This direct link to the earlier experience is apparent with several of those in positions of prominence at Norfolk. William Lamb had served as a secretary to the 1857 Knoxville convention. John Brown Baldwin of Staunton, Virginia, who served on the Business Committee, had attended at both Richmond and Savannah. Jeremiah Watkins Clapp of Memphis, also on the Business Committee, had participated at Memphis, Charleston, and Knoxville. Judge Robert J. McKinney of Knoxville, temporary chairman of the Norfolk convention, had attended the session in his hometown. Thus it is not surprising that the Norfolk meeting concluded with a call for a commercial convention to be held in Memphis the following spring.

The chamber of commerce in Memphis took responsibility for organizing the next event and issued invitations that listed several issues to be discussed: direct trade with foreigners, a Pacific railroad, Mississippi River levees, and immigration into the South. Over eight hundred delegates had registered when the session convened on May 18, 1869. They deliberated for four days, voted to continue to use the name Southern Commercial Convention, and set a date for the next meeting to be held in the city of Louisville, during October of 1869.[11] The Memphis convention served as a linchpin in the movement: sixty-seven of its delegates had participated in at least one convention held before the war, and over one hundred southerners were there attending their first convention who would go on to attend at least one other convention in the ensuing three years.

Not by coincidence, the New Orleans Chamber of Commerce had

planned a convention for May, 1869. Organizers took advantage of the fact that a Memphis convention was also scheduled and set a date for their session that would enable many of the participants at Memphis to travel immediately on down to New Orleans for a second assembly. General Cyrus Bussey, representing the New Orleans Chamber of Commerce, issued an invitation from the floor of the Memphis convention to all interested parties. He was rewarded by seeing eighty-nine delegates make the trip.[12]

Organizers of the New Orleans convention, many of whom had been active in the antebellum series, intended it as a forum on the task of improving the Mississippi River valley's economy, and they directed special attention to the importance of the area's interregional grain trade. Nine of the seventeen states represented were located in the valley. The convention opened with the temporary chairman, General William Vandever of Iowa, offering the enticement that wheat would be shipped to New Orleans by water rather than to New York by rail if the Mississippi River could be cleared of obstructions. This convention adjourned without setting another session, but its delegates were reminded of the upcoming Louisville convention in October, and they were urged to attend.[13]

When the Southern Commercial Convention met at Louisville in October, 1869, twenty-eight states were represented. The presiding officer of this third postwar convention was former president Millard Fillmore, who cautioned the delegates against allowing politics to interfere with their work. After seven days of deliberations, the Louisville convention voted to move north of the Ohio River, to Cincinnati, for the next meeting. Despite the fact that the convention met outside the geographic boundaries of the South in 1870, it assembled under the name of the Southern Commercial Convention. The majority (66 percent) of delegates represented southern states, cities, towns, or companies. The chairman of the convention, John Work Garrett, hailed from Baltimore. However, from the outset a movement began to change the name to the National Commercial Convention. On the first day of deliberations, the Committee on Rules of Order and Order of Business recommended in favor of the name change. Too many delegates objected, and the resolution was laid on the table informally. By the fifth day, resistance had been worn down as the convention had supported measures aimed at national reconciliation. The name change resolution was reintroduced, accompanied by a preamble declaring that representation at the convention had become more national, lending the body a national character and importance. The delegates agreed and voted to hold the 1871 meeting under the banner of a National Commercial Convention.[14]

The final chapter in the story of the commercial convention movement took place in Baltimore. Responding to a call from the Cincinnati convention, more than three hundred delegates, less than one-half of whom were from the South, assembled at the Masonic Temple on September 25, 1871. All of the southern states were represented, along with eighteen outside the South. The president, Richard M. Bishop, was from Cincinnati. In keeping with the tradition of other conventions, this session issued a call for a subsequent session, to be held in St. Louis in November, 1872. The St. Louis session met on December 11, 1872, but it scarcely resembled other sessions in the movement. Although fifteen states were represented, it attracted fewer than one hundred delegates, and of those, one-half came from only two states, Missouri and Ohio. The convention was not even well supported by local St. Louisans, according to the *Missouri Democrat*, and it is not included in this study as one of the official conventions in the Southern Commercial Convention series.[15]

Throughout its twenty-six-year lifetime, specific features unified the separate meetings held from year to year. Geographically, the movement was a southern one. All sessions except one took place within the geographic confines of the South, and the vast majority of the delegates resided in the fifteen southern states. The organizational structure remained virtually unchanged once established in 1845. The sessions were well publicized in advance, and for most sessions a planning committee was designated to bridge the interval from that session to the next. The primary objective of each session seldom varied: to seek ways to increase the prosperity of the South. And, as is discussed later in more detail, the many characteristics of the men who attended fit a pattern that remained consistent throughout the entire life of the series.

For these reasons, the convention movement can be thought of as an institution. The movement persisted for a considerable time, its appeal drew back appreciable numbers of delegates to more than one session, and it involved thousands of individuals who represented a particularly prominent stratum of their society. All geographic areas within the South sent delegates, and the major urban centers of the region were represented on a regular basis.

One claim for significance can be made based on sheer size. Throughout the life of the conventions, the southern delegations numbered more than 6,400 for the entire 1845–1871 series, according to newspaper reports, accounts published in *De Bow's Review*, and printed copies of official proceedings. This number, however, does not measure individual participation in the movement, as it includes those men who attended more than one session. In terms of individuals, a total of 5,716 southerners have been identified for this study as attending at least one session. Just as the majority of the sessions took place before the Civil War, so too the majority of these individuals attended only prewar sessions: 4,039, or 71 percent. The number who attended only postwar sessions was 1,566, or 27 percent. A group of 111, or 2 percent, attended sessions held in each of the two time periods. The size of this entire study group can better be appreciated by comparing it to other important, contemporaneous groups of southerners. Southern states held 1,351 seats in the United States Senate and House of Representatives during the years 1845 to 1871, and the number of individuals holding those seats was fewer due to multiple-term officeholding. The number of delegates to the fifteen southern state Secession Conventions and Secession Legislatures was 1,859. Two hundred and sixty-seven men served in the Confederate Congress during its lifetime.[16]

Another facet of the continuity of the conventions as an institution can be measured by the extent to which geographic areas were repeatedly represented at the sessions. While the individual delegates might change from one session to the next, it is important to realize that there was a high degree of recurrence of locale representation. At its most general level, this can be measured by representation of states. In a culture where the debate on states' rights took on major significance, each of the southern states was well represented at the conventions over the lifetime of the institution.

In general, the conventions drew their delegates fairly equally from the four northern/southern and eastern/western regions of the South (table 1.1). Five of the eleven prewar conventions were held in cities of the South Atlantic region. The remaining six took place in South Central states. Proportionately, 47 percent of the delegates resided in the South Atlantic and 53 percent in the South Central states. Six prewar conventions were held in cities of the Lower South and five in the Upper South. Among all prewar delegates, 53 percent resided in the Lower South and 47 percent in the Upper South. The most evenly distributed delegations were those at Knoxville in 1857: they split between Upper and Lower South by 51 and 49 percent respectively, and they split evenly between South Central and South Atlantic residences.[17]

The concept of locale representation can be taken down to the county level, and there is still striking repeat participation, especially from the most urban counties of the South. Home county has been ascertained for 3,466 delegates, 61 percent of all delegates. Hence, any generalizations about home county will probably underestimate a given county's representation. Even so, it is clear that urban centers of the South were well represented in the movement. Those counties of the very largest cities, Baltimore, New Orleans, and St. Louis, were represented at over one-half of the sessions: specifically, at 56 percent, 81 percent, and 56 percent respectively. Cities of medium size also sent regular delegations. Richmond led all urban centers in the number of conventions its citizens attended, 94 percent. Charleston and Memphis sent delegates to 81 percent of the sessions, and the relatively small Vicksburg had citizens present at 63 percent of the conventions. Nashville, Knoxville, and Montgomery representatives were present at 56 percent. Columbia (S. Carolina), Alexandria, Atlanta, Galveston, Natchez, and Savannah had delegates at 50 percent, and Augusta, Louisville, and Norfolk at 44 percent.

When the conventions resumed after the war, a slightly different pattern emerged as the conventions opened their forums to northern as well as southern delegates. Still, the movement remained predominantly a southern one in that the majority of the delegates came from southern states. Of the total number who have been identified as attending at least one of the five postwar sessions, there were 1,676 south-

TABLE 1.1
Southern State Representation

State	Percentage of Conventions Where Represented	Total Prewar Delegate Slots	Total Postwar Delegate Slots
Alabama	88	232	129
Arkansas	75	97	29
District of Columbia	50	17	12
Florida	63	34	13
Georgia	88	454	209
Kentucky	69	59	133
Louisiana	88	501	158
Maryland	56	79	45
Mississippi	88	349	117
Missouri	63	92	64
N. Carolina	63	77	16
S. Carolina	88	592	45
Tennessee	100	833	375
Texas	69	37	31
Virginia	88	671	285

erners and 265 northerners, or 86 percent southern and 14 percent northern. Sessions drew more heavily from areas closest to the host city. Four of the five conventions met in cities of the South Central region, and 62 percent of the southern delegates at postwar sessions represented South Central states. Four of the five sessions were also held in the Upper South, and 58 percent of the southern delegates lived in that region. Similarly, most northern delegates represented states of the Midwest and mid-Atlantic regions: Ohio, 110; Pennsylvania, 33; Indiana, 30; New York, 28; and Illinois, 25.[18]

Another dimension of the movement is frequency of attendance. What was the personnel overlap, or put another way, how many individuals chose to attend more than one convention? Comparisons of delegate lists show that out of the entire set of 5,716 men, 648, or over 11 percent of the individuals, were present at more than one session. This can be considered a core group in terms of involvement in the movement. How frequently did these repeat delegates return for subsequent sessions? Most of those who attended more than one convention attended only one other. The total of those attending two sessions was 531. Of the remaining core group, seventy-nine individuals attended three sessions, twenty-seven attended four sessions, seven participated in five sessions, and three persons attended six. De Bow himself, the chief proponent of the movement, attended ten sessions.

On the average, approximately 22 percent of the delegates at each convention attended more than one session (table 1.2). This repeat participation was not, however, a matter of an individual simply attending one session, being interested enough to travel to the subsequent session, and then dropping out of the movement. Only 3 percent, on the average, followed the movement just to its next stop. The majority presumably attended additional sessions for reasons such as expectations about the issues to be discussed, the geographic location of a session, or the demands of one's own personal schedule.[19]

Specific personnel links can be traced between pairs of conventions. In effect, repeat attendance between pairs of sessions serves as one measure of the closeness of ties between any two meetings. The matrix of pair-by-pair delegate overlap, or how many delegates chose to attend both conventions in a pair, is presented in table 1.3. One pattern that clearly emerges is geographic. When a city hosted more than one session it drew many of the same delegates to its succeeding conventions. Forty-eight individuals attended the two conventions held in Memphis in 1845 and 1853. Sixteen years later, in 1869, the third convention at Memphis drew sixteen delegates who had been at the 1845 session and twenty-two who had been there in 1853. Out of this group, four men

TABLE 1.2

Convention Size and Delegate Repeat Attendance

Convention Session	Total Number of Delegates Present	Percentage Attending At Least Two Sessions
Memphis, 1845	545	16
New Orleans, 1852	408	19
Baltimore, 1852	60	30
Memphis, 1853	588	24
Charleston, 1854	985	17
New Orleans, 1855	230	33
Richmond, 1856	244	21
Savannah, 1856	556	19
Knoxville, 1857	804	15
Montgomery, 1858	95	36
Vicksburg, 1859	62	26
Memphis, 1869	835	23
New Orleans, 1869	371	31
Louisville, 1869	319	29
Cincinnati, 1870	231	27
Baltimore, 1871	136	32
Average	404	22

were present at all three Memphis conventions. Similarly, forty-four men attended both the New Orleans session of 1852 and that of 1855. By 1869, when the city hosted its third convention, seven of the delegates had been at the 1852 session and five at the 1855 meeting. Of these, only one attended all three Crescent City gatherings. The only exception to this geographic overlap was that none of the delegates to the last convention, that held in Baltimore in 1871, had also attended the earlier Baltimore session of 1852. The strong linkage between sessions at Charleston and Savannah can also be attributed in part to proximity of the two cities.

This matrix also illustrates that factors other than geography were at work, as there are cases of notable delegate overlap in cities far apart from one another. One's interest in particular issues probably played a part in the decision to attend or not. Major regional newspapers and *De Bow's Review* carried complete enough advance coverage of each session that anyone interested in particular subjects could reasonably predict their debate at an upcoming convention. The convention organization formalized this process as a standing committee from one session handled preparations for the subsequent meeting, including lists of committees appointed on specific issues. Delegates, then, could elect to attend an upcoming session having some indication of the subject matter to be discussed.

Sessions held in the mid-1850s devoted attention to a set of issues of interest to the entire South. Up through 1857, ties between several key conventions stand out, and Charleston proved to be a pivotal session. Despite the distance between Memphis and Charleston, the convention of 1854 drew forty-eight delegates from the earlier 1853 session. The sessions that followed at Savannah in 1856 and at Knoxville in 1857 attracted thirty-nine and forty-three delegates respectively of those who had participated at Charleston. Within this group, eight men attended all three sessions. Similarly, the overlap between the Savannah and Knoxville sessions was forty-four, again suggesting a commonality of issues between the two conventions. Conversely, the sessions held in 1858 and 1859, which sanctioned extreme proslavery positions, stood alone in the series, sharing low overlap rates with earlier 1850 sessions. Those at Montgomery who participated in other conventions limited their involvement mainly to the 1857–1859 time frame.

The earlier mid-1850s pattern resumed after the Civil War, as sessions held between 1869 and 1871 witnessed strong repeat attendance. The two sessions in 1869 at Memphis and New Orleans were held liter-

TABLE 1.3

Convention Pair-by-Pair Delegate Overlap

Convention and Year	New Orleans, 1852	Baltimore, 1852	Memphis, 1853	Charleston, 1854	New Orleans, 1855	Richmond, 1856	Savannah, 1856	Knoxville, 1857	Montgomery, 1858	Vicksburg, 1859	Memphis, 1869	New Orleans, 1869	Louisville, 1869	Cincinnati, 1870	Baltimore, 1871
Memphis, 1845	8	0	48	14	6	5	2	5	1	5	16	3	1	2	1
New Orleans, 1852		1	16	10	44	5	2	5	2	2	4	7	2	3	1
Baltimore, 1852			6	3	4	5	3	1	0	0	1	0	2	0	0
Memphis, 1853				48	19	6	5	8	2	7	22	8	5	5	3
Charleston, 1854					15	16	39	43	9	5	11	3	7	3	0
New Orleans, 1855						2	4	1	2	2	3	5	1	0	0
Richmond, 1856							18	12	2	1	6	2	1	2	2
Savannah, 1856								44	12	3	6	2	3	1	2
Knoxville, 1857									18	2	12	2	7	4	0
Montgomery, 1858										4	1	0	4	0	0
Vicksburg, 1859											1	1	1	0	0
Memphis, 1869												89	39	14	12
New Orleans, 1869													16	8	3
Louisville, 1869														27	12
Cincinnati, 1870															21

ally days apart, making it possible to combine visits to both sessions into one trip. This in large part accounts for the fact that eighty-nine delegates attended both meetings. But still, the overlap of thirty-nine delegates between the Memphis and Louisville conventions and that of twenty-seven between the Louisville and Cincinnati gatherings show a sense of commitment to the movement on the part of a sizable group of participants and suggest a commonality of issues about these postwar conventions.

When one focuses on the entity of the convention subset, a broader time slice of activism than just a single convention, it is again apparent that delegate participation spanned the various stages of the movement. Within the entire series of sixteen conventions there were four identifiable groups, or subsets, of sessions. They were distinct from each other chronologically and differed from each other in terms of the scope of their interests. The grouping labeled the Internal Improvement subset is the 1845 session and the January, 1852, session; the Mid-1850s subset comprises the seven sessions concerned with a broad range of economic issues lasting from December, 1852, through 1857; the third subset is the Montgomery-Vicksburg subset, comprised of two aberrant, disunionist sessions of 1858 and 1859; and the Postwar subset is the series of five sessions held when the movement resumed following the war. If a delegate attended any convention in the series that made up the subset, he is included as a member of the subset. It is possible to trace attendance at sessions outside of a member's own subset, and while instances of individual participation from the earliest conventions to the latest are few, such cases did exist (table 1.4). Most important for appreciating the broad degree of personnel crossover, all subsets except that of the Montgomery-Vicksburg series were represented at every convention outside their own.[20]

As might be expected, the two subsets with the greatest number of conventions tended to see instances of repeat attendance occurring at another session within the same subset more so than did the subsets of fewer conventions. This is especially true for the Postwar subset, where over 60 percent of those who attended more than one convention did so only within the Postwar series. The linkage from the Internal Improvement subset is strongest between that series and the later sessions held

TABLE 1.4

Subset Member Attendance at Non-Subset Conventions

Convention	Internal Improvements Subset Delegates (N=945)	Mid-1850s Subset Delegates (N=3,218)	Montgomery-Vicksburg Subset Delegates (N=153)	Postwar Subset Delegates (N=1,677)
Memphis, 1845	N/A	65	5	18
New Orleans, 1852	N/A	65	3	14
Baltimore, 1852	1	N/A	0	3
Memphis, 1853	62	N/A	9	29
Charleston, 1854	23	N/A	12	19
New Orleans, 1855	49	N/A	4	8
Richmond, 1856	8	N/A	2	10
Savannah, 1856	3	N/A	12	13
Knoxville, 1857	9	N/A	18	19
Montgomery, 1858	2	28	N/A	5
Vicksburg, 1859	6	13	N/A	2
Memphis, 1869	18	53	2	N/A
New Orleans, 1869	10	17	1	N/A
Louisville, 1869	3	22	5	N/A
Cincinnati, 1870	5	10	0	N/A
Baltimore, 1871	2	6	0	N/A

in the same cities, Memphis (1853 and 1869) and New Orleans (1855 and 1869). Even though the actual number of delegates from this group who attended the last postwar conventions is small, it is noteworthy, given the nineteen-year lapse between 1852 and 1871. The Mid-1850s subset was well represented at sessions in all three other subsets. Those who attended either one or both of the conventions of 1858 and 1859 had, by contrast with the three other convention subsets, less personnel overlap with the main body of commercial conventions. The involvement of this subset group was apparent though limited at the 1854 Charleston meeting, more substantial at the 1857 Knoxville session where the radical wing of the delegate body noticeably built up their presence within the institution, but especially weak at any of the postwar conventions. Of particular interest is the fact that the first postwar convention, that in Memphis in 1869, drew more delegates from the Mid-1850s subset than did the radical Montgomery-Vicksburg, 1858–1859, series. As expected, the links between the Postwar subset and earlier conventions are strongest in those cities hosting conventions both before and after the Civil War, but significant ties exist as well to two key conventions, those in Charleston and Knoxville.

What does this information about personnel overlap and locale representation tell us about the conventions? Clearly, the commercial conventions were not monopolized by any particular group of individuals traveling from session to session. Rather, the vast majority of delegates at any given convention attended only that one session. From the total series, 5,068 delegates attended one time, though only 1,954 did so at a session held in their hometowns. Yet neither can the overlap that did occur be ignored. The convention movement attracted 648 individuals to participate in at least two sessions, and the attraction bridged the chasm of the Civil War for 111 of these. While some conventions may have been geographically limited in their delegate draw, the entire series' participants came from all sections of the South. Importantly, the less political of the sessions, those held between 1853 and 1857 and those held after the war, drew from a balanced cross section. Taken as a whole, all of the conventions together contributed to a total roster of participants in the movement that is far larger than could ever have been assembled by any single southwide gathering of its time.

If one looks at the convention movement through its organizational structure, it appears as a dynamic institution that modified its framework to meet a broadening agenda. The convention movement grew from an effort to address specific economic problems of a limited region into a national forum, addressing a wide spectrum of economic issues. In the course of this evolution, the institutional structure of the conventions became more formalized, and promotion of upcoming sessions was handled increasingly more professionally. The delegate selection process also changed. The earliest sessions reached out to individuals, who would participate as concerned private citizens. However, as the convention movement evolved into an institution in its own right, its organizers actively sought a more official representation from other recognized institutions: state governments, urban civic organizations, and private industry.

Starting with the Baltimore convention of 1852, future planning became a responsibility of those present as each session determined what city would host the next convention. Detailed arrangements for logistics of each gathering, with its attendant social events, were left to local committees in the host city, and existing business associations often took an active part in planning the conventions. Notices of meetings of these arrangement committees appeared in the host city's presses prior to the conventions. The job of publishing advance notices and issuing invitations was assigned to a specific committee from the sitting convention. Judged from the turnout and press coverage, the committees seem to have done a good job for most sessions, although back-to-back sessions in 1855 and 1856 at New Orleans and then Richmond were not as well publicized as most, and attendance was down for both conventions. In an effort to fix the next convention on delegates' calendars well in advance of the meeting, each session held after Richmond established the date, as well as the place, for the subsequent session. Postwar sessions were particularly well organized at the local level, and the elaborate planning for postwar conventions might reflect a growing strength and sophistication within urban civic business associations.[21]

Conventions actually placed no restriction on who could attend, but organizers included guidelines in their promotional material on how the public should approach their right to representation. These guidelines ranged from the earliest sessions' suggesting representation at the judicial-district level, to postwar sessions' calling for representation from states, counties, cities, business associations like chambers of commerce or boards of trade, and even from private corporations. Convention organizers also sought to contact directly those individuals whom they assumed would be interested in the convention by sending them invitations. Additionally, they appealed to the general public through newspapers and, in its lifetime, through *De Bow's Review*.[22]

The postwar convention organization process disclosed an urban orientation that did not supplant, but supplemented, the historic emphasis on state entity participation. In this, the convention movement reflected the transition from antebellum South to postwar South when urban centers like Atlanta, Nashville, and Birmingham experienced explosive growth. One impact of the abolition of slavery was to transfer southern wealth from labor to land, and a new emphasis on land values in turn prompted boosterism of towns in an effort to enhance property values.[23] The members of the Southern Elite who participated in the postwar commercial conventions recognized this reality in the way they modified representation guidelines, thus keeping the convention in step with a changing world. The change was apparent in the self-descriptions of the delegates, for the antebellum practice of listing delegates by home state, and perhaps also by home county, gave way in 1869 to listing the home city and even the particular private company or civic organization an individual represented. By the time of the last two conventions, delegate lists were no longer grouped by state, but organized strictly alphabetically.

The postwar shift in emphasis to appeal to an urban South presented an interesting method of balancing size and importance. Guidelines for delegate selection called for participation from cities, from established commercial associations, and from active businesses and corporations. Organizers implemented a weighting system for the ratio of delegates per represented body, and that system favored larger urban centers and successful business enterprises. The only changes made were to require greater population or capitalization per delegate. Whereas each city of five thousand could send two delegates to Memphis, it took a population of ten thousand to send one delegate to Baltimore in 1871. And while any corporation or transportation company could send a delegate to Memphis, only those with a base of $100,000 in "cash capital" could qualify for representation at Baltimore. Also, by the time of the postwar series, delegates were required to present their credentials to the local Arrangement Committee in order to be issued a badge for admittance into the convention, suggesting a higher degree of sophistication than had prevailed previously.[24]

While women were not restricted from participation in the conventions, women had no direct role in the commercial convention movement. No woman was ever listed as a delegate, and no woman addressed the convention sessions as an invited speaker. Yet, while women lacked official status in the institution, they were not barred from its proceedings. Reports of many of the sessions specifically mentioned the presence of women spectators and the fact that they were usually placed in a seating area apart from that designated for use by the delegates. Several conventions voted resolutions of thanks to the "ladies" for their presence. Such resolutions, worded in courtly fashion, spoke of the grace and beauty of the female audience. At the 1853 Memphis convention, President William C. Dawson turned to the women, seated to his right, and thanked them "in his own peculiarly happy style, gracefully attributing to their ever-welcome presence all the order and harmony which had characterized the deliberations of this vast body." Officials at the 1855 New Orleans session went so far as to pass a resolution on the first day officially inviting the "ladies of New Orleans" to attend the meetings and decreeing that the gallery be set aside for their accommodation. On the third day, the report indicated that a large number were present, and they were welcomed with a special speech by President Mirabeau B. Lamar, a "short but eloquent and flowery speech." Henry W. Hilliard remembered the women who visited the 1858 Montgomery session with more respect for the seriousness of their involvement: "[S]eats were crowded with ladies who felt as deep an interest in political affairs as the friends of contending statesmen in England did when those of the highest rank thronged the hustings." A report in the *Chicago Tribune* noted that many southern delegates at Louisville had brought their families, and that it might serve as a signal that the proceedings would extend several days.[25]

The presence of women in the audience as participants in the convention experience, albeit in a restricted role, suggests that time spent at the commercial conventions presented the delegates with something more than merely a business occasion. The convention consisted not only of the daily debate sessions but also of a span of several days of travel and social activities. For those attending from a distance, the travel allowed for rides—often complimentary rides—on the very railroad and steamship lines that the sessions supported so enthusiastically. Once arrived, visitors were honored with entertainment that ranged from banquets in Baltimore to balls in Charleston. Postwar sessions added gala public processions and side trips to points of commercial interest. Such activities added to the impact of attending the convention, providing a chance to socialize with prominent southerners outside, as well as inside, the halls of the daily debates.[26]

Despite the air of festivity that was portrayed in newspaper accounts of the conventions, convention participants intended that their deliberations and resolutions be taken seriously by government officials and by the public at large. They formalized proceedings by adopting clear rules of order and careful internal organization so that floor debates would be orderly and businesslike. Debate was restricted, committees became increasingly powerful, and voting procedures were clear-cut. Officers of the conventions developed means of gaining closer control in order to avoid disruption from those who sought to publicize political causes and distract attention from commercial subject matter. One sees evidence of strong, active committees with the ability to bury disquieting resolutions and usually a firm insistence from the presiding officer that delegates adhere to the rules of order.

The voting procedure was based on the concept that the convention derived from a regional representation of southern states. The total number of delegates sent from each state varied, but the size of state delegations did not determine the voting power of the state. Rather, for the sessions between 1853 and 1856, each state had one vote per resolution. Beginning at the Savannah convention in 1856, the more populous states gained advantage by expansion of each state's vote to match its total votes in the federal electoral college. The postwar conventions called for both per capita voting and voting on a state basis, with the later procedure to be implemented upon request.[27] The emphasis was on the regional character of the conventions, and organizers worked to prevent dominance of any session by local area delegations.

Officials on those central committees with power to channel and often control debates were drawn equitably from all state delegations. As early as the conventions of the 1830s, real control over debates resided not with the presiding officer, but instead with a single committee, variously known as the Select Committee, General Committee, or Committee of Twenty-One. By the time of the 1845 Memphis convention, the structure expanded, adding a Nominating Committee to select the president and vice-presidents and creating subcommittees to handle individual topics of debate. Membership on subcommittees was balanced to reflect participation of all states represented at the convention. This multitiered officer system enabled the organizers to filter endorsements by the convention through carefully selected buffers. Additional control came from adoption of Jefferson's Manual of Parliamentary Rules, a time limit on speechmaking, and a cap on floor resolutions once the standing committee handling that subject had made its report.[28]

Remaining conventions patterned their internal organization after that at Memphis. The president retained broad appointive powers, honorary vice-president positions were awarded to distinguished delegates from each state, and a central committee or business committee, along with its subcommittees, to some extent designated which issues would be given floor debate. Starting with the 1853 convention, state delegations selected their own vice-presidents and members of both the powerful central committee and of the more important subcommittees. Resolutions introduced from the floor went to the appropriate committee, which could then decide whether to recommend them to the general body. The time limit on debates was not always invoked, but most resolutions went through the committee structure prior to consideration by the delegates.

This format worked relatively smoothly to channel debates at sessions held between 1852 and 1856 and at the postwar conventions. However, between 1857 and 1859 the framework of the organization crumpled in the face of challenge from disunionist contingents. Pressured by demands for unrestricted debates that could be used to introduce the topic of reopening the foreign slave trade, presiding officers and central committees gradually lost control of the sessions. The Montgomery convention dissolved into a single-issue debate on this highly charged political question after radicals insisted on per capita voting and rules allowing unrestricted debate. At Vicksburg the central Committee on Resolutions was stripped of power, and resolutions were debated as introduced from the floor. In its closing chapter, the final antebellum commercial convention was seen by many as a poor example, if not a perversion, of the original intent. Even De Bow felt compelled to excuse the "excitable temperaments" on display at Vicksburg.[29]

Several conclusions can be drawn from this review of the format and structure of the conventions. Participants wanted their efforts to be taken seriously by the public. The formal structure, the careful rules of procedure, and the businesslike use of committees to keep the debates within desired bounds all illustrate the intention of the delegates to appear professional and respectable. They took extreme care to maintain a regional profile, rather than allowing local crowds to dominate. True, the carefully constructed machinery broke down between 1858 and 1859 in the face of an emotional onslaught from disunionist forces. But then, so did many other institutions. The majority of conventions demonstrate that participants took their job of debating the needs of the southern economy quite seriously, and that they strove to position the commercial convention institution clearly within the mainstream of reputable associations.

The commercial convention movement spanned more than a third of a century, originating in the late 1830s, expanding through sessions held in the 1840s, and reaching maturity with the Southern Commercial Convention that began in 1852 and ended in 1870, closing with the National Commercial Convention in 1871. This enterprise involved more than 5,700 southerners and 265 northerners, met in eleven different cities, and told its story to thousands of interested onlookers through the pages of newspapers across the country. In 1852, De Bow had anticipated such a body and shared his dreams with the delegates at that year's New Orleans convention:

Thus this Convention will become in time the great centre of the industrial interests of this region. It will collect through its committees and correspondence extensive information, which will be distributed gratuitously at the annual meetings. No one can estimate the good that will be effected. It will be the focus to which leading practical minds will be drawn. It will be in session always by its committees. It will be felt each moment, and throughout all our limits. No more powerful agency could be devised.[30]

The power of its agency can be debated, but its existence as an ongoing, regularly recurring assembly came to be just as De Bow had hoped, withstanding the turmoil of secession, Civil War, and Reconstruction. In its forums leaders from the South expressed their hopes and dreams, and within its assemblies they reached out after the war to northern delegates in an effort to bind the commercial wounds of the nation. The commercial convention proved to be an institution of significant size, with strong durability against extreme changes in the world of its participants. The next chapter introduces the delegates themselves, presenting a group portrait of those distinguished southerners who created the institution. That portrait reveals how much of a personal stake those individuals had in their region's future by exploring the extent of their achievements and community involvements and the degree to which their fellow southerners entrusted them with leadership authority in arenas outside of the commercial conventions.

2

Delegate Profile
Southerners of Distinction

Delegate rosters at the commercial conventions sparkled with well-known names: Mississippi's James L. Alcorn, Jeremiah W. Clapp, and John A. Quitman; Virginia's Joseph R. Anderson and Roger A. Pryor; Louisiana's Judah P. Benjamin and James Robb; Georgia's William C. Dawson, Alexander H. Stephens, and Eugenius A. Nisbet; South Carolina's James Gadsden, Benjamin F. Perry, and James L. Orr; Alabama's Henry W. Hilliard and Clement C. Clay, Sr.; Tennessee's John Bell, James C. Jones, and Aaron V. Brown; North Carolina's Romulus M. Saunders; Arkansas's Albert Pike; Texas's James W. Throckmorton and Mirabeau B. Lamar; Kentucky's John C. Breckinridge and Joseph R. Underwood; Maryland's John W. Garrett; and Missouri's Thomas Allen and Francis Preston Blair, Jr. Throughout its history, the commercial convention movement drew southerners who enjoyed public honors and trust, southerners of distinction. The presence of such men demonstrates that the commercial conventions were a part of the lives of some members of an elite group.

In order to understand more fully the linkage between the convention movement and the society it sprang from, it is important to identify more precisely the shared attributes and accomplishments of the men who attended the conventions. Did the conventions attract a cross section of southerners, or did they appeal to men with particular experiences? What personnel links existed between the conventions and other southern institutions? What experiences outside of the con-

ventions did the delegates share? What common background characteristics might help explain the delegates' opinions and perceptions as
voiced on the floors of the sessions? Just how representative of all delegates were the movement's leaders? Did such men attend regularly, and
were they there as working members of the organization, or were they
making perfunctory appearances? In what ways did the leadership of the
convention movement resemble other groups holding positions of power
and authority in the South? The answers lie in a collective biography, or
a prosopography, of the membership of the convention movement. The
profile that emerges reveals what a cursory glance at the convention
rosters suggests: a distinguished membership body and a leadership
corps with clear elite status.

Before studying the delegates systematically, two sets of criteria are
needed. The first pertains to the question of prominence and the general definition of elites: how best to determine which background characteristics of the delegates should be studied in order to measure the
elite status of the convention membership as compared to the general
population. The second criteria relates to delegate involvement in the
convention movement: a method has to be established to identify the
convention leadership as distinct from the delegate population. For
each task, social scientists' study of elite development proves useful in
identifying those delegates who wielded power, both within the broad
confines of the nineteenth-century South and within the narrower
bounds of the institution of the commercial conventions.

Elite study since the 1950s has focused on defining elites, defining
power, and determining how to identify members of an elite should one
exist. Modern studies of elites have generally taken one of three positions: the emphasis on institutional access to power as argued by C.
Wright Mills, the importance of the reputation of a powerful individual
as emphasized by Floyd Hunter, and further elaboration of the concept
that the decision maker is the one with power, as most notably presented by Robert A. Dahl. For the purpose of this study, to assess the
historical importance of the commercial convention movement through
analyzing the group profile of the convention participants, it also proves
helpful to consider the definition of a political elite offered by Peter
Bachrach. He defined political elites as comprising those individuals or

institutions who regularly have the capacity to wield a great amount of power and authority in the form of decisions and nondecisions that significantly influence the values of a society; to Bachrach, the search for a power elite should delve beyond the ranks of political officeholders in seeking those who shape a society's values.[1]

From a combination of Bachrach's broad definition of power with elements from the concepts of Mills, Hunter, and Dahl, the premise used here is that three criteria are to be considered in qualifying an individual or a group as powerful. They must occupy positional access to power, preferably in both political and nonpolitical institutions. They should carry a reputation for influence wielding among fellow members of the elite and among nonelite members of their society. Finally, members of such a group should differ markedly from the general population in shared social characteristics and social background that together would help shape their concept of a "good society" and provide them with a resource in defining proper behavior.[2]

A number of different personal characteristics are selected here for study to help determine the elite status of members of the convention movement within the broader southern society. Most of these characteristics relate directly to the positional approach: elective and appointive political officeholding, occupation, property holding and slave ownership, and political party affiliations. A delegate's reputation is judged from his multiplicity of officeholding, from his membership on the governing boards of educational institutions and other voluntary associations, from what was said and written about him in public, and from what his contemporaries said about him in private correspondence. Social background characteristics include education and religion, as well as age, state of birth, and geographic mobility.

The process for identifying convention leaders is based on the organizational format of the conventions themselves. Those who served in positions of leadership at the conventions derived their power from their ability to select those issues on which the conventions would express opinions, as well as what those opinions would be. True, the conventions could make no actual policy decisions for their society. Rather, their role was that of an advisory body whose recommendations served as a source of public opinion to those who would make decisions, either as members of policy-making institutions within state and federal governments or as members of influential social and economic institutions within the private sector. The fact that the conventions maintained a clear hierarchy of internal structure and placed real authority in the hands of presiding officers and committee members means that the leadership of the conventions obviously included those who held such offices, but it included those who influenced the outcome of convention deliberations in other ways as well.

The Convention Elite is identified here as those who exerted power, and power is measured in three specific ways. The first measurement is a delegate's personal decision-making authority, the second is a delegate's skill in persuading others, and the third is a delegate's ability to elicit deference from others as a sign of respect. A ranking system divides the powerful into degrees of influence wielding. The most powerful men were in positions to make decisions by virtue of serving in the office of president, holding seats on the central business committee, or being appointed to organize the succeeding convention. Such men receive the highest ranking on the power scale. Holding a lesser degree of decision-making authority are those who served as members of secondary committees: the standing committees, nominating committees, credential committees, or committees on permanent organization. They are assigned the second highest ranking on the power scale, along with those delegates who were able to persuade others to take a specific position by arguing in floor debate on behalf of a controversial resolution that was later adopted by the convention. Finally, those who are given the third power ranking filled the ranks of the temporary officers and the permanent vice-presidents and secretaries. These positions carried no real decision-making authority, but they marked a man as having a notable public reputation, as these men had been accorded an honorary distinction by their fellow delegates. The remaining delegates fall into the fourth or bottom level.

As a general rule, the number of leadership posts per session increased over time as the convention structure became more complex. The two Internal Improvement Conventions in 1845 and 1852 selected first thirty-two, then thirty-three leaders among the total delegates, a percentage of six and eight respectively out of each total. Succeeding conventions held between 1852 and 1857 saw some variance in proportion of leaders to delegate ranks when the total number in attendance was slight at Baltimore and Richmond, but the number of leadership positions grew in these years from twenty-seven at Baltimore in 1852 to sixty-eight at Knoxville in 1857. The average number of leadership positions in this series was fifty, or 10 percent. The sessions at Montgomery and Vicksburg drew a smaller than average number of delegates, but they retained the same levels of leadership slots, forty-nine and thirty-five respectively. Conventions held after the war followed the established pattern, and they offered between thirty-four and fifty-two leadership positions, an average of 23 percent of the total delegates attending.

By assigning each delegate a score on the four-position power scale, 596 members are identified here as the Convention Elite, the leadership of the convention movement. Within the Convention Elite, a total of 264, or 44 percent, are assigned the highest power ranking at least once in the course of their convention participation. Second-level designates number 170, or 29 percent. Those holding positions rated at the third power ranking number 162, or 27 percent. An individual qualifies for membership of the Convention Elite if he held a position of power at any convention, even if he attended only one convention. If an individual attended more than one convention, he might be assigned more than one power rating, but the group is divided on the basis of the highest rating an individual can be given over the course of his convention association.

As one would expect from the overall pattern of frequency of attendance, the majority of Convention Elite members attended only one convention. But although a majority, it is not as overwhelming a majority as found for the delegates outside of the Elite, a group that will be referred to as the Delegate Ranks. Sixty-one percent of the Convention Elite were present at only one session, contrasted with 92 percent of the Delegate Ranks. Within the ranks of the Convention Elite, 25 percent attended two conventions, 8 percent were at three conventions, and 4 percent participated in four conventions. Beyond that, five Elite members attended five conventions, three attended six, and one, De Bow, was present at ten meetings. By contrast, only 7 percent of the Delegate Ranks attended two sessions, and 6 percent attended more than two sessions. So while the leaders followed the general pattern in that most of them were active in the movement just one time, a higher proportion of leaders became involved a second time, a third time, or more. This indicates a stronger commitment to the institution on the part of leaders than most delegates showed.

Various biographical records were consulted for information about the convention delegates. The first record sets searched were those most readily available and those dealing with men of obvious prominence. The entire list of 5,716 delegates was checked against inclusive rosters of specific officeholding levels. The information was found to be complete on whether convention delegates belonged to the following groups: members of the United States executive branch and the Congress of the United States, members of the Confederate executive branch and the Confederate Congress, state governors, and members of Secession Conventions. Delegate names were compared to the list of military leaders of the Confederacy. The convention delegation list was also checked against a file of records about southern state legislators, executive officers, and county officials for the years of 1850 and 1860, which included data from the manuscript census as well as information about officeholding experiences. Finally, the delegate list was compared to a file of records taken from the manuscript census for individuals whose 1860 estate was valued at $100,000 or higher. These sources have allowed for a firm conclusion about what proportion of commercial convention delegates held positions of obvious visibility.[3]

The search for data about members of the Convention Elite was extended beyond these sources to numerous other biographical records. Such sources could be feasibly checked against a delegate list of 596 names, but not against the larger list of 5,716 names. These sources included national and state biographical collections, individual biographies, published speeches and writings by the delegates, state histories, manuscript private correspondence, and the collection of pardon requests received by President Andrew Johnson after the Civil War. Other sources consulted for information on officeholders among the Convention Elite included rosters of state legislators, executive officers, and delegates to state conventions. The primary source for measuring wealth and slaveholding levels was federal manuscript census records for 1850 and

1860; when other information was found, it was used if no census data could be obtained. Occupations of group members were found in the census, in the general biographical sources referenced above, and in studies devoted to particular industries. Information on prewar and postwar party preference and on secession position was obtained from both biographical sources and from a large number of studies of specific parties or political bodies.

Not every characteristic could be identified for every delegate in the entire set. In a sense, the number of delegates for whom substantial biographical information could be obtained was, to a large extent, predetermined by their social visibility, as the very sources of such information deal, by and large, with those of some prominence in the field under examination. Many delegates left no readily obtainable record of their lives, though one may safely assume that if their profiles were found they would show less distinction than those of the men about whom much is known.

Since the data collected does not make up a sample, the generalizations offered here necessarily apply only to those individuals for whom information has been obtained. Each of the biographical characteristics measured has been located for less than 10 percent of the Delegate Rank members but, predictably, for much higher percentages of the Convention Elite. Hence generalizations about member characteristics for the Convention Elite have the most supporting evidence. Nevertheless, so much information has been assembled for many hundreds of men that very definite patterns of status and achievement can be traced for far more than an insignificant scattering. The results make it clear that the convention movement was not conceived and executed by those out of touch with other institutions and other arenas of decision making in the South.[4]

A major finding from evaluation of the information collected is that conclusions regarding the member characteristics studied apply generally to participants at any stage in the movement. Whether one is considering delegates active in the Internal Improvement subset of 1845 and 1852, in the mainstream, Mid-1850s subset of 1852–1857, in the Montgomery-Vicksburg subset of 1858–1859, or in the Postwar subset of 1869–1871, the member characteristics of the subsets are remarkably similar. By focusing on profiles of each of the four individual subsets, one can, in a sense, look at a composite photograph of the delegates at each stage in the movement's history. Clearly, the subset pictures resemble each other more than they differ from each other. Despite noteworthy variances pertaining to some of the background characteristics discussed in the ensuing presentation, generally the similarity of characteristics among all subgroups makes it possible to apply the findings to those active at any time.

Equally important, the findings indicate a closeness between the Convention Elite and the Delegate Ranks in most areas. In order to further evaluate the relative prominence of members of the Convention Elite, their group profile has been compared to those of two other groups whose members were singled out for distinction in the same southern society and whose membership has been the subject of similar collective biographies: members of the Confederate Congress and delegates to southern state Secession Conventions or Secession Legislatures. All three groups can be distinguished from the general southern population in one way or another. That alone would have made them attractive comparisons. More pragmatically, these particular political elites are the largest southern groups of that era to have been systematically studied in a manner similar to that employed to study the commercial convention delegates.

It should not be surprising to find that there were personnel overlaps between the two political groups and the commercial convention delegation. Out of the total of 267 Confederate congressmen, forty-eight attended at least one commercial convention; a smaller proportion of secession body delegates were involved with the movement, 121 out of 1,859. Thus, while there was an overlap, the degree of overlap can be judged insufficient to weigh against the value of comparisons. Additionally, in an effort to analyze their relative level of wealth accumulation compared to that of other large bodies of southerners, the commercial convention delegates are compared in that regard to farm operators of economist Gavin Wright's Cotton South.[5]

Discussion of the group profile begins with the topic of age. Evidence indicates that the commercial conventions involved individuals who generally were in their mature years. They were not young men, still seeking their places in society, but rather men few of whom would have held expectations of profiting extensively in their own lifetimes from any improvements in the southern economy effected by convention activity. Their convention involvement was probably thought of more as public service than as an opportunity for short-term private gain. Year of birth is known for the majority of Convention Elite members, 350, or 59 percent, and employing their age in 1850 as the vantage point from which most began service in the commercial conventions, well over one-half, 59 percent, were already thirty-five years old. Most of those who were over thirty-five in 1850 were under age fifty, as only 14 percent were by then fifty years old or older. The median age in 1850 of the Convention Elite was thirty-five. The Delegate Ranks reflected a slightly younger age cohort, as the 436 delegates for whom age is known had a median age in 1850 of thirty-two. As did the Elite, this group split fairly evenly over and under age thirty-five at the 1850 bench mark. And too, as with the Elite, most of those who were over age thirty-five were under age fifty. Only 12 percent of this group was older than age fifty in 1850. Another way to evaluate delegate maturity is through median delegate age for the four convention chronological subsets, a way of depicting age at the time of convention activity. Age levels increased slightly as the years of convention occurrences continued, but subset median ages of forty, forty-two, forty-six, and fifty-two respectively show how the conventions attracted men of experience rather than men in early adulthood.

In this respect, the commercial convention participants were quite similar to those in comparative elite groups. Close to three-quarters of the Confederate congressmen ranged between age thirty and age fifty. Likewise, the median age of delegates to the various state secession bodies ranged between age forty and age forty-nine. For these three southern elites then, most members can be described as middle-aged, but not elderly. Maturity in years was a common characteristic of these particular leaders, while not necessarily a prerequisite for elite status.

Information on delegate occupations indicates that there was always a large number of lawyers and commercialists present at the conventions, and that together, representatives of these two groups outnumbered agriculturalists among those for whom occupations could be determined (table 2.1). Information on occupations also points to one clue about the leadership selection process: membership of the Elite included a larger proportion of lawyers than did that of the Delegate Ranks. Antebellum occupation is known for 361, or 61 percent, of the Convention Elite, and postwar occupation is known for 168, or 28 percent, of the group. Among the Delegate Ranks, antebellum occupation has been ascertained for 427 men and postwar occupation for 119. The comparative preponderance of lawyers within the Elite is clear: among those for whom the information has been gathered, a total of 42 percent of the Elite were lawyers in the years before 1860, 46 percent after the war. The comparative lawyer proportion for the Delegate Ranks contingent was 30 percent in the antebellum period, and it was 36 percent after 1865. The two groups compared more equally in the share of commercialists within their two ranks. Thirty percent of all delegates for whom occupation could be identified were commercialists before the war, increasing to 40 percent after the war. Likewise, the share of agriculturalists was almost equal in the two convention groups in both time periods. But unlike the case with commercialists, the proportion of agriculturalists declined in both groups after 1865, decreasing from slightly over one-third of each convention group to less than one-fifth. Aggregate information for each convention subset parallels the occupational divisions of the general delegate population. Interestingly, though, the delegate group active in the postwar conventions contained the lowest proportion of agriculturalists, before the war and after. Conversely, the group active in the 1858–1859 series had the highest proportion of agriculturalists in each time period.[6]

Within the larger classification of commercialists are three major subgroups: merchants; bankers, railroad promoters, insurance representatives; and manufacturers. The evidence suggests that a shift occurred after the war in that there was a decrease in the proportion of merchants present after 1865, and an increase in the proportion of men associated with finance and railroads. The proportion of manufacturers remained fairly constant between both time periods, accounting for less than 15 percent of all commercialists. The small number of delegates for whom evidence of involvement in manufacturing could be found,

TABLE 2.1
Delegate Occupations

Occupation	Convention Elite:		Delegate Ranks:	
	Antebellum Occupational Distribution (N=361)	Postwar Occupational Distribution (N=168)	Antebellum Occupational Distribution (N=427)	Postwar Occupational Distribution (N=119)
Lawyer	31%	40%	25%	34%
Agriculturalist	18%	9%	32%	12%
Commercialist: Merchant, Manufacturer, Banker, Railroad, or Insurance Industry	25%	36%	26%	38%
Professional: Editor, Educator, Medical Doctor, etc.	8%	5%	9%	13%
Lawyer-Planter	9%	5%	4%	2%
Planter-Commercialist	5%	4%	1%	1%
Lawyer-Planter-Commercialist	2%	1%	1%	0
Miscellaneous	2%	0	2%	0
Major Subgroups: Lawyer and Lawyer-Combination	42%	46%	30%	36%
Agriculturalist and Planter-Combination	34%	19%	38%	15%
Commercialist and Commercialist-Combination	32%	41%	28%	39%

TABLE 2.2

Antebellum Occupations Among Comparative Elites

Occupation	Commercial Convention Elite	Confederate Congressmen	Secession Body Delegates
Lawyer	31%	35%	29%
Agriculture	18%	10%	41%
Commerce	25%	7%	9%
Lawyer-Agriculture	9%	41%	2%
Other	17%	7%	19%
Combined: Lawyer and Lawyer-Agriculture	40%	76%	31%

less than 4 percent of the total convention delegates, helps explain the low level of enthusiasm for industrialization voiced by convention speakers. Apparently few personal ties to expansion of the manufacturing sector were represented within the membership of the convention movement.[7]

When the group composite of the Convention Elite is compared to those of the two southern officeholding elites, Confederate congressmen and secession body delegates, differences emerge (table 2.2). All three groups included a large number of lawyers, but when the number of those who were lawyers and combination lawyers-planters is totaled and compared, the overwhelming dominance of lawyers among Confederate congressmen is clear. Also there were evidently proportionately more who were engaged in agriculture in each of the officeholding elites than in the Convention Elite. The Convention Elite showed the strongest ties to the commercial arena of all three groups.

Thus far the group portrait of the commercial convention delegates, and especially that of the Elite corps members, is one of individuals of maturity involved somewhat more often in nonagricultural than in agricultural occupations. To these qualities can be added affluence. When material achievements are assessed by property holding levels and slave ownership, the impression that emerges is of a group that included many men of significant wealth. Six specific measurements of wealth are collected: individual (total) estate value in 1850; real, personal, and total estate value in 1860; and numbers of slaves held in 1850 and in 1860. Estate values are depicted in the form of median values, quartile value breakpoints, and quartile distribution; slaveholding levels are grouped into specific categories. Gauging from the known age range of the delegates, one would expect that the majority of any wealth accumulation would occur during the decade of the 1850s, in excess of inflation. So, it is not surprising to see large increases in estate values between 1850 and 1860. In this respect, the Elite and the Delegate Rank members shared the same experience. The median estate value in 1850 for both groups was slightly under $15,000, while the median estate value in 1860 (table 2.3) had climbed to $72,500 for the Elite and $118,500 for the Delegate Ranks.[8]

These increases of five- and eight-fold in a decade far exceed that reported for all southern states where estate values did not quite double, with the 1860 average state value at 188 percent of the 1850 value. Higher increases were reported for southcentral and southwest states than for the older states along the Atlantic seaboard. By comparison, the median 1860 value of the Elite delegates was 496 percent of the 1850 value, while the 1860 median value of the Delegate Ranks was 801 percent of the 1850 value. Among the four convention subsets, only the Postwar subset had a median 1860 Total Estate Value lower than that of the Elite. Yet even here, the median of $64,500 compared favorably to estate values of both Confederate congressmen and secession body delegates. The higher estate values of the Delegate Ranks is not unexpected as the analysis of occupations shows that a larger proportion of them were engaged in agriculture, with its attendant property holdings and slave ownership, than were members of the Elite. In those 438 cases where both prewar occupation and 1860 Total Estate Value are known for individual delegates, the evidence points to higher levels of wealth among those in agriculture than those engaged in either the legal pro-

TABLE 2.3
Delegate 1860 Estate Value

	Median Value	Lowest Quartile Upper Limit	Second Quartile Upper Limit	Third Quartile Upper Limit	Highest Estate Value
Elite (N = 188)					
Total Estate	$72,500	$23,000	$72,000	$160,000	$835,000
(Personal)	($30,500)	($9,000)	($30,000)	($89,000)	($700,000)
(Real)	($29,813)	($11,000)	($27,000)	($80,000)	($500,000)
Quartile Share:					
Total Estate		3%	11%	24%	62%
(Personal)		(2%)	(8%)	(22%)	(68%)
(Real)		(2%)	(7%)	(24%)	(67%)
Delegate Ranks (N = 276)					
Total Estate	$118,500	$35,000	$118,000	$225,000	$1,000,000+
(Personal)	($60,000)	($17,000)	($58,000)	($118,000)	($750,000)
(Real)	($41,167)	($13,000)	($41,000)	($100,000)	($1,000,000+)
Quartile Share:					
Total Estate		2%	14%	30%	54%
(Personal)		(2%)	(10%)	(24%)	(64%)
(Real)		(2%)	(8%)	(23%)	(67%)

fession or in commerce. Even so, within that same set of delegates, lawyers and commercialists accounted for over half of those holding estates valued at more than $100,000 in 1860. Clearly, material success among convention delegates was not limited to delegates in agriculture.[9]

Both delegate groups not only experienced increases in the levels of wealth but also showed similar concentrations of wealth (table 2.3). In each group, over one-half of the total wealth in 1860 was owned by the top 25 percent of the delegates. An even slightly higher degree of concentration characterized the Elite, where the top one-quarter owned 62 percent of the total wealth. At the other end of the scale in both groups, only a fraction of the total wealth, 3 percent or less, was in the hands of the lowest one-quarter of the delegates. Evidence about the convention delegates suggests that while wealth was concentrated, the degree of concentration lessened in the decade between 1850 and 1860 within both delegate groups, from a condition in 1850 where over 80 percent of the wealth was controlled by the top 25 percent of the delegates, to one in 1860 where approximately the same share of wealth was controlled by one-half of the delegates. Taken together, the overall increase in estate value between 1850 and 1860 indicated by median values and top limits of each delegate quartile, coupled with the downward spread of wealth among this group, demonstrate that for those individuals active in the commercial convention movement, personal experience buoyed their expressions of optimism about southern economic growth potential.[10]

A large percentage of convention delegates had accumulated startlingly valuable estates by 1860. That degree of affluence is further highlighted by comparisons with other historical study groups. Many commercial convention delegates had 1860 estates the value of which exceeded median values of estates held by Confederate congressmen and secession body delegates, and moreover the Confederate Congress median at $47,335 was above the average estate of their home county. Median values of 1860 personal property only for members of state secession bodies ranged from $5,000 to $50,000; the Convention Elite's median value was $30,500. Median values of 1860 real estate for those officeholders ranged from $4,500 to $30,000; the Convention Elite's median value at $29,813 was at the top of that range.

To capture the distinctiveness of the Convention Elite compared to the secession body delegates in yet another way, the Elite can be profiled by the number at the top wealth level. A total of 5.4 percent of secession delegates held 1860 real estates valued at more than $100,000. The comparative number among the Convention Elite was 22 percent. In the category of personal estate values, 7.4 percent of the secession delegates ranked at or above the $100,000 level, compared to 21 percent of the Convention Elite. Even the slaveholding farm operators within the Cotton South study group discussed by Wright had a far lower average 1860 estate value at $24,748 than did these convention delegates (Convention Elite at $114,197, Delegate Ranks at $159,399). Further, the Cotton South study group evidenced a higher degree of wealth concentration than did the Convention Elite. The richest 10 percent of the Cotton South planters held 53.4 percent of the group's agricultural wealth in 1860. The richest 10 percent of the Convention Elite held 35 percent of that group's total 1860 estate value. On the other end of the spectrum, the lower one-half of Cotton South planters held only 5.6 percent of the group's total wealth while, by contrast, the lower one-half of the Convention Elite held 14 percent of total 1860 estates.[11]

Members of the commercial convention delegations, as well as those in each of the other elite comparison groups, resided in a society that used slave labor and protected ownership rights of slave property. Yet, slaveholding was not universal throughout the South. On the eve of the Civil War, in 1860, just one-quarter of all southern white families used slaves, and only a small portion of them could be considered major slaveholders. Among the more than 384,000 slaveholders in 1860, the median number owned five slaves, and 72 percent of slave owners held fewer than ten slaves. Only 12 percent fit the planter category by owning twenty or more slaves, and just 3 percent were major slaveholders with fifty or more slaves. While it is not possible to state categorically what percent of the commercial convention delegates owned slaves on the basis of information collected for this study, the convention delegate slaveholder profile is that of an elite firmly entrenched in the economics of slave investments. There were only nine delegates for whom it could be determined that they held no slaves in 1860, and all findings pertaining to slaveholding almost certainly underestimate the number of slaveholders among convention delegates as the slave schedules of the census were not systematically examined. Records of 1860 slaveholding levels were obtained for 323 individual delegates, 98 of whom belonged to the Convention Elite.[12]

The median among convention delegate slaveholders fell at the point of owning twenty-seven slaves, and the Convention Elite and Delegate Ranks were identical in this measurement. That is over five times the median level of all southern slaveholders. Furthermore, there was a higher proportion of medium and major slaveholders among the convention delegates than among all slaveholding families (table 2.4).

TABLE 2.4

Comparative 1860 Slaveholding Levels

	Slaveholding Level:				
Group:	1–10 Slaves	11–19 Slaves	20–49 Slaves	50–99 Slaves	100 + Slaves
All Southern Slaveholders	72%	16%	9%	2%	1%
Elites:					
Confederate Congressmen	28%	20%	23%	13%	16%
Secession Body Delegates	36%	21%	24%	13%	6%
Convention Elite	34%	9%	14%	27%	16%
Average Among Elites	33%	17%	20%	18%	13%
Delegate Ranks	25%	17%	19%	22%	17%

Fifty-eight percent of convention slaveholders held twenty or more slaves, almost six times the comparable percentage of the slaveholding population. Finally, 16 percent of the Convention Elite and about the same percent of the Delegate Ranks belonged in the class that held one hundred slaves or more, a proportion far beyond the same share of the slaveholding population. While all of the elite groups outranked the general slaveholder population in terms of levels of holdings, among the four elite groups the Convention Elite slave owners included the highest proportion of those holding fifty slaves or more, and the second highest proportion of those holding twenty slaves or more.[13]

In view of the fact that debates at the antebellum conventions evidenced some concern that slaveholding was becoming too concentrated, it is useful to know that among members of the Convention Elite slaveholding appears to have been equally as concentrated as was the broader wealth index, total estate value. Where the top one-half of Convention Elite delegates for whom such information was obtained possessed 86 percent of total 1860 estate values, the top one-half of slaveholders in the Elite held 90 percent of all slaves owned. The quartile shares of slaves held by slaveholders within the Confederate Congress match the Convention Elite percentages exactly. The same information is not available for secession body members or slave owners of the Cotton South, but Wright found a decline in the proportion of those who held slaves between 1850 and 1860, and a general trend toward consolidation in large holdings within some of the most valuable cotton areas.

Taken together, the affluence depicted by 1860 total estate values and 1860 slaveholding occurrence among commercial convention delegates suggests that the convention movement attracted representatives of the top strata of the South's wealthy residents. Furthermore, such men took a leadership role in the movement as seen from the fact that the Convention Elite included a sizable portion of such men. The convention leadership had high personal stakes in securing southern property values. Their achievements no doubt gave encouragement to others still engaged in a struggle to prosper, and their continued presence on the floor of succeeding sessions must have confirmed to many the reality of the movement's affirmation of rich potentials offered by the South's economy. As a part of the broader segment of southern leadership, the Convention Elite included many who equaled or exceeded personal wealth levels of members of other power groups. Just as those men selected to deliberate in state Secession Legislatures and Conventions and those men who governed the Confederacy through its national legislature well represented the top wealth strata of the South, so did the top ranks of the commercial convention activists. This very commonality speaks to the issue of expected qualifications for leadership in that antebellum society. There is further evidence in Wooster's studies that the presence of slaveholders was increasing among the powerful. He found that slaveholders dominated the ranks of all southern state legislators and governors by 1860, and only in the states of the Upper South did less than one-half of the county government officials own slaves. Certainly the elite of the conventions and the political elite of the region must be thought of as men of affluence whose personal property holdings exceeded those of their fellow southerners by a long measure.[14]

Two additional elements of the social backgrounds of commercial convention delegates give further evidence of their upper-class representation: education and religious preference. In the antebellum South, formal education was generally an experience limited to the few. While information on the extent of training received by commercial convention delegates is limited, the 287 delegates for whom educational experience could be identified had generally been well trained before their convention service, and education evidently did not serve as a distinguishing factor between the Convention Elite and the Delegate Ranks. Among those for whom such information is available, more than two-thirds had attended college, an additional slightly more than one-fifth had received at least some formal training at academies or common schools, and only a small minority in each group had been self-taught. These convention delegates matched the profile of the Confederate Congress, whose members could also be described as well educated. Information about the educational levels of members of secession bodies is not available. Those convention delegates for whom religious affiliation is known number 109, and their association with smaller, more exclusive denominations is clear. Whereas three-fourths of 1860 church seating capacity in the South was divided nearly equally between Baptists and Methodists, the convention delegates among this group of 109 came predominantly from the ranks of Episcopalians and Presbyterians, with some Methodists.[15]

Apparently, participants in the commercial convention movement reflected a native-born southern orientation. Among those 748 delegates for whom state of birth is known, the overwhelming majority, 83 percent of the Elite and 85 percent of the Delegate Ranks, had been born in a southern state. Most of these native southerners hailed from the South Atlantic seaboard, as 60 percent of the Elite and 55 percent of those in the Delegate Ranks originated from that older southern region. Northern-born delegates made up just 14 percent of the Elite and 10 percent of the Delegate Ranks. In both convention groups only a small number of delegates, less than 5 percent, were born in foreign countries. Records compiled on a subset basis generally show the same proportions. Only among the disunionist sessions of 1858–1859 was there a higher proportion of natives of the Southwest and a lower share of northern-born delegates than among the general convention delegations.

Even if many of the delegates started out in areas of the South Atlantic, for the most part they did not stay there. A comparison of birthplace to residence at the time of convention participation illustrates that the general population movement within the South toward the new lands of the Southwest was an experience shared by commercial convention delegates. While the majority of both convention group members for whom birthplace has been ascertained were born in the Southeast, the majority of both groups, 56 percent of the Elite and 53 percent of the others, resided in the Southwest prior to the Civil War. Specifically, 58 percent of the 346 Elite for whom birthplace is known had found a new home outside of the state of their birth by the time of their convention participation.

Leaders of the commercial conventions, in their South Atlantic origins and their high degree of geographic mobility, fit the general profile of comparative southern elites. A majority of Confederate congressmen were born in states along the east coast of the South, and these politicians were highly mobile as three times as many moved to a different state during their lifetime as did not. Secession body delegates also reflected a pattern of higher proportions of native-born members among Atlantic seaboard state delegations than among deliberative bodies in the Southwest.[16] Among those in the Convention Elite for whom birthplace is known, more men were born in Virginia than in any other state or country, followed by a much smaller number of South Carolina natives and an even smaller number of Georgia natives. In fact, South Carolinians numbered exactly the same as those born in a northern state. Virginia claimed the largest number of native sons among Confederate congressmen, too, with Georgia and North Carolina in second and third order. Notably higher proportions of commercial convention delegates were born in the North or abroad than were Confederate congressmen, only 2 percent of whom were born outside the South.

Various political viewpoints were voiced on the floors of convention sessions, but the conventions do not appear to have been monopolized by followers of any one party. Political party affiliation of delegates paralleled reasonably well the South's party divisions for the time. Thus, with certain suggestive exceptions, the inclination of men to take an active role in the convention movement was not strongly related to party preference. During the 1840–1860 period, the Democratic-Whig division in the South was approximately 60 percent Democrat, 40 percent Whig. Antebellum party preference has been determined for 389 delegates, 189 of whom belonged to the Elite. In both convention groups, delegates were divided along the lines of the general population. Among the Elite, 62 percent were Democrats, and among the Delegate Ranks, 60 percent were Democrats. In this study, delegates are classified as Democrat if they always were Democrats, if they switched from opposition to Democrat prior to 1850, or if they left the opposition party after 1856 to join the Democrats. Similarly, in addition to those who were active in the Whig party exclusively prior to 1856 and in the opposition party thereafter, delegates are classified as Whig if they left the Democrats prior to 1850 to join the Whigs. Under this system, 33 percent of the Convention Elite and 37 percent of the Delegate Ranks were Whigs. Three percent of each convention group could only be determined as belonging to the American party, while 1 percent of the Elite could only be placed in the Free-Soil party and another 1 percent of the Elite belonged to both the Democrat and Whig parties with the timing of each membership unknown. The difference in percentage points between Democrats and Whigs within the Elite is twenty-nine, and that among the Delegate Ranks is twenty-three. Both differentials exceed the southwide presidential popular vote differentials for elections of 1852, 1856, and 1860, which were respectively eight percentage points, twelve points, and fifteen points. Thus, the commercial convention groups showed a somewhat higher Democratic proportion than did fellow voters in the South. This may largely be the result of the fact that 53 percent of the delegates resided in the Lower South.[17]

The exceptions referred to above concern convention subsets, and three sessions in particular. The early sessions in the convention series, those held between 1845 and 1852, were primarily concerned with development of the South's transportation facilities. They seem to have attracted more who were then or would later become Whig or American party members than Democrats by a margin of 54 percent to 46 percent. The late antebellum conventions of 1858–1859, at which spokesmen for extreme proslavery positions took control of proceedings, included the highest percentage of Democrats, 65 percent, and the lowest percentage of Whigs or American party members, 35 percent, among all convention subsets. In three of the conventions, antebellum Whig party members seem to have outnumbered Democrats, albeit by only a slight margin of less than 10 percent; two of these conventions were held in New Orleans in the years 1852 and 1869, and the third was the 1853 convention held in Memphis.[18]

Convention delegates' political ties on the eve of the Civil War may be probed by identifying their choices in the 1860 presidential election and their positions on the issue of secession. Evidence about support for candidates in 1860 has been ascertained for sixty-seven members of the Convention Elite and twenty-seven members of the Delegate Ranks. Findings follow in line with those relating to party preference. Among all delegates for whom the election choice is known, the majority of support went to the two Democratic candidates, Stephen A. Douglas and John C. Breckinridge. The Elite split seventeen votes for Douglas, sixteen for Breckinridge, and seventeen voted Democratic with choice of candidate unknown. Among the remaining share of members, 19 percent voted for the former Whig John Bell, and 6 percent voted for Abraham Lincoln. This information suggests that a lower than expected proportion of the Convention Elite supported Breckinridge, as among general southern voters the Kentuckian garnered 45 percent of the popular vote.[19]

The number for whom a position on the issue of secession could be determined is larger, 269, of whom 149 belonged to the Elite. In both delegate groups, the majority came to favor secession at some point, while only a small percent could be counted as Unconditional Unionists. Evidence suggests that just over three-quarters of the Convention Elite came to prefer secession. Yet few had belonged to the vanguard of that movement; less than one-fifth of all 269 delegates qualified as Immediate Secessionists, favoring disunion at the earliest official deliberation of the issue prior to President Lincoln's call for troops on April

15, 1861. The balance of the Elite took less determined positions on the secession issue. The hard core of Unconditional Unionists was small, only 8 percent. Among the Delegate Ranks, 17 percent could be labeled Immediate Secessionists and 6 percent could be considered Unconditional Unionists.

The commercial convention movement witnessed a growing support for disunion in the rhetoric and resolutions of those sessions held after 1856. Tabulation of secession positions taken by members of the convention subset of 1858–1859 reveals that these two final antebellum conventions did attract a higher proportion of Immediate Secessionists than did earlier or later conventions, a proportion twice as high as would be expected from knowledge of the Convention Elite profile. When the presidential election of 1860 came, members of this final antebellum subset also supported the candidacy of Breckinridge more heavily than did the general Convention Elite. Such findings support the conclusions drawn by some historians, including Wender, that the sessions held after 1857 were dominated by disunionists. Still, a sizable share of men within that final antebellum subset for whom political affiliations and position on secession could be determined had roots in the Whig party and continued to espouse the cause of Unionism in the face of the crisis. For this reason, it is difficult to agree with other historians who have claimed that these final prewar conventions were nothing more than gatherings of disunionists. Rather, the fact that delegates representing both sides of the political spectrum continued to participate speaks of the way that the conventions mirrored the diversity of opinion among southern leaders in general.[20]

The Convention Elite was rated not as strongly secessionist as delegates to secession conventions of the Lower South, among whom 71 percent can be classified as Immediate Secessionists and 29 percent as either Cooperationist or Conditional Unionist. Yet, commercial convention delegates seem to have been more supportive of secession than Confederate congressmen or secession body delegates in the Upper South. The Lower South residency of the majority of commercial convention delegates helps in part to explain this secessionist stance. Another factor might be the strong affiliation with the Democratic party among commercial convention participants. Alexander and Beringer found a high degree of association between a Confederate congressman's former political affiliation and his congressional behavior, especially in regard to views on secession, where over 80 percent of former Whigs were Unionists, and the same proportion of former Democrats were secessionists. Within the Convention Elite this high association held true for those in the majority, the Democrats. Among the 107 Elite members for whom both prewar party affiliation and position on secession are known, the Democrats split 79 percent in favor of secession while the Whigs divided more equally on the issue, with 56 percent taking a Unionist position.

Evidence on participation in the Confederate government and political affiliations made after the war shows that these areas did not distinguish members of the Elite from their fellow delegates. Once the war began, and the Confederate government was selected and its armies assembled, representatives from the commercial conventions took their places in that effort. They served at the highest levels—as vice-president, officers of the cabinet, members of Congress, diplomats to Europe, judges and other officials, and on the fields of battle. Those from the Elite held the more prominent offices, but both convention groups sent members into the war effort. A more detailed discussion of Confederate officeholding by convention delegates will follow, but the evidence is clear that many played important roles in that new nation.

Information about political affiliations after the war is not as plentiful as that pertaining to the antebellum period; still, it offers evidence that convention delegates became active in the Republican party. Among those for whom 1866 political alignment is known, in both delegate groups the largest proportion were active in the National Union movement, indicating a conservative political complexion at the start of postwar politics. Information about choices in the presidential elections from 1868 through 1876 suggests that members of the Convention Elite remained aligned with the Republicans by approximately 45 percent, while Republican ties among members of the Delegate Ranks declined from 57 to 50 and then to 17 percent. Separate from information about election preferences, affiliation with a national party in the postwar era has been determined for ninety-nine individuals; again the Republicans drew 50 percent of those in the Delegate Ranks and 40 percent of those in the Elite for whom that information has been obtained. This represents a strong showing for the Republican party. A measurement of postwar party affiliation at the state level indicates that the Republican party attracted 37 percent of the Delegate Ranks and 27 percent of the Elite members.[21]

The portrait of the commercial convention participants drawn to this point presents specific characteristics about those involved in the movement. With few exceptions, those member characteristics are evident during all chronological stages of the convention series, and generally the description of the group in regard to each characteristic applies equally well to members of the Convention Elite and members of the Delegate Ranks. So far, the qualities and experiences of these men offer little in the way of explanation for the fact that some were elevated above others within the convention movement. Members of the Convention Elite might have been slightly older than their fellow delegates, but the general age profile of both groups is that of men most of whom were in their mid-forties at the time of their convention involvement. Each convention group included many who rated far above the general southern population in property holdings and slave ownership, and both groups exhibited similar patterns of wealth concentration. Both groups included men who shared upper-class experiences in education and religion. Each group drew many members who had roots in the oldest southern states, and who had then moved west with new opportunities. Antebellum political alignments among members of both groups matched those of the South in general, and the members' support of secession generally did not place them in the radical vanguard. As they had been split politically before the Civil War, they continued to take different political positions after 1865. No convention session appears to have been completely dominated by members of either party, before or after the war.

Among those characteristics reviewed so far, the major distinguishing feature between the Convention Elite and the Delegate Ranks is occupation. The Convention Elite substantially outranked the Delegate Ranks in its share of lawyers, before and after the Civil War. Lawyers accounted for a sizable share of the Delegate Ranks, too, albeit a smaller share than within the Elite. Furthermore, the two groups included equal proportions of commercialists. So, selection of leaders must not have been made on the single basis of occupation, even though occupation seems to have played a role of some kind. Rather, the experience that seems to have distinguished the leadership group from the other was political officeholding. When the membership roll of the Convention Elite is compared to lists of southern officeholders, the presence of the convention leaders in the halls of national government and in the statehouses and courthouses across the South is apparent. By contrast, the Delegate Ranks had a far smaller proportion of officeholders in their number. Just how greatly the two groups differed in this respect, and how significant was the officeholding experience the Convention Elite brought to their unofficial job, will be addressed in the next chapter.

3

The Convention Elite

The commercial conventions attracted many men of distinction, so many that it does not appear to have been a coincidence that each convention session drew representatives of the top strata of the wealthy slaveholding class of the Old South. Again and again, a great number of attendants shared upper-class status in their home communities. In the group portrait of the commercial convention delegates as presented in the previous chapter, evidence of accomplishment and prominence stands out. And, in most ways, the 596 leaders and those remaining delegates for whom biographical records have been assembled seem to have resembled each other more than they differed. Yet, in one important respect there was a major distinction between the two groups. That difference was the political officeholding experience that leaders brought to the floor of the conventions.

Members of the Convention Elite held political office at a higher level and a higher frequency than did other delegates. At least one instance of political officeholding was discovered for 279 members, or 47 percent, of the leadership group. By comparison, the same information was found for only 6 percent, or 325 members, of those in the Delegate Ranks. Part of this difference is to be explained by the greater number of sources consulted for information on leaders. Where the same sources were consulted for both groups, however—generally sources pertaining to higher-level offices for which incumbency by any convention delegate is certain to be known—a decisively larger percent of leaders were found by a ratio of 1.7 to 1. Among those delegates for whom instances of officeholding were established, at every government level the Elite made up the majority: majorities of 64 percent of all federal national offices held, 62 percent of all Confederate offices held, 54 percent of all state offices held, 55 percent of local offices held, and 66 percent of instances of military experience. Most importantly, the Elite share of the more highly ranked offices was at much higher levels: 72 percent of the highest federal offices, 75 percent of the highest Confederate offices, and 73 percent of both the highest state offices and those who served as military generals. When officeholding occurred made little difference between the groups. In both groups the majority, or 77 percent, of instances of officeholding took place before 1865. Less than one-fifth, 17 percent, of officeholding was limited to the time after 1865, and only 6 percent of the time was an office held in both time periods.

A group-by-group comparison of those holding each rank of political office thoroughly demonstrates the greater public visibility of the Convention Elite (table 3.1). At the highest rank, each of the three who served as vice-president of his nation belonged to the Elite: John C. Calhoun, John C. Breckinridge, and Alexander H. Stephens. At the second rank, fifty-four of the seventy-six held Elite status. Eight of the twelve who served on the United States Supreme Court or in the federal cabinet ranked in the Elite. All six commercial convention delegates who served in the Confederate cabinet belonged to the Elite. The Elite claimed twenty-six of the thirty-nine convention participants who went to the United States Senate, and five of the eight Confederate senators. Among diplomats posted to major assignments, there were six Elite members out of seven in the United States service, and three of the four in the Confederate service. At the third rank, Elite outnumbered Delegate Ranks 161 to 96. Sixty-nine out of 109 convention delegates who served in the United States Congress or who sat on high federal court benches came from the Elite. The Elite sent twelve out of twenty-two delegates to the Confederate Provisional Congress, and only slightly less than one-half of the members of either the Confederate Congress or Confederate district judgeships. Elite members outnumbered fellow delegates at positions of command on the battlefields

TABLE 3.1
Political Officeholding Instances

Office Ranking	Elite	Delegate Ranks
Highest: USA or CSA President or Vice-President	3	0
Second: USA Supreme Court Justice, Cabinet Officer, Senator, or Diplomat at Major Post. CSA Cabinet Officer, Senator, or Minister to Major Post.	54	22
Third: USA Congressman or Judge. CSA Congressman or district Judge. USA or CSA military General.	161	96
Fourth: USA Diplomat, Postmaster or Customs Collector at major city, or Territorial Governor. State Governor, Supreme Court Justice, Statewide Official, Senator, member of Constitutional Convention or Secession Convention, or Presidential Elector At-Large. USA or CSA military Field Grade Officer.	222	203
Fifth: USA lower court Judge, Commissioner, District Attorney, or minor appointee. CSA Agent, Postmaster, or other minor appointee. State representative, lower court Judge, District Presidential Elector, or minor official. County Judge, Attorney, Sheriff, or Mayor of large city.	344	249
Lowest: County minor official, Mayor of small city, or city official. USA or CSA military Company Officer.	64	50

by two to one, furnishing 96 out of 142 generals. At the fourth rank, the Elite outnumbered the Delegate Ranks by a slim margin of 222 to 203.

As one would expect if political officeholding served as a dividing factor between general participants and leaders, members of the Elite who held political office were most likely to have held that office prior to attending a commercial convention. The order of this process has been ascertained for 184 officeholders within the Elite, most of whom held multiple offices. The great majority, 78 percent, came to the convention having already served in public office, and, for most, a commercial convention appearance did not mark the end of a political career. Over one-half of those who had already held one office prior to a convention went on to hold another. The leader whose political officeholding lay solely in the future was the exception, as this described just 22 percent of all officeholders among the Elite. In their high incidence of political officeholding experience, commercial convention leaders resembled members of the Confederate Congress.[1] Like those elected to steer the new southern ship of state, members of the commercial conventions who were elevated to positions of decision making and prominence within that voluntary association had already been entrusted with similar distinctions in public life. Although many among the entire delegate pool qualified as members of a southern socioeconomic elite, the leaders brought more; they brought a record of prior public service and a degree of renown that was not shared by all delegates.

A brief glance at the lives and careers of those who ranked at the very top level of convention leadership brings the Convention Elite profile to a personal focus. Individuals have been selected from each of the chronological convention subsets, all of whom held a leadership position at one or more convention. These short descriptions illustrate how the commercial convention movement acted as a magnet to attract leaders of southern society as the delegates assembled and reassembled from city to city.

The name of John C. Calhoun is certainly one of the most familiar of the Old South. In some respects it is surprising that Calhoun, the preeminent states'-rights Democrat, chaired a convention devoted to development of internal improvements. Yet, Calhoun fit the profile of convention leadership quite well. He was sixty-four in 1845, somewhat older than most delegates, but he was a native of the Atlantic seaboard, had attended college, practiced law, and had already held significant public offices prior to his convention appearance. His friend James Gadsden had convinced him to attend the convention. Also a native of South Carolina, Gadsden was fifty-seven when he first joined the convention movement at that same Memphis session. A college-educated planter, Gadsden had a personal interest in railroad promotion as he had served as president of the South Carolina Railroad in the 1840s. As minister to Mexico under President Franklin Pierce, Gadsden successfully negotiated a treaty that insured future railroad access to the Pacific along a southern route. He advocated construction of such a southern railroad at the conventions of 1845, 1853, and 1854 prior to his death in 1858. Clement Comer Clay served as vice-president from Alabama at the 1845 convention, was called to the presidential chair when Calhoun had to leave the convention prior to adjournment, and would return to the 1854 session in Charleston. Clay was fifty-six in 1845, a Virginia-born, college-educated lawyer. He had served his state in high public office prior to leading the state delegation at Memphis, as United States senator and congressman, as governor, and as justice of the Alabama superior court. Clay prospered as a lawyer and planter, holding an estate valued at $145,000 in 1860, which included more than fifty slaves.[2]

The president of the second convention, that held in New Orleans in 1852, was one of his state's most prominent citizens. Alexandre Mouton had served as a Louisiana state legislator and state senator, and he had then been sent to the United States Senate in 1837 as a Democrat. Mouton returned to sit in the governor's office until 1846, and he would later serve as president of the Secession Convention. He was a native of Louisiana, a combination lawyer-planter who owned 120 slaves in 1860 within an estate valued at $201,000. He was to write to De Bow of the high honor he felt having been selected to serve as president of the convention. One of the most active railroad promoters in the Southwest joined the convention movement at the New Orleans session, James Robb of Louisiana. This Pennsylvanian had left home at age thirteen and settled briefly in Virginia before moving to New Orleans in 1837. Robb was thirty-eight in 1852, and he had already made his mark in the Crescent City as owner of the New Orleans Gas and Banking Company, as a highly successful private banker, and as the newly installed president of the New Orleans, Jackson and Great Northern Railroad. Robb used the convention floor to argue in favor of public tax support for railroads, and he later worked beside Judah Benjamin in the Louisiana Senate to secure enabling legislation for public railroad investment. Despite delays in payments from his public stockholders, Robb completed his railroad to its Mississippi terminus by 1858. He was to lose his personal fortune in the wake of the Panic of 1857 and to leave the South prior to the Civil War, but Robb was an example of energetic entrepreneurship and an advocate of diversifying the southern economy.[3]

While Robb concentrated on railroads to service the interior markets, Albert Pike dreamed on a grander scale. He first participated in the convention movement at New Orleans, where he served on the Nominating Committee as a delegate from Arkansas. At succeeding sessions in 1854, 1855, and 1856, Pike would stand as a prime spokesman for a southern Pacific railroad. Born in Massachusetts, Pike moved west to Arkansas, where he practiced law, wrote poetry, and rose to prominence within Freemasonry. He served as reporter of the Arkansas Supreme Court prior to his convention activity, negotiated Indian treaties during the war as a brigadier general, and ended his Arkansas career on the state supreme court prior to the close of the war. Pike settled briefly in Memphis after the conflict, then relocated permanently to Washington, D.C., where he practiced law until his death in 1891. His poetic talents were evident in the many speeches he made on the convention floors and in his advice to President Johnson imparted within his pardon request: "It is not wise to furnish a conquered people with martyrs, more potent dead, than when alive. Living, we shall have no influence: by dying, we should become immortal and omnipotent, eternal inciters of future insurrections. . . ."[4]

William Crosby Dawson was fifty-four years old when he took the chair as president of the 1852 Baltimore convention. He would go on to preside at the two subsequent conventions as well, but he died in 1856. This Georgia native had been educated at Franklin College and practiced law in Greensboro. Prior to his involvement with the convention movement, he had staked out a political career of prominence, serving as a Whig in the United States House of Representatives from 1836 to 1841, returning to be unsuccessful as state gubernatorial candidate, moving to a bench on the circuit court, and returning to Washington as a senator in 1849, where he remained in office during the years of his commercial convention appearances. James Lyons of Virginia presided over the 1856 Savannah convention after having held prominent convention offices at Charleston in 1854, New Orleans in 1855, and Richmond in 1856. This Virginia native practiced law in Richmond, and he was age fifty-five at the time of the Savannah convention. Lyons had once aligned himself with the Whig party, but he changed allegiance in 1852 to the Democratic party. Prior to his commercial convention activity he held public office at the state level, serving in both houses of the legislature. He would go on to represent Virginia in the Confederate Congress and later to serve as defense counselor to Jefferson Davis. His 1850 estate was valued at $60,000, and he owned twenty-seven slaves as of 1860.[5]

James ("Lean Jimmy") Chamberlain Jones of Tennessee became involved with the conventions early on, holding a leadership post at five conventions between 1845 and 1856. Jones was thirty-six years old in 1845, born in Tennessee, attended public schools, and practiced law in Memphis prior to his death in 1859. A member of the Whig party, Jones held high-level political offices. He served in the Tennessee legislature prior to becoming governor in 1841, was reelected in 1843, and would sit in the United States Senate from 1851 to 1857. Jones had a personal interest in convention debates over railroad promotion, as he was president of the Memphis and Charleston Railroad. The commercial conventions attracted another prominent southern Whig, Judah Benjamin, who attended the 1852 New Orleans session and served on the Business Committee of the 1856 meeting in Richmond. Benjamin was born in the West Indies in 1811, raised in North Carolina, and attended Yale prior to beginning his law practice in New Orleans. His officeholding began in the Louisiana legislature in 1842, and from there as a Whig he was elected to the state constitutional convention of 1844 and then represented Louisiana in the United States Senate from 1853 until he supported the Confederacy. He assisted Jefferson Davis as attorney general, then secretary of war, and finally secretary of state. He chose to remain in Europe after the Civil War, where he enjoyed a legal career of prominence in London until his death in 1884. In the years before 1860, Benjamin promoted railroad expansion, as a director of the New Orleans, Jackson and Great Northern Railroad and as counsel to the Tehuantepec Company in its quest to acquire transit rights through Mexico.[6]

Matthew Fontaine Maury, international oceanographer and meteorologist, a native of Virginia born in 1806, chose a career in the United States Navy. Maury was an advocate of direct trade with Europe, and he supported government assistance in developing internal improvements. He served in leadership posts at the 1852 Baltimore convention and the 1854 Charleston convention. He brought technical expertise as superintendent of the United States Naval Observatory, and as vice-president of the Charleston convention he suggested that the delegates think of railroads as "iron rivers" flowing to the world marketplace. Maury resigned his commission to join the Confederacy and, like Benjamin, left the United States immediately after the war. Maury, unlike the Louisiana senator, would return to his native land. He signed on as an instructor at Virginia Military Institute in 1868, and from there he promoted the cause of steamship lines between Norfolk and Europe.[7]

The list of leaders from the conventions held prior to 1858 includes other prominent southerners as well. John Bell of Tennessee, nationally known leader of the Whig party and presidential candidate in 1860, attended two conventions in Memphis, in 1845 and in 1853. Prior to 1853, Bell, a college-educated lawyer, had served in both houses of the Tennessee legislature and in both houses of the United States Congress. He was fifty-six years old in 1853, and by 1860 he had accumulated an estate valued at $325,000. Tristam Burgess Bethea of Montgomery, Alabama, was active in the commercial conventions of 1856, 1857, and 1858. He had served in the Alabama Senate for two terms starting in 1853, and at age forty-six in 1856 was well on his way to becoming one of the wealthiest lawyer-planters among the delegates. By 1860 his estate was valued at $439,000 and included 221 slaves. Bethea, born in South Carolina, supported the secessionist cause and voted for Breckinridge in 1860. John Minor Botts attended the 1853 Memphis convention and that of 1856 in Richmond. He came to the conventions from various public offices, including a seat in both the Virginia legislature and the United States House of Representatives. This Whig planter-lawyer was born in Virginia in 1802, and he would take a strong Unconditional Unionist position during the war. Aaron Venable Brown, a Virginia-born lawyer-planter who resided in Nashville, where he was a law partner of James K. Polk, had served his state as representative, senator, and governor prior to 1848. His national officeholding came in the House of Representatives between 1839 and 1845, and he held the post of postmaster general from 1857 to 1859. Brown was a wealthy man, with an estate of $243,000 at the time of his death in 1859. He attended the 1852 New Orleans convention, and he held office at the 1854 session in Charleston.[8]

Nicholas Daniel Coleman attended five commercial conventions, and he held leadership positions at four. Born in Kentucky in 1800, where he served in the state legislature and was elected to the United States House of Representatives in 1829, this college graduate moved to Vicksburg, Mississippi, in 1832, where he practiced law and served as postmaster in the 1840s and as president of the Vicksburg, Shreveport and Texas Railroad. Coleman possessed an estate of $73,000 by 1860. A Democrat, he would later join the National Union movement in 1866 and support his state's National Union Republican party. David Hubbard held high convention offices at the sessions of 1856, 1857, and 1858. He was born in Virginia, and he moved to Alabama, where he had relocated at least four times prior to 1830. This farmer-merchant owned thirty-one slaves in 1860 and had held office in the Alabama legislature since 1827. He served in the United States House from 1839 to 1841, and after two defeats he won back his seat in 1849. He was a states'-rights Democrat, a Breckinridge supporter, and would later serve the Confederacy as commissioner of Indian affairs.

Luther Martin Kennett represented St. Louis at three conventions, those of 1845, 1853, and 1856. Kennett was born in Kentucky in 1807, attended private schools, and relocated to St. Louis in 1825, where he became a prominent merchant, mine owner, and president of the St. Louis Iron Mountain Railroad. By 1860 his estate was valued at $210,000. His political career began at the local level as a St. Louis alderman in 1843, then mayor in 1850; from there he was sent to the House in 1855 as a

member of the American party. Kennett left America after the Civil
War to live in France until his death in 1873. John Moore, a lawyer-
planter in New Iberia parish, Louisiana, attended four conventions and
held office at each: 1852 in Baltimore, 1853 in Memphis, 1855 in New
Orleans, and 1856 in Savannah. He served in the Louisiana legislature,
represented his state and the Whig party for three terms in Congress, was
elected to the state senate in 1860, and was a member of the Secession
Convention. Tench Tilghman of Maryland presided over the 1856 convention in Richmond, held office at the preceding session in Charleston,
and would attend the Savannah convention later that year. He was
forty-six years old in 1856, a native of Maryland. Tilghman was a planter
and railroad promoter, and he served as superintendent of the United
States Military Academy from 1847 to 1857 during the years of his convention involvement.[9]

Leaders of the Montgomery-Vicksburg conventions did not have the
national prominence of those from earlier sessions. The president of the
1858 convention was Andrew Pickens Calhoun, the forty-six-year-old
son of John C. Calhoun. A cotton planter, Calhoun had by 1858 returned to live at Fort Hill in South Carolina after his father's death, but
he retained property in Alabama valued at almost $300,000. In con-
trast to the prominence of his father, this Calhoun held no national
public offices and no state offices that have been determined. The president of the 1859 convention in Vicksburg was, like Calhoun, not a
prominent officeholder. Charles Clark was forty-eight in 1859, born in
Ohio but established in Mississippi as a planter. He owned 149 slaves in
1860, and he held an estate valued at $270,000, "acquired by my own
industry," as he told President Johnson. Clark had held state offices,
serving in the legislature in 1838 and again in 1856. He had been a
member of the Whig party, and he would hold the office of governor
during the Civil War.[10]

The most notable protagonists in action at these last two antebellum
conventions were William Lowndes Yancey, who instigated a convention debate over reopening the African slave trade, and his debate opponents Roger A. Pryor and William Ballard Preston. Yancey had served
one term in Congress and had sat in the Alabama legislature, but he
held no office in 1858. He was a Georgia native, educated at Williams

College in Massachusetts, and a planter-lawyer practicing in Montgomery. Yancey the orator was one of the South's most outspoken secessionists. He would later serve in the Confederate Senate prior to his death in 1863. Roger Atkinson Pryor, a Democrat, represented Virginia in the United States Congress in 1859 in his first and only term in that office. Previously he held the post of United States minister to Greece from 1854 to 1857. Like Yancey, Pryor was an extreme pro-South orator. Unlike Yancey, Pryor disputed the desirability of reopening the African slave trade. He would later serve the Confederacy in the Provisional Congress and as a brigadier general. After the war, Pryor moved to New York, where he eventually sat on that state's supreme court. In contrast to these two, Preston was not regarded as a radical secessionist and his profile more closely resembles that of the Convention Elite. A native of Virginia with prior officeholding experience in both houses of his state legislature, Preston served one term in Congress as a Whig in 1847, and then he held the post of secretary of the Navy under President Zachary Taylor. He was a wealthy planter-lawyer with an 1860 estate of $383,330, including fifty slaves. Preston resisted secession until after Lincoln's call for troops. He would serve in the Provisional Congress of the Confederacy prior to his death in 1862.[11]

Southerners outnumbered northerners among the total list of delegates at the commercial conventions held after 1865, and three of the five presidents of those sessions represented southern states. However, all three of these southerners had sided with the Union during the war. And, with the exception of Millard Fillmore, who presided over the Louisville, 1869, convention, the postwar convention presidents had only limited political officeholding experience prior to the time of their convention appearances. Charles Anderson presided over the first postwar convention. Before the Civil War, he had lived in Dayton, Ohio, and speaking to a crowd there in 1863, he made a virulent speech against southern slaveholders. Anderson served one partial term as Republican governor of Ohio in 1865; that came after he was elected to serve as lieutenant governor and the elected governor died in office. By the time of the 1869 Memphis convention, he had returned to live as a stock breeder in his native state of Kentucky, and he was evidently willing to look at former slaveholders in a different light. Chauncey I. Filley, former mayor of St. Louis and prominent Missouri Republican, presided over the New Orleans convention of 1869. This forty-year-old merchant had supported Frémont in the 1856 election and had served as an elector for President Grant in 1868. John Work Garrett, who chaired the 1870 session in Cincinnati, was one of the wealthiest men of the South, and he was one of its most successful entrepreneurs. A native of Baltimore, Garrett was at that time president of the Baltimore and Ohio Railroad and had been since 1858. Although not known as a politician, his name was mentioned among Democrats as a possible conservative presidential candidate for 1872. The final convention, that held in Baltimore in 1871, was presided over by Richard Moore Bishop, former mayor of Cincinnati and a Democrat who would later be elected to the Ohio governorship.[12]

While neither Filley, Anderson, nor Garrett had the stature conferred by national officeholding experience, they did share Unionist credentials, a not unimportant element in their elevation to leadership at conventions sympathetic to sectional reconciliation. The same cannot be said about other southern members of the postwar series Convention Elite, who more closely resembled the prewar leadership in both their officeholding experience and their differing attitudes toward the late conflict. They included Thomas Stanley Bocock of Lynchburg, Virginia, who served in the Virginia legislature both before and after the Civil War, represented his state in the United States House as a Democrat from 1847 to 1861, and then served as Speaker of the House for the Confederacy. Alexander M. Clayton of Mississippi served as a state vice-president at the 1869 Memphis convention. He was a Virginia-born lawyer-planter with an 1860 estate valued at $350,000, including 142 slaves. Clayton served in state government, as a supreme court judge and member of the Secession Convention, and in 1866 as a circuit court judge. He was associated with the Memphis and Charleston Railroad as well. Thomas Hardeman was one of the leaders in the postwar Democratic party in Georgia and an advocate of state aid for railroads. He attended the Louisville convention, and he would serve in the United States Congress twice. Other prominent participants in the postwar series were General Clinton Bowen Fisk of Missouri, United States attorney general and senator Reverdy Johnson of Maryland, United States congressman and diplomat Pierce M. B. Young of Georgia, United States congressmen Edwin Obed Stanard of Missouri and Charles Edward Hooker of Mississippi, Confederate congressman Robert Benjamin Hilton of Florida, and Governor James Webb Throckmorton of Texas.[13]

The members of the Convention Elite whose association with commercial conventions bridged the transition from Old South to New numbered forty-five. These men attended at least one convention held before 1860 and at least one other held after 1865. In most ways, they resembled their fellow leaders. They were men of maturity at the outset of the Civil War, and their ranks included far more lawyers and commercialists than agriculturalists. Their wealthholding was in line with that of the general Convention Elite. The group included twice as many antebellum Democrats as Whigs, and few could be considered Immediate Secessionists. Among all characteristics measured, that which most set these men apart from other delegates was the fact that so many of the bridging group held public office: there were 42 percent for whom at least one instance of public officeholding could be determined. Another characteristic that set them apart is not as easy to measure, but it recurs in their life stories. Among this group of men who returned to the commercial conventions after the war can be seen a demonstrated ability to adapt to change.

Robert M. Patton was the governor elected to office during Presidential Reconstruction in Alabama. He had attended the 1853 Memphis commercial convention and would serve as temporary president and state vice-president at the 1869 session in Memphis. Patton serves as an interesting example of a southerner who was willing to adjust to changed circumstances. He was born in Virginia in 1810, and he settled in northern Alabama. Patton was a planter who owned 117 slaves in 1860, possessed an estate valued at $248,607, and also dabbled in railroad promotions. He represented his county in the state legislature for many years, and he was serving as president of the Alabama Senate when he finally resigned in 1862 under a desire to discontinue association with the Confederacy. As a Unionist and former Whig, Patton had supported Douglas at the 1860 Democratic convention in Charleston. He was among those who joined together to rebuild the state's government in the short period of Presidential Reconstruction. He succeeded Provisional Governor Lewis Parsons as governor in 1866 to serve until displaced during Congressional Reconstruction. Patton continued to be personally involved in railroad promotion and industrial development in the years after 1865 as president of the Central Mining Company and of the Wills Valley Railroad. He was an optimist about the opportunities awaiting the South in 1865, challenging delegates to the 1869 convention not to despair, but rather to look to the South's great energy for hope.[14]

Henry Stuart Foote was also a survivor. Foote was forty-nine years old in 1853 when he first participated in a commercial convention. By that time he had moved across the South from his birthplace in Virginia to Tuscumbia, Alabama, in 1825, and then to Vicksburg, Mississippi, in 1826. Foote had attended Washington College, and he was able to establish himself as a preeminent criminal lawyer. He switched political parties throughout his life. Starting as a Democrat and Polk elector in 1844, he served in the United States Senate from 1847 to 1852, where he supported the Compromise of 1850. He then served as Whig governor of Mississippi from 1852–1854. He waged an unsuccessful bid for another senate seat in 1854 and left Mississippi for California, where he became involved with the Reform party. Foote returned to Vicksburg briefly in 1858, and he remained long enough to attend the Vicksburg commercial convention, where he led minority forces against those who took a radical disunionist position. He moved on to Nashville in 1859, and it was the Nashville district that he represented in the Confederate Congress. During the war he acted as a foe of President Davis, and he even went so far as to have conducted his own peace mission. Foote reminded President Johnson of his many efforts to thwart the Confederate government, of his wartime actions on behalf of peace, and admitted that he "cannot say that I at all lament the destruction of a system [slavery] which has been so long a prolific source of discord and unbrotherly feeling. . . ." Foote represented the city of Nashville at two postwar commercial conventions, those at Memphis and at New Orleans in 1869. He later left Nashville for Washington, D.C., and by 1878 he was sufficiently supportive of the Republican party to be appointed as superintendent of the mint at New Orleans under President Rutherford B. Hayes.[15]

Robertson M. Topp represented his hometown of Memphis at each convention held in that city, as well as at the 1871 Baltimore convention. Topp was born in Tennessee and was self-taught and studied law, but he branched beyond a legal practice into planting, finance, and railroad promotion. He ran the Memphis and Ohio Railroad, later to become a part of the Louisville and Nashville Railroad. He was thirty-eight when he attended his first commercial convention in 1845. A Whig, Topp had served in the Tennessee legislature prior to 1845, and he would later sit in that state's Secession Legislature. Topp prospered, securing an estate valued at $120,000 in 1860. After the war, he continued to practice law and joined the Democratic party prior to his death in 1876. He represented the Memphis Chamber of Commerce at the 1870 annual meeting of the National Board of Trade, along with another commercial convention activist, John Timothy Trezevant. Born in Virginia in 1814, Trezevant attended the 1845, 1852, and 1853 conventions along with the 1869 Memphis session. He was a business associate of Topp, a lawyer and railroad promoter, a Democrat who later joined the American party of 1856 and served as mayor of Memphis in 1847 and 1848.[16]

Milton Brown of Jackson, Tennessee, also a prominent lawyer and railroad promoter, served as president of the Mississippi Central and Tennessee Railroad Company from 1854 to 1856, and then president of the Mobile and Ohio Railroad from 1856 to 1871. He amassed an 1860 estate valued at $306,000. Like other leaders, Brown had spent time in public office prior to his appearance at a commercial convention. Brown had served on the Tennessee chancery court between 1835 and 1841, and at the time he attended the 1845 Memphis session he was serving as a Whig in the United States Congress. Brown continued his interest in the commercial convention movement after the war, serving as Tennessee state chairman at both the 1869 Memphis session and the succeeding New Orleans convention. Henry Hilliard, another Whig lawyer, was born in North Carolina, attended college in South Carolina, and taught at the University of Alabama before the start of his political career. Serving first in the state legislature and standing as a Whig presidential elector in 1840, Hilliard was appointed chargé d'affaires in Belgium before winning a seat in Congress. He was a long-standing political opponent of Yancey's. Still, this did not stop him from admiring Yancey as a speaker, for forty-four years after Hilliard's time at the Montgomery convention he recalled the debates as a prime example of Yancey's "power as a tribune of the people." He resisted the tide of the secession movement for as long as he deemed it politically feasible to do so, and he described his final decision as a "transient error" to President Johnson. During the war he served the Confederacy as brigadier general and commissioner to Tennessee. Hilliard left Alabama to practice law in Georgia after the war and represented his new home state at the 1869 Louisville convention. He affiliated with the Republicans, unsuccessfully ran for a seat in Congress in 1876, and at the age of sixty-nine he was appointed minister to Brazil by President Hayes.[17]

James Lusk Alcorn of Mississippi attended two conventions, both in Memphis, first in 1853 and again in 1869, where he served as chairman of the Committee on Mississippi River Levees. His age in 1853 was thirty-seven, and this native of Illinois had resided in Kentucky prior to settling on his Mississippi plantation. He attended an academy, then studied law and served first in the Kentucky legislature, then in office in Mississippi as state senator prior to his 1853 appearance in Memphis. By 1860 he had accumulated an estate valued at $250,000, including ninety-three slaves. Alcorn served as Whig presidential elector-at-large in 1852, but he voted with the secessionists as a delegate to the Secession Convention. He joined the Confederate army as brigadier general of the Mississippi militia. Alcorn understood his ability to influence others, and he explained to President Johnson in a request for pardon after the war that he voted in favor of the secession ordinance "to avoid what he [Alcorn] considered worse consequences, and to hold a position with the people whereby his influence would not for future usefulness be wholly lost. . . ." Alcorn did not lose his public standing, and he reached the zenith of his political career after the war, serving as Republican governor of his state from 1870 to 1871 and as its representative in the United States Senate from 1871 to 1877.[18]

Joseph Reid Anderson of Richmond, Virginia, contrasted in some interesting ways with Alcorn. Anderson attended six conventions, five between 1852 and 1857, and the 1870 Cincinnati session. This Virginian was native born and college educated. He was thirty-nine at the time of his first commercial convention, and he was placed on the powerful General Committee at his second. Anderson never held a United States federal office, but he served in the Virginia House of Delegates and attended the Secession Convention. He was a member of the Democratic party, and he vigorously supported the Confederate war effort as owner of one of the largest ironworks in the South. Anderson used slave labor in his shop, and he personally held sixty slaves in 1860. His prewar estate was valued at $200,000. He was found in the Conservative party after the war, and he was esteemed by Governor Francis H. Pierpont, who recommended that President Johnson grant Anderson a pardon in this way: "I have thought much about this case, and it strikes me under all the circumstances, it is not policy to strike down men of great energy like Anderson where his skill and talents are engaged in developing the country. . . . Perhaps I have a false estimate of this class of men, if I have it is because they are scarce. I would not give one of them for as many politicians as will fill an acre field."[19]

Jeremiah Watkins Clapp maintained a high profile in the convention movement. He held top posts in 1853, 1854, and 1857, and he returned as a delegate to three postwar conventions. Clapp was Virginia born, college educated, and settled in Holly Springs, Mississippi, to practice law. He served his neighbors in the Mississippi legislature in 1856 and again in the state Secession Convention. A one-time Whig, Clapp turned Democrat before the war and voted for Breckinridge in 1860. He advocated secession prior to Lincoln's call for troops, and he went on to serve in the Confederate Congress. Clapp belonged to the slaveholder class, owning sixteen slaves within an estate valued at $167,000 in 1860. He was only one year younger than Anderson, and he was also a pragmatist. He wrote President Johnson that he deserved a pardon, in part because he "recognizes as a practical result of the late contest the necessity of a hopeless abandonment of the [secession] theory. . . ." Clapp left Mississippi after the war to practice law in Nashville, but not before offering his thoughts on the late conflict to the graduating class of the University of Mississippi in June of 1866. Speaking on behalf of the board of trustees, Clapp cited proof of "southern honor" in the way many had "adapted themselves to the new condition of affairs" and had accepted defeat with a "chivalrous fidelity to the terms of surrender." Clapp charged his student audience with the duty of regenerating pros-

perity, and he encouraged them by painting a picture of new opportunities to diversify capital investments.[20]

These vignettes confirm that the public stage of the commercial convention was for many participants an extension of their lives in the
larger public arena. Key leaders among the Convention Elite did not
find within this particular institution recognition otherwise unavailable
to them. The data collected about those who made up the leadership
corps of the conventions indicates that they were men of distinction in
their world: sharing experiences common to members of the South's
privileged few and succeeding in carving out a life of prosperity. Many
among them took on the obligations of public service within local, state,
and national governments. They represented all political factions, differed among themselves, as did other southerners, on the reasonable-
ness of secession, and for the most part rebounded after the war to resume
positions of public attention. Delegates to the commercial conventions
availed themselves of its forums, using such opportunities to outline
their hopes for the future of their South. Once there, participants in the
movement exercised an authority that was based on reputation and personal achievement. Delegates rotated convention responsibilities among
themselves, one time the job of one man, another time the job of some-
one else. No evidence has been found that the movement was controlled by a small cadre. Rather, it attracted many who resembled each
other in private and public achievement, and it most frequently elevated those with experience in other positions of public trust.

Debates at the commercial conventions were conducted by men of
note, men who represented the top economic strata of white southern
males and men who in other capacities stood at the forefront of their
society. The credentials of the leadership of the commercial convention movement pass the test for membership in a broader ruling elite.
This institution was created by and existed with the support of men
who were in a position to have done otherwise. It evidently served their
purpose, and their involvement can be interpreted as one of the many
manifestations of the activism of the Southern Elite. They took the
lead, in this institution as in so many others, seizing the opportunity
to share their vision for the South in the hopes it would one day be
fulfilled.

II.

THE
ANTEBELLUM CONVENTIONS

4
Economic Policy

Calhoun must have begun to feel the excitement of the 1845 Memphis convention by the time his riverboat, the *Maria,* had passed Natchez on its journey upriver from New Orleans. His trip had been delayed by a mechanical problem, and a stop planned for Vicksburg had to be canceled. Still, residents of that town were not going to let the chance to greet this eminent South Carolinian literally pass them by. They crowded onto the riverboat *Ambassador,* band and all, and met the *Maria* midstream. The boats were lashed together, the cotillion music began, and Calhoun was feted all the way to Memphis. Within sight of their eventual destination, the joined boats were met by a third, the *Memphis,* whose decks were thronged with a delegation from her namesake city. Accompanied by an onboard band, the crowd on the *Memphis* joined their cheers to those of the thousands lining the river bluffs. In this way Calhoun was escorted into the city of Memphis to preside over the Southern and Western Convention.[1]

What Calhoun enjoyed in 1845 exemplified the drama of succeeding gatherings as well. Convocations of the commercial conventions had a festive air. It was evident in the ceremonial pomp of opening day, in the glowing resolutions of thanks on closing day, in the banquets and balls accompanying the official proceedings, and even in the decorations adorning the various meetinghalls. These occasions were celebrations of the South's glories, and the rhetoric of the movement's leading speakers as well as the preferences indicated in key convention resolutions bespoke a shared confidence on the part of the movement's leadership about the South's economic future. After all, these men were living proof of the many economic opportunities open to southerners. Achievers, they reflected the flush society of the 1850s cotton boom.

Speakers at the conventions did not evidence anxiety about whether the South would continue to enjoy prosperity under her existing economic framework. To them, signs such as the South's rich agricultural bounty, her cotton-crop income, her expanding transportation network, her plentiful but as yet untapped mineral resources, and the enthusiasm of her inhabitants all indicated an assured future of expanding economic opportunities for enterprising southerners. The job of the conventions, as its promoters outlined it to each other and to the public, was to explore ways to guide the South to its maximum potential. Self-complimentary about the South's progress, and yet critical, too, of areas where southerners lagged behind, the commercial conventions presented a public forum in which it is now possible to trace the evolving definition of a "good society" as perceived by leading southern statesmen and businessmen.

The call to the movement heard in 1845 was echoed and reechoed through succeeding meetings: let us assemble together as reasonable men to map out strategies to increase southern prosperity. The impetus for convening was not to foment economic revolution or to revamp the southern economy. In that sense, the men were conservatives. Yet, these were not antimodernists. Rather, content with the South's basic structure but desirous of keeping pace with new opportunities, they hoped to augment the region's wealth. As producers, they sought improvements to an agrarian-based economy that would allow them to increase profit margins on exports. As traders, they proposed that the South take a more direct role in marketing both its own exports and those of the West. They looked for ways to reduce that share of southern profits that went to others, especially to northerners.

Strains of sectional resentment against the North came through quite clearly in each of these areas, but the recourse this movement sought was economic, on the field of commerce, not politics. The delegates looked to fellow southern investors for aid in this campaign, and they urged government action as well. Before 1856, the conventions laid recommendations for public aid on the doorsteps of both the federal government and the southern state governments. After 1856, acting to defend slavery against what they perceived as a growing threat to its existence emanating from the national government, the convention delegates tempered their economic liberalism by limiting appeals for public aid to state resources alone.

The prominence of the commercial convention movement in the years before the Civil War provides support for those who have emphasized both the pivotal decision-influencing role played by southern slaveholders and the region's commitment to slavery as the basic source of southern wealth. Despite the fact that the leadership ranks of the conventions were not dominated by agriculturalists, the conventions presented a consensus on the profit potential of the South's agricultural-based slave economy and on the need to protect slave property from any and all attacks. Notable among recent historians who have placed slaveholders at the center of authority in the Old South is Eugene D. Genovese, but the list includes William L. Barney, Randolph B. Campbell, William J. Cooper, Jr., Carl N. Degler, James Oakes, Michael Wayne, and Ralph A. Wooster. Their work emphasizes the power and prominence of slaveholders, which Genovese went so far as to characterize as "planter hegemony."[2] That the conventions attracted a great many slaveholders who held far above the average number of slaves and that they presented a proslavery argument time and again show that the conventions had the support of slaveholders, whose interests they acted to protect.

Whether or not their attachment to slavery was a rational economic decision is a different question, as the relative prosperity of the antebellum South has been a divisive issue for historians. Recently, econometric analysis has been used to support the contention that the slave South enjoyed a thriving economy and that slavery was profitable. Robert W. Fogel, in the forefront of those who have concluded that southern cotton planters acted rationally in investing in commercial agriculture based on its profit level, ranked the antebellum South as fourth in the world at the time in its state of economic advance. John Hebron Moore's recent history of the cotton southwest similarly contends that southerners of that region shared a widespread belief that the

South was riding on a wave of prosperity that was limited only by the size of its cotton crop. While economist Gavin Wright concluded that slavery eventually weakened rather than strengthened the southern economy, preventing the development of a free-labor market positioned to take advantage of opportunities to diversify, he described the southern antebellum economy as prosperous and growing at comparatively strong rates. This prosperity, according to Wright, derived not from the efficiency of the application of slave labor, but from an increasing world demand for cotton that sustained its price level. Wright argued that slavery was profitable in the antebellum South because slave prices were increasing, making an investment in slavery one that promised to provide capital gains. In his analysis, that economic reality provided a unifying factor among all slaveowners and potential slaveowners, regardless of their direct involvement in cotton production. Any situation that they perceived as threatening the future of slave property values was one to be resisted, even if that meant breaking the ties of the federal Union.[3] The actions of the commercial conventions demonstrate a perception of an association between slavery and prosperity. Clearly, the sanctity of the slave economy lay at the crux of the convention movement's definition of a good society.

The convention movement's consensus on slavery did not close the delegates' eyes to their economy's weaknesses, for also at the center of their notion of the good society was the need to be receptive to opportunities for improvement. The historian to write most recently in some depth about the conventions, Laurence Shore, saw the commercial, railroad, and planters conventions of the 1840s and early 1850s as efforts at reforming the southern economy, and he traced the antecedents of the 1881 Atlanta International Cotton Exposition back to these prewar commercial convention efforts to encourage diversification. Shore described the conventions' proponents as neither typical planters nor typical leaders, and yet they were not outsiders either, as they were well respected. The evidence collected for this study supports Shore's contention that commercial convention proponents were well respected, but not his premise that they were not typical leaders. If anything, they represented the very highest strata of the South's wealthy, political activist echelon. The most serious question about Shore's interpretation, however, arises from his emphasis on the reformist drive of the convention movement leaders and the negative bent of their evaluation of the South's progress. He argued that much of their impetus came from pro-slavery leaders' drive to erase the stigma of a perceived economic inferiority, and he included the convention movement in what he labeled as a "flood of criticism."[4]

Were they, as Shore argued, seeking reform of the southern economy? The delegates did not discuss agricultural reform, and they did not demand so much a cessation of what basic economic activities already existed as an expansion of the commercial delivery network. Harold Woodman seems closer to the mark in his assessment of the antebellum conventions. He claimed that they promoted a more rounded economy through development of manufacturing and railroads. Staunch defenders of slavery, they were nevertheless receptive to introducing into the region nonslave industry with its free-labor artisans. They did not begrudge the North its wealth, as long as that wealth did not come at the expense of southern producers. In fact, they admired northern commercial enterprise, but they saw no reason southern traders could not service southern producers equally well. They admonished fellow southerners for making few investments outside of agriculture, but they did not go so far as to argue that agricultural investments were in and of themselves bad. In summary, their efforts were directed at preserving the slave-based agrarian South, not replacing it. Yet, the South was not to be preserved pristine, untouched, and proudly distinctive from the modern economy of the North; it was to be brought forward with the times, as long as the additions did not undermine the basic structure.[5]

The debates of the conventions offered little evidence of deep divisions within southern society over long-term economic goals. Most speakers appeared eager to experience the benefits of limited modernity within the confines of a slave economy. They provided a supportive chorus to the forces that were changing the face of the South in the 1850s. Industrialists were praised, not ostracized. Railroads were deemed desirable because of the links to the world market they could bring to remote agricultural producers. If, as some have suggested, the southern yeomen resisted this intrusion, their objections were not aired on the convention floor.[6] Direct trade with Europe and South America was attractive because it would enhance southern profits, making funds available for further internal improvements. Urban commercial centers were to be expanded, not feared.

Those who stood behind the commercial convention movement did not seek to create a premodern island in the midst of a commercially interactive world. Even the politically explosive sessions of the late 1850s outlined the same economic priorities as had earlier conventions. As they moved the convention movement onto a track leading to acceptance of disunion, the leadership of the meetings held after 1856 offered a vision of a southern nation that met all the criteria for progress so long endorsed at these annual sessions. Unlike the portrait drawn by J. Mills Thornton of radicals in Alabama, the convention leadership did not evidence anxiety over cultural changes wrought by expanded transportation networks and a growing urbanization of the southern interior. In their positive attitude toward modernizing features such as railroads, towns, and general improved market access, the commercial convention leadership conforms more closely to the economic elites of North Carolina and the South Carolina up-country so well described by John Inscoe, Paul D. Escott, and Lacy Ford.[7] As they moved toward southern nationhood, these defenders of slavery moved in step with the rhythm they had long been beating on the drums of progress.

Another basic belief that the convention leadership shared, although it must be inferred from their action as much as from their words, is that those members of the society with high personal stakes in its continued prosperity had a responsibility to help direct public policy. Ford found evidence of the same philosophy among the businessmen of the South Carolina up-country. He referred to it as their Victorian belief in progress, their conviction that men of talent and resources must be committed to implementing changes needed for long-term growth and prosperity.[8] This assumption underlay the official statements of purpose made by those leading the convention movement, statements found in preconvention materials published by planning committees, in letters sent to the convention planners by prominent southerners in advance of the opening session, and in speeches made by presiding officers at the outset of the meetings.

These documents emphasized two primary responsibilities: to investigate the facts pertaining to the South's resources and what had been done to develop those assets, and to set forth directives for public consideration that would meet the long-range economic objectives delineated by the convention participants. Typical of those to follow was the overview presented by John C. Calhoun in 1845. To him, the purpose of the Memphis convention was to determine what the resources of the Southwest were, how they could best be developed, and how far the aid of the federal government might be invoked for that purpose. Maunsell White, a wealthy, sixty-nine-year-old planter-merchant from Plaquemines, Louisiana, evoked the enthusiasm of the association in his opening remarks to the delegates assembled for the first day of the 1852 New Orleans convention: "This friendly meeting of representatives of popular interest for the common consideration of so profound a question, is entirely in accordance with the character of our age and day; and we sincerely trust, gentlemen, that the result of our deliberations will be equally compatible with the all-accomplishing genius of our country." "They met not for idle purpose; not for the mere expression of opinion," proclaimed James Robb to that same convention assembly, "but to accomplish results. . . ."9

Edward Bates, Whig legislator and previously congressman from Missouri, wrote to De Bow apologizing for the fact that he would not be able to attend the upcoming 1852 New Orleans convention. In that letter, Bates envisioned the catalyst effect of the convention: "It proposes to develop and put into useful action the boundless resources of the South and West; to stimulate enterprise and wealth . . . and to make transportation rapid, safe and cheap. . . ." The official report of the Baltimore convention of 1852 outlined the purpose of the assembly as "stimulating the Commercial progress of the Southern, Western, and Southwestern States in their direct intercourse with Europe, and in regard to their Internal Trade. . . ." When a Baltimore delegate objected to a resolution appointing a committee to publish freight rates into and out of Baltimore as asking for something that already existed, Joseph Rogers Underwood, senator from Kentucky, defended the resolution and challenged the convention as to its real benefit unless it could provide needed information. In an article for his *Review* about the 1853 Memphis convention, De Bow assessed the conventions as being "deliberative assemblies, which, coming fresh from the people, and embodying their sound practical sense and native energies, tempered by the judgment of leading men, leave an impression not easily effaced, even where the desired results are not immediately accomplished." William C. Dawson opened the 1853 Memphis convention with this charge to the delegates: "We are here to ascertain how we can best develope [sic] our vast resources, and fulfil [sic] the duties incumbent upon us, by leaving a rich heritage to our children."[10]

Starting with the 1854 session, promoters began to introduce a sectional slant to their statements of purpose. While these leaders did not state this directly, the flare of sectional animosities generated by the Kansas-Nebraska controversy and the strong showing by the precursors of the Republican party in the 1854 congressional elections lay behind the sense of urgency heard at these and succeeding antebellum sessions. Job responsibilities to collect and disseminate information and to present concrete suggestions remained the same, but the long-range economic goal was not only to increase southern prosperity, but also to seek economic retribution against northern economic and political aggression. Newspapers alluded to this change as they discussed the upcoming meeting.[11]

De Bow could not be present at the 1854 Charleston session, but he communicated by mail to its organizers, who then read his message to the delegates on the floor. His letter was in part an effort to review the history of the convention movement and, therein, to demonstrate that the movement had supported measures that had strengthened the South's power and thereby its claim to an equal rank in the Union with attendant equal rights. De Bow hoped that in the discovery process that had unfolded at these annual sessions the South had come to realize the extent of its lingering vassalage to the North. The sectional overtones of subsequent actions taken by the Charleston convention did not go unnoticed by the press. Nine months later General Mirabeau B. Lamar defended the New Orleans convention against unnamed detractors who would impute to it motives other than "virtue, patriotism, and improvements within the limits of the Constitution," but he admitted "we are driven to our present post from a stern necessity of self-preservation."[12]

Bad winter weather in Virginia and a rumor of smallpox in Richmond restricted attendance at the 1856 Richmond convention. The delegates on hand adjourned the session hardly into the first day, deciding to wait until the second day to begin business in the hope that more delegates would arrive in town overnight. At the second day's session, De Bow proposed that the convention adjourn and meet again there in May, but the delegates decided to proceed, in part to avoid the appearance of failure. In his preamble to the resolution for adjournment, De Bow again summarized his perception of their purpose, conveying an aggressive sectionalism not heard in introductory remarks by speakers at previous conventions. He told his audience that they met for the usual purpose of securing the prosperity of the South as a part of the Union, but he added that they met also to "vindicate and maintain their rights and institutions whether that Union shall subsist or not." De Bow's position was counterbalanced by a Unionist proclamation from President Tench Tilghman, but even he acknowledged they met amid circumstances in the country "of the most peculiar and momentous interest."[13]

James Lyons, a Virginia Democrat active in state government and brother-in-law of Governor Henry A. Wise, took the president's chair at the second 1856 convention, that held in Savannah in December after the presidential election. His opening address set forth the convention's task: to make the South more comfortable, strong, and equal in all respects. While Lyons claimed the session would not discuss politics, he set the stage for just such a debate when he cast the North in the role of the enemy and referred to the recent federal election as a "war" to be renewed in 1860. Lyons asked the delegates to "obtain some practical result" to rekindle the South's urban growth and commercial activity.[14]

De Bow was in his full glory at the 1857 Knoxville convention. His presidential address began with an observation that a convention forum had often been used to prepare the public for great emergencies, and then he exhorted his audience to proceed with talks and plans to strengthen the South. They did, and the committee created to address the public on results of the 1857 Knoxville session stated its belief that the convention movement had met annually in order to gather information pertaining to trade and to discuss plans to alleviate the condition of sectional economic inequality. While the committee admitted that the imbalance had not been remedied by 1857, they laid the blame for shortcomings not on their own failures, but rather on congressional and state legislative inactivity. Ominously, they charged the convention move-ment with a duty to prepare the South for commercial independence as she would soon, in all probability, seek political independence.[15]

Rather than take on that broad assignment, the last two conventions held before the Civil War shifted the attention of the movement almost exclusively to the topic of reopening the African slave trade. During the course of debate on this issue, many perceptions about the nature of the South's political economy were revealed, but they were not deliberated in the usual convention context (these perceptions are discussed in greater detail in later chapters). The 1858 Montgomery convention was little more than an extended debate on reopening the slave trade with a short digression to the topic of filibustering in Nicaragua. The 1859 Vicksburg session did focus on other commercial topics, but by com-parison to earlier conventions little work was done. Yet interestingly, General Charles Clark, presiding at that last antebellum convention, defended the institution's reputation against those who by 1859 were charging it with exceeding its recognized role of promoting commercial independence. He acknowledged that the delegates met as commer-cialists, but he added that they had the right to delve into seemingly political questions that were tied to the needs of southern commerce.[16]

What General Clark claimed as a right was something that conven-tions held between 1845 and 1856 had deliberately avoided. While dis-cussions on the expansion of direct trade with foreign countries and debates on the best route for a Pacific railroad led the delegates to express political and sectional opinions, over the course of eight sessions held in the years prior to 1857 the convention movement sought ways to enhance the South's prosperity in a forum that was determinedly non-partisan. Statements by participants, made in public and private, under-lined their determination to steer their debates away from the disagree-ments of party politics and the emotions of sectional animosities. This resolve was applauded by the southern press. Evidence cited earlier in Chapter Two indicates that the movement was not dominated by mem-bers of either major political party. Nor were most of the delegates for whom biographical information could be obtained politicians. The leadership did include many who brought political officeholding experience to their convention post, yet the percentage of identifiable political officeholders among all delegates remained relatively stable between 1845 and 1857, averaging 17 percent per session until 1858, when the percentage of politicians climbed to 40 percent, and the leadership's intentions were overtly political, rather than commercial.[17]

Despite the increasing politicalization of the movement, the vision of the good society they sought to improve, or defend, remained intact: it was a society whose economy revolved around commercial agriculture. A resolution adopted at the 1856 Savannah assembly summarized this outlook: "That in the opinion of this Convention there is no truism in political economy which addresses itself more forcibly to the favorable consideration of the slaveholding States at the present time, than that by agriculture we live, and by commerce we thrive." Historians have debated the soundness of this choice, but clearly the conventions offer proof that the welfare of agriculture was a central concern.[18]

Nevertheless, the conventions left to others the task of improving agricultural production methods. Despite the sizable number of planters among participants in the convention movement, other than endorsing the need for better public education on the subject, the conventions seldom discussed farming methods. This was due no doubt in part to the existence of the Agricultural Association of the Slave-holding States, founded in 1853 at Montgomery, Alabama, and active throughout the years before the Civil War. The Charleston commercial convention of 1854 did call for the merger of the two associations, since their objects coincided and many planters found it difficult to attend both annual meetings. No reference, however, was made to the merger at any later session. In one of the few instances of specific recommendations on farming concerns, the Savannah convention of 1856 endorsed public assistance to southern agricultural and mechanical associations in their efforts to provide fairs easily accessible to the public.[19] Evidence about occupations of the delegates suggests that the majority of those involved in the movement were not themselves agriculturalists, but as lawyers and commercialists their service-industry ties to an agricultural economy made them dependent upon its prosperity. As partners with producers, their efforts were directed toward an expansion of the commercial facilities of the South.

In surveying the southern economy, the conventions listed agricul-ture as the South's basic strength. They listed its primary weaknesses as surplus agricultural production with insufficient access to markets, a diminished level of commerce passing through the major southern trad-ing centers, and a failure to develop mining and manufacturing. While the leaders sensed that the South seemed to be missing valuable oppor-tunities to remedy these deficiencies, they suspected that the North, and specifically New York and Boston, seemed to be pressing its com-mercial advantage to the detriment of southern agricultural investors. To remedy these conditions, as investigative researchers and as eco-nomic planners the convention movement participants set about sug-gesting ways for the South to expand its agricultural markets, create a transportation infrastructure sufficient to reinstate their section to its earlier commercial preeminence, and extract full value from natural resources that could sustain a more diversified manufacturing economy. The leadership of the movement focused its attention clearly on the marketplace. These were not dreamers who sought a society that would live apart from the world. As representatives of an economy based on staple-crop production, these men looked to demand from consumers worldwide to sustain high prices for southern exports. To expand their market presence, the conventions focused on several basic strategies, all of which will be discussed in the next chapter.

Starting with the 1856 Savannah convention, leading spokesmen for southern independence sought to persuade the delegates to envision a future South, independent and separate from the North. Still, in many ways, the South they described was the South the conventions had sought to create all along. Addressing the participants of the 1857 Knox-ville session, De Bow pictured what would follow independence. The South would see the emergence of great interior towns and seacoast cit-ies engaged in trade sufficient to fund any need of a central government despite a reduction of trade duties below current levels. The new coun-try would enjoy strong economic and hence strong diplomatic ties with England, and through free-trade policies its major rivers would trans-port talented, skilled immigrant artisans. Eventually, it would be joined by Mexico, Central America, Cuba, and the West Indies, and its slave labor force would grow by natural increase and by a reopened slave trade. De Bow's presidential address at that 1857 convention was in an important way a far cry from his address to delegates five years earlier at the 1852 New Orleans gathering. Back then, De Bow asked the convention to banish commercial apathy with four remedies: railroads, manufacturing, foreign commerce, and annual sessions of the Southern Commercial Convention. In 1852, De Bow was appealing to his fellow southerners to stand up forcefully within the Union. By 1857, he was enticing them to step away from it. At Knoxville, looking to a new nation, he enumerated all that had been accomplished to place the South in readiness for departure: networks of railroads, a more vigorous shipping industry, factories, and new southern colleges. The South could now stand alone without the Union. Her economic agenda had remained the same, but her political agenda had changed.[20]

During the course of the time between the Savannah convention in December of 1856 and the Knoxville convention in August of 1857, the direction of the commercial conventions reversed irretrievably until after the Confederacy's defeat. No longer did the conventions devote the majority of their time to exploring various possibilities for economic growth. Rather, they became virtually single-mindedly engaged in an introspective review of the peculiar needs of their slave economy as it defended itself against what was perceived as a mortal challenge. Gone until 1869 was the commercial focus of the movement. Gone also was a willingness to seek federal involvement in the South's economy. In part due to a states'-rights mentality, but more as a result of fears of federal intervention into slavery, the conventions after 1856 resisted the chance to seek help from the national government for large-scale internal improvements.

Whereas participants at sessions held before 1856 spoke to a national audience of like-minded men of business, North and South, and to national party officials reaching into all sections for support, the attention of the movement shifted inward after 1856. Leaders of the conventions were now speaking primarily to the South, and their subject was the very future of the South's existence as a unique culture. As they debated the issue of reopening the African slave trade, the conventions were actually dissecting the very economic logic of the institution of slavery.

In that sense, even though it was a breech in the tradition of the commercial convention movement, this debate marked a continuation of the Convention Elite's action to fulfill their self-appointed task of defining a good society. The final stage of the antebellum commercial conventions was a journey into the vortex of the southern slaveholder's dilemma.

5
Economic Building Blocks

The conventions held between 1845 and 1859 advocated a policy of economic liberalism, a belief that public policy should actively promote economic growth. This belief applied to all the major strategies the conventions presented to the South: to modernize her transportation networks, to secure a more profitable international trading basis, to supplement the economy with manufacturing, and, last but not least, to protect the region's investment in slavery against internal and external threats. This is not to deny that many who participated in the sessions disagreed with the philosophy of economic liberalism and spoke in opposition to resolutions calling for public aid to various projects, but the majority of votes were cast in favor of an activist public policy.[1]

The basic transportation mode in the antebellum South was its water network, and the convention movement recognized that the task of keeping the major rivers and harbors clear of obstructions lay beyond the means of private industry. Convention spokesmen generally looked to the federal government to assume responsibility for aid to navigation at locations of national importance. This solution struck at the heart of partisan politics and constitutional interpretations, but most conventions took their lead from the 1845 Memphis convocation, where John C. Calhoun told the delegates that as a result of the invention of the steamboat he considered the Mississippi River to be an inland sea, and that therefore the federal government had a constitutional duty to secure its open navigation. The delegates agreed with Calhoun, and they expanded the concept to include safe communication between the Gulf of Mexico and the interior via the waterways of the Mississippi and the Ohio. They called for federal funding of navigational improvements on those two rivers and their principal tributaries, and they called specifically for federal action to deepen the mouth of the Mississippi River. They endorsed the need for federally financed lighthouses and beacons along the Gulf, and even federal funding of a canal that would link the Mississippi with the Great Lakes and then, through the St. Lawrence, with the Atlantic. Eight years later in Memphis, delegates recommended that the federal government fund engineering reports on flooding patterns of the Mississippi and install a system of permanent hydrometers to record water levels and channel changes. Despite some disagreement between New Orleans forces, led by General John A. Quitman, and St. Louis forces, led by Francis P. Blair, Jr., the 1853 convention endorsed a resolution calling for increased federal appropriations to clear the Mississippi River at both New Orleans and Des Moines, along with federal appropriations to clear other southern harbors.[2]

The 1854 Charleston convention did not endorse federal aid to navigation, but a close study of the debate indicates the delegates acted not so much out of opposition to the principle of federal funding as out of determination to keep the convention from becoming mired in a partisan debate. William Dawson, as presiding officer, opened the convention with a request that the delegates endorse federal assistance to Mississippi River navigation, and De Bow sent a letter asking for the same. The Business Committee reported out favorably a resolution recommending federal assistance for navigational improvements; however, on the convention floor, a number of delegates, led by William H. Polk, brother of former president James K. Polk, disagreed with this proposal. While a majority of delegates supported the committee's resolution, they were unwilling to divide the convention over the issue, and the resolution was withdrawn on the suggestion of a bipartisan delegation.[3] Clearly, leading members of the Convention Elite continued to recognize the need for federally provided navigational improvements, but they made the harmony of the convention an even higher priority.

Sessions held between 1855 and 1859 firmly endorsed the need for federal action. In 1855 at New Orleans, Albert Pike alleged that at Charleston the needs of the western states for navigational improvements had been voted down by delegations from the Atlantic seaboard states. As if to counter the earlier choice, those in attendance at New Orleans went firmly on record in favor of federal aid to navigation for several specific projects: the Louisville and Portland canal, Galveston harbor, the harbor of any city engaged in direct trade with Europe, improvements along the Red River, a federal navy yard at New Orleans, marine hospitals at New Orleans, and a canal that would stretch across Florida. A resolution appealing for federal improvements to deep water ports at Port Royal in South Carolina, Beaufort Harbor in North Carolina, and Mobile, Alabama, was adopted at the 1857 Knoxville convention. Specifically, the delegates wanted to see establishment of federal coaling stations at these locations. At the last antebellum convention, a majority of delegates set aside southern paranoia, invoked Calhoun's definition of the Mississippi as an "inland sea," and voted in favor of a resolution seeking federal aid to clear obstructions at the mouth of the Mississippi despite a recommendation to the contrary from the Committee on Resolutions.[4]

Communication networks were considered similarly vital to commerce, and the conventions were willing to hold the federal government responsible for seeing that mail service and telegraph access were provided on an equal basis to all sections of the country. The 1845 Memphis convention adopted a resolution charging that the southern and western regions suffered from poor service, and that the federal government should act promptly to extend the magnetic telegraph into the Mississippi valley. The topic came up again at sessions in 1853 and 1854. Each time, the convention noted that southern mail service was insufficient, and that the government had an obligation to improve it.[5]

Every antebellum convention devoted attention to the need to improve southern land transportation. The mania for railroad building was national, and the rate of southern railroad growth was explosive during the years of the prewar commercial conventions. The South almost quadrupled its railroad track miles in the decade of the 1850s, from 2,133 miles to more than 7,400. Yet, according to analyst John Stover, there were problems with the southern roads. Most lines were concentrated in the South Atlantic, and southern railroads were generally heavily dependent on local, not interstate, traffic. Compared to northern roads, they were inferior in construction, power, and rolling stock, and they lacked bridges and depot connections.[6] Even so, discussions at the conventions focused not on problems such as these but on the more basic necessity of securing public support for funding of initial construction.

The delegates were unanimous on the importance to the region of railroad expansion, and there were those among the audience who had a personal stake in expansion of this network. Many of the South's leading railroad entrepreneurs took part in the convention movement, and these key industry representatives were elevated into the Convention Elite: John Work Garrett of the Baltimore and Ohio; James Gadsden of the South Carolina; John P. Screven of the Savannah, Albany and Gulf; Milton Brown of the Mobile and Ohio; James Robb of the New Orleans, Jackson and Great Northern; Judge Harvey W. Walter of the Mississippi Central; Dr. Morris Emanuel of the Southern Railway of Mississippi; Nicholas Daniel Coleman of the Vicksburg, Shreveport and Texas; Samuel Tate of the Memphis and Charleston; Edwin Cole of the Nashville and Chattanooga; and Luther M. Kennett of the St. Louis Iron Mountain.[7] They brought personal experience to the debate and, together with those who would benefit in other ways from increased railroad facilities, led the commercial convention discussion about railroad development by focusing on two subjects: what benefits the South would derive from railroad construction, and to what extent construction should be funded with government assistance.

To railroad proponents, an expanded railroad system was a basic attribute of the good society, and the primary benefit it offered the South was market linkage, both within the South and between the South and the outside world. Secondarily, they believed that railroad networks created valuable by-products in their wake. Civic boosters and representatives of railroad companies took advantage of convention sessions to entice potential investors from both the public and the private sectors.[8] As a result, the railroad debates at the conventions often read like promotional brochures for specific projects. But rather than allow deliberations to dissolve into open haggling about the better route or the better road, the conventions assigned the task of recommending specific investment opportunities to general railroad committees, who more often than not recommended all projects called to their attention.

The general philosophy seemed to be that any expansion of the South's railroad facilities was a positive step, especially when it linked the South with the West, or the South Atlantic with the Mississippi River valley. At the 1845 convention, Calhoun predicted that a railroad link between the Atlantic and the Mississippi River would create a new and vast internal market for the South, and he proposed a route with main terminus points at Atlanta, Chattanooga, Nashville, Vicksburg, and New Orleans. Looking westward, Albert Pike of Arkansas suggested to the 1852 New Orleans session that railroads could link western trade to New Orleans rather than to commercial centers along the Atlantic coast. De Bow told the same audience how railroads could allow southern agriculturalists direct access to markets at their best prices, freeing them from shipping schedules, which were often disrupted by foul weather or geared more to the inventory needs of southern merchants than to the needs of southern exporters. He also foresaw other by-products of railroad expansion: increasing land values, urban development, and expanded manufacturing opportunities made possible by railway's reliability, speed, and economy of transport. The 1852 New Orleans convention voted in favor of better interstate cooperation and exchange of information in the task of completing trunk lines, and it assigned a committee the job of consulting with engineers about conversion to a standard track gauge. Delegates who convened in Baltimore on December 18, 1852, congratulated their hosts on the upcoming completion of the first railway linkage between Baltimore and the Ohio River, and they noted how the project had enjoyed much public support. Recognizing the importance of western trade, the 1855 New Orleans convention endorsed state aid for completion of a railroad from New Orleans to the Ohio River. Similarly, the 1856 Savannah session recommended favorable consideration of state aid to railroads that would link the Atlantic and Gulf States, and more specifically it requested the Kentucky state government's assistance in linking the Chesapeake with the Ohio River by means of a railroad through the Cumberland Gap.[9]

Railroad promoters cast their eyes beyond the shores of the South, to an international link across the Isthmus of Tehuantepec in Mexico. Judah Benjamin spent more than twenty years on this endeavor, and he used the 1852 New Orleans convention forum to publicize the project. There, delegates approved of a resolution presented by Joseph Anderson of the Tredegar Iron Works of Virginia that labeled the construction of a railway and water communication across the Isthmus of Tehuantepec to be of "national importance." Tehuantepec promoters gained the support of the 1853 Memphis convention as well, despite a spirited attempt by Missouri forces to prevent it. The 1855 convention endorsed state government assistance to efforts to construct a Tehuantepec road, the 1856 Savannah convention endorsed an appeal for a federal mail contract to the project, and in 1857 delegates endorsed negotiation of a right-of-way across both the Central America Isthmus and Tehuantepec and federal assistance to a completed road.[10]

Railroads were prized not only for the way they linked various geographic points, but also for their ancillary impact on social development: railroads could civilize, they could spread republicanism, and they could open the South to diversified economic enterprises. In speeches to the 1852 New Orleans assembly, both James Robb and Judah Benjamin projected the importance of railroad development as essential to mankind. Robb called it "a civilizing and conquering power, greater than that of all the cannon that ever belched forth destruction on the battlefield. The rail-road is the greatest of all missions, save that alone of our Saviour." Benjamin saw in it a chance to accomplish the American mission of spreading republicanism by successful example rather than by warfare. A Mississippi delegate summarized his perception of the importance of railroads to society this way: "We live in an age in which the rail-road system is the great labor-saving machinery in the way of transportation and travel, controlling directly the commercial world, and indirectly affecting all the pursuits of life. . . ." The Charleston convention focused on yet another social function of railroads, the way that railroads would serve to draw the "bonds of union" together within the South and to "perpetuate our social and other institutions."[11]

The fact that railroads could be associated with both national linkage and sectional separation seems illogical, and yet the story of what position the conventions took on the issue of federal assistance to railroad growth is the story of their growing sense of southern separateness. At every session but one prior to 1857, participants in this movement endorsed federal aid. Whether it was to be in the form of land grants, reductions of tariffs on railroad iron, or direct funding of road construction, the commercial convention delegates agreed that there was justification for government action. This did not relieve state governments, municipal governments, or private investors from a responsibility to secure funding themselves, but clearly the mainstream conventions spoke with one voice in insisting on federal assistance. However, at the last three conventions, held in 1857, 1858, and 1859, the majorities rejected the principle of federal aid to railroads and concentrated instead on state aid. Their shift in position was not a retreat from support for a liberal state economy, but rather a political statement pertaining to a much larger issue, the rights and duties of the South as the delegates perceived them.

The Memphis convention of 1845 went on record in support of federal land grants of alternate sections and granting of rights-of-way to roads. The attendants urged citizens to support the issuance of state charters for railroad construction and any such aid as the states, "in their discretion, may deem proper and necessary. . . ." The 1852 New Orleans convention body voted in favor of both federal land grants to railroads and the levying of property taxes to fund municipal subscriptions to private railroads. Similarly, the assembly at the 1853 convention endorsed federal land grants to the states for use in construction of the Mississippi Valley Railroad. The 1854 convention had been unwilling to endorse federal aid to navigation, and similarly it rejected resolutions for federal land grants to railroads and lower duties on railroad iron imports. It did, however, endorse a general policy of state financial aid to railroads, cautioning that such state credits be "properly grounded." Not unexpectedly, the New Orleans convention held the following year was not as encumbered by restrictive constitutional interpretations, and it endorsed grants of alternate sections of federal lands to southern railroads. The delegates at New Orleans also took an extremist position in favor of total abolition of duties on railroad iron and materials, and the Richmond convention of 1856 followed suit. The 1856 Savannah meeting passed no general resolution on railroads, but it did endorse limited federal assistance in the form of land grants to be exchanged for the provision of sites for military defenses along a proposed Pacific railroad line.[12] By the time of the Montgomery and Vicksburg conventions, the subject of federal aid to railroads was a dead issue, never even broached. However, the Vicksburg session did agree on the merits of a southern Pacific railroad, as will be discussed below.

Navigational improvements, communications technologies, and railroad expansion: these formed the basis of the infrastructure that the commercial conventions envisioned. An additional major transportation project had a strong coterie of supporters at the conventions, a southern Pacific railroad. As they offered the vision of a South linked to Mexico, to California, and to the Far East, the conventions provide yet another manifestation of the drive to expand southern markets. They also provide compelling evidence that the conventions were for many an appropriate place in which to map out long-range economic strategies for the South.

In their quest for a southern Pacific railroad, the conventions followed a path of retreat away from federal involvement, just as they had done with the issue of federal aid to general railroad development. But in the case of the transcontinental railroad project, the reasons seem to have had less to do with symbolism and more to do with pragmatism. No issue stirred the fervor of the conventions as much as did the drive for a Pacific railroad. By 1852 the project had drawn the attention of railroad promoters across the country, and the vision of such an accomplishment intrigued every commercial convention from that time forward.[13] Early on, the delegates agreed on the necessity of such a railroad, but throughout most of the history of the antebellum convention movement, they failed to agree on which of three terminus points, New Orleans, Vicksburg, or Memphis, would be the most desirable. Not surprisingly, boosters from all these cities lobbied hard at the convention sessions.

The 1852 New Orleans convention recommended that two roads be built, each terminating at the Mississippi River, one to the north and the other to the south of the Ohio River. The Baltimore convention spent little time on the subject, but it did vote in favor of the project as important for "national defense." By the time of the 1853 Memphis convention, Congress had appropriated money for a War Department survey of four routes, including a southern one, and many southerners had faith in Secretary of War Jefferson Davis to issue a survey report favorable to the South. James Gadsden was involved in negotiations with Mexico over land deemed attractive as a southern route for the railroad, and the Texas legislature had promised state aid to those who would build such a road through Texas. Two companies, the Vicksburg and El Paso Railroad and the Atlantic and Pacific Railroad, had obtained state charters from Texas. It was fairly well known that the subject of the Pacific railroad would be a key topic at the Memphis convention, and in the days prior to the opening of the convention, newspapers in Memphis and New Orleans agreed on the choice of the same route, one that would terminate at Memphis.[14]

As it turned out, the 1853 convention did not argue over routes but rather over funding. Democrats, led by John Quitman of Mississippi, took the side of private funding assisted by government surveys and land grants while Whigs, led by John Bell of Tennessee, argued for not only generous land grants but even government construction of the main trunk line. The General Committee's report took the Whig position, but Democrats won out in floor debate, and the convention recommended to Congress only that the government take some "prompt and efficient steps for its speedy completion" along a route with "genial and temperate climate."[15]

Beginning in 1854, the conventions, probably less due to a shift in constitutional scruples than to a judgment that the likelihood of securing federal assistance for a southern route was remote, were willing to move forward without federal aid. Once organization of the Kansas and Nebraska territories had made both a northern and a central route not only possible but also the most likely candidates for federal assistance, the conventions united behind a drive to secure support throughout the South for a privately funded railway. They had concluded that if such a road were to be built, it would have to be done independently of the federal government. Such a conclusion may have led them to chase an impossible dream, but nonetheless it seemed the only way open to them.[16]

As the action taken at the 1854 convention marked a turning point in development of a strategy for securing a southern transcontinental, it is helpful to review circumstances surrounding the Charleston decisions. True to the hopes of the South, James Gadsden returned from Mexico with an agreement in treaty form, and it was in the hands of President Pierce on January 19, 1854. Two more railroads had been chartered with plans to build in Texas: the Mississippi and Pacific Railroad and the Mississippi, Shreveport and Texas Railroad. However, between the June, 1853, convention and the succeeding session in April, 1854, at Charleston, other events transpired that threatened the plans of southern promoters. By April of 1854, the Kansas-Nebraska Bill had been passed in the Senate, and it was under deliberation in the House. President Pierce's annual message, delivered in December of 1853, had advocated a Pacific railroad but not government construction of the project. Gadsden's treaty was under debate in the Senate, with its approval not assured. As the convention opened, the *Charleston Mercury* reported, erroneously as it turned out, that on April 12 the Senate had changed the Gadsden Treaty boundary so as to cut off the southern railroad route.[17] The delegates to the commercial convention, not at all convinced of the probability of government aid to a southern Pacific road, split into three conflicting camps: those who held a Whiggish insistence on government construction of a southern road, those who took the Memphis convention's compromise position calling for indirect government assistance to builders of a southern road, and last, those who came to endorse the proposition that was to take the delegates by storm, that the South tackle the project completely on its own.

Railroad promoter and Whig senator James C. Jones of Tennessee opened debate on the Pacific railroad issue at Charleston, serving notice on the second day that he would argue for full government responsibility to construct a southern Pacific road. Albert Pike of Arkansas, an advocate of a Pacific railroad since 1847, stepped up in the wake of applause for Jones to offer his own resolutions, which completely denounced reliance on the federal government. Pike's speech was also greeted with applause. On the third day of the convention, General Leslie Combs, a Kentucky Whig, laid a groundwork for Pike by urging that southerners act on their own to build a road that would run through slave territory and take advantage of Texas land-grant offers. Pike spoke next, delivering an even harsher message. He looked to the population growth in the

North as clear evidence of increasing northern political power, and he went so far as to say that if Congress ever did build a road, it would be a northern one built in part with southern tax dollars. He went on to declare that the South must become independent within the Union, and it must take on this task alone, even if it meant negotiating with Mexico directly. Pike was asking for the delegates' support for the concept of a southern corporation, to be formed by a union of southern states, southern railroad companies, and individual southern investors.[18]

Pike's bold suggestion drew support from James Gadsden, in the audience as a South Carolina delegate. Gadsden assured the assembly that the treaty he had negotiated provided for acquiring a right-of-way from Mexico for a railroad. He also admitted that there was "imposing and violent opposition" to the treaty's ratification. Others leveled criticism at Pike's idea, objecting to its suggestion that a corporation negotiate a treaty with a foreign power and dismissing the plan as impractical. Pike rejoined in defense of his plan. He emphasized that it called for a corporation, which states could or could not join, but which could also attract individual investors. Its success was not, in his mind, totally dependent upon cooperation from all southern states. Pike admitted he was worried that northern companies would seize the Texas land grants before a southern company could be organized, and he asked the delegates to give the plan their endorsement in order for him to seek a corporate charter from Virginia in short order. His pleas won the delegates over, and the convention voted unanimously in favor of a Pacific Railroad resolution, which recommended his plan and created a committee to implement formation of a corporation.[19]

Southern press reaction to Pike's plan was mixed. Because of the delegates' approval for Pike's resolution, the *Richmond Enquirer* labeled the convention an "abortion, if not worse." The *Charleston Mercury* suggested that Atlantic and Gulf interests preferred the Tehuantepec route to that through Texas, and that the vote in favor of Pike's scheme was a political response to the rumor that the Senate had modified the Gadsden Treaty. Similarly, the *New Orleans Picayune* saw the vote for Pike's resolution as an indicator of how much faith the South placed in the Gadsden Treaty and how much southerners would resent its rejection. The *New York Times* ridiculed the convention. Wishing them luck on building a Pacific road with southern funds, it offered an opinion that Congress could not fund such a sectional project, and ominously, it forecasted that a southern Pacific railroad was becoming too sectional an issue and would never be built. The *New York Tribune* berated the convention's "silly impractical Southern Pacific railroad scheme."[20]

The Gadsden Treaty was ratified on June 29, 1854. However, in the aftermath of northern disapproval of the possibility for extension of slavery into the territories that the Kansas-Nebraska Act provided, the Republican party claimed 45 percent of the House membership after the 1854 congressional elections.[21] The strong showing of this northern party dimmed prospects for federal funding of a southern road. By January of 1855, Pike seemed even more determined, and he resubmitted his resolution to the New Orleans convention, this time proposing to seek a charter through the state of Louisiana. Pike suggested that one-half of the funds needed could be gotten within the South and the balance in New York. He admitted that his hopes might prove "chimerical," but that if so, it would be the fault of the southern people. At this point, Albert Pike made a speech that would be paraphrased by Hinton Rowan Helper in his famous 1857 publication, *The Impending Crisis*:

It is time that we should look about us, and see in what relation we stand to the north. From the rattle with which the nurse tickles the ear of the child born in the south to the shroud that covers the cold form of the dead, every thing comes to us from the north. We rise from between sheets made in northern looms, and pillows of northern feathers, to wash in basins made in the north, dry our beards on northern towels, and dress ourselves in garments woven in northern looms; we eat from northern plates and dishes; our rooms are swept with northern brooms, our gardens dug with northern spades, and our bread kneaded in trays or dishes of northern wood or tin; and the very wood which feeds our fires is cut with northern axes, helved with hickory brought from Connecticut and New York. And so we go on from the beginning to the end. We hardly put any thing on or *in* ourselves that does not come from the north. It is high time these things were changed.[22]

Pike drew criticism from members of the audience, yet the convention voted in favor of his proposition. Still, the New Orleans assembly seemed unwilling to relinquish all hopes for federal aid, and this 1855 convention inserted a plank calling for the federal government to aid the endeavor by every constitutional means in its power. The same week that the New Orleans convention met, Douglas introduced his Pacific Railroad Bill in the Senate, a bill that provided for three roads, with exact route selection left to the discretion of the contractor. His bill passed in the Senate, but it failed by one vote in the House. Shortly thereafter, Secretary of War Davis announced the survey report, and he recommended the Gila River route for military reasons. Pike, meanwhile, secured a charter from the Louisiana legislature for the Southern Pacific Railroad Company, capitalized at one hundred million dollars and required by charter to begin construction within three years and to reach the Pacific coast in fifteen years.[23]

Pike did not attend the 1856 Richmond convention, and in his absence a resolution was passed that had been introduced by Thomas J. Green of Texas, recommending that southern and western states provide assistance to construction of the Texas Western Railroad, a railroad with which he had been affiliated and which was reorganized in August of 1856 as the Southern Pacific Railroad. Its organizers planned to link up with Coleman's road, the Mississippi, Shreveport and Texas Railroad, at the Texas border. Meanwhile, before the time of the second 1856 commercial convention in December at Savannah, the House Special Committee on the Pacific Railroad had issued a recommendation for three routes, noting that both major political parties had adopted a pro–Pacific railroad plank in their national conventions. However, the Republican plank favored the central route, and the Democratic plank advised proper constitutional limits on federal assistance to a Pacific railroad.[24] So, once again, the chance of federal construction of a southern transcontinental railroad hung in doubt, while private roads in Texas looked like they might be positioned to build important links.

Pike appeared at Savannah, this time representing the state of Louisiana, asking the convention to support his joint-stock company. The ensuing debate centered around the issue of the constitutional power of the federal government to construct a road, with the fear expressed that if the South endorsed federal action it might end up seeing federal funds build a northern road. The convention took a position in general support of a Pacific railroad along the Thirty-Second Parallel, and it urged southerners to assist any railroad company or companies willing to complete this project. Yet the convention did not turn its back on federal aid completely, as the resolutions acknowledged that it would be reasonable that such a road receive federal land grants in exchange for services the company might render the government.[25]

President James Buchanan went on record in favor of the Gila River route in his first annual message, and John B. Floyd of Virginia was in position as secretary of war to implement that choice should Congress take action on the Pacific railroad, but consideration of a transcontinental railroad bill was put off until the 1858–1859 session. By February, 1857, the Southern Pacific Railroad Company had completed its first ten miles of track, thereby qualifying for a Texas land grant. As the 1857 commercial convention gathered in Knoxville on August 10, the Pacific railroad connection was still very much an issue. In his presidential address, De Bow spoke proudly of how the Southern Pacific Railroad was being "vigorously prosecuted," and he assured his delegate audience of its "demonstrative certainty of success." The convention endorsed the need for a southern Pacific railroad, along with the proposition that Congress organize the territory of Arizona, through which lay the route for such a road.[26]

Then came the Panic of 1857, taking both the Southern Pacific Railroad Company and the Vicksburg, Shreveport and Texas Railroad into debt and further reorganization. The 1858 meeting at Montgomery, mired in the debate about the African slave trade, took no action on the subject of a Pacific railroad. The final prewar commercial convention session at Vicksburg convened at the time the Southern Pacific Railroad Company was undergoing its reorganization. By then, President Buchanan had taken a position in favor of private, not public, construction of a Pacific railroad. Congress was deadlocked over a pending Pacific Railroad Bill, with southern representatives unwilling to vote for a bill that would probably result in a central road, the route preference of the Republican party. Not surprisingly, the Vicksburg convention pinned its hopes on private roads. Delegates voted in favor of a resolution sponsored by Coleman calling on southern state governments to assist his road and the Southern Pacific Railroad in their efforts to link up and build a transcontinental. Still, reluctant to give up completely on Congress, the 1859 convention authorized a lobbyist committee to petition Congress for assistance if they deemed it necessary or proper.[27] Whether or not the conventions thought construction of a Pacific railroad without federal assistance was realistic is not clear. They certainly did not prefer to forge ahead without a commitment of government aid, but they seemed to believe that the possibility of securing such aid was remote after 1854. And so, they pinned their hopes on the efforts of ongoing roads operating in Texas. After all, southern roads might not have had the financial resources on a level with northern roads, but the South experienced considerable railroad expansion in the years between 1845 and 1859. True, by the start of the Civil War there was no railroad connecting the Mississippi River with Texas, but there were five major lines running across the South, from Charleston to Memphis, Alexandria to Mobile, Louisville to Charleston, New Orleans to the Ohio River, and the Potomac to the Gulf.[28] From their own perspective, participants in the convention movement could be proud of the South in this regard, and they could also take pride in their own role in promoting that expansion. Viewed from this perspective, the convention movement's support for construction of a southern Pacific railroad should be seen as something more purposeful than an exercise in symbolism and sectional pride. Though it may have been unrealistic to have believed the road could be built without federal funding, it was also unrealistic to have believed that federal funding could be obtained from the Congresses in session after 1854.

Just as the conventions pressed to improve physical access to markets, they sought to build up direct financial access to world consumer markets. They thought southerners were too heavily dependent upon the services of northern merchants, and they called for southern merchants to take action to improve their position. What they did not discuss was how to replace the lines of credit northern merchants provided the South. Rather than directly facing the issue of how to fund the operation of southern merchants in light of limited southern consumer demand, the conventions seemed to blame the merchants themselves and to argue that if the South could only establish direct physical contact with foreign markets then somehow thriving commercial enterprises would follow. They also argued that the federal government was not awarding a fair share of mail contracts to steamship lines that served southern ports. So, their solution to both problems was to create steamship lines out of the South. Such an advocacy flew in the face of reality, but it drew tremendous support from convention participants.[29]

William Dawson led the delegates at the 1852 convention in Baltimore to vote in favor of a resolution encouraging Baltimore merchants to establish steamship lines to Liverpool. Also, the assembly heard a long report from the consul of the Netherlands, prepared in response to a request made by the Baltimore Board of Trade, on various advantages to trade with Rotterdam. The 1853 convention called for government mail contracts to aid expanded direct trade to Europe from southern ports, and delegates at the 1854 Charleston convention voted for state government tax abatements and importer bounties. They also added a provision requesting federal mail contracts for southern steamship lines to a resolution that had endorsed promotion of direct trade in very general terms. The 1855 New Orleans convention recommended that southern merchants and capitalists take it upon themselves to establish steamship lines, and it added a request for federal appropriations to improve southern harbors.[30]

Most of the fourth day of the 1856 convention at Richmond was taken up by a debate on the constitutionality of federal appropriations for mail contracts with steamship lines running between America and Europe. A resolution had been reported on favorably by the central committee that called for southern congressmen and senators to refuse to vote for funding of any mail contract with a northern line unless an equal sum was appropriated for a contract with a southern line. Various amendments were offered to weaken this resolution, and some in the audience criticized the very fact that the convention was mired in such a political discussion. In the end, the original resolution was passed. In addition, the delegates at Richmond appointed a committee to solicit assistance from all southern state governments for a project promoted by Ambrose Dudley Mann, former assistant secretary of state, which would create a steamship line between Hampton Roads and Europe. The Savannah session too endorsed the scheme of Mann and recommended it for public investment. In further support of direct trade, this 1856 convention

recommended the establishment of schools to train future southern sea-
men and a provision of state and municipal public assistance to southern shipbuilders. The Knoxville session witnessed a debate over the
general question of federal mail contracts as the convention considered
a resolution supporting such contracts for southern steamship lines.
Eventually, the session passed a resolution favoring the use of public
funds to aid steamship transportation and one requiring the federal government to award contracts to southern and northern lines equally. The
Vicksburg convention passed no similar resolution, but it noted with
enthusiasm the upcoming arrival in Memphis of trading vessels from
Belgium.[31]

Due largely to the efforts of oceanographer Matthew Fontaine Maury,
the convention movement championed the cause of expanded trade
between the South and South America. At the 1852 Baltimore meeting, he cited statistics to prove the vast potentials of such trade, and he
won approval of a resolution in support of additional steamship lines to
that market. Maury was named as official emissary from the 1853 Memphis convention to the federal government charged with promoting free
trade along the Amazon. As it had done for steamship lines between
the South and Europe, the 1853 Memphis convention endorsed the
need for federal mail contracts to steamship lines running out of New
Orleans to South America. Maury attended the 1854 convention at
Charleston, and he again boosted the advantages of increasing trade
between the South and Brazil. That assembly, like its predecessor, voted
to seek congressional support for establishing mail steamers engaged in
South American trade. Finally, the 1856 Savannah convention recommended to Congress a petition seeking award of a mail contract to a
steamship line operating between Savannah and South America.[32]

Advocates of a general free-trade policy did not find a receptive audience within the convention movement. Despite the efforts of a minority
segment within the body to secure endorsement of tariff eliminations, no
session voted in favor of such a policy. However, the participants did evidence a desire to see tariffs reduced. At the 1854 Charleston meeting, a
proposal advocating free trade was quashed by the central committee
prior to floor deliberation, and in its stead the committee reported favorably on a recommendation for lower duties. The Savannah convention

was divided over whether to support a policy of free trade. The central Committee of Twenty-One reported out a series of resolutions favoring lifting of all federal trade restrictions, but their report was initially tabled against the wishes of state delegations from South Carolina, Georgia, and Louisiana. The assembly compromised by delaying the decision and appointing a committee to report to the next convention on the subject. The committee was composed of the same men who advocated the holding of debates on reopening the foreign slave-trade.[33]

At the 1857 Knoxville convention, a proposal in favor of elimination of tariffs was presented by William W. Boyce, a lawyer-planter congressman from South Carolina, who had not been present at the Savannah convention. The Business Committee considered the proposal, but they did not report it out to the delegates. This engendered long debate on the merits of direct taxation in lieu of tariffs, including comments on the reluctance of slaveholders to see the federal government given any right to define taxable property. In the end, this convention, like its predecessor, postponed a vote on the question until the next convention. At Vicksburg in 1859, a resolution in favor of free trade and direct taxation was tabled at the request of its sponsor.[34]

The conventioneers seemed to view tariffs in a negative light, as adding to the price of imports, not in a positive way, as protective tariffs offering inducement to domestic manufacturing. The resolution that was tabled at the Savannah convention indicated a clear realization of the way that tariffs acted as bounties to home manufacturers, but the delegates nonetheless focused on the price-additive nature of trade barriers. Those instances where conventions voted in favor of adding tariffs for protection of industry were limited to duties affecting agricultural products. Delegates at the New Orleans convention, sensitive to the needs of the sugar industry, voted in favor of federal tariffs on sugar and molasses, "in justice to the people of the south, as equals with the people of the north in this great confederacy of States." The 1857 Knoxville convention appointed committees to petition Congress to repeal fishing bounties and to seek repeal of foreign duties on American tobacco exports.[35]

This lack of interest in protective tariffs is not surprising. The commercial conventions were not industrial expositions. The attitude of

the conventions toward southern manufacturing and mining development can be described as friendly and supportive, though not insistent.
The debates reflected a favorable disposition toward adding industry to
the southern economy, at times suggesting that such diversity was essential. The sessions encouraged those so inclined to pursue expansion of
industry, but they did not devote a majority of their time and energy
to this campaign. The delegates seemed to believe that growth would
occur in selected industries naturally, as resources were abundant and
the profitability of investment in manufacturing was proven. The southern press noted the convention's advocacy of manufacturing in a positive way, with no mention of possible social disruptions to follow. By the
time of the 1858 Montgomery convention, the New Orleans press concluded that the convention movement had succeeded in its quest to
convince investors to diversify into industry.[36]

The convention debates reveal a perception among southern leaders
that manufacturing was an attractive addition to the South's economy,
but that it was not a replacement for the agrarian mode. In this respect,
the debates were representative of the South in general, if historian
Larry Schweikart's analysis of southern banking investment choices is
accepted. He argued that southern investors had a bias in favor of agricultural lending, for its practical, proven, short-term return and for
social reasons. As southern manufacturing was not widespread enough
to make risk and return rates predictable, investors chose the known
over the unknown. Schweikart's argument reinforces that made by historians Bateman and Weiss, that the low level of involvement in manufacturing was a conscious choice on the part of planters, who were
constrained by a social hierarchy, the fear of risk, and the fear of social
havoc to be wrought by industrial change.[37] Nevertheless, there was no
criticism of manufacturing at the conventions, and there was little evidence at these sessions to suppose that these southerners feared changes
that industrialism would bring. When they spoke of manufacturing, it
was in a positive way.

By far, most of the interest in manufacturing was directed to those
industries that tied in directly to the objective of expanding the southern
agricultural economy: mining and iron manufacture, cotton textiles,
lumber milling, and shipbuilding.[38] The delegates spoke to each other,

and to their broader audience, as potential investors in this regard, and as men able to bring influence to bear upon state governments that could assist fledgling southern manufactures. Proponents of diversification seemed aware of the need for skilled artisan immigrants, but they did not explore how to attract them to the South. The delegates saw no reason slave labor could not be used in southern industry, but they did not squarely debate the dilemma of mixing free and slave labor side-by-side.

Their discussions of cotton textiles illustrates how they blended industrialism with the agrarian base. Those who encouraged cotton manufacturing centered their rationale around three objectives: to increase southern capital pools through highly profitable investments, to afford employment for skilled white laborers, and to maximize the profit from production of the cotton staple by eliminating costly transportation expenses loaded onto the export price of this southern crop. In the last regard, textile plants were also presented as ways to employ slave labor throughout the lay-by season, thereby further reducing staple-crop production costs.

Tennessee Governor Aaron V. Brown corresponded with the promoters of the 1852 New Orleans convention in advance of its opening on the subject of cotton manufacturing, and his letter was published as an appendix to the proceedings. Brown urged that southern planters invest in building cotton mills, and he advocated the use of slave labor to avoid the capital outlay of wages to white laborers. William Gregg, South Carolina textile pioneer, likewise wrote to the same promoters, urging the South to begin manufacturing, lest her soils wear out, her commercial centers languish, and her investment capital be sent elsewhere after more profitable opportunities. He proposed that the South adopt a new motto: "The Plow, the Anvil, and the Loom." James Orr spoke at the postconvention banquet in Baltimore and criticized the region's overinvestment in agriculture, especially in light of available capital. In 1853, both John Bell and President William Dawson drew the delegates' attention to the need to expand southern investments in manufacturing. That session appointed a committee to publish a report, intended for circulation in European manufacturing regions, detailing the opportunities to build cotton mills throughout the South. William Gregg was named to the committee.[39]

Delegates who met in Charleston recommended both cotton manufacturing and mining as being investments with low risk, providing
uniform incomes. They named a committee to collect statistics on existing manufacturing and mining establishments, along with information on internal improvements in the South, and to present the case for
expanded manufacturing to southern state legislatures. The convention
endorsed state financing of geological surveys and agricultural exhi-
bitions. It even called for formal training in the field of commerce at
southern colleges. The 1856 Savannah session appointed a research
committee, which was assigned to report to the next convention with
statistics on existing manufacturing and mining operations in the South.
The same group of delegates endorsed the proliferation of cotton manufacturing, reminded the public that manufacturing and mining brought
uniform and rewarding returns on investments, and encouraged southerners to establish locomotive and machine works. General support for
growth of southern manufactures and mining was endorsed by the Knoxville convention on the basis of the "highest considerations of patriotism,"
and a committee from the 1859 Vicksburg convention was assigned the
task of researching ways to develop manufacturing resources.[40]

The lack of discussion about either the advantages or the disadvan-
tages of using slave labor in industry is curious in light of how historians
have found considerable evidence of the use of slave labor in southern
manufacturing. As the comments made by Governor Brown and other
advocates of diversification indicate, adherents of manufacturing at the
conventions did not seem to feel the need to refute the notion that slave
labor could be used successfully in industry. The only convention to
entertain a suggestion that slave labor should not be used in manufacturing was the final antebellum session of 1859. However, even there
the delegate who presented a resolution condemning the practice, "fast
becoming prevalent," of elevating slaves to nonagricultural mechanics
realized that the convention body would not endorse such a condemna-
tion. He introduced the resolution by requesting that it be immediately
tabled without reading. Significantly, his objection to the use of slaves in
industry was not based on an inherent problem with slavery, but rather
on a perception that industrial slavery antagonized white artisans.[41]

Slavery. That was the basic component that set this particular agrarian economy apart. In other respects, the voices at the commercial conventions were not so very different from their fellow Americans. They thrilled at the potential contained within the land's abundant resources; they joined in the transportation revolution with high expectations about the power of steam to enrich those it served. As capitalists they pondered the promise of high returns on investments offered in manufacturing, and they recognized how industry could be used to diversify the profit opportunities of staple-crop production. They prided themselves on the existence of large commercial and cultural centers, and they sought to regain former levels of trade. They were willing to invoke government assistance to private enterprise when it benefited a broad segment of the population. Yet, shadowing all of these objectives was the overriding concern about the sanctity of slavery. The conventions were united in protecting this institution and hoped to blend the best of what was new with what was most cherished about what they had: a society anchored in a land-based economy using slavery to control the bulk of its black laborers. With the vision of hindsight, historian Herbert Wender saw the delegates' unwillingness to question either the sanctity of slavery or the "despotism of cotton" as the convention movement's major failure.[42] From the perspective of the 1850s, however, the delegates saw their devotion to both slavery and staple-crop agriculture as a sure strategy for southern prosperity.

In the years between 1845 and 1856, convention managers sought ways to preserve and enrich the South within the framework of the federal Union. Even so, rhetoric became more stridently sectional. Conservative voices like those of William Dawson, Nicholas Coleman, "Lean Jimmy" Jones, John Trezevant, and Tench Tilghman were drowned out after 1856 by those pushing the South toward aggression. Heated by the flames of the November, 1856, elections and the strong showing of the Republican party under John C. Frémont, this southern institution could no longer avoid the political conflagration.

6
The Mandate of Slavery

Many ties bound leaders of the commercial convention movement. A great number of them shared access to decision-making institutions, material success, recognized status within their home communities, and often a common social background. More, these men of prominence were united in a purpose, a drive to modernize their region's access to the marketplace, to benefit from new technology that could link them as producers and consumers to national and international trade flows. Such ties joined them together as a group and drew them into the national economic and social mainstream, for in their homage to the gospel of prosperity they followed in the footsteps of many other Americans. As John Bell reminded those at the 1853 Memphis convention, rather than see such enterprise as hostile, liberal northerners should appreciate southerners' efforts to follow the example set by the North in building commerce and manufacturing.[1] Yet, these Americans were also bound by a distinctly regional tie, southern slaveholding. This shared institution, this peculiar institution, made them unique, and their allegiance to it created a divergence between these southerners and men with whom they otherwise shared much in common.

The commercial convention discussions of slavery, and specifically the prolonged debate over the issue of reopening the African slave trade, provide further evidence of how southern slaveholders lived in a society of contradictions. These businessmen, proponents of an economy based on widespread commercial agriculture with ties to world markets, lived on both sides of the dividing line between premodern or prebourgeois society and capitalism. As historian Elizabeth Fox-Genovese has phrased it, they were "in but not of the bourgeois world." As they relate to markets and marketing strategies, convention proposals and programs recognized the degree to which the southern economy was dependent upon world capitalism. However, as they relate to labor and the social network that buttressed southern slavery, the delegates' rhetoric and the policies supported by their resolutions suggest that the conventions stood in the vanguard of a southern proslavery defense.[2]

As the conventions juxtaposed their economic agenda against an increasingly self-conscious defense of slavery, they turned their backs on those whom they believed posed a threat to their society. Most notably, they rejected federal assistance for southern internal improvements and trade expansion for reasons having little to do with the desirability of federal aid per se. Rather, after the startling congressional victories of the Republican party in 1854, the sectional animosity released by the controversy surrounding Kansas, and the strong showing by Frémont and other Republican party candidates in 1856, the conventions lowered the signal flag for federal economic intervention and hoisted that of proslavery aggression. Not retreating from a drive to modernize the South, they redirected their economic appeals to proslavery southern state governments rather than to an unfriendly national one. Gradually, at their annual sessions held between 1856 and 1859, in advance of what would culminate in 1861 in formal declarations of secession by state government entities, the commercial conventions edged toward economic separation from a government deemed hostile toward slavery.

As their demands for economic aid diminished, the delegates' insistence on political rights as slaveholders increased. Eventually, the conventions divided over the extent to which they would push a proslavery confrontation, but they never backed down from a position of unquestioned commitment to protecting slavery. Increasing after 1854 both in quantity and in stridency, the proslavery speeches voiced the convention movement's insistence on this most distinctive southern right, and that insistence came to separate the movement's protagonists from the very world they had been reaching out to since 1845. The slavery issue brought talk of disunion to the conventions as extremists aired a defense of slavery against what was perceived as a growing assault on the institution. Proponents of disunion argued that the people of the South had a shared destiny because of slavery and, regardless of their differences, this single institution unified all slaveholding states. Further, the South had a common enemy in those who sought to deny the region political power, because as a legal institution slavery was vulnerable to political interference at the national level.

A further contradiction was revealed at the conventions. Even the most adamant defendants of the system acknowledged that it was not universally supported at home in the South. Historian William W. Freehling focused on the division of southern slaveholders between those who believed slavery to be perpetual and those who preferred to envision it as having some conditional termination. He even suggested that this one dilemma goes a long way toward explaining southern radicalism: "The history of southern extremism from Jefferson's day to Jefferson Davis's could be summed up as one long, losing campaign to extinguish Monticello's master's vision [conditional termination] in more northern sections of the South." Certainly, many statements of those in the proslavery vanguard at the conventions included direct discussion of the perpetuity of slavery, the immutability of the "God-given" institution. Those who waged the proslavery crusade at the commercial conventions took care to affirm their own complete loyalty to the system, to explain the racist and religious basis of their conviction quite clearly. Also, they openly described a diminishing incidence of slavery in the border South and challenged border-South representatives to disavow the notion that the change was due to any hesitancy about the rectitude of slavery. Some did make such disavowals, but in a few instances speakers disclosed a clinging to the thought of conditional termination made in tandem with their defense of the existing circumstance of southern slavery. Thus, the proslavery drive appeared to be waged in large part to reconfirm to slaveholders the justifiability of their institution in the face of doubts from within as well as in the face of northern assaults.[3]

Early indicators of a siege mentality were observable in conventions held before 1856, but they surfaced infrequently and almost as an aside to the main issue at hand, the quest for economic prosperity. At the

1845 Memphis convention, the only admission of sectional tension occurred when railroad promoter Thomas Allen of St. Louis accused the national government of appearing to be neglectful of the West. Even then, he backed away from further attack because he said he knew the convention did not wish to engender sectional prejudices. The 1852 New Orleans convention witnessed several instances when speakers tied their particular economic proposals to a general need for the South to expand economically in order to keep the balance of political power between the sections on an even basis. Louisiana banker James Robb spoke of an "uneasy feeling" that had recently sprung up as a consequence of slavery agitation, which he blamed on the "wicked and insane meddling of the enemies of our institutions." De Bow suggested that as slaves were presently underemployed and fast becoming more significant as consumers than producers that they be used in ways to diversify the economy, such as building railroads.[4]

The Baltimore convention was generally free of talk of sectional hostility, but nuances of tension surfaced. Local civic booster Brantz Mayer made an explicit reference to the mutual stake that his city shared with the South in the "security of our labor." William M. Burwell of Virginia chided the convention for not devoting sufficient attention to ways for the South to expand her population, as he believed that "population is power." Senator Solomon W. Downs of Louisiana, called upon to speak at the postconvention banquet, gave his view of sectional economic competition: he felt it was a friendly competition, but nonetheless a real one in which the South was lagging behind. Muted though it was, such sectionalism caught the eye of both the *Richmond Whig* and the *New York Times*.[5]

President William Dawson opened the 1853 Memphis convention with a specific denial of sectional antagonism, claiming instead that the delegates met as members of one family entitled to an equal share of their common heritage. He returned to that point in the final section of his presidential address, signaling the delegates to proceed with their business "with no sectional feelings." Delegates responded by twice tabling a resolution sponsored by John S. Thrasher, a New Orleans resident who had been imprisoned in Cuba and who was supported at the convention by John Quitman, advocating acquisition of Cuba. Some from the Lower South states explained that they were interested in the subject but felt it "impolitic" to include it in commercial convention deliberations. Several newspapers took note of the deliberate inaction on the Cuba resolution and interpreted it as a move to engender consensus. Aside from sectional rhetoric about a southern Pacific railroad and river and harbor improvements, the issue used most clearly in a sectional way was education. The delegates replaced a resolution in general support of free common-school education with one loaded with sectional meaning. The substitute called for home education, employment of native teachers, encouragement of a home press, and the use of home-published school books "adapted to the educational wants and the social condition" of these states.[6]

Sectionalism escalated at the next year's session in Charleston. Heard first and foremost in the extensive debate over the southern Pacific railroad, it was also interwoven in speeches of leading activists on other subjects, such as proposals designed to protect the rights of southern slaveholders and endorsements for home education. De Bow assumed a decidedly aggressive posture on southern rights. He hoped that the conventions had "torn the veil from the eyes of the South" to see herself as the "willing vassal of other sections" and as the victim of a power "grown wanton and arrogant . . . pressing upon her rights and institutions . . . through its 'provisos,' " presumably a reference to the Wilmot Proviso.[7]

Shortly after De Bow's letter was read, Nelson Tift, wealthy Democratic merchant from Albany, Georgia, introduced a proposal that was purely sectional and political. Tift asked the convention to name a committee to report on the "most simple, practicable, and Constitutional means in the reach of the Southern States, which would defend and secure their rights in the Union." After some debate, it was referred to the Business Committee, which later allowed Tift to report it out for consideration by the entire convention. Tift suggested that if Congress were to abolish slavery in either the District of Columbia or in United States territories, southern states had the right, in turn, to impose an import tax on northern goods. The convention took no action on Tift's resolutions, but the fact that the central committee allowed him to present them to the entire assembly indicates the issues he addressed were of great interest to the leadership. In a similar vein, the convention endorsed Virginia Democrat Shelton F. Leake's resolution for southern states to take additional legal action to protect slaveowners against abduction of their slaves at sea while within the confines of southern seaports.[8]

At Charleston, as they had done at Memphis, delegates adopted a pro-South education agenda that would provide replacements for teaching materials deemed by Reverend Charles K. Marshall of Mississippi to be "not well adapted to our latitudes, nor always teaching the doctrines of philanthropy and Providence, on which we rest for our support, defence [sic], and responsibility." Additionally, the convention created a special committee to prepare a report on the state of southern publishers, on the basis that to patronize nonsouthern educational facilities was "fraught with peril to our sacred interests, perpetuating our dependence on those who do not understand and cannot appreciate our necessities and responsibilities; and at the same time fixing a lasting reproach upon our own institutions, teachers and people."[9]

Press reaction to this convention varied according to how generally supportive the paper was on southern rights. The *Charleston Mercury* concluded that there had been disagreements among the delegates, but that sacrifices had been made for the sake of harmony. The *Richmond Enquirer* was unhappy with the speeches of Whig politicians, but it reprinted a story from the *Charleston Standard* that concluded that the convention had made a positive contribution in its "developing and maturing of southern sentiment." At the other extreme, the *Missouri Democrat* saw the effort as a disunionist operation, and the *New York Tribune* decided that the convention had sworn "a new fealty to slavery."[10]

The New Orleans convention assembled in January of 1855, in the wake of the November elections of the previous fall, and the sectional tension that had been evident but somewhat suppressed at Charleston became more openly expressed. General Mirabeau Buonaparte Lamar, former president of the Republic of Texas, opened the session with a call for harmony and for Union. The delegates proceeded with routine business on commercial matters until the third day, when Albert Pike rose to defend his Pacific Railroad plan, and to define the rights of the South within the Union, rights which included freedom to form a union of southern states meeting in periodic conventions. Pike's words were not designed to foster sectional harmony: "We know, Mr. President, that the prejudices of the world are against our southern institutions, and that all the world is prepared to war against these institutions." He posed two alternatives, either to help the South strengthen itself within the Union, or to resort to dissolution "which may Providence avert!"[11]

The next assault wave came in the form of a resolution on the subject of repeal of laws against the foreign slave trade, marking the first instance that the association considered the issue. The New Orleans assembly did not actually debate the subject, as that resolution was never reported out of the General Committee, but the issue had now ominously been brought into the commercial convention forum. As they had done in 1853, extremists precipitated a brief debate about acquisition of Cuba before their resolution was passed on for burial by the central committee. Finally, Reverend Charles K. Marshall of Mississippi prompted delegates at New Orleans to reaffirm his own Charleston resolutions on southern home-education, to keep southern youth out of the hands of northern "fanatic" professors who taught them that slavery was wrong. Many newspapers covering the convention took no special notice of debate of these topics; however, the *Charleston Mercury* reacted positively to both Marshall's speech and the Cuba debate, while the *Missouri Democrat* disdained the presence of Quitman (who did not attend) and other filibusterers among the convention's leadership.[12]

The 1856 Richmond convention was dominated by Virginians, as bad January weather prevented the normal complement of delegates from participating. The abbreviated session was short on commercial debate but open for discussion of political topics due no doubt in large part to the presence of many members of the Virginia legislature, who adjourned their own session to attend the convention. President Tench Tilghman's opening remarks were intended to set a moderate tone to the meeting, which he clearly saw as a political exercise in light of the "circumstances which exist in our country at this time. . . ." However, he believed that southern interests still lay with the Union. "It will be time enough to talk of a dissolution of the Union when the circumstances shall leave no other alternative—and God forbid that the time shall ever arrive."[13]

De Bow, however, would not let Tilghman's sentiments stand unchallenged, and as he offered a resolution to adjourn and reassemble another time, he inserted his belief that a legitimate object of the association was to secure southern prosperity either within the Union or outside of the Union. Those who fought against adjournment used the convention floor to air feelings of sectional discord. John H. Gibbon, supervisor of the United States Mint at Charlotte, North Carolina, wanted to remain in session and took the floor to rail against abolitionists. Dr. William Brewer of Maryland also opposed adjournment as the South had no time to lose. "Her interests were interfered with and her rights trampled upon."[14]

The convention decided not to adjourn, and the delegates were honored at a public dinner that night. The dinner toasts carried warnings of sectional complaints. From Maryland, that she shared tides, wind, and sun with Virginia and "may we still share together, when we must, the triumphs of war—while we can, the victories yet, more renowned, of Peace." From North Carolina, that "her history attests that she knows alike *how to wait* and *when to strike.*" From Texas, "If driven to separation, the southern republic, bounded on the north by Mason and Dixon's line, and on the south by the isthmus of Tehuantepec, including Cuba and all the other islands upon the southern shore which threatens Africanization." From President Tilghman, to the Judiciary, "the bulwark against encroachments . . . the power in the Republic that says to the tumultuous tide of unconstitutional agitation, 'Thus far shalt thou go and no farther.'" Slavery, the "institution of the South, approved by man and sanctified by God—all the powers of Hell cannot prevail against it."[15]

On the last day of the meeting, delegates at Richmond passed a series of pro-South resolutions, which called upon the public to use southern manufactures, southern books, and southern resorts. They appointed a committee to address the people of the slaveholding states about the next convention, and its membership included De Bow, Tilghman, and the man who would preside at the Savannah session, Virginia Democrat James Lyons. Printed in *De Bow's Review* and elsewhere, the address echoed the belligerent tone of the convention. In recounting a history of the convention movement, it portrayed the association as marked by respectability, ability, and patriotism, but now subjected to the "insolent and aggressive spirit exhibited at times by the free States, sufficient in other countries to have led to open hostilities. . . ." The group presented a list of recommendations for consideration by the Savannah convention, and these included the usual topics of agriculture, internal improvements, domestic and foreign trade, mines, manufactures, and the arts.[16] To a large extent, the message in each subject area was the standard one of the convention movement, a balance of congratulations on the status quo with encouragement for improvement.

What was not typical in this message, however, was its incorporation of sectional and proslavery references. The Savannah convention was charged with determining the means for "promoting the best condition of their operatives" in agriculture. It was to discuss extending internal improvements to make southerners "as indeed we ought to be, one in interest and in sentiment." The South should pay heed to the lesson that "it is as dishonorable to purchase the wares and commodities of an abolitionist, knowing him to be such, as it would be to give aid and countenance to the enemy during the pressure of actual war." Moreover, to the standard litany of meeting topics were added two subjects clearly intended to politicize the upcoming convention: the social system and institutions of the South and education. In each case, the rationale for placing the topic on the convention agenda was loaded with danger flares. That on education promulgated sending students to southern institutions rather than to northern, "where the most sacred associations of their homes are denounced as those of the savage and the barbarian, the heritage of guilt and crime. . . ." Northern professors and clergymen, it charged, left their pulpits and desks to circulate "incendiary political addresses, substituting rifles for Euclid or the Bible, and finding in Kansas, fields more classic and consecrated than were ever before furnished to them by Attica or Palestine." That on slavery maintained that one of the purposes of the convention was to see that the institution remained intact, as its existence was basic to the South in this way:

This system and these institutions have ever been ours and those of our ancestors, including the very founders of the Republic. They have given us all of opulence that is enjoyed. They have raised us to ten millions of freemen, and enabled us to bring under Christian influences four millions of happy, well-protected and contented laborers, descendents of barbarians, thrown upon our shores by the hands of Providence, making use as instruments of Northern ships and Northern cupidity. . . . Domestic quiet and repose are invited to give way to agrarianism, socialism, spiritualism, and all of the other infinitely diversified *isms*, which agitate and keep in continued turmoil, what is called by an abuse of terms, free society. Reforms there may be—improvements; time and experience develop these in the machinery of all societies. Should such at any time be necessary at the South, it is ours and ours only, in assemblies and conventions, to discuss and pronounce upon them, indignantly repelling the impudent interferences of our neighbors.[17]

Within this declaration are many of the standard proslavery arguments that had evolved by the 1850s, treating slavery as a positive good. Slavery had legitimate links to the republicanism of the American revolution. Slavery was economically viable, and even more, brought not just prosperity but "opulence." Morally, slavery elevated "barbarians" to the redemption of Christendom, thereby also elevating the good Christians who saved their bondsmen's souls. Socially, slavery brought order and freedom for whites to indulge in "repose" rather than drudgery. Moreover, it protected the South from the "turmoil" common in the free-labor North. This was no apology for slavery, just as the commercial convention movement was not an apologist for southern expansion of a staple-crop economic base. Rather, it was a clear attempt on the part of leading southern public figures to elucidate the ties between slavery and the basic values and achievements of their society.[18]

Thus began the convention movement's proslavery crusade. While sessions held prior to 1856 had certainly linked slavery with southern prosperity and shown an awareness that northern abolitionist and political organizations opposed the institution, the address of the leadership of the Richmond convention marked the start of an aggressive defense campaign. From this point forward until the close of the last antebellum session in 1859, the commercial convention movement pushed the proslavery argument to the top of its agenda. Leading spokesmen of this effort did not always take the next step and proclaim that attacks on slavery were sufficient cause for disunion, but they made this suggestion often enough that it is clear the causal relationship was becoming more and more widely accepted among the more radical southern-rights advocates within the convention movement. An attack on slavery was, in their minds, an attack on the whole of southern society: its economy, its morality, its social fabric.

Once the convention movement had staked out a determined proslavery advocacy, it attracted others who were similarly intentioned, including many from among the radical fringe of southern public figures who generated an extremist proslavery doctrine by advocating reopening the African slave trade. In the most extensive historical study of that advocacy to date, Ronald Takaki found that its leaders emphasized three reasons for reopening the trade. First, doing so would eliminate the threat to slavery posed by the federal government. This would occur either by using newly imported slaves to increase the South's representation and power within Congress, or by creating such national discord over the policy so as to bring about secession. Second, reopening the trade would counter an internal threat to slavery from a non-slaveholder class. Without slave importations, southern labor shortages might draw European immigrants, who were known to chafe at the power of slaveholders. Also, a reopened slave trade would reduce the purchase price of slaves and thereby broaden the slaveholder base. Third, reopening the trade would force the sometimes hesitant South into taking a firm stand in defense of the morality of slavery. Historian Freehling would have us believe that advocates of reopening the trade correctly understood the twofold damage its prohibition did to southern slavery. For, he maintained, not only did the federal action assume that slavery in America was transitory and need not be permanently resupplied, but it also did in fact prevent slavery from spreading further in the South. Opponents of reopening the trade, according to Takaki, defended slavery just as strongly as did proponents. Many of them rested their best hope for the future of slavery with the protection offered by the Union, and to that end they sought to shield the national Democratic party from schism over the issue. Others, like many of those who advocated reopening the trade, sought to foment secession, but from within a united South, not one divided by such an imbroglio.[19]

All of these arguments and more were brought into play on the floors of the commercial conventions in the years between 1856 and 1859 as the association deliberated, or, more precisely, was stampeded by those determined to deliberate this extreme proslavery position. Takaki, William Barney, and J. Mills Thornton have concluded that most of the proponents of the drive to reopen the slave trade were young Democrats, raised in years of heightened sectional tension, who sought to gain social prestige and were reacting to social tensions created by declining economic mobility. Some evidence supports that conclusion in the story of how the convention movement was overtaken by proponents of the positive proslavery cadre, but much evidence suggests that men who were neither young nor social outsiders were similarly drawn to defend the South's right to dictate national policy concerning this aspect of the institution of slavery. Laurence Shore referred to the reopening debates at the last four antebellum commercial conventions as a dialogue among the "ruling elite." The fact that the 1856–1859 sessions became forums for proslavery thought, through the device of debating the issue of reopening the African slave trade, shows that the defense of slavery was foremost on the minds of many influential southerners by then, and it also suggests how prestigious the conventions were if radical pro-South politicians believed they could further their cause through controlling the convention association.[20]

The drive to popularize the idea of reopening the slave trade began in the state of South Carolina, in the pages of editor Leonidus W. Spratt's *Charleston Standard* and thereafter in the *Charleston Mercury*. In November of 1856, Governor James H. Adams advocated the proposal in his annual message.[21] Thus the stage was set for public debate, and the commercial convention association was not allowed to avoid the issue. The last four commercial conventions witnessed a full airing of the issue of reopening the slave trade. Many of the leading proponents of debating the topic appeared on the floor of the conventions to plead their case in front of this large and well-respected body. They drew fire from opponents of their cause, but they came back again and again a step further each time, until gradually the entire convention agenda was jettisoned to accommodate the debate. The story of how this came to pass is the story of how the commercial convention institution became transfixed with the emotionalism of the proslavery cause. In the end, a resolution advocating a lifting of prohibitions against the African slave trade was approved, but this was not accomplished without a long and vigorous fight. The manner in which the conventions confronted the subject of reopening the African slave trade evidences both the issue's powerful attraction and its fearsome repulsion among southern leaders in the years between 1856 and 1860.

The second 1856 commercial convention assembled on December 8, at Savannah, after the results of the November national elections were known, and after Governor Adams had advocated reopening before the South Carolina legislature. Although he claimed that they met to discuss securing the commercial independence of the South, President James Lyons of Virginia quickly moved the convention into politics and contemplation of the upcoming electoral "war" facing them in 1860. Repeatedly, Lyons accused the northern opposition of attacking southern "institutions," and he charged the delegates with generating ideas on how to keep the South independent within the Union.[22]

When the Savannah assembly convened the second day, despite the fact that a central committee was already functioning, the convention adopted a resolution from the floor naming a committee to report to the succeeding convention on the extent of financial inequality between the North and the South. This was followed by the standard exhortation in favor of southern home-education, with an added endorsement for using southern labor and machinery in the construction of southern railroads. Then came the first salvo from those seeking to debate reopening the African slave trade: a resolution advocating repeal of federal laws prohibiting the trade and negotiation of a fugitive slave treaty with Canada. The convention tabled the resolutions "by a decided vote." On the third day, with a motion to take the resolution from the table, the radicals made another try to force the convention to debate the question. They lost the vote, but they had won the support of the South Carolina, Tennessee, and Texas state delegations.[23]

Four days into the convention, the advocates of debate gained strength. Led by Virginia delegate A. L. Scott, they secured enough votes to schedule a debate over a resolution creating a committee of inquiry into the subjects of slavery in general and the propriety of reopening the African slave trade in particular. When that resolution was debated on the fifth day, it was defeated by a vote of sixty-one to twenty-four. In the two-day interim, proponents had picked up support from the Alabama and Louisiana delegations and had lost the support of the Tennessee delegation.[24]

During the course of that debate, which was reprinted in full by De Bow, it became evident that one strategy of those leading the drive for open discussion of the issue was to ask the convention only to sanction inquiry into the subject, rather than ask it to take a position for or against the propriety of the policy of reopening the trade. Scott and South Carolina planter John A. Calhoun requested the convention not to place a gag rule on debate of the topic, maintaining it was important that the issue be addressed openly by such a respectable, public body. Another strategy was to suggest that repeal of laws prohibiting the slave trade was first and foremost a matter of southern rights. Leonidus Spratt, appearing at his second commercial convention since 1854, told the Savannah audience that it should be the right of the South to decide whether or not to reopen the trade, without interference from Congress. Likewise, William B. Goulden of Georgia made this claim: "If they were right in the matter of slavery, now was the time to say to the North and to the whole world that they would have their right, their whole right, and nothing but their right." As for himself, he believed "in his inmost soul that slavery was an institution from God, and therefore could be defended."[25]

Even though the Scott resolution would have committed the convention only to investigate the propriety of reopening the African slave trade, several of these speakers went further and spoke in favor of that public policy. Their stated rationale was often a mixture of politics and economics. Scott himself said he was afraid that as slaves continued to be taken out of the border states and transported to the deep South, European immigrants would be brought in to meet the resulting labor shortage. With fewer slaveholders, and with large numbers of white laborers known for their affinity for free-soilism, the northern tier states might no longer feel a strong allegiance to the institution of slavery. If instead, African slaves were added to the existing border-state populations, the South would increase its numerical power in the House of Representatives by means of a nonvoting population. Goulden hinted at an awareness of the potential conflict between slaveholders and non-slaveholders should slave ownership become too concentrated when he maintained that importation of African slaves would lower all slave prices and diffuse slave ownership.[26]

Judged from the votes, opponents of this drive were in the majority at Savannah. They were represented by a group of speakers who, like the proponents, split into two basic camps: those opposed to any debate of the issue at the convention, and those actually opposed to reopening the trade. Thomas S. Gholson, a slaveholding Whig lawyer-banker from Virginia, objected to even broaching discussion of reopening the trade, as a world that could not possibly accept that policy on the grounds of humanity would impute disunionist motives to the convention. Another Virginia delegate, Andrew Hunter, felt that it was still too soon after the South had been taken aback by South Carolina governor James H. Adam's message, which "came like a thunder clap in a calm day upon a large portion, at least, of the South," for the convention to take a position on the issue.[27]

Most of the speakers who objected to creating a committee were quite ready to take a stand against reopening the trade for a number of political and economic reasons. First, there was a moral argument against the trade. Albert Pike felt the South could not defend itself against the charges of inhumanity that would be levied by the rest of the world should she engage anew in the African slave trade. Pike also geared his opposition to those who would defend slavery in the South as a positive good, suggesting that influxes of African slaves would retrograde the institution that they had nurtured in the South, changing it to one no longer defensible on humanitarian grounds. If that was not enough of a reason to oppose the trade, Pike appealed to their investor mentality, asking why would it benefit the South to wipe out its existing property value?[28]

Gauged from reaction of the southern press to the Savannah convention, the opposition majority had the support of other public spokesmen. Members of the southern press who commented on the debate did so disapprovingly. Both the *Charleston Mercury* and the *Missouri Democrat* referred to the "desultory" debate on the slave trade, and the *Richmond Whig* called Lyons a "bag of wind" and ridiculed the convention for those "idle and ridiculous" discussions. Otherwise, the southern press reported the convention proceedings without comment on the subject, except both the *Richmond Enquirer* and the *Savannah Daily Morning News* applauded evidence of pro-South sentiments. The *New York Times* ridiculed the convention as motivated by jealousy of the North.[29]

If proponents of bringing the debate to the floor of the convention had hoped it would elicit strong proslavery statements, they were proved right. Sentiments expressed in the report issued by the Richmond convention had been echoed in speeches at Savannah. Slavery was moral in that a barbaric race was thereby elevated by its contact with a Christian and "superior" race. Slavery benefited all southern whites in the way it restricted "menial offices" to slaves. These were the proslavery basics, that slavery was good for the souls of the slaves and the lifestyles of all whites, slaveholders and nonslaveholders alike. Hugh McLeod, a Democrat lawyer-merchant from Texas, summarized the impact of the debate on the convention when he remarked that it had aroused an ardent defense of slavery, especially among "many of the lukewarm, that they were stronger in their opinions than they had supposed themselves to be. They had at least not heard in the Convention any attack upon the institution of slavery."[30]

Yet, statements also revealed disagreement over the perpetuity of slavery in the South, a disagreement seemingly not aligned with opinion about reopening the trade. Pike, an opponent of reopening the trade but a defendant of slavery, phrased his view of the future this way: "He did not think there was a slaveholder present who would not be glad to believe that in some good time every man on the face of the earth, who was fit to be free, would be free. That was for the future to bring forth." In reply, Alabaman R. B. Baker contested that notion and announced he did not believe God intended the African to be free. A fellow Alabaman concurred with Baker on the perpetual nature of slavery as an "immutable truth derived from the counsels of heaven," but like Pike, he opposed reopening the slave trade. David Funsten of Virginia opposed reopening the trade, and like Pike, he saw an end to slavery when, after having educated and Christianized the Africans, American slaveholders would return them "in good time" to civilize their native country.[31]

The debate on reopening the slave trade was not the only evidence of growing sectional hostility at Savannah. A resolution was brought to the floor that spoke of the South's interest in keeping "domestic tranquility" in Cuba in the face of European efforts to interfere with slavery there. The Committee of Twenty-One presented a series of resolutions about the South's equal rights to settle slaveholders in western territories so as to increase the number of slaveholding states, and it specifically encouraged southerners to go to Kansas to protect slaveholding interests in that territorial battle over a state constitution. A special resolution was passed that put the convention on record in sympathy with expansion of slavery into Central America. Ominously, at the behest of the central committee, the Savannah delegates requested southern congressional representatives to see that federal arsenals located in the South received their full quota of arms and munitions and that plans be devised to fortify southern harbors against attack. Another resolution called for the establishment of southern foundries and works for the casting of cannons, and urged that states encourage the manufacture of arms.[32]

Once the effort to bring discussion of reopening the slave trade to the Southern Commercial Convention had been successful, the convention movement leadership acted to keep the issue on the agenda. A committee of five, headed by De Bow but otherwise a conservative group, was named to prepare the address heralding the next convention; they inserted the topic in a backhanded way by listing it as part of the Savannah convention's unfinished business, thereby guaranteeing it a further hearing at Knoxville. When the advance planning committee published its call for the upcoming assembly, it was a call for a meeting aimed toward "advancement and security of the South," yet still "consistent with and promotive of the peace and welfare of the Union."[33]

Despite having made such a Unionist appeal, De Bow, as convention president, opened the 1857 meeting with a ringing call for defense of all southern rights. His list included distribution of a fair federal tax share to the South, mail contracts for carriers serving the South, justice in Kansas, a fair distribution of public arms to southern forts, repeal of laws providing a monopoly to United States registry vessels in coastal traffic, and recall of the American naval squadron from the African coast. Most important was the right to retain their slave institution, despite the opposition of those whose true purpose was "the extinction of slavery."[34]

Shortly after his speech had been concluded, in a harbinger of the proceedings to follow, a disagreement broke out among the delegates on seating members of the northern press, in reaction to unfavorable reports that had been published about the Savannah convention. James Lyons of Virginia hinted that his intentions for the Knoxville session were to push the convention debates even further than had been done in 1856. In advocating unrestricted press coverage, Lyons said, "So far from excluding the reporters of the Northern papers from this floor, I would rather they should come here. All I would ask of them would be to report us truly and fairly to the North; and then I would say to the sound sense of the North—read that report and take warning from it."[35] By the close of the first day the delegates were still unable to reach agreement on this matter.

Having warmed up in this skirmish, the radicals soon engaged the convention in the battle over debating reopening the slave trade. Edward B. Bryan, a South Carolina legislator who supported his governor on this issue and represented his state delegation on the convention's Business Committee, offered a resolution calling for recall of the American naval squadron from the coast of Africa. Its proponents fought off an attempt to table the resolution and secured enough votes to send it to the convention's central committee. Next, they overcame a movement to impose a gag rule on debates, limiting speakers to twenty minutes per speech and two speeches per issue. This was followed by a second skirmish on seating members of the northern press, specifically on seating the press representative from the *New York Tribune*. Those opposed to extending the courtesy referred to the paper as a Black Republican press; those who favored allowing the reporter to be seated wanted a full hearing for the convention in the North as well as in the South. All reporters were seated, but not without opponents insisting on a state-by-state polling.[36]

Roger Pryor, who was at that time editor of *The South*, an extremist southern-rights paper, made his first commercial convention appearance at the Knoxville session and secured a spot on the committee responsible for nominating convention officers. Quick to make his presence known on the convention floor, he joined in the fray over press privileges, and then at the close of the morning session on the second day he introduced a resolution recommending that southern states exempt one or more slaves from debt liability. A Virginia colleague moved its adoption with an interesting comment on the politics of slavery in the South: "He did not agree with some that there was a class of population in the Southern States opposed to slavery. But he desired to have all more directly interested in its maintenance than they were at present." The resolution was sent to the Committee on Business.[37]

The Committee on Business reported out Bryan's resolution pertaining to withdrawal of the American naval squadron from the shores of Africa. After speaking at length in defense of his resolution, the sponsor then requested that rather than act on it then, the convention make it a special order of business for the following day. Clearly, the radicals wanted to prolong the debate. On the following day, Richard S. Gladney, owner-operator of the largest cotton gin in Mississippi, joined the debate and offered a substitute resolution for Bryan's resolution, which captured most of the proslavery, pro-South sentiments offered to date: that slavery was not evil in any way, that it followed that the slave trade was not wrong, that the South had the resources to become independent, and that the South ought to fight the evils that threatened the Union by providing for its own educational and theological needs. Before the convention could vote on the substitute, Whig congressman William H. Sneed of Tennessee offered his own substitute, which objected to enforcement of the 1842 treaty, but recommended that the African slave trade should remain prohibited. Gladney rejoined with a defense of his resolutions, a defense which incorporated an elaborate moral argument on the positive good of slavery and the positive good to be accomplished by civilizing African slaves within the South. Bartholomew R. Carroll of South Carolina explained that he too favored the return of the American squadron; however, he was not in favor of reopening the trade, and he would not vote for Bryan's resolution if its real intent was to signal the convention's desire to do just that. Still, he was not afraid to stand up for the defense of slavery: "I am prepared to write for the system of slavery, to speak for it, to fight for it, and if necessary to die for the maintenance of the institution of slavery."[38]

Democrat Robert G. Payne of Memphis, Tennessee, soon to be elected to the state senate, urged the convention to "quit this discussion." That was not to happen. The discussion was too significant and too interesting. Leonidus Spratt rose to respond to Payne and those who disapproved of reopening the trade. Spratt spoke openly of a class conflict in the South between those who owned slaves and those who did not because they could not afford to purchase them. The price of slaves was too high because the supply was too scarce. That was one reason to reopen the trade; another was that the South must fight any law restricting slavery if she was to defend her right to own slaves, for if the slave trade was wrong, then slavery was wrong.[39]

Congressman Sneed related what had been discussed in the last session of Congress on the slave trade issue, and he acknowledged that the congressional debate was a direct consequence of the 1856 Savannah convention. His point was that the overwhelming majority of southern representatives had voted for a disavowal of any desire to reopen the slave trade. Sneed believed the convention should not stake out a position that was contrary to public opinion. William Waters Boyce, congressman from South Carolina, reconfirmed Sneed's reading of congressional opinion. He too was opposed to reopening the trade, but for reasons not previously outlined on the floor of the convention. Boyce feared that the influx of Africans would swell the black population to such a point that America, either as it was presently constituted or if divided into separate entities, would witness Civil War among the races for control of the land. That was the worst fear he had; even should that not come to pass, Boyce harbored a foreboding about the future. "I look forward to the future and see nothing but the severest struggle that any people have ever had to encounter. It is my earnest conviction that we shall have to defend our altars and our fire-sides by our arms. The struggle may not come to-morrow, or next year, under this administration, or under the next. But the time must come, and will come, when the people of the South must do one or two things—submit or draw the sword."[40]

Sneed's substitute amendment, which specifically disapproved of reopening the slave trade, was rejected, and Bryan's resolution in favor of recall of the American naval force passed by a vote of sixty-six to twenty-six. These were significant victories for the radical forces, but they alienated the border-state delegations, as those from both Tennessee and North Carolina, along with one-half the Maryland delegation, voted against the Bryan resolution. In yet further acts of sectional defiance, the convention approved a resolution presented by the Committee on Business that southerners should "under no circumstances" deal in trade with a known abolitionist, and another that southern state governments exempt one or more slaves from debt liability.[41]

Before the conclusion of the convention, Spratt of South Carolina introduced a resolution, like that rejected at Savannah, that the convention establish a committee of inquiry to study both the condition of slavery and the question of the slave trade. De Bow quashed the effort by invoking a parliamentary rule, but his move drew an outcry from Benjamin C. Yancey, who accused President De Bow of constituting himself an "autocrat." The Committee on Business reported out a resolution asking that the convention release the committee from further consideration of the issue as "the time has not yet arrived for the consideration, in this body, of the propriety and policy of reopening the African slave trade. . . ." Spratt immediately moved, as an amendment, his own resolution to create an investigative committee, and his supporters bullied the convention into its adoption by charging that to do otherwise was to doubt the rightness of the institution of slavery. Those named to the committee of inquiry included noted radical pro-South politicians: Spratt, Thomas L. Clingman of North Carolina, Robert Toombs of Georgia, William Yancey of Alabama, John Quitman of Mississippi, and Roger Pryor of Virginia. The significance of this membership is that only Spratt and Pryor were present at Knoxville. Clearly, the committee was intended to provide a political platform, not to function as an investigative body drawn from the ongoing convention association.[42]

Interestingly, unlike the case at Savannah, all speeches at Knoxville that touched on the issue of the future of southern slavery endorsed its perpetuity. Bryan of South Carolina was most direct, declaring that no longer did the South look forward to the time when slavery should be abolished but rather "now that our opinions have changed; now that we do not regard slavery an evil, and are resolved that it shall not be abolished," their duty was to "cut loose" from any further connection with those who disagreed. Likewise, Gladney of Mississippi proclaimed slavery was "right, and will be immortal, that it is neither a social, political nor moral evil." A. W. Starke of Alabama sought continuation of discussion of reopening the slave trade with this reasoning: "Now if slavery is right, we ought to perpetuate it; if it is wrong, we ought to abolish it." As for himself, "I believe that it is a Heaven-born and a Heaven-prospered institution notwithstanding the assaults of the fanatics of the North."[43]

The reopening debate and the proslavery declarations of various delegates drew most of the attention of the press. As would be expected, the *Richmond Whig* was upset by the "high emotion" of sectional bitterness aggravated by party politics and "politicizing" of the slavery question. At the other end of the political spectrum, the *Richmond Enquirer* editorialized that this convention had been more practical and comprehensive than others, even though the paper thought De Bow's presidential speech was a bit too radical. The *Missouri Democrat,* quoting the *Knoxville Whig,* labeled the debate "exceedingly rendolent [*sic*] of gas and bosh." The *Charleston Courier* passed on reports of daily sessions without further comment. It was the *Charleston Mercury,* sensitive to the nuances of the issue of the slave trade, that fixed on that part of the proceedings most closely. The editor believed that Boyce of South Carolina had spoken for the majority of delegates in his fear that it was too divisive an issue around which to rally the South, and that the audience's reaction to the entire debate indicated that men in both the border states and the cotton states might be driven to Unionism over this issue. Despite the controversy over seating its representative, the *New York Tribune* issued only a brief series of reports on the convention; it did, however, note the debate on Bryan's resolution to recall the squadron. The *Boston Evening Transcript* told its readers that the convention went on record in favor of withdrawal of the naval forces. The *New York Times* printed an editorial about the convention, "The South and the Slave Trade," wherein it observed that the resolution on the slave trade "indicates a southern hope to incite a fierce political conflict on the slavery question."[44]

The radical forces had scored a big victory at Knoxville by demonstrating their ability to use the commercial convention forum to air the issue, with all of its proslavery underpinnings. Men like Pryor, Spratt, Boyce, and Bryan must have relished the attention they drew for their radical cause. They had effectively taken over the movement in the way they had claimed a vast amount of time and energy of the Knoxville session in the proslavery crusade, and they had come away from Knoxville firmly in the driver's seat for the upcoming 1858 session. These pro-South extremists had used the slave trade debate both to take a sounding on public sentiment on the issue and to push the southerners in attendance to commit to insisting on the right of the South to demand recall of the federal naval squadron.

The convention's reaction to their efforts provided several clues about southern attitudes, clues which should have been important to both radicals and moderates within the Democratic party. Public opinion was far from supportive of the policy of reopening the slave trade. Even those willing to proclaim the South's right to demand withdrawal of the navy, such as Sneed and Carroll, were not willing to also advocate reopening the slave trade. The border-state delegates in particular rejected the notion that an aggressive stance on any aspect of this inflammatory demand was in the South's best interests. On the other hand, the radicals had been able to elicit fervent declarations about the positive good of slavery and the willingness of many southerners to defend their right to maintain the institution. In his closing remarks, De Bow admitted that the convention had been a long, arduous, and exciting contest.[45] That seems an understatement.

Starting in 1856, the real intensity of the convention had shifted from the field of commercial planning to that of sectional politics. Politicization of the movement, first evident in the resolutions offered by the postconvention summary of the Richmond convention and next by the subject matter and emotionalism of the Savannah session, had continued unabated at Knoxville. The change in the convention agenda might well be interpreted as an effort on the part of radicals to stir up political controversy by pushing proslavery advocates to an extremist defense, making an already volatile sectional tension even more so. This does not necessarily argue that all who defended slavery or even the reopening of the slave trade on the floor of the commercial convention did so in an effort to disrupt the national party structure, but rather that by getting this respectable institution to agree that slavery was under attack from the North, the radical southern-rights element gained further, important legitimacy for their cause.

7
Radical Agendas
1858–1859

The call to assemble at Montgomery in 1858 made it clear
that leadership of the Southern Commercial Convention
movement sought to make that meeting a southern-rights rally.
A committee chaired by James Lyons of Virginia, and otherwise
composed of East Tennessee Democrat and former congressman William M. Churchwell, former Alabama state senator
and planter Tristam Bethea, who had defected from the American party over the issue of states' rights, William Waters Boyce
of South Carolina, and Benjamin Yancey of Georgia solicited
representatives to come forward and continue to work for southern commercial independence, since it was probable they
would soon have to seek political independence. "For a number
of years, not only the most offensive denunciations have been
poured out upon the South, but the most wanton aggressions
upon her constitutional rights, have been committed. . . ."
Specifically, they charged that northern radicals had resisted
the Fugitive Slave Act, had refused to accept the Kansas Le-
compton Constitution, and had castigated the federal judiciary for its proslavery Dred Scott decision.[1]

The alleged wrongs perpetrated on the South were political
acts. Nevertheless, as southerners had heard time and time
again from the commercial convention movement, while the
agents of sectional disruption were political, the South's re-
taliation should be economic. This call to the Montgomery
session argued that now that the fate of the Union was in the
hands of the majority, the free states, the South must arm

itself to meet the crisis with restoration of her commerce and encouragement of home manufactures. According to the committee, contrary to what opponents of those who sought to protect southern rights argued, the convention would not "consider the question of disunion, or any question tending to produce that result." The people should send their "ablest, best tried, and most trusted sons" to Montgomery, and should "shrink not under the cry of 'Disunion.'"[2]

However, other information coming from the movement's chief proponent hinted at a quite different intention. As published in the *Mississippi Free Trader*, De Bow's own list of topics worthy of consideration by the convention had only one item that could be considered a strictly commercial topic, that of increasing agricultural production and manufacturing. The other items were all politically explosive: physical and religious improvements resulting from slavery, reclamation of slave property, the African apprentice system, the South and the tariff, independent southern literary and educational systems, and the political relation of the South under the Constitution.[3]

The combined effect of the emotionally sectional tone at Savannah, the victory of the radicals at Knoxville in securing a debate on the slave trade, the message of further disunionist steps to come buried within the facetiously nonpolitical posture of the Montgomery planning committee, and the brazenly sectional agenda drawn up by De Bow, proved to be too much for most conservatives among the commercial convention movement's leadership. They opted to avoid further risk of inciting disunion, or of polarizing the Democratic party, and boycotted the next convention. By May of 1858 the mood of much of the South was conservative. Democrats had gained renewed faith in their party's congressional power. Buchanan had brought the Kansas debacle to a close by April of 1858, securing a compromise that convinced many southern Democrats that they had a champion in his administration. Former Whigs took heart from results of the 1856 elections, as Fillmore won close to 40 percent of the vote in the South, and they now worked to rebuild a national Unionist party by 1860. Leaders such as James H. Hammond, Jonathan Worth, Benjamin F. Perry, James L. Orr, Howell Cobb, and even Jefferson Davis professed a new conservatism against the fire-eater branch of the Democratic party and the states'-rights factions among the opposition.[4]

Those southerners who had concluded that the commercial convention movement was in the hands of the radicals were proved right by events at Montgomery. The delegates were called to order on May 10, 1858, by one of Alabama's most prominent southern-rights Democrats, William Yancey. He welcomed their association to his state as the foreshadowing of a more important body that "must, ere long, assemble" to devise means for southern sovereignty. President Andrew Calhoun hoped that if the assembly would be able to "unite the South to act with half the energy in defence [sic] of her rights that the people of the non-slaveholding States evince in attacking and subverting them, we would at once achieve independence within or without the Union." What, exactly, did the enemies of the South attack? "The slaveholder and his slaves, the slave States and their institutions, are the objects of their remorseless hatred."[5]

Once Calhoun had set the stage accordingly, the first step taken by the radicals was to sweep away the normal rules of order and to substitute a process whereby resolutions could flow directly from floor debate to final vote without passing through a centralized committee. They met with resistance but had enough votes to win. Once this had been accomplished, the way was clear for discussion of the slave trade. Spratt took the floor to read the report his Knoxville committee of inquiry had prepared. Apparently, Spratt had not worked with the other committee members on this, as both Pryor and Yancey rose to object to the reading as they had not yet reviewed the contents. Both asked that the report be tabled and printed. However, both also let their own opinions be known immediately: Pryor stated his opposition to a policy of advocating reopening of the slave trade, and Yancey voiced his conditional approval.[6]

Spratt's report was made the order of business for the second day. However, the debate took not only the second day but also every one of the five days of the convention, morning, afternoon, and evening. Spratt and Yancey teamed up to demand that the convention address the topic of reopening the slave trade. They met with formidable opposition: Pryor of Virginia, who was soon to be elected to Congress; Virginia's former Whig congressman and at that time Unionist William Preston; fellow Virginian and radical secessionist Edmund Ruffin; and Yancey's long-time political opponent in Alabama, Henry Hilliard.

Pryor admitted that he had previously been attracted to the policy of reopening the trade as an act of defiance, but upon further reflection he had concluded it was wrong. Pryor said that if the South needed more population to increase its congressional strength she should seek free whites, not slaves, who counted only as three-fifths of a resident. Furthermore, he disagreed that the South needed more agricultural labor. Pryor also attacked Spratt's contention that the South had a disloyal class of nonslaveholders, and he challenged the argument that it was in the interests of slaveowners to reduce the value of their slave investment. In fact, Pryor called that policy a form of abolitionism. The Virginian seemed uneasy over the prospect of moving "a hoard of barbarians" into the South as doing so would upset her "patriarchal institution." Even more dangerous, it would shift in-place field hands into the household, and it would push owners to train more slaves in mechanical arts, which ran counter to the South's interest as that would "imply a certain degree of accomplishment and instruction" and give slaves "an opportunity for brooding and meditation, and the fermentation of discontent."[7]

Though most of Pryor's speech related directly to why the trade should not be reopened, his sharpest attack was mounted over the desirability of even debating the issue. After all, the idea was impractical since the North would never agree to reopen the trade and southern states would not act independently to override the very Constitution they were demanding be upheld by the North. The rest of the Christian world was not ready to see the trade revived, even though France and England seemed to be moving in that direction. If the hope to reopen the trade was unrealistic, what could be gained by such a debate? Pryor suggested that one certain result would be to sacrifice the Democratic party. He concluded that Spratt's real intent was to instigate disunion, and he warned the advocates that Virginia would not leave the Union over this issue.[8]

Yancey responded to Pryor, first attacking the Democratic party. The Alabaman saw no need to protect a party that did not defend southern rights in Kansas; he charged the southern Democratic congressional delegation with caving in "under the influence of the Federal City." Yancey targeted his invective at the North, and he presented a resolution calling for repeal of the laws prohibiting the slave trade on the grounds such laws were unconstitutional and did injury to the honor of the South. He summarized his resolution as a proposal to "wipe out from our statute books the mark of Cain which has been placed upon our institutions, that we may stand in the Government as equals."[9]

Yancey did not argue in favor of reopening the trade; rather, he wanted to make elimination of its prohibition a rallying cry for the South. As he explained to an admirer in a letter written after the convention, he had hoped to use that issue to force southerners to see that law as one more in a series of congressional acts used to increase northern power and stigmatize the South. Yancey's mission at Montgomery, in his own words, was to "strip the Southern ship of State for battle." He employed the same tactic in his contest for the Alabama Senate seat with Benjamin Fitzpatrick, a contest he was deeply enmeshed in at the time of the Montgomery convention, when he insisted that southern states and only southern states had the right to determine the legality and desirability of reopening the slave trade. To Yancey, proponents of southern rights had to demand northern recognition of their privileges and not mere promises of noninterference with their existing institution.[10]

Yancey's target in his campaign to use this particular occasion to prepare the South for secession seemed to be the Virginians. He tried to goad Pryor, on behalf of Virginia radicals, to say what issue, if not this one, would drive him to support secession. Pryor admitted, and then retracted, that it would be election of a Republican president and a Republican majority in Congress. Edmund Ruffin of Virginia, who was otherwise united with Yancey in an effort to promote disunion, told the convention that he was opposed to reopening the trade on practical grounds, and he defended the reputation of Virginia slaveholders by claiming the vast majority among them hoped to retain, not sell, their slaves. Hilliard of Alabama disputed the unconstitutionality of laws against the slave trade and offered his opinion that the government was moving to protect southern rights, as evidenced by the Dred Scott decision. He spoke against reopening the trade, and he spoke against agitating the issue in Congress. Further, he did not want to outrage Christendom with such an impracticality. Then Hilliard admitted what Pryor had already confessed and subsequently retracted: that for him, election of a "Black Republican" to the presidency would be sufficient cause to abandon the Union. As if to stem this tide, Pryor tried to have the debate postponed indefinitely, but he did not succeed, and it continued.[11]

Virginian William Preston wanted the South to remain united, and he feared the issue was too divisive. For those sensitive to the charge that the South's honor was at stake, he sought to prove that the original law prohibiting the trade had been constitutional, and that it had been concurred with by honorable southern representatives. He also defended Virginia's reputation against Yancey's charge that she had a financial interest in building an internal southern slave trade. Yancey rejoined, seeking the Virginia delegation's forgiveness, yet stressing that he saw prohibition of the slave trade as one in a series of wrongs against the South and certainly not as an issue that in and of itself would justify disunion. In his best fire-eater rhetoric, Yancey claimed that the "young men of the present day" were in a better position to judge what was in the interest of the South than were those leaders of fifty years prior. The convention should not disparage his cause just because it was a new idea, rather than "old fogydom."[12]

Buried within the Yancey-Pryor debate about the slave trade was a dialogue about the status of slavery in the border states. Yancey pressed the convention to consider that slavery was not secure in the South's northern tier. He told a story of a New Orleans ship captain who was perplexed as to why it was morally wrong to buy slaves in Cuba for six hundred dollars each but not in Virginia for fifteen hundred dollars each. Later, Yancey was more direct: "There is no denying that there is a large emancipating interest in Virginia and Kentucky and Maryland and Missouri, the fruits of which we see in Henry Winter Davis, Cassius M. Clay, and Thomas H. Benton." Pryor's own views justified Yancey's disquiet. While he defended nonslaveholders as having an interest in the future of slavery, Pryor argued that slavery was strongest when concentrated rather than diffused as it was in Missouri. "While he admired the genius and patriotism of Jefferson, he must at the same time confess, with humiliation and shame, that he was the most intelligent and efficient adversary of slavery that the world has ever produced." Yet this Virginian seemed to have not entirely come free from Jefferson's sway, for as he boasted of the present result of slavery, he cautioned against dividing slaveholders over debating the slave trade with these words: "Let us rather wait, and let an overruling Providence guide our institutions to their natural culmination."[13]

In the end, Yancey challenged those present to call a convention of all southern states to consider the question of whether the South had sufficient cause to leave the Union. He then yielded the floor to Spratt, who admitted that even within his own South Carolina delegation there was disagreement over reopening the slave trade. Spratt suggested the convention should postpone further discussion of the issue until the next year's meeting in Vicksburg, which it chose to do. Yancey, however, made sure that opponents of the report did not get credit for that decision, so that minutes could not be interpreted to show that the convention disapproved of the policy.[14]

In the course of the debate at Montgomery, the radicals saw that the convention was divided not only over the policy of reopening the trade, but even over the politically symbolic proposition of calling for an end to federal prohibition of the trade. By deliberately avoiding a vote on either proposal, they had kept the convention's internal disagreement out of the public record. Disunionists could claim a victory, for as Edmund Ruffin confided to his diary, they had "fortunately, avoided exhibiting to our northern enemies the division of the south." According to Ruffin, President Calhoun had come away from the convention with the impression that the delegates had been unified in favor of disunion. Certainly, radical forces had seized the opportunity of the convention session to goad southerners into further consideration of disunion. For even those such as Pryor and Hilliard who tried to eliminate the issue of reopening the slave trade from the convention's discussions of southern rights were forced to chalk in a defense perimeter behind which southerners could rally: constitutional equality and political balance. Looking back on the convention thirty-four years later, that is how Hilliard remembered the event: as a meeting of some of the ablest statesmen of the South at which Yancey and other radicals were preparing the people of the South for disruption of the Union.[15]

While the Montgomery convention conducted little commercial business, it delved into one other highly charged political issue, expansion of slavery into Central America. The delegates gave a warm welcome to William Walker, who had been ousted from Nicaragua in December of

1857 and who was traveling through America on a speaking tour. Alabama congressman Percy Walker, who had deserted the Know-Nothing party over the issue of southern rights, sponsored a resolution in support of the filibusterer's efforts. The text was loaded with sectional flash points: that southerners regarded federal actions against Walker as indirect insults to themselves, and that further persistence would "most certainly dissolve the Union itself." Conservatives moved to table the resolutions, but they failed. They did succeed in watering down the disunionism by eliminating that particular warning, but the overall vote of confidence in Walker remained on the convention record.[16]

Reaction from southern newspapers was mixed, but generally it was not as positive toward this convention as toward earlier sessions. The *Charleston Mercury* believed that had there been no congressional compromise on Kansas, the Montgomery convention would have "left its mark in history." As joyful as this South Carolina paper was at the disunionist spirit of the assembly, it was not pleased at the dissention created by the debate on the slave trade. The convention proceedings were followed by the Richmond press, and the *Whig* came out in favor of reopening the slave trade, seeing that as "the great substantial and vital issue before the South. On this she will win or lose all." In St. Louis the *Missouri Democrat* took note of Spratt's argument, but it maintained that his opinion did not represent the general consensus. Other southern papers charged that the convention did wrong by moving away from its commercial focus. In the words of the *Mississippi Free Trader*, there had been "too much talk, not enough action," and the convention had done nothing to further southern prosperity except "let loose gas and theory." Similarly, the *New Orleans Picayune* cautioned that the convention movement, which had been regarded with general favor, could now bring harm if allowed to "degenerate into political assemblies."[17]

If the radicals had hoped to incite the anger of the North by the debate, the reaction of the New York press to the convention must have given them immense satisfaction. The *New York Times* made the first day's convention news its front-page story, and it warned advocates of reopening the trade of the impracticality of their cause, as the North and Europe would act to prevent the "crime." By the time of its correspondent's final report, the paper was reacting emotionally to the proceed-

ings. Never in the history of the Southern Commercial Convention
had there been such an "exhibition of low, contemptible, demagogueism
and political cant." Once commercial conventions, the meetings were
now political conventions. To his readers the reporter confided that
"the scene was loathsome to me from the beginning." The *New York
Tribune* did not mince words either, describing the slave trade as "that
branch of commerce with which the members of this convention are
more familiar than any other." The *Tribune* editorial advised that the
convention had grown more and more "ignorant, gassy and absurd,"
but that northerners should give it their attention as it served as an
exponent of southern ideas.[18] James Lyons's hopes had been fulfilled.

In the wake of the high drama of Montgomery and the indication
that the next convention would in all probability be a repeat of the last,
the convention movement lost its border-state participants. The final
antebellum session was strictly a Lower South phenomena, and a poorly
attended one. According to a report in the *Jackson Mississippian*, there
were only twenty-five delegates from outside of Mississippi in attendance at Vicksburg, and the total number of delegates was not even 10
percent of the total who had been present at Knoxville two years earlier.
None of the border states sent delegates. The largest delegation outside
of that from Mississippi was the South Carolina contingent. Not only
was the convention small, but it was also lackluster. Gone were the
notables and nationally prominent politicians. The few such men as the
convention did attract were locals: former senator Walker Brooke, former governor and senator Henry Foote, and former congressman Hendley S. Bennett. De Bow was the only member of the official planning
committee to come to the convention; William Yancey, Guy M. Bryan
of Texas, and William H. Chase of Florida did not attend. The absence
of well-known regional politicians suggests that many in the South's
political parties had decided that the commercial convention was a
dangerous place to be.[19]

The presiding officer, Charles Clark of Mississippi, a Whig turned
states'-rights Democrat, officially opened the floor to any subject. Clark's
speech was followed by the reading of a message from Mississippi's former governor, Congressman John J. McRae, who had been asked to sit
on the planning committee following the death of member John Quit-

man. McRae told them his wife's illness prevented his appearance, but he had a number of items he recommended for their approval, all of them political: repeal of the laws prohibiting the foreign slave trade, an expansionist policy of southern "ascendency of the United States in the Gulf of Mexico," and consideration of southern options and duties should the Republicans win the 1860 election. Leonidus Spratt, present once again to initiate debate, offered three resolutions: that slavery was right and so were the means to its formation, that the convention should support reopening the slave trade, and that a committee should be named to investigate the issue further. Floor debate ensued, in which De Bow supported reopening the trade against opposition led by former governor Foote. Early on, it was clear that delegates at Vicksburg, like those at Montgomery and Knoxville, disagreed over the policy of reopening the slave trade and over the propriety of even discussing the issue.[20]

When the Committee on Resolutions presented its recommendation on the issue, it was obvious that the disagreement witnessed on the floor of the session ran through the central committee membership as well. The committee presented three separate reports. A majority report favored repeal of all laws prohibiting the trade. One of the minority reports demanded that the convention drop the subject entirely; the other suggested the South institute an African apprentice system, different in legal respects from slavery. For the next two days, debate over these reports was interspersed among discussions of various commercial matters.

Spratt and Foote, the key debaters, disagreed about reopening the slave trade, but they agreed on the benefits of slavery to the South. Spratt based his argument favoring reopening the trade on strict political economy: the difference between the North and the South was a clash of two philosophies. The North believed that equality among men was universal, while the South believed that equality could only occur among equals and that some races were inferior to others. He contended that to win, the South must gird the institution of slavery with a moral strength through an aggressive attitude, culminating in a demand that the slave trade be reopened. The North was committed to eliminating slavery, and the South must be equally committed to defending it: "All that is vital to the South is slavery, and that South will

not be divided on this question." Spratt admitted that he had decided
to force the South to confront the morality of slavery so directly out of
his fear that some slaveholders, particularly those in Virginia, leaned
toward emancipation. Foote also sought to defend slavery, "the best institution for the African," but he named its two most important sources
of protection as the Union and maintenance of high slave prices. In his
opinion, the slave trade, even if it could be reopened, would introduce
more problems to the South than opportunities. While he deprecated
the politics of William H. Seward, he remained optimistic about the
South's chances in the upcoming election, and he felt the convention
should not agitate this issue as it would "concentrate the energies of the
whole North for our overthrow."[21]

De Bow argued in favor of the Spratt resolution, and he contended
that it did not necessarily mean one favored reopening the trade. His
belief was that any decision to reopen the trade lay within the purview
of the states. Walker Brooke, a Whig, quoted from South Carolina's
leading opponent of reopening the trade, J. Johnston Pettigrew, on the
way the introduction of masses of Africans would dehumanize American slavery. Brooke explained to the convention that to keep slavery
alive, it must be kept profitable, and its greatest profit derived from cotton production. Any prospect of an increase of world demand for cotton
was insufficient to justify adding to the numbers of slaves in that industry. South Carolinian James Farrow, a member of the state legislature, noti-
fied the delegates that there were five out of the South Carolina delegation of eleven who would vote against the resolution because they knew
that the vast majority of residents of their state also opposed it; he worried that their opposition would not be otherwise known as the convention intended to vote on that resolution by states.[22]

The convention accepted the measure calling for repeal of all laws
prohibiting the African slave trade. It passed by a total of forty votes in
favor, nineteen against; Tennessee and Florida delegations voted unanimously against it, and the South Carolina delegation was divided, as
Farrow had warned. Later, the assembly supported a resolution calling
for the federal government to withdraw the American naval patrol from
the African coast and notify England it would abrogate the treaty. A
committee was assigned to investigate the legality and expediency of an

African apprentice system, and Henry Hughes was assigned to its membership. He had presented a lengthy report to the convention on that system, in which he described American slavery as moving toward "warranteeism," wherein slaves had all the rights justly due them, masters owned not slave property but slave labor obligations, slaves were remunerated by wages in the forms of housing, board, and necessities, and the master-slave relationship was regulated by the state. Warranteeism's rationality was based on racism, and Hughes argued that Africans could be constitutionally brought into America within that system. Those who had opposed the majority report advocating repeal of laws prohibiting the foreign slave trade rose in protest at creation of the African Apprentice Committee, but they were ruled to be "indecorous and disrespectful" by the chair. This was enough to cause Henry Foote and his ally, I. M. Patridge, who was the editor of the *Vicksburg Whig*, to resign their seats.[23]

The protest made by Foote and others provides further insight into the fringe character of this last convention. The protesters, who included Walker Brooke, objected to the convention's call for repeal of laws prohibiting the slave trade because they felt the convention was not truly representative of public sentiment on this issue, and because the convention consisted for the most part of men who, however "respectable in private life," had not the experience in "management of public concerns" that would qualify them to make pronouncements of public policy. Furthermore, they charged that the proponents were avowed disunionists, whose only hope in agitating the issue would be to thereby insure a Republican victory in 1860, giving southerners a pretext to dissolve the Union.[24]

Two other radical propositions, immediately tabled, were introduced not for serious consideration but rather just for public airing. John A. Jones, a Georgia Democrat and state legislator, called for total nonintercourse between people of the North and South in wake of northern efforts to entice slaves to run away. A Mississippi delegate, H. J. Harris, introduced a resolution that opposed Stephen A. Douglas's Freeport Doctrine. Before adjourning, the delegates set their next convention for the second Monday in November, 1860, when results of the presidential election would be known. President Clark ended the Vicksburg session on a note of foreboding, when he bade farewell to those traveling home to distant places, whom he would not see again unless it was to be march-ing together "shoulder-to-shoulder" in that "great contest that may arise hereafter."[25]

De Bow seemed to have had misgivings about the outcome of the Vicksburg convention. He introduced his series of reports of its pro-ceedings with an admission that the debates had provoked heated re-sponses, but he reasoned that southerners were by their nature prone to such high temperament within public assemblies, and that in every other respect the delegates responsible for the disruption were "law-abiding men and good citizens." By contrast, Ethelbert Barksdale of the *Jackson Mississippian,* who had served as a convention delegate and who would support Breckinridge in 1860, defended the delegates' "patriotism and sagacity" against "weak-headed editors and broken down political hacks" who defamed them "out of envy that they are not in [their] com-pany." He saw the delegates' vote on repealing the prohibitory laws as "an important step in the right direction." The *Natchez Courier,* how-ever, agreed with the protesters that the delegates did not fairly repre-sent public sentiment on the issue.[26]

The *Richmond Enquirer* reported the convention, with its "exciting debate," and noted passage of the radical resolution. The *Richmond Whig* took no notice of the convention whatsoever. The *Charleston Mer-cury* did not change its position in favor of reopening the trade as a result of the convention, but it suggested that that subject was one to be considered later, "when the South shall have control." The *New Orleans Picayune* gave the convention lengthy coverage, and it included reports of both sides in the debate. Speaking, perhaps, for those in the commercial convention movement who were absent from Vicksburg, the *Lynchburg Daily Virginian* concluded that the people were losing confidence in the conventions since they had been "perverted" from commercial assemblies to political assemblies. The *New York Tribune* did not report the convention, but the *New York Times* applauded the efforts of Henry Foote and other conservatives, as "the first time that one of these sorry bands of crazy conspirators has had the truth told in its own den."[27]

Those who led the drive for the convention's endorsement of reopening the African slave trade had waged a four-year battle for their cause. In the end, they could claim a victory, but it was not by any means a clear victory. The commercial convention movement never officially endorsed reopening the African slave trade as a public policy. Rather, it approved of the political demand that the federal government relinquish the right to make the choice on that policy. Moreover, the final vote on whether to demand repeal of existing federal laws was split, just as every body of delegates had been divided over each resolution having to do with the issue presented at the last four antebellum convention sessions.

The fact that the proposition to reopen the slave trade had been so vigorously debated all along the way is strong evidence of widespread disagreement over its many political and economic facets. Yet, the most prominent politicians who took the floor in the matter seemed primarily concerned with the effects that holding such a debate would have on national political parties. Thomas Gholson, William Preston, Roger Pryor, Henry Hilliard, and Henry Foote feared that publicizing the issue would lend vast strength to the Republican cause and fracture the Democrats if advocacy of either the policy of reopening the slave trade or the right of the South to determine federal policy on this issue were ever used to measure northern loyalty to fellow Democrats in the South. Yancey and Spratt seem to have had just such a purpose in mind as they succeeded in provoking the convention delegations, and, through press reports of the debates, thereby the public at large, to enumerate the rights of southern slaveholders.

Laurence Shore has concluded that the way the debate exposed defects in slavery led southern leaders to create economic justifications for their continuing right to rule.[28] Certainly, the debate revealed uneasiness over some aspects of the institution. Yet, it also elicited emotional declarations of loyalty to that system. Widespread opposition existed among participants at the convention to each of the three radical positions: using debate of the issue for the purpose of eliciting a united proslavery South, making repeal of federal laws restricting the trade into a political demand more difficult for Democrats to agree on than expansion of slavery in the territories, or actually advocating the policy of reopening the trade. However, the opposition did not dispute the sanctity of slavery.

Perhaps the most important result of that debate was to bolster among these southerners, and among those who followed their actions, a perception of slavery as being under attack. Even those who fought against the radical proslavery resolutions in an effort to shield their party from the strain of extremism did not question the need for protection of the institution. Whether it was pictured as threatened internally by a growing number of nonslaveholders, as being in danger from northern and worldwide foes bent on a moral crusade, or as losing ground politically to a growing number of northerners who sought to impose legal limits on its expansion, the outcome of the long confrontation was the same. Leaders and delegates who took part in the final four years of the antebellum commercial conventions evidenced a vision of their section being under siege because it insisted on the right to maintain slavery. Whether it was that the master-class defined itself and ruled through slavery, as Genovese has argued, or that they believed that slavery sustained white freedom, as Oakes has concluded, there is no doubt that proponents of the commercial convention movement took the defense of slavery to be the most overriding issue facing their collective body between 1856 and 1859.[29]

The perceptions of the leadership about the priorities of their convention association changed in line with their perceptions of the changing situation of the South. As they moved the defense of slavery to the forefront of their concerns, they accordingly devoted their time together to discussion of that consideration. Because there was a dramatic shift in subject matter at the sessions that met from 1856 to 1859, it is important to realize that those involved in these late antebellum sessions shared many of the same background characteristics with the men involved in the convention movement prior to 1856 or after 1865. They did, however, evidence important differences. The single most important difference was that the share of leadership slots held by delegates from states of the border South declined precipitously, from a share of 26 percent at Savannah to 18 percent at Knoxville, 15 percent at Montgomery, and none at Vicksburg. By the time of the Vicksburg convention in 1859, the movement, its focus altered, had been abandoned by the border states.

Generally, the leadership at the final four prewar sessions reflected the same age distribution of the general Convention Elite, with the majority of leaders older than age forty. The occupations of these four leadership corps were also in line with those of the general Convention Elite, with this exception: the percentage of commercialists among leaders at Knoxville, Montgomery, and Vicksburg ran considerably below that of the Convention Elite. This perhaps helps to account for the fact that the amount of time devoted to commercial discussions became increasingly restricted after 1856. Also, all four of these late 1850s conventions attracted proportionately larger numbers of major slaveholders than usual. The Convention Elite included among its slaveholders 57 percent who ranked in the planter class. Among slave-holders at the Savannah, Knoxville, and Montgomery sessions, those who held more than twenty slaves accounted for 86, 79, and 78 percent respectively, and 67 percent of the Vicksburg slaveowners fit that classi-fication. Clearly, and not surprisingly, the leadership at each of the last four antebellum conventions included a sizable number of slaveholders who had a significant investment in that institution.

Information about political affiliations among these leaders suggests that they fit the general pattern evidenced by the total Convention Elite, with one interesting exception. The leadership ranks at the Sa-vannah session included a higher than would be expected proportion of Democrats: 87 percent. That suggests that in 1856 it was the Democrats who took a high public profile at occasions of sectional display. The share of former Whigs and of American party members climbed in lead-ership ranks at sessions held after 1856, moving closer to the levels of the total leadership group. This reflects the resurgent strength of opposition parties throughout the South between 1856 and 1858. The formerly Whig opposition did not abandon the commercial convention movement in the end. They continued to participate, and many, such as Henry Foote, Walker Brooke, William Preston, and Thomas Gholson, vigorously took on the fight against the radicals.

As time progressed from 1856 to 1859, the movement's leadership included a higher than normal share of officeholders, but a declining number of national officeholders as opposed to state and local govern-ment officeholders. While the percentage of those who held office at some time in their lives was higher among the leadership at all four of these late conventions than among the total Convention Elite, the major distinction lies in the nature of officeholding experience. In the end, at the final convention, in terms of political profiles, Vicksburg did not attract prominent politicians from outside of the host state. Even among the South Carolina delegation, the second largest, there were no nationally known officeholders.

This information allows for conclusions about the late antebellum conventions, some of which conflict with standard historical depictions. While the last two convention agendas were monopolized by radical political issues, the conservative political element in the South did not desert the convention movement, contrary to what historians Russel and Craven have concluded. And McCardell was wrong when he claimed that only the most hardened secessionists bothered to attend the Vicksburg convention, as was Van Deusen in describing Vicksburg's assembly as composed almost entirely of radicals. For, even as late as that last session in 1859, conservatives were still engaged in a contest against proponents of disunionist policies. Wender's description of the debate over reopening the slave trade as a Unionist-secessionist battle is closer to the mark, although there were enough intricacies attached to that debate that such a clear-cut conclusion is difficult to make. There is some justification, however, for the notion that politicians had replaced businessmen among the movement's leadership, as Van Deusen, Davis, and Wender have claimed. As Matthew Fontaine Maury, a leading proponent of direct trade with South America and a frequent speaker at conventions held before 1856, told his audience at a state agricultural bureau meeting in October of 1859, "Look to your commercial conventions, and take warning. Keep men from the political commons out of your meetings."[30]

Starting in 1856, the signs appeared that some leaders hoped to use the commercial conventions to explore issues beyond southern business matters. While the Savannah and Knoxville sessions devoted the majority of their time to discussing economic improvements, by 1858 the normal course of commercial concentration had ground to a halt, replaced by a fixation on the subject of slavery. The underpinnings of the commercial convention movement gave way against an assault by the proslavery vanguard. The long battle that had been waged by the Dawsons and Colemans and Robbs and Clapps and Maurys to keep the course charted on a commercial path, above the political fray, was lost against the storm of the politics of slavery. The radicals worked within the structure of the conventions to attain their objectives by creating committees to investigate reopening the slave trade and by debating resolutions on that subject. They even used the standard public calls to assemble to their advantage. Their success says much about the power and momentum of the proslavery drive, and their relentlessness indicates how all consuming this defense became to many southern leaders.

Given the heightened sectional tensions that followed in the wake of events such as the rift within the Whig and Democratic parties over the Kansas-Nebraska Act, the obvious vitality of the Republican party in the North after 1856, the publicity of alleged bloodletting in Kansas, northern reaction to the Dred Scott decision, and a growing perception throughout the South that an antislavery fringe was gaining acceptance among more and more northern voters, there were not many southern institutions that could have withstood the call to rally around the cause of southern rights. The very fact that the conventions were targeted underscores the prominence of this particular institution, a prize deemed worth winning.

The radicals succeeded in capturing the convention association, and in the process they learned much about southern popular opinion. Because of the conventions, by 1859 they knew that only a small minority among those southerners inclined to take an active role in public affairs would agree to insist on the right of the South to determine federal policy on the legality or propriety of reopening the African slave trade. They knew that former Whig spokesmen were generally united in opposition to such a stance, and that it was sufficient cause for disruption among Democrats that the party leaders could never endorse such a plank. Very few among the convention body actually supported the policy of reopening the trade, and those who did could not be described as men who had been entrusted with positions of public responsibility. The convention delegations seemed to reflect a widespread and general southern opposition to reopening the African slave trade. Not even the Confederacy would adopt the policy. When Yancey led dissenting Democrats out of their Charleston national convention in 1860, he did not champion the cause of reopening the slave trade, but rather the issue of slavery expansion in the territories.

Judged from the rhetoric of border-state Virginia and Tennessee politicians who had remained active at the conventions through 1858, those who advocated secession could conclude that they stood a better chance attracting fellow southerners to that cause by emphasizing the general threat to slavery posed by antislavery forces in the North. From the border-state spokesmen they might have seen how anxious many southerners were about the prospect of a Republican win in the presidential election of 1860. That lesson was not lost on Breckinridge's supporters. Moreover, the fact that each of the conventions from 1856 to 1859 witnessed heated debate and lack of unanimity on every slave issue except the sanctity of slavery should have persuaded radicals that, while they still had their work cut out for them, they should keep their focus on the fears of slaveholders. Moderate southern-rights advocates could have concluded from the same circumstances that southerners were firm in their insistence that slavery survive, and they were unsure that it could do so in the highly volatile national political environment.

If those members of the commercial convention movement who sought to expand the South's access to the marketplace were planners and dreamers, their dreams were to enhance the South but to do so not necessarily at the expense of the North. Within a framework developed over the years between 1845 and 1856, advocates of southern economic expansion insisted that the Union could only be strengthened if the South increased its prosperity as a section. This is not to say that the primary purpose behind the effort was to foster Unionism, but certainly the projected outcome of the commercial convention movement's agenda could have moved the two sections closer to each other rather than further apart in terms of their economic advances. Such an outcome would have pushed the South further toward the experiences that economic modernism might bring.

If the attraction to benefits of commercial modernization acted as a national unifying factor for the conventions, this was countered by the conventions' statements of southern distinctiveness due to its peculiar institution, and a pride in that distinctiveness as well. While the convention leaders revealed an envy of northern prosperity, they did not expand their preference for emulation of northern activities beyond those changes that would enhance rather than erase their regional distinctiveness. They did not urge southerners to become northerners, to give up the agricultural base of their economy, or to subject their communities to the "isms" that seemed to accompany free-labor society. They were not anti–free labor, but they were adamant in insisting that slavery was essential to southern progress. The commercial conventions clearly represented the interests of the slave power. What seems to have happened between 1856 and 1859 is that the movement's leadership got caught up in the politics of slavery, along with the other activists among the Whigs, the Know-Nothings, the Americans, the Constitutional-Unionists, the Democrats, and the Republicans. The momentum of sectional antagonism over this basic difference swept away any semblance of "business as usual" repeatedly within the halls of Congress and eventually on the floors of the conventions. In the end, those who preferred that the commercial conventions preach the gospel of prosperity were outnumbered, outmaneuvered, and upstaged by those who sought to make the prominent commercial convention institution stand up to defend the South's peculiar institution of slavery against what was rightly perceived as a mortal attack.

III.

THE
POSTWAR CONVENTIONS

Introduction to Part III

For most of its lifetime, the Confederate States of America
existed in wartime, and because of that it is difficult to trace
how the economic policy proposals generated at the antebellum commercial conventions may have influenced decision
makers in the southern nation. Certainly men who had taken
part in the antebellum convention movement also played key
roles in matters relating to the Confederate economy: Alexander Stephens as vice-president; cabinet officers Judah Benjamin, John Breckinridge, Christopher G. Memminger, John
H. Reagan, and George A. Trenholm; diplomatic agents William Yancey and A. Dudley Mann; Quartermaster General Alexander R. Lawton; William S. Ashe and Frederick W. Sims,
who supervised military railroad transportation; state governors Charles Clark, Andrew G. Magrath, and Thomas O.
Moore; the eight members of the Confederate Senate, the
thirty members of the Confederate House, and the twenty-
two members of the Provisional Congress; and men like Joseph
Anderson of the Tredegar Iron Works. The basic tenets of the
antebellum conventions appear to have been shared by many
in the Confederacy. These precepts included a belief in the
crucial importance of staple-crop agriculture to southern economic profitability, even to the detriment of supplying food-
stuffs, coupled with high expectations about European market
demand for southern cotton. Added to this was a conviction
that government should intervene in the economy to spur commerce, manufacturing, and railroad expansion.[1] The degree to
which any one of these policies contributed to the Confederacy's defeat is arguable, but they suggest a consistency in economic philosophy between the pronouncements at the con-

vention forums and some of the policies pursued by the independent nation. That the Confederacy did not survive the war ended any opportunity to forge a peacetime economic policy fashioned to serve the needs of the slave South, and those who survived the war faced a new set of political, economic, and social circumstances. The story of the postwar commercial conventions provides evidence that many survivors of the Old South brought perceptions from their antebellum experience that had significant bearings on the manner in which they confronted the new conditions of the postwar South.

8
"The New Condition of Affairs"
1865–1869

The history of the antebellum commercial convention movement illustrates how loyalty to the institution of slavery as it had evolved in the particular historical setting of the Old South circumscribed the economic and political choices open to members of the southern leadership elite. Clearly, the leadership of the conventions recognized the way that their economy was tied to a worldwide marketplace. They agreed among themselves that their own best interests, and those of their constituents, would be better served by a drive to improve market access than by resistance to modernization. They called for railroads, shipping facilities, open-mindedness to the opportunities to be offered by manufacturing, a more direct and presumably more profitable trading relationship with European consumers, and a general enthusiasm for progress as defined by these improvements. Yet, as slaveholders or as men whose self-interest lay with enrichment of the slaveholding class, these public spokesmen could not avoid, however reluctantly on the part of some, the political choices that defenders of southern slavery eventually faced.

The dilemma of slavery rechanneled the focus of the conventions. The attraction to growth and change that characterized the conventions held in the decade between 1845 and 1855 shifted to a more pressing concern after the dramatic emergence of the Republican party between 1854 and 1856. As the commercial conventions thereafter retreated from national economic and political linkages and turned to find southern re-sources with which to build the economic edifice they sought, they limited their options. For once that restriction had been accepted, southern progress could only move at a rate commensurate with regional economic resources rather than at a pace set by northern enterprise. Delegates at the final meeting, that held in Vicksburg in 1859, talked of expanded trade with Brussels, of tapping the wealth of the Amazon, and of a southern Pacific railroad, but somehow their boasts sounded hollow. Their real enthusiasm was reserved for the debate on reopening the African slave trade, a policy which, if adopted, could only have further separated the South from the modern world of its marketplace.

After the defeat of the Confederacy, once again the set of choices open to these men was circumscribed, limited no longer by the needs of slavery, but limited in important ways by the legacies of slavery. To the extent that the Civil War itself was a legacy, the South faced serious devastation. The scarcities wrought by death and destruction on a massive scale constrained the actions of southern leaders. As the war-imposed deprivation was an aftermath, so was the political condition of the country in 1865. Here, southern leaders presumed that they had some choices, but they also soon had to face the real possibility of loss of control of their state governments to a federal government dominated by a party with yet undetermined political intentions. Certainly one of the most dramatic changes in their circumstances resulted from emancipation. They had inherited an economy formerly based on the existence of a large slave labor force and fashioned to serve the interests of a slaveholding society, but that economy was no longer buttressed by the legal support mechanisms that slavery had brought to the relationship between labor and capital. Still, some way had to be found to produce the crops because in the short run the South had few ways to survive other than by agriculture. Socially, the South had lived with a concept of race relations that was based on the notion of racial differences and inequalities, and this impression had not been weakened by defeat of the Confederate armies. This notion would in turn further limit the economic and political options available to the decision makers of the New South. As veterans of the convention movement surveyed the social, economic, and political landscape of the South in the years immediately following the war, the problems at hand must have seemed far greater than the opportunities.

Many choices would be made by many people in the years between 1865 and 1869, the year marking reactivation of the commercial convention movement. An understanding of the choices made and the results of those choices can illuminate the actions of the five conventions that met between May of 1869 and September of 1871. Any history of the postwar commercial convention movement can be enriched by taking into consideration events of the four years between the end of the Civil War and the first meeting of the commercial association, just as it should build from an understanding of the precedents set by the antebellum conventions. Apart from their historical context, the optimism of the convention movement can not be fully appreciated, nor can the list of options presented by the convention leadership be understood. To that end, a brief foray into postwar events witnessed by convention delegates is in order, as is an effort to gain some insight into the perceptions of the participants of the convention movement during this time of transition.[1]

At the close of the Civil War, some of the most pressing problems facing southerners were life threatening: physical survival in the face of drought and food shortages and protection of life and property against the forces of lawlessness and violence. Wartime death and destruction of property had left the region critically weakened, and these conditions were made even more devastating by both pervasive debt and the legal uncertainties over the status of that debt, much of which had been incurred during the war. Furthermore, that both land and personal property that survived relatively intact were subject to confiscation was more cause for uncertainty. The South's railroad network, much of it still in ruins, was badly in need of capital despite the limited federal assistance that had already been provided. Extensive stretches of levees along the Mississippi River had been washed out during the war. In the state of Mississippi, the severe floods of 1865 had been made more catastrophic by the fact that the federal armies had deliberately made cuts in the levee system to reduce Confederate cotton supplies. Landowners dependent upon former slaves to farm the land could not be sure of securing their labor, either because the former slaveholders believed the former slaves not willing to work under a free-labor system or not able to work effectively without the direct management provided by the system of plantation slavery, or because the landowners lacked the resources to compensate nonslave labor. To all these fears was added the fear inherited from a legacy of racial repression, the belief of many southern whites that southern blacks would rise up against them.[2]

In the months after Appomattox, one comfort southern political leaders had was the way that President Andrew Johnson seemed to support restoration of white southern-directed civil government. However, as part of his policy, Johnson insisted that those who had held office under the Confederacy and those whose taxable property in 1860 had been valued at more than $20,000 must individually seek a presidential pardon. That he did so has provided us with a valuable historical resource, for one way to seek an understanding of the perceptions of future commercial convention leaders as they faced the immediate aftermath of the Civil War is to read their requests for presidential pardon, written in the summer and fall of 1865. Requests for pardon from forty-four members of the postwar convention leadership were found among the federal Amnesty Records Group. True, there is a large degree of self-serving motivation behind what thoughts the men conveyed to President Johnson, but their perspectives illustrate their readiness to face the future, having come to terms on an individual basis with the past. Writing to a man whose political policy held out hope that individuals such as themselves would have a meaningful role in the future of their region, they often revealed the conclusions they had reached about the history they had lived through.

James Lusk Alcorn, like some others, justified his past acceptance of secession on the basis that while he did not flee his homeland over the issue of secession, he gave little support to the Confederate government in its effort to wage war against the Union. Several others indicated they had quietly retired from public life during the years of the armed conflict: John L. Morehead of North Carolina, H. L. Hart of Florida, William S. Hastie and George W. Williams of South Carolina, and William McKendree Byrd of Alabama. David P. Lewis of Huntsville boasted of how, as a state judge, he had contested government conscription efforts and had sought the safety of federal lines once he received notification he would himself be conscripted. William Miller, a merchant in Mobile, claimed he had risked his safety by making Unionist speeches during the war. Others, like Generals Robert D. Lilley, Winfield S. Featherston, and Harry T. Hays, maintained they ended up in the army because they had little choice.[3]

Most who acknowledged they had supported the Confederate effort said they had done so out of loyalty to their state. Joseph Anderson of the Tredegar Iron Works in Virginia admitted his choice had been to remain loyal to his state and to assist in the war effort even though he felt sectional differences could have been settled amicably. As one not accustomed to succumbing to obstacles, Anderson had faith in his ability to restore his business in an effort to build up his "broken down section." Thomas Branch, a Richmond merchant, reported that while he had as a delegate to the Virginia Secession Convention voted to secede, it was done at the bequest of his constituents rather than out of personal preference. Once his state had joined the Confederacy, Branch, as a loyal Virginian, felt he had no recourse but to do "what the circumstances and position in which he was placed required of him." General William J. Hardee, as the head of the Selma and Meridian Railroad, admitted he had sided with the Confederacy but that he now sought reconciliation with northerners as "our best friends are among those who fought us hardest." General Nathan B. Forrest told the president he had joined the army as a private citizen out of loyalty to his state, as any true Democrat would have done. Elbert Hartwell English of Arkansas, who had been chief justice of that state's supreme court in 1861, conveyed a similar belief that his position at the time of secession required him to remain dutiful to his state responsibilities under a new confederation government. He made no apology for continuing to serve as a state judge until surrender of the Confederate armies. In an accompanying letter to President Johnson, the commanding major general of the Union Army testified as to English's prominence and to his acceptable attitude and "good taste" as presented in an 1865 Fourth of July celebration speech.[4]

Several drew the president's attention to their personal importance for the recovery process. Morris Emanuel, president of the Southern Railroad, operating out of Vicksburg, felt that his membership in the antebellum Whig party seemed political justification enough for a pardon, and the pressing needs of his railroad for his personal involvement provided further pragmatic reason to grant clemency. Samuel Tate explained how he had gone South with the Confederate army to accompany the machinery of his railroad company, the Memphis and Charleston Railroad, in the hopes of preventing its destruction. Like Emanuel, he now asked for pardon so that he could get about the business of rebuilding the road. Benjamin H. Micou of Tallapoosa, Alabama, enclosed a petition signed by 360 residents of his county attesting to their desire that he be pardoned in order to keep his textile mill open, a mill which employed more than three hundred residents. Similarly, William B. Johnston of Macon wrote to the president of the public trust in his charge as he attempted to keep the Central Railroad and Banking Company of Georgia operating. Thomas Hardeman of Georgia, who was to emerge as one of the most prominent members of the Democratic party, argued for his pardon in light of his ability to wield public influence and to carry the message that the South should turn swords into plowshares and ships of war into merchant vessels, and in that way southerners would once again enjoy civil government along with peace and prosperity.[5]

A few admitted they had supported the war movement, but they seemed remorseful. Henry Hilliard commented to the president that he regarded the effort to divide the Union as "the most fatal blunder of statesmanship that has ever occurred in the annals of the world," and that he hoped to make amends for any role he had played in the tragedy by a "consecration of my whole future life to the advancements of the best interests of his country." The Reverend Charles Marshall of Mississippi sought solace in his wartime efforts to alleviate suffering among the soldiers, perhaps in atonement for what he so cautiously described as having "sympathized in the late war," somewhat of an understatement from the man who had pushed so strongly at antebellum commercial conventions for a policy of "home education" for the children of southern slaveholders.[6]

Robert Patton, soon to serve as governor of Alabama, told of how he had resisted secession until at the end, he too, in common with nearly all of the Alabama Union men, "fell into the current" and went along with the rebellion. Harvey Walter of Mississippi admitted that he had voted in favor of secession at his state's convention, but also said he had been surprised when war followed. From that point forward, he took an active role in the military action because otherwise he "would have felt dishonored in avoiding the hardships and perils which his vote had in part provoked." The same sense of honor would commit him to observe the terms of the pardon he sought. Benjamin Yancey, on the other hand, seemed to approach the prospect of reunion with enthusiasm rather than primarily out of a sense of duty. He wrote that now that slavery as a cause of dissention was removed, he could "very cheerfully acquiesce in the new condition of public affairs."[7]

Here, in the words of those who would four years hence meet together at the commercial conventions to formulate public policy through its debate process, we see common perceptions about the South as it existed in 1865, about a society wherein such men had come to terms with their role in the secession effort. Many of these men justified their present suitability for leadership largely on their resistance to early southern initiatives for secession; in their minds the fact that they finally followed their states was more an honorable reaction to circumstances than a personal choice in favor of secession.[8] They also based their application for pardon, and thus their appeal for a decision-making role in the South's future, on an open-mindedness about the fact that the Union would be reconstituted by a joint North-South effort. In 1865, after all, they had little reason to fear that Johnson would lose control of the reconstruction process or that southern state governments would operate with any voter constituent groups other than those long known to all parties.

This group of men in many ways fit the pattern of the conservatives who took control of the southern state governments under Johnson's presidency described by historians Thomas Alexander, Dan Carter, and Michael Perman as reluctant rather than strident secessionists, often former Whigs, and men with enthusiasm for economic modernization.[9] In these pardon applications, they told of personal economic hardship and of the fear that their remaining property might be subject to confiscation, but they seemed intent on staying in place within the South to weather the storm. Often, they spoke of the future in terms of opportunity rather than misfortune. Most acknowledged they carried influence with the public which could prove useful to the president in his effort to administer Reconstruction.

The thoughts of one man in particular, Jeremiah Watkins Clapp, seem particularly instructive in understanding the motivations and the intentions of those who continued to be attracted to the institution of the commercial convention in the years following the Civil War. Clapp had taken a leadership role in three commercial conventions, those held in 1853, 1854, and 1857. He would go on to attend three more sessions after the war. He is of particular interest because he was selected to give the featured speech at the opening of the first postwar convention, that in Memphis in 1869. As a wealthy lawyer-planter and former slaveholder, Clapp had been firmly entrenched in the economic elite of the Old South. Active in state politics in the 1850s as a member of the states'-rights faction of the Democratic party, he had represented his neighbors in the Confederate Congress for one term, and thereafter served the Confederacy as a cotton agent in Louisiana and Mississippi. After the Civil War, Clapp moved to Memphis to continue his law practice, and he resided there until his death in 1898. Clapp's thoughts come to us through four sources: two letters, one of 1865 and one of 1866, to President Johnson seeking pardon; a speech he delivered in Mississippi on June 29, 1866; and his May, 1869, address to the Memphis convention delegates.

On July 26, 1865, Clapp wrote to President Johnson of his activities under the government of the Confederacy, and he confided that he had lost his property "by the casualties of war." Unable to practice law pending clearance through executive pardon, he appealed for release and promised to abide by the terms of his oath of allegiance "in good faith." As of one year later, Clapp had still not been granted pardon. A longtime trustee for the University of Mississippi, Clapp addressed the graduating class at their commencement ceremony on June 29, 1866. To his audience, this man surely represented much of what had been swept away with the victory of the Union armies. Clapp had lived the dream of the old gospel of prosperity, and the outcome of the war had brought considerable upheaval to his life. Yet, Clapp's speech to the graduates carried the message of hope rather than a sad reminiscence. He praised those who had "adapted themselves to the new condition of affairs." Cognizant of the "oppressive sense of a great public sorrow," yet proud of the way that southerners were behaving honorably in accepting defeat with their "manhood unsullied," Clapp offered the graduates his vision of an opportunity to regenerate prosperity. Now that slavery was abolished—that "insuperable barrier to the introduction of foreign labor"—southerners could invest surplus capital in more than just "land and slaves." They could establish manufacturing enterprises and gain economic independence. They could find dignity in depending on their own labor. Clapp held out little hope that former slaves, members of an "inferior" race, would continue to provide the region with a dependable labor supply in the light of the interference posed by government intervention. His remedy was to bring in white laborers and to treat blacks with "kindness" but "keeping the social distance." His closing remarks were an ode to southern women, who had once as guardian angels soothed dying soldiers and who now stood watch over memorial graves.[10]

As of the time of that speech, former leaders of southern society like Clapp still faced uncertain futures. The southern state governments, with many of these very men in influential positions, were moving toward two major goals designed to revive the old economy: controlling the labor force through such means as Black Codes, and introducing economic programs designed to encourage expansion, such as aid to railroads and manufacturing. However, there were signs that members of the Thirty-ninth Congress were not going to let President Johnson's policies stand unchallenged. They had blocked the seating of southern congressmen, had created a Joint Committee on Reconstruction, had extended the life of the Freedmen's Bureau, and had framed the Civil Rights Act and the Fourteenth Amendment. President Johnson, in turn, had issued a call for a National Union Convention to prepare for the upcoming federal elections.

Clapp's original request for pardon had evidently not reached President Johnson, so on September 11, 1866, he made a second appeal and conveyed a strong sense of foreboding to the chief executive. He wrote that at stake in the success of Johnson's Reconstruction policy was "not only the preservation of the Southern States from spoliation and degradation, but also the preservation of the Union from dismemberment, the Constitution from desecration, and public liberty from anarchy and despotism." Despite this anxiety, Clapp made no effort to blur the evi-

dence of his own part in the coming of the Civil War. He freely acknowledged that at the time of secession he believed the political and
property rights of his section were being threatened by the "new England school of politics" and that the act of secession was a legitimate
and legal recourse. Clapp added that he did not at that previous time see
that civil war would necessarily follow. He reminded Johnson the Democrat that many prominent southern Democrats had shared those beliefs.
As to the result of secession, Clapp was still not ready to admit that
a philosophy was unsound because its adherents had suffered military
defeat, but he was also a practical man, and he accepted the outcome of
the war as a "final result."[11] Perhaps in these bold admissions one can
gain further insight into why the southern state governments resisted
the Republican insistence on acceptance of the terms of the Fourteenth
Amendment.

After a two-year period, Presidential Reconstruction came to an end
in 1867. The efforts of southerners to reinstate home rule under terms
amenable to white conservatives failed. The governments created under
the presidency of Johnson were swept aside as Congress took over formulation of national Reconstruction policies. The national Republicans
reclaimed the office of president, and southern state governments came
under the control of state Republican parties elected largely by black
voters and included among their elected and appointed officials numerous former slaves. Ratification of the Fourteenth Amendment changed
the basic political configuration of the South, and many white southerners who had held office before 1865 were subject to disenfranchise-
ment under its provisions. However, Republican Reconstruction did not
evolve without its own conflicts. Both political parties were split between
extremist and conservative factions. Southern Republicans divided into
those who hoped to enlarge the party's base of support among white
voters, and those more interested in seeing blacks and existing party
regulars retain control. Southern Democrats were similarly divided into
a centrist faction that had adopted the rhetoric of "New Departure"
politics, advocating that the South put the war behind her and accept
political reality, including the reality of black voting, and a more conservative group unwilling to abandon the party traditions of states' rights
and white supremacy. By 1869, much of the South was racked by violence

as secret societies such as the Ku Klux Klan emerged to belie the seeming acceptance among white southerners of changed circumstances and to further challenge the legitimacy of the Republican governments.[12]

What had been done to rebuild the South's economy? Despite the hardships of the droughts, floods, and insect infestations of 1866 and 1867, the agricultural South was back in operation but under greatly transformed conditions from those of the slave South. Lacking any massive redistribution of land from landowners to former slaves, the new relationship between these two sets of southerners was generally that of white landlord and black laborer, both theoretically operating under the natural laws of a free-market economy. Actually, within the agricultural economic sector, the transition from slave labor to free labor had produced many varieties of economic arrangements.

Sugar production had shifted to the use of wage labor, and large plantation operations remained intact; large rice plantations had been split into small parcels of land, and former slaves worked the crops, largely unsupervised, under the old task system. In tobacco and cotton production, white landowners competed with each other for laborers, and several forms of agricultural production arose simultaneously during this time: large-scale business plantations where black laborers were paid as sharecroppers but white owners continued to be responsible for marketing the crop, tenant plantations with absentee landlords where the tenants financed their crop production through liens and usually marketed the crops themselves, and small farms where landowners similarly relied on liens or mortgages. While tenancy provided landowners with dependable labor and provided tenants with some control over their work, it also burdened tenants with debt, which kept them in poverty. Jonathan Wiener has described the result as the "Prussian road," a social and political system, imposed by a planter-dominated state, designed to control labor. One student of the history of the postwar agricultural South, James Roark, has argued that as this particular system of labor relations evolved, landowners looked upon sharecropping as a temporary solution, not as the wave of the future. Even if it was developed to serve as a temporary solution to the problem of farming, it had critical impact on the development of the South's economy in many ways, not the least of which was that it prevented the tenant farmers from devel-

oping entrepreneurial skills and gave southern white landowners a distorted understanding of the realities of free labor.[13]

The Freedmen's Bureau had been instrumental in bringing whatever
stability existed in labor relations, but the labor contracts in force provided only meager incomes to farm laborers. Politicization of the freedmen through contact with the Union League and other similar bodies
increased the level of agitation for new work autonomy rights, and control by the tenant over the day-to-day organization of work became a
central feature of decentralized tenant farming. In return, many former
slaveholders felt themselves released from whatever sense of paternalism
they had felt toward their slaves. Still, as there had existed in some ways
under slavery, there was a vital dependency between worker and landowner: the landowner was dependent on labor that would remain in
place for the entire crop-life cycle, and the farmworker was dependent
on a source of income or credit to sustain life.[14]

To the extent that Republican governments came to the aid of farm-
workers in these years, they heightened the perception on the part of
white landowners that there was no dependable supply of labor in the
South. Republican lawmakers swept away the Black Codes, ameliorated
the harsh legal treatment of vagrants and criminals, and refused to enact
fence laws. The rights of tenants were protected by laws giving them
first lien on the crop and some recourse against uncompensated evic-
tion. Debtor relief legislation protected minimal property holdings
against debt collections.[15]

The white landowner's perception that the labor supply was unreli-
able was made the more frustrating by the region's drive to increase cotton production. Eventually, cotton prices would start a decline in the
1870s, but in the immediate period after the war, steep declines did not
seem likely. And, even when prices did decline, cotton production was
an immediate source of cash, so vital to the debt-ridden South. So whether
it was a decision made by the landowner, by the tenant, or for the tenant, the result was an increase throughout the South in the production
of cotton. The cotton culture had begun its spread into the southern up-
country in the years before the Civil War in the wake of an expanding
railroad network, and this phenomena would increase in the years of
Reconstruction. The import of all this for understanding the commer-

cial convention debates is that, if anything, more southerners than ever before were anxious about the needs of commercial agriculture. For planters especially, the interest in securing improved access to the world market was almost certainly more intense than before, as the primary asset of such a planter now lay with his land.[16]

As they had done for many antebellum southerners, railroads still held the promise of prosperity to many in the South after the war, and enthusiasm for railroad building had continued unabated in the years immediately following the war. As they sought financing with which to rebuild, southern railroad companies turned initially to private investors, both local investors and European investors who had purchased bonds before the war. They appealed, too, to state governments for help, and they were not disappointed. The Republicans who assumed control of state politics after 1867 actually continued a policy supported by Presidential Reconstruction state governments: providing both indirect and direct state aid to railroad development. Charter provisions were amended to allow for extension of credit, state governments assisted roads in securing public bonds, and specific lines were often granted tax exemption.[17]

Planter-landowners may have had cause for concern between 1867 and 1869, but those southerners anxious to bring railroads and industry to the region found reason to support Republican governments. In the years following Presidential Reconstruction, moderate Republicans and conservative Democrats alike appealed to prospective party members, especially to former Whigs, in a campaign to bring industry, urbanization, and some degree of diversified farming to the South. Under constitutions devised by Republican-controlled governments, both laws limiting personal liability and general incorporation laws were enacted, paving the way for business expansion. Government support for railroads reached an all-time peak under the Republicans. Every state allowed the government to assist internal improvements. In his history of how Reconstruction governments aided railroads, Mark W. Summers concluded that in the end, the state governments' largesse resulted in more roads than the southern traffic volumes could support, but at the time every city and town was clamoring for railroad connections to the broader market in the hopes of generating local prosperity. State government support included bonds, grants, and tax relief. While the railroads were able to rebuild and even expand, the government involvement proved detrimental in the long run, as railroad finances became intertwined with state politics, and this relationship in turn ushered in a period of corruption and indebtedness that would to some degree assist in bringing down the Republican governments. Historian Michael Perman concluded that the support that Republicans gave to railroads pushed them in a conservative direction and made them less responsive to the demands of their poorest constituents.[18]

If the South was still land rich, it was cash poor. Those southern banks that had survived the war were now subject to the credit restrictions imposed under the National Banking Act, and historian Larry Schweikart has estimated that banking capital in the South dropped from an 1860 level of sixty-one million dollars to an 1870 level of seventeen million. Harold Woodman found that much of the northern money that had come South immediately after the war for the purchase of cotton had been used to repay old prewar debts and was not available to fund the cost of current crop production. Despite appeals from bankers for laws that would release them from personal liability for bank debt, the southern state governments initially refused. Under Republican governments, usury laws were repealed in many states, which drove the cost of money up. Vital cash was drained from the region by another direct consequence of the war, the federal Cotton Tax, a tax on raw cotton. The tax had been imposed in 1863 and continued until its repeal in 1868. An estimated total of sixty-eight million dollars was paid out by the South in that five-year period. This aggravated an already critical shortage of working capital in the region.[19]

Thus we come to May of 1869. In the midst of profound change, in the wake of uncertainty about what further changes the South might witness, a large number of southerners assembled under the umbrella of an association long familiar to them, a regional commercial convention. In response to an appeal from a commercial gathering held in Norfolk the previous October, the Memphis Chamber of Commerce had invited representatives from the South, especially from those states along the Mississippi River, and representatives from all states along the Ohio River, to convene on May 18, 1869, assembling in an advisory capacity. Adopting a format comfortably reminiscent of antebellum gatherings, the delegates organized themselves into officers and committees. The order of business listed topics long of interest: the southern Pacific railroad and general railroad development, direct trade with Europe, manufactures and mining, and river and harbor improvements.[20] Except for introduction of the topic of immigration, one might as well have been looking at the order of business from the Memphis convention of 1853 as that of 1869.

The commercial convention of 1869 was followed by four more, with the last session held in 1871. All five of these conventions promoted the same core of policies, all designed to lead the South back into the national economy and into a resurrected political alignment with moderates in both major parties. Southern participants at these sessions hoped to rebuild their bridge of communication with like-minded representatives from the North in an effort to ease the travail of the uncertainties of Reconstruction. Their presence at the conventions testifies to the persistence of their belief that leaders must take action to influence public policy, including ways outside the normal bounds of party politics. These men who met together during the three years of the convention movement's revival repeatedly disavowed partisanship. Like their predecessors at the conventions of the first half of the decade of the 1850s, they were united by a shared economic philosophy and by an optimism about the South's ability to enjoy prosperity once again.

The leadership of the postwar convention series was drawn from the membership rosters of both political parties, Republicans and Democrats or Conservatives. Political affiliations of the three southerners who served as convention presidents after the war illustrate this diversity: Charles Anderson and Chauncey Filley were Republicans, and John Work Garrett a Democrat. Notably, however, all three had been Unionists. Other Republicans among this postwar convention elite included James Alcorn and Arthur E. Reynolds of Mississippi, Cyrus Bussey of Louisiana, Carleton B. Cole of Georgia, former Alabaman and now Georgian Henry Hilliard, Clinton Fisk and Edwin Stanard of Missouri, David Lewis and Robert Patton of Alabama, and Logan H. Roots of Arkansas. Prominent Democrats or southern Conservatives among the convention officeholders included Joseph Anderson, Thomas

Bocock, and Thomas Branch of Virginia; David E. Butler, Thomas Harde-
man, and Pierce M. B. Young of Georgia; Jeremiah Clapp, Edwin Cole,
Henry Foote, Nathan B. Forrest, Thomas A. R. Nelson, and Robertson
Topp of Tennessee; Alexander M. Clayton, Winfield Featherston,
Charles Hooker, and Edwin M. Yerger of Mississippi; Reverdy Johnson
of Maryland; Robert B. Lindsay of Alabama; James Throckmorton of
Texas; and Erastus Wells of Missouri.

While the delegates from northern states have not been included in
the biographical study group, it is evident from a cursory examination of
the list of 265 individuals who represented northern communities at the
postwar conventions that they too came from both political parties.
Among the Republicans attending the conventions were Massachusetts
senator Henry Wilson and Congressman Nathaniel P. Banks; Roscoe
Conkling's brother and former congressman Frederick A. Conkling of
New York; Ohio congressman Benjamin Eggleston; coal industrialist
and leader of the Western Pennsylvania Republicans John F. Dravo; former Ohio Superior Court judge and later United States Supreme Court
justice Stanley Matthews; Ayres P. Merrill of New York, who would
serve as minister to Belgium in 1876; congressman from Pittsburgh and
president of the Atlantic and Ohio Telegraph Company (Western Union)
James K. Moorhead; prominent Pittsburgh iron industrialist Henry W.
Oliver; United States Senator William Sprague of Rhode Island; and
former congressman William Vandever of Iowa. The Democratic party
was represented by former mayor of Cincinnati and later governor of
Ohio Richard Bishop; New York state assemblyman Erastus Brooks;
railroad president and Ohio state legislator Hugh Jewett, who would
later serve in Congress; the founder of Dubuque, Iowa, and former United
States senator George W. Jones; former federal judge and Indiana congressman John Law; New York congressman John Van Schaick L. Pruyn;
Pennsylvania railroad promoter and later congressman John Reilly; railroad promoter and prominent lawyer Breese J. Stevens of Madison,
Wisconsin; and extremist southern sympathizer and former congressman Clement L. Vallandigham of Ohio.

Obviously, as both southern and northern lists indicate, the conventions continued to attract men of influence, including many who were
active in politics. Also, the organization continued to elevate those

who either already had held or would hold public office, especially at the Memphis convention, where at least one instance of officeholding could be determined for 59 percent of the leadership. Apparently office-holding experience declined among leaders at the final four conventions, but that might be partially explained by the fact that most of the biographical information used in the study that related to officeholding at the state level pertained to the antebellum period, and thus postwar officeholding at the state level may be understated. Even though instances of officeholding declined among leaders at succeeding postwar conventions, their combined average of 37 percent compared to an average officeholding experience of 10 percent among all postwar delegates indicates that political officeholding continued to be an important criteria for elite status. The majority of those postwar leaders who held public office had done so prior to the time of their commercial convention leadership designation.

As might be surmised from reading the list of southerners who composed the postwar leadership, it appears that these conventions did not involve black southerners in their meetings. Information about race was not recorded as a part of the delegate registration process, nor was it noted in delegate listings by the local newspaper accounts. The delegate rosters have been checked against historical references to black individuals of prominence during the Reconstruction years without finding matches. Also, no speaker in the five-session series made reference to there being black members in the audience. One newspaper report of the Louisville convention emphatically remarked that "not one single colored person" was to be found among the delegates.[21] What comments were made about black southerners spoke of them as laborers, not as participants in the conventions or potential participants.

The convention revival was engineered by native southerners, not transplanted northerners. Of those 270 delegates for whom antebellum residence is known, only 3 percent resided in states outside of the South. The percentage of former northerners, or carpetbaggers as they are traditionally labeled, ran slightly higher among the leadership echelon, at 8 percent. The convention held in Cincinnati included the highest portion of carpetbaggers among its southern leadership, 10 percent. That held in New Orleans included the lowest share, 4 percent.

Based on that information, it is reasonable to suggest that the convention membership did not shun carpetbaggers, but that they played a minor role in the association.

Occupational information about the postwar leadership indicates that its members shared much in common with the antebellum leadership. Lawyers and those engaged in commerce continued to play a predominant role at the commercial conventions. A comparison of postwar occupations among postwar convention leaders has been made to antebellum occupations among antebellum leaders in an effort to describe the occupations of the convention leadership at the time of its members' convention involvement. The percentage of lawyers among leaders averaged 33 percent at postwar conventions, slightly lower than the 48 percent at antebellum conventions. The proportion of commercialists among leaders at the postwar conventions averaged 56 percent, compared to 30 percent at antebellum conventions. The largest contrast between antebellum leadership and postwar leadership is in the agriculturalist category, as only an average of 13 percent of leaders at postwar conventions were involved in agriculture compared to an average of 41 percent at antebellum meetings.

The gain in commercialists and the decline in agriculturalists suggest that the leadership of the commercial conventions shifted after the war to men less directly involved in agricultural production than had been their antebellum predecessors. In that respect, the commercial conventions present evidence of historical change in the postwar South. The postwar leadership was more urban, more commerce-oriented. However, within the information about occupations of postwar leaders is also evidence of historical continuity. The pattern of occupations of postwar leaders did not change from the antebellum period to the postwar period. Men who held leadership posts at the postwar conventions had long been involved in law and commerce rather than agriculture. Among those for whom earlier occupations have been determined, 31 percent of the postwar leaders had been lawyers in the antebellum period, 46 percent of them had been engaged in commerce, and just 15 percent in agriculture. For these men, as a group, the postwar period did not mean a drastic change in their personal world in terms of how they made a living or where their financial interests lay. They had been engaged in the emerging modern world all along.

If postwar leaders differed, as a group, from antebellum leaders in their fewer agricultural ties, does this mean that differences in occupation might account for the fact that some antebellum leaders chose not to return to the commercial conventions? Apparently not, for among men who took leadership roles in the antebellum convention movement but not in the postwar movement and for whom there is no evidence of death prior to 1869, there appears to have been a shift after the Civil War into the same types of occupations represented by those who were leaders of the postwar conventions. Among those such antebellum leaders were 179 for whom antebellum occupation is known. Of these, 44 percent were antebellum lawyers, 27 percent were engaged in commerce, and 37 percent were engaged in agriculture. Out of the same group of antebellum leaders there are eighty for whom postwar occupation is also known. Here is seen the same pattern as with postwar leaders, movements into law and commerce and a decline in agriculturalists. Among these eighty men, 59 percent were postwar lawyers, 26 percent were in commerce, and 19 percent in agriculture. Thus, men attracted to the movement at various times throughout its history evidenced similar behavior in the aftermath of war and disruption, and they gravitated increasingly toward those occupations that had attracted a majority of their membership prior to the war.[22]

As was true in the years before 1861, the majority of leaders at the conventions were older than age forty. The prewar conventions as a group averaged 61 percent of their leaders over age forty; the postwar conventions as a group averaged 76 percent over age forty. One interesting difference between the two time periods of convention activity is that the postwar leader groups, and especially the groups from the three conventions held in 1869, included proportionately more men over age fifty at the time of their convention participation than did the antebellum leader groups. This is understandable partly in light of the fact that many who were in attendance at the postwar sessions had also attended at least one prewar session, and there was a ten-year gap between antebellum and postwar conventions. The last two conventions, those of 1870 and 1871, more closely matched the leadership age distribution of antebellum sessions in that they attracted more men below age forty.

Just as the conventions continued to attract men of maturity, they also continued, initially at least, to attract men who had enjoyed wealth in the years before the Civil War. When median values of 1860 estates held by leaders at each of the antebellum conventions are averaged, they yield a mean estate valuation of $86,000. When median values for leaders at the three 1869 conventions are averaged, the comparable value is $85,000. Only the last two conventions seemingly differed from the previous sessions as the median 1860 estate values of convention leaders in 1870 and 1871 dropped significantly below the median of the previous groups, down to medians of $9,000 and $5,000 respectively. Here, age must be considered. Anyone younger than age forty in 1870 would have been younger than age thirty in 1860 and unlikely to have inherited or made much progress yet toward building an estate. That is important for understanding the lower antebellum estate values at these final conventions, because 37 percent of the leaders fit that age category, whereas only 15 percent of the leaders at the three 1869 conventions would have been younger than age thirty in 1860.[23]

Party affiliations among postwar convention leaders show an expected pattern, with more antebellum Democrats among the group than opposition party members, and more postwar Democrats or Conservatives than Republicans. Generally, their politics was not as distinguishing as was their economic orientation. To an even larger degree than had their predecessors, delegates at the conventions meeting after the Civil War placed mature commercialists and lawyers at the helm of the association as it met to inquire into what could be done to regenerate the South's economy.

The resumption of the commercial conventions involved a sizable number of individuals who had been active in the movement prior to the Civil War. Sixty-seven men present at Memphis had attended a prewar session, and in all, a total of 111 members of the antebellum delegations would return to the association after the war. Forty-five out of this 111 would hold a convention leadership post at some time. Of course, many who had taken a prominent role in the prewar series were no longer alive by 1869. De Bow had died in 1867 and William Dawson in

1856. Gone also were Clement C. Clay, "Lean Jimmy" Jones, James Gadsden, Mirabeau Lamar and Memucan Hunt, and Edmund Ruffin and William Yancey. At least sixty-four members of the antebellum Convention Elite had died by the time of the 1869 Memphis session. Others had left the South: James Robb and Roger Pryor for New York, Albert Pike for Washington, D.C., and Judah Benjamin for Europe. Still, there were 11 percent of the surviving antebellum leaders who participated in the postwar movement, a further indicator of individual persistence reinforcing evidence of persistence of men who shared common biographical characteristics.

This evidence of continuity of leadership suggests that the commercial convention movement matches a general pattern of the period, that leaders from the slave South took positions of responsibility in the postwar South. The issue of continuity has at least two dimensions: political leadership and economic elite status. While both political parties in the South attracted black members who had obviously not been politically active in the years before the war, and while the Republican party included many white males who had moved to the South from the North after the war, still both parties had among their leadership a large number of men who had attained varying degrees of political prominence in the antebellum South. The previously discussed studies of Thomas Alexander, Michael Perman, Dan Carter, and Laurence Shore all give heavy emphasis to the leadership vitality of antebellum men of prominence in the years after the war. Other historians, studying particular groups in geographically limited areas, have also found considerable evidence of persistence of members of the respective local economic and political elites: Alabamans studied by Jonathan Wiener and Sarah Woolfolk Wiggins; North Carolinians traced by Dwight Billings, Gail O'Brien, and John J. Beck; the Virginians detailed by A. Jane Townes; Conservative party members of North Carolina and Virginia described by Catherine S. Silverman; and the portrait of Natchez planters painted by Michael Wayne.[24]

The leadership of the postwar commercial conventions lend further credence to these findings of historical persistence. On an individual basis, many who had held positions of leadership within the antebellum convention movement returned to lead the effort after the Civil War. In terms of group representation, many of those postwar leaders who had not previously participated in the convention movement shared similar biographical characteristics with their predecessors, characteristics which merit classifying them as members of an economic elite. This is not to claim that their personal circumstances, as well as those of their constituents, had not changed. In the historical debate over persistence, historians Eric Foner and Harold Woodman, as well as economist Gavin Wright, have stressed the importance of recognizing just how changed these circumstances were.[25] The fact that the Confederacy had been defeated, that slavery had been abolished, and that Republican party policies had been enacted marked major changes. Nevertheless, the discussions at the postwar commercial conventions reveal that those taking a prominent place among public statesmen carried many of the same perceptions and beliefs about their South that had guided their actions before the war.

The debates at the postwar commercial conventions parallel those held at the antebellum series. Delegates who met together at the sessions held between 1869 and 1871 brought back the same sense of optimism about the economic opportunities open to southerners and the same determination to press for public policies that would bring prosperity to the region. As they reached out symbolically to effect reconciliation with northerners at each convention session, these southern leaders sent the message that they expected real help in return. Such assistance was a major component in their definition of national reconstruction, and they clung to hope for its realization throughout the entire three-year period of postwar convention activity.

Yet, in their own limited vision of the "good" economy for the South, they served to reinforce a dependence on agriculture and to present a definition of progress that fell far short of a radical rebuilding of the region. For they brought to the postwar South the same perspective about the relationship between agriculture and prosperity that had driven the policy formulations of the antebellum conventions, and the old racism that sustained the existence of the institution of slavery. To that end, not only was the instrument of the commercial convention familiar to southern business leaders, but so was its message, and so would be its result.

9
A Bid for Reconciliation
1869

A good starting point from which to begin analysis of the postwar commercial convention debates is with Jeremiah Watkins Clapp, for in his address to the Memphis convention are many of the major themes of the entire postwar convention movement. As mentioned in the previous chapter, the Memphis Chamber of Commerce called upon Clapp, then a resident of that city, to speak as the featured orator at the opening day session of the Southern Commercial Convention in May of 1869. His target audience was the 879 delegates from both South and North assembled for what was to be the largest postwar convention. Clapp was as optimistic with these listeners as he had been with the University of Mississippi graduates in 1866. He reminded the Memphis convention of the abundance of the South's natural advantages: her salubrious climate, fertile soil, mineral and forest treasures, and her "almost" monopoly production of four of the world's great staples—cotton, tobacco, sugar, and rice. As he had done in 1866, Clapp focused on two key objectives: securing both adequate and "well directed" labor and capital. With these needs met, he asserted, the South would see repair of levee systems and economic expansion of the Mississippi River delta region through control of floods, creation of a regional railroad network, construction of a southern Pacific railroad, proliferation of shipping lines providing direct trade with Europe and South America, and establishment of manufacturing enterprises employing "Old World" operatives. Not incidentally, he urged more effective use of both the southern press and various educational and religious institutions to bring a restraining influence on former slaves who exercised a "fearful preeminence as the controlling interest in our political affairs."[1]

Here, in the speech of this Memphis lawyer, it is evident that foremost among the ideas carried across the Civil War experience was a continuing belief in the gospel of prosperity and in the potential of the South to achieve success. Others addressed the delegates that opening day with similar optimism. Robert Patton, former governor of Alabama who was temporarily serving as chairman of the convention, assured the delegates that they should not despair, but rather be optimistic, as the South had "great energy." General Robert E. Lee, who could not be there in person, communicated with the delegates by letter in support of their efforts, and the audience responded to his message with "great cheers." The convention's presiding officer, President Charles Anderson of Kentucky, admitted that the job of removing the ruins of wartime destruction was a "huge task," but he declared that he held high hopes that the future prosperity of the South might surpass all her past experience.[2]

Just as speakers at the antebellum conventions had done, the postwar convention leaders revealed that their hope for prosperity was grounded in a perception of the richness of the South's natural resources. As Missouri congressman Erastus Wells succinctly told the 1869 Memphis convention, "We must pay our way out of debt by the soil."[3] In their investigation of what was needed to draw full benefit from the South's natural bounties, the conventions focused on the two priorities that Clapp had asked his Memphis audience to consider: to secure both adequate and well-directed labor and capital. Throughout the three-year discussion, delegates showed that the war had in one respect freed them, and in another respect it had changed little.

As they sought capital with which to fund their economic expansion, the delegates moved beyond the restraints that delegates at conventions of the late antebellum years had imposed on themselves. Free of the need to avoid federal involvement in the southern economy out of the fear of federal interference with slavery, the leaders of the postwar conventions revealed that they expected much from the federal government. They recognized that the national government had, since the years before the war, taken on a more active role in the economic development of the country, and they seemed to expect that as a part of the process of returning to the national economy, the South would benefit accordingly. In that respect, they had emerged from the war with heightened expectations about the positive aspects of change that the war had brought.

For many of these delegates, it appears they believed that another result of the war was to bring the South more fully into the modern world. In one of the few direct references made to the Civil War, a convention report concluded that it had produced a revolution, a "stupendous event of modern history." By bringing about the elimination of the country's "conflicting institutions," the American people had been made homogeneous, with the potential to become a "colossal power, destined to carry the blessing of civilization as far as the arm of aggrandizement may reach. . . ." As one St. Louis delegate put it, Congress needed to provide those improvements that were "calculated to stamp the word progress" on every town along the Mississippi River valley.[4]

By contrast, their perceptions about labor were still constrained by racism and a distorted view of work incentives left with them from their experience with slavery. The spokesmen for the propertied class who led these gatherings were painfully aware of the importance of securing dependable agricultural labor, and they evidenced mixed feelings about the willingness and ability of former slaves to supply the need. They were attracted to immigrants, both as potential landowners and as farm laborers. They seemed to prefer European immigrants for political and social reasons, but they also discussed immigration of Chinese laborers. By their attraction to an external remedy for an internal problem, the convention activists exhibited what Harold Woodman has described as an inability of native southern whites to come to terms with the reality of free labor. At times they held out the possibility for racial cooperation among native southerners, and at other times they admitted to a fear that any free-labor relationship between former slaves and former slaveholders could not be sustained. Despite the fact that efforts to attract immigrants to the South by and large failed, and that those immigrants who did arrive in these years seldom stayed in the region, the conventions of 1869–1871 voiced enthusiasm about the possibility of drawing foreign immigrants. Perhaps the enthusiasm was real, or perhaps the immigration campaign was being used as a threat against reluctant black laborers. The fact that the 1869 conventions clung to immigration as a panacea for a perceived dilemma might serve more as a measure of their fears than of their hopes.[5]

The postwar commercial conventions sought capital with which to enhance the South's contact with the world marketplace, to implement those improvements that would broaden the agricultural production base, and to make delivery of southern products less costly. Thus, as delegates had done at meetings held before the Civil War, these assemblies spoke of the need for railroads, river and harbor improvements, a southern railroad connection to the Pacific, and steamship lines to connect the South with Europe and South America. They recommended limited diversification into mining and textile manufacturing, but they did not in any way propose radical surgery intended to replace staple-crop agriculture with industry. A resolution adopted at the Memphis convention phrased it this way: "Agriculture—This is the first, last, and greatest employment of our people, and lies down under all other pursuits. The rich productions which its diversification gives to the country are the main springs to all the machinery of domestic, social and commercial life."[6] They saw opportunities to spread commercialization of agriculture by extending railroads into the southern interior, and they recognized the benefits to be derived from modern farming methods such as using fertilizers and machinery. They sought ways to repair levees along the Mississippi River in order to expand the cotton culture across flooded lands.

From the outset of the first postwar commercial convention, it was evident that those southern leaders active in the convention movement expected substantial economic assistance from the federal government as a part of the process of national reconciliation. The New Orleans report on the Southern Pacific Railroad includes a history lesson that explains why such men anticipated a munificent federal economic reconstruction policy. They likened their situation to that of the Roman Empire, and they recalled that a large part of the greatness of the Empire had resulted from its policy of extending internal improvements to those whom it conquered in war. So, as a conquered people, these representatives of the South suggested that the government act in a rational way, in a way calculated to enrich the entire country in the long run.[7]

Commercial convention appeals for federal aid reinforced those made by southern congressmen. In the years between 1869 and 1871, both groups acted in a bipartisan way to express a unified southern appeal for economic assistance. The representatives of southern business interests who assembled at the commercial conventions echoed the sentiments of the public officeholders, most of whom were Republicans, that a part of the rationale behind southern acceptance of the aftermath of the war was the hope that the South could reap some of the same benefits from nationhood that the states of the North had come to enjoy. In his study of the return of the South to Congress, historian Terry L. Seip found that southern Republicans and Democrats often united to seek federal funding for river and harbor improvements, but they met with little success until after 1876. He concluded that the refusal of northern Republicans to provide the federal economic aid that the congressmen sought contributed substantially to the failure of Republican Reconstruction. Richard H. Abbott, observing the reluctance to meet southern requests for congressional aid, concluded that northerners remained ignorant of the conditions in the South, and that they had few chances outside the halls of Congress to meet with southerners to hear of matters first-hand. To the extent that the conventions reiterated the same expectations about federal economic involvement that southern congressional leaders presented, they lent further weight to such official appeals and provided evidence to leaders of both national political parties that public opinion across the South favored federal economic activism. Therefore, while northern congressmen chose not to extend federal largesse to the former Confederate states, it seems unlikely this was done out of ignorance. If, as Richard F. Bensel suggests, the finance capitalists of the northeastern commercial centers were determined to see federal economic retrenchment and reduction of expenditures for local internal improvements, then the commercial conventions and southern congressmen were pitted against formidable opposition within the Republican party in their quest for federal financing.[8]

The postwar conventions eagerly sought reconciliation and northern economic assistance, whether from public coffers or private investors. Southerners cordially welcomed northern delegates to the assemblies, and the northern delegates returned the enthusiasm, perhaps with visions of their own enrichment in mind. The majority of the northerners who attended the conventions represented midwestern constituencies: of the 265 northern delegates participating at the five sessions, 74 percent were from Ohio, Pennsylvania, Indiana, and Illinois. New York delegates alone represented 11 percent of the northern total, but the remaining numbers of northeasterners accounted for only 3 percent. Eight percent came from the states of Michigan, Wisconsin, Iowa, and Kansas, and less than 3 percent from far-western states. Historian George Woolfolk has traced the postwar effort of merchants of the Midwest to shift southern trade out of New York into the interior. Organizing into trade associations, which worked to change federal trade regulations so as to allow interior cities to serve as ports of entry, they supported expansion of northern railroads into the South.[9] While he did not discuss these five commercial conventions, they were part of that drive, providing northerners with the opportunity to establish direct contacts with southern men of influence and to marshall public opinion favorable to expansion of southern-midwestern trade flows.

The movement was off to a strong start with the first convention, that held in Memphis. It attracted 835 southerners and 44 northerners. Though Tennesseeans were the largest contingent, 258 delegates, they did not dominate the group, nor did representatives of the Upper South. While Virginia sent 192 men, Georgia sent 94, Mississippi 88, and Alabama 81. In addition to the prominent southerners mentioned above in connection with the opening-day speeches, the meeting drew senators and congressmen, governors and generals, and many with high-profile name recognition, at least within their own states: Tennesseeans Senator Joseph S. Fowler, Thomas A. R. Nelson, Isham G. Harris, Nathan Bedford Forrest, John Trezevant, Robertson Topp, Henry Foote, Milton Brown, William T. Dortch and Edwin Cole; Virginians John Tyler, Jr., Samuel B. French, and General Robert Lilley; Mississippians James Alcorn, Winfield Featherston, and Charles Hooker; Alabaman William Byrd; Kentuckians E. Kirby Smith and Warren Mitchell; Georgians

General Alexander Lawton, Duff Green, Nelson Tift, and William G. McAdoo; and South Carolinians William Hastie and George Williams.

The Memphis convention adjourned on Friday, May 21, 1869, and a group of eighty-nine southern delegates and seven northern delegates journeyed to New Orleans for a second commercial convention, which was to open on the following Monday. There, as at Memphis, the local Arrangements Committee had made extensive preparations for the occasion. At noon on opening day, the delegates who had come from Memphis joined the more than three hundred additional delegates at the chamber of commerce offices and formed a parade to march to the Mechanics Institute, where the convention was to meet. The conventioneers were led by a silver cornet band, and once inside the hall they beheld a display of banners, flags, and mottoes that symbolized what the convention debates would also reveal, a blend of grand ambition and practicality. These were their messages: "The West and the South Join Hands; God Helps those who Helps Themselves; The River to the Sea, the Sea to the River; Punctuality is the hinge of business; The Mississippi Valley only seeks her own—this she demands; and Trade knows neither Friends nor Kindred."[10]

This New Orleans session of 1869 harkened back to the earlier New Orleans conventions of 1852 and 1855 in several ways: a large amount of time was spent discussing specific concerns of the city of New Orleans, the general topic of commerce was the overriding theme of the meeting, and the delegates strongly endorsed a policy of federal aid to internal improvements. Of all the conventions, those in New Orleans were most westward focused, and in 1869, the highest ranking officers of the convention represented the interests of the Mississippi Valley: General William Vandever of Dubuque, Iowa, and Chauncey Filley of St. Louis.

However much it resembled earlier New Orleans meetings, this session differed in reflecting the new urban character of the postwar movement. As had been the case with the Memphis convention, the New Orleans report of the convention proceedings listed the cities that the delegates represented. Only a few delegates were listed as representing a county or state. Naturally, the largest delegation was that from the host

city, New Orleans. Not unexpectedly, the second largest group represented Memphis. The other sizable contingents were those from cities of
the Upper South: St. Louis with twenty-two, Louisville and Norfolk with
twelve each, Petersburg, Virginia with ten, and Nashville with eight. Although fewer in number, cities from the Lower South sent delegations
too: Mobile, Huntsville, Savannah, Atlanta, Charleston, Vicksburg,
Galveston, and Houston, among others. There were fewer northerners
and westerners at New Orleans than at Memphis, a total of twenty-seven,
with the states of Ohio and Illinois claiming eleven each. In the speeches
and in the resolutions adopted by the delegates, this convention evidenced a positive attitude toward urban development in the South, and
a bourgeois appreciation of the attributes of successful commercialists.

General Vandever explained that the purpose of the meeting was to
consider how to eliminate problems that infringed on the valley's growing commerce: obstructions along the length of the Mississippi River,
particularly at the mouth of the river, and improvements at the falls of
the Ohio River. He contended that western grain producers needed a
water transportation network as an alternative to a Chicago-route railroad system that had become too costly, and that the federal government had not yet given the West its fair share of aid for internal improvements. To that end, he hoped their meeting would create an awareness of
public support for such federal assistance, and that it would forge an association of men "bound together by mutual interests, forgetting the troubles and animosities of the past. . . ."[11]

Though the General had wasted little time getting to the practical
issues facing the convention, the other speakers on opening day waxed a
bit more poetic. Judge Alexander Walker of New Orleans, an attorney
and former slaveholder who had been sent to the Secession Convention
as a secessionist and who had since come back to political life as a participant in the National Union movement of 1866 and a Conservative, had
larger goals in mind for the convention: to promote the "increased greatness, glory and wealth and enlightenment of this magnificent
region. . . ." The convention's president, Chauncey Filley, a Republican,
asked the delegates to consider that they faced "the new dawn of Western
commercial life." Among the opportunities available to them were the
manufacture of iron barges and steamers, cotton textile manufacturing,

direct importation of foreign goods, and establishment of steamship lines
to Europe to be used to transport immigrants. Following that speech, a
list of recommendations was submitted from the New Orleans Chamber
of Commerce, most of which called for federal expenditures for internal
improvements. Of interest in understanding the intentions of leaders of
the postwar convention movement is the closing section of that message.
It called for the convention to exert its influence in carrying the message
of the "supreme importance of commercial harmony" as the first step
toward the Reconstruction so "earnestly" desired by "patriots, capitalists,
and business interests throughout the Union."[12]

With the third convention, that held in Louisville in October, 1869,
there were even stronger signs that the convention movement was drawing those interested in forging a commercial reconciliation. The Louisville session attracted the most northern delegates to date, 112, and they
accounted for almost one-quarter of the entire assembly. The largest contingents came from Indiana, Ohio, Pennsylvania, Illinois, and New York,
but a total of thirteen states from outside of the South were represented.
Every southern state sent delegates, but the majority of southern delegates came from the Upper South, with large delegations also coming
from Georgia, Alabama, and Louisiana. The urban orientation was again
evident, for in almost every case there was a city listed as the residence of
the delegate rather than a county. Among northern cities, Cincinnati,
Philadelphia, Evansville, Chicago, and New York City sent the largest
delegations. Outside of Louisville, the southern cities sending the largest
number of representatives were Memphis, Baltimore, and New Orleans,
followed by Atlanta, Augusta, Nashville, and Norfolk. It seems to have
been a bipartisan gathering, as it drew both Republicans and Democrats
from each state, although there appears to have been more Democrats
among the southern delegates than Republicans. The Georgia delegation, as an example of bipartisanship, included both Republican Governor Rufus Bullock and the leader of the state Democratic party, Thomas
Hardeman.

Just as the banners at the New Orleans convention conveyed much
about the purpose of that meeting, the decorations and ceremonies of the
Louisville convention were symbolic of its major theme, reunion. At the
Opera House, site of the convention, the local Committee of Arrange-

ments decorated the interior with American flags: large flags hung on the stage behind the president's chair, and small ones were stuck into evergreens all around the seating area. As the Democratic *Louisville Courier-Journal* described it, ". . . the most intensely national delegate must rest satisfied of the wholesome national influences of his surroundings." The citizens of Louisville organized a parade for the delegates, and at a prominent position they placed an omnibus, purportedly the largest one in town, drawn by a team of eight horses and filled with schoolgirls. Each girl bore a sign with the name of one of the states of the Union, and atop the carriage was a statue of the goddess Liberty.[13]

The speeches of the dignitaries who appeared at Louisville were filled with references to reconciliation and reunion. The man chosen to preside, former president Millard Fillmore, brought Whig credentials untarnished by postwar political affiliations. When he made his first public appearance in association with the convention on Monday, October 11, at the courthouse, his speech began with a declaration that he belonged to no political party and that he was thrilled to see a "deliberative body, gathered from every state in the Union." Charles Anderson, who had presided at Memphis and subsequently attended the New Orleans session, made the official welcoming speech on the first day, and he shared his hope that this convention, like its predecessors, would work to "restore this country in all its parts to its pristine industry, wealth, and worth." The governor of Kentucky, John W. Stevenson, a Democrat, greeted them next, on behalf of the host state. He described the delegates as men of "virtue, wisdom, and practical experience," who met from "no motive of political supremacy," but rather out of a hope to attract capital to the South and to inspire new energy in all sections. When Fillmore took the chair as president, he began his remarks with a celebration of peace, and he drew applause when he declared that wartime bitterness lay behind them. He ended his speech by asking the delegates to conduct their deliberations "outside of and above all political considerations." As a conclusion to the opening ceremony, a telegram from President Ulysses S. Grant was read aloud, in which he endorsed the work of the convention as a means of bringing the citizens of different sections of our own country together in "interest and friendship . . . to the allayment [sic] of sectional prejudice and bad feeling."[14]

Opening-day rhetoric about reconciliation ran poetic, but the proposals generated by all three 1869 conventions were quite to the point, and most involved the federal government in some way. One of the key areas in which the conventions sought federal action was fiscal policy. With enactment of the National Banking Act during the war, the government had taken responsibility for banking regulations. Accepting that reality, the delegates targeted the government for banking solutions; specifically, they hoped to convince Congress to make bank capital more readily available to southern producers and investors. They also sought revisions in federal revenue policies deemed punitive to the South: they asked for return of the monies collected under the federal cotton tax, and, while continuing to espouse a general southern preference for free trade, they sought changes in tariffs that would encourage expansion of the American shipbuilding industry so as to increase trade between the South and Europe.

The Memphis committee charged with making recommendations on matters of finance and banking issued a report critical of the National Banking Act, blaming it for shortages of capital in the South and the West. The report recommended that the entire banking system be reorganized, but it admitted that the committee was not prepared to present a detailed plan to accomplish that goal. Committee chairman, banker David N. Kennedy of Clarksville, Tennessee, reported that there had been a general consensus among committee members that the national currency should be based on gold rather than on credit, but he also shared with his audience the committee's fears that converting to a gold standard would bring short-term hardships. Unable to suggest a solution, the committee argued that the convention should at least demand a fair share of the present allocation of capital, which would translate into credit potential for southerners. In another segment of its report, the committee offered a resolution that while the national debt must not be repudiated, it should be reduced.[15]

At the Louisville session, the Finance and Banking Committee report, which called for government action to distribute more currency throughout the South and the West, elicited much discussion—so much discussion that the delegates determined that the report should be printed before a vote was taken, thus delaying its consideration. The report took a more belligerently antigovernment stand than the majority of delegates could support. The report was a call to return to specie payments, but it was more than that. It suggested that since under federal banking regulations southern banks had limited access to capital, private citizens should establish southern banks under state laws, and that those banks should then issue currency based strictly on specie. Furthermore, the report called on southerners to conduct all business on the basis of specie payments, including what they would accept in payment for their agricultural production, as well as what they would use for wages to their laborers. This proved too harsh a recommendation for most, and when the report was presented to the delegates, they voted to postpone discussion of the entire subject, effectively taking no action. Nevertheless, the debate at these 1869 conventions reflected public support for concurrent bipartisan efforts of southern and western congressmen to seek redistribution of currency, efforts credited by historian Seip with passage of the National Bank Currency Act of 1870. The conventions, then, were appealing to different factions within the Republican party on each issue: to the northeastern commercial center representatives who favored return to the gold standard and, on the question of capital distribution, to their opposition in the capital-poor West and upper Midwest.[16]

The conventions of 1869 adopted the general policy of the conventions held between 1845 and 1855 when it came to federal aid for river and harbor improvements. On those projects deemed to have national, or at least multistate impact, the conventions insisted that the federal government had an obligation to fund improvements. To the long-standing list of problems, which included the Mississippi River, the Tennessee River, and major southern ocean harbors, the postwar sessions added the need for improvements on the Ohio River and construction of levee systems along the Mississippi River. They paid particular attention to obstructions at the mouth of the Mississippi, and they reminded their northern audience that the natural obstructions to harbors was not the only problem, for the East Coast harbors of Richmond, Charleston, and Savannah remained choked with the debris of war.[17] The conventions also supported canal construction along the Gulf

Coast to complete a protected marine trafficway stretching from the Atlantic to Texas.

Delegates at the Memphis convention called upon the government to assist the South in completing massive internal improvements. The Committee on Mississippi River Levees, chaired by James Alcorn of Mississippi, who would spend a great part of his political career fighting for levee improvements, called upon the central government to assist southern states in levee construction by providing federal bonds to fund the work. Similarly, the Committee on Tennessee River Improvements appealed for federal aid in the construction of a series of canals at Muscle Shoals in order to serve the agricultural and industrial producers of that multistate river valley. The Committee on General River Navigation, Canals, and Internal Improvements, through its chairman, Winfield Featherston, advocated federal action to complete the canal around the falls of the Ohio River, and it proposed that the government take control of the operation of the canal and reduce its tolls. Resolutions from the floor were adopted that suggested Congress set standards for bridge spans across the Mississippi and Ohio rivers and that Congress consider "annexing" the telegraph system to the existing federal postal service.[18]

The twin themes of economic liberalism and optimism about the future shaped the policy presented in the New Orleans convention's recommendations. The list of items requiring federal aid was long, and it encompassed levees, river and harbor improvements, and railroads. This second postwar convention endorsed many of the same proposals made by the first, and it added a few of its own as well. Delegates at New Orleans agreed with the Memphis group that the federal government had a responsibility to help rebuild levees through issuance of federal bonds, even though they backed down from asking for a federal water-gauge system, which could be used to warn of impending flooding. They also agreed that the federal government should take control of the canal at the falls of the Ohio River. Much of the convention's time was spent discussing navigation problems at the mouth of the Mississippi River, a discussion which was in part a dispute between delegates and the New Orleans Chamber of Commerce over who should coordinate with Congress to resolve the problems. The final vote favored leaving the responsibility for solving the problems in the hands of the United States government engineers. The convention endorsed a list of other Gulf harbor improvement needs for the attention of Congress, under the supposition that the responsibility for all harbor defense and improvement lay with the federal government.[19]

Louisville participants accepted reports that took the same outlook as had previous postwar convention resolutions: that the federal government should take responsibility for navigational improvements on major rivers, including the job of regulating bridge construction. The delegates voted in favor of a more limited federal role in levee construction than had previous conventions, preferring to recommend private efforts. The Committee on Harbors gave the delegates a long list of harbors needing improvements, complete with technical information relating to each case, and this session, too, approved of seeking federal expenditures in this area.[20]

The postwar meetings resumed the antebellum commercial convention movement's campaign for a southern Pacific railroad, but by 1869 it was a campaign waged under a new set of circumstances. When the earlier call for a southern transcontinental had gone out from the antebellum conventions, it had placed those southerners in direct competition with proponents of northern routes in the race to be the first to the Pacific. Since that time, the northern road had become reality in the Union Pacific and Central Pacific Railroads, and the actual completion of the combined line had been made on May 10, 1869, a week prior to the first postwar convention. It was also clear by then that the Union Pacific would not be the only line to cross the country. The Northern Pacific Railroad had received its federal charter in 1864 to run between Lake Superior and Portland; the Atchison, Topeka and Santa Fe Railroad had in 1863 been granted federal land allocations for its construction between the Missouri River and Santa Fe. Under terms of the Railroad Act of 1866, the Atlantic and Pacific had been chartered to traverse the Thirty-fifth Parallel between Springfield, Missouri, and the eastern California border on the Colorado River, where it would join Collis P. Huntington's Southern Pacific Railroad. Also, the Atlantic and Pacific, under the leadership of John C. Frémont, had in May of 1866 bought the old South-West Branch Railroad of Missouri, completing the link between St. Louis and Springfield. Given the federal largesse to these interstate lines, the southerners who met together at the conventions of the postwar series perhaps expected they could plan on equitable federal aid to a line that could serve the South, and at each of the five sessions between 1869 and 1871, they indicated that they expected federal subsidization of a privately constructed road positioned along the Thirty-second Parallel.[21]

As the old commercial convention dream of a southern Pacific railroad was revived at Memphis, delegates called for construction of a trunk road stretching from San Diego, through El Paso, then to "a convenient central point near the thirty-second Parallel east of the Brazos River" in eastern Texas, with branches to St. Louis, Cairo, Memphis, Vicksburg, and New Orleans on the east, and San Francisco on the west. Without specifying exactly how the national government should assist the project, the committee report called upon the convention president to forward that proposal to the president of the United States, the vice-president (as Senate president), and the Speaker of the House.[22]

The New Orleans assembly did not spend as much time as the Memphis convention had discussing railroad matters, but it did endorse the need for a southern Pacific railroad. Despite a disagreement during which Kentuckian Charles Anderson accused the Texans of having caused the Civil War and Texan Caleb G. Forshey invited those who would insult his state to "retire from the hall" with him, the delegates voted to ask congress for federal right-of-way and subsidies to a trunk line along the Thirty-second Parallel with branch connections to St. Louis, Memphis, Vicksburg, and New Orleans.[23]

The debate over the Pacific railroad continued at the Louisville session, and the discussion again was far from harmonious. The battle lines were drawn where they had been at earlier antebellum commercial conventions: between those favoring the route along the Thirty-second Parallel and those advocating a more northern route along the Thirty-fifth Parallel. The committee in charge of the issue made two reports: the majority report supported the southern route and was endorsed by committee members from most of the states represented at the convention, while the minority report argued for the central route and was signed by committee members from Missouri, Maryland, Kentucky, and Pennsylvania. As noted by the *Washington Chronicle*, the minority sponsors included representatives from the Pennsylvania Central Railroad. After an acrimonious debate the delegates voted to accept the majority report.[24]

The discussions and disagreements over routes for a southern Pacific railroad does not provide evidence of sectional antagonism at the postwar commercial conventions. Rather, the debate was a scene from a different play, the competition between railroad rivals and their supporters, which permeated national and state politics throughout these years. By the time of the Louisville convention, Tom Scott of the Pennsylvania Central had begun his campaign to build a southern transcontinental, having incorporated the Texas and Pacific Railroad, and having signed on both Grenville Dodge, of Union Pacific fame, and John Frémont.[25] Despite the obvious disagreement among delegates over where to build the road, the conventions provide further insight into the widespread and continuing enthusiasm across the South for securing a southern transcontinental road with multiple eastern branches.

The 1869 conventions also provide evidence of a continuation of an antebellum convention policy of urging state government assistance to railroads. The Memphis committee in charge of reports about railroad matters offered a list of specific roads that merited aid. While the New Orleans assembly did not spend as much time as had the Memphis convention in discussing railroad matters other than the southern Pacific railroad, it expressed a general belief that railroads were critical to southern economic development. The Louisville committee charged with reviewing resolutions on the subject of railroads in general avoided the pitfall of seeming to favor one company or another at the expense of various competitors, and it addressed only those areas of generic railroad interest. As presented by its chairman, Edwin Cole, president of the Nashville, Chattanooga and St. Louis Railroad, it supported the use of a standard gauge in future construction and asked that both federal and state governments assist railroad construction as they deemed fit. The committee did suggest that Congress be petitioned to reinstate antebellum land grants made to southern lines, grants which had lapsed for want of road construction during the war years, and it asked railroad companies in the South to cooperate in providing cheap transportation to immigrants.[26]

However, the third 1869 convention also entertained decidedly anti-railroad talk, providing some evidence that the southern romance with railroads was wearing a little thin. The report from the Tennessee River Improvements Committee struck a responsive chord among the floor delegates in its recommendation for federal improvements at Muscle Shoals, but it also spoke directly of the problem of railroad monopolies, and suggested that one benefit from increasing navigational access along the river would be to provide competition to railroad networks serving the area, which subjected their users to the "grasping spirit of railroad monopoly." The River Navigation Committee echoed that antirailroad sentiment, reporting that railroads abused monopoly power, especially that of eminent domain, and that improved navigational systems could bring welcome competition to the southern transportation industry.[27]

The suggestions that came from committees charged with matters of trade contain some of the most practical suggestions the commercial conventions had made to date, and they demonstrate that the conventions saw a major role for government in this arena. The New Orleans Committee on Western Trade, concerned primarily with trade along the Mississippi River, made four specific recommendations: that a subcommittee study a report from engineer James B. Eads on the feasibility of manufacturing iron barges and steamers for use in river shipping, that towage rates in New Orleans be lowered, that local governments resist the temptation to impose local taxes on river commerce, and that western merchants establish better contact with merchants from the Ohio Valley. The list of proposals from the Committee on Foreign Commerce and Postal Subsidies was even longer, and it was targeted at public and private entities. It called on the federal government to clear navigational obstructions on the Mississippi River and at the falls of the Ohio River, to establish interior ports of entry, to negotiate more favorable foreign trade treaties, to grant more postal subsidies to shippers who served the South and West, to complete a federal survey of a proposed Florida shipping canal, and to support the movement for a Central America canal. Local municipal governments were asked to provide better port facilities by lowering towing rates and by allowing location of railroad depots and storage elevators near wharves. Private shippers and factors were enlisted to make through bills of lading more available to those engaged in foreign trade. The Louisville convention took a more typically proactive stand in regard to federal efforts to increase the volume of direct shipping between the South and Europe, calling for issuance of more mail contracts to carriers who served southern ports, for abolition of tariffs on shipbuilding materials, and for creation of ports of entry at cities of at least 100,000 population.[28]

Discussions relating to manufacturing would have sounded familiar to delegates knowledgeable of antebellum conventions. The Memphis report made three points: that manufacturing was a valuable addition to the South, that state governments should provide tax relief as incentive for such investments, and that if information about the feasibility and profitability of southern manufacturing be made known, investors could be found. To that end, the committee members volunteered to investigate the topic further and report back to the succeeding convention. No special committee on the subject of manufacturing was named at the New Orleans convention, but a delegate from Columbia, South Carolina, merchant Edward H. Heinitsh, read into the minutes a report from another South Carolinian, John B. Palmer of Columbia, pertaining to textile manufacturing. Palmer had previously read this report to the South Carolina State Agricultural Convention in April of 1869. In it he provided information and statistics explaining why southerners should establish cotton manufacturing, and he included interesting references to the southern labor supply. Palmer pointed out that not only were members of the southern labor force willing to work for low wages, but also they were "frugal and industrious" and "easily controlled." It seems he was clearly referring to native southerners, for Palmer said they would be otherwise unemployable and a burden on the country. While he never specified their race, he did remark that they were "principally females, from ten years of age up, and small boys." He admonished southern planters to move fast and to establish mills before northerners could beat them to it. The report from the Louisville committee charged with the subject of manufacturing and mining concerned itself with how to realize the maximum profits from agricultural products by processing them, or using them in manufacturing, close to the fields. It also gave a general endorsement to encouragement of mining and to actions on the part of state and local governments to assist those individuals who were willing to establish either manufacturing or mining operations.[29]

Many delegates seem to have shared a conviction about the need to secure foreign laborers to alleviate what was perceived of as a labor shortage in the South. The shortage was judged so severe that the Memphis Committee on Agriculture concluded that over one-half of the land in the South lay idle, awaiting labor. Its report endorsed a recent publication by Matthew Fontaine Maury favoring immigration and direct trade, and it assigned the task of publicly circulating the report to a special committee. Organization of the Immigration Committee generated one of the rare instances of sectional feelings to occur at the postwar meetings. The delegates at Memphis seemed to disagree among themselves whether the subject was truly a matter for joint northern and southern deliberation, or a matter to be handled strictly by southerners. Despite a move to keep northern delegates off the Immigration Committee, a majority of those present voted to include representatives from both sections on that body. At least one northern speaker seemed genuinely concerned about the need to secure dependable labor in the South: Senator William Sprague, cotton textile manufacturer from Rhode Island, spoke openly of the "want of labor" created by abolition of slavery.[30]

The delegates looked to immigrants from Europe as the best new source of labor, but they realized that they faced a challenge in attracting Europeans to their region. The convention focused its main attention on how to attract and transport European immigrants, rather than on how to provide employment for them once they had settled in the South. The delegates seemed to be aware of the South's having a bad reputation among Europeans as an unsafe place to live, and to counter this, the Immigration Committee recommended that immigration agents be sent to Europe carrying the message of a positive image of the region. It also recommended that prospective immigrants be transported directly into the South through southern ports, where they "would not be exposed to the influence of the North." To help keep the new arrivals in the South, the committee urged southern railroad companies to lower fares for immigrants. Other committees, too, voiced an interest in immigration. The Southern Pacific Railroad report noted that a southern transcontinental line would encourage "the greatest necessity of the hour, immigration and direct trade with Europe." Delegates were appealed to on behalf of the majority report of the Direct Trade Committee with a sense of urgency about getting a prompt start on providing such transportation to immigrants.[31]

Edward Yerger, editor of the *Vicksburg Herald*, and former Whig who had supported Douglas and the Mississippi Constitutional Union movement, was chairman of the Immigration Committee at Memphis. His speech, reprinted in full in the *Memphis Appeal*, presented a perception of scarcity of labor in the South. It also revealed his attitude toward former slaves as free laborers, as well as his perceptions about the political reality of 1869. Yerger welcomed the addition of white immigrant laborers to the South, whose labor would allow the region to maximize production of her staple crops and other natural resources, giving her power over the North in the form of "a victory sweeter than any military victory. . . ." In his opinion, the current government of "strangers and inferiors" threatened the South's liberty, and additional numbers of whites could lend the region more forceful "power of people to protect her liberty." To assist the region in attracting such immigrants, Yerger proposed formation of joint-stock companies, which would invest in land and then resell it in forty-acre parcels to the immigrants. Furthermore, he recommended that such land should be made tax exempt for a "long period." As for the former slaves, Yerger presented a not entirely negative scenario. Southerners should work with former slaves, to educate them "if possible, to the rational enjoyment of freedom" and to "relieve them from the unwise counsel of adventurers." For slaves, formerly "a charge upon the land," will now become consumers, laborers, and land purchasers.[32]

The report of the New Orleans Committee on Immigration concentrated on the need for a labor force for agriculture and reflected mixed feelings about how best it should be secured. Chairman James O. Noyes, who was the Louisiana Commissioner of Immigration, submitted a report that began with the premise that development of the South's resources required a large influx of population from "the older and more densely populated portions of the world," and it went on to make suggestions about how to attract European immigrants to the South. The committee expected these immigrants to become landowners and farm laborers, and it urged southern state governments to send official agents to Europe, who could arrange safe passage to the South and who could oversee operation of labor exchanges and land registration operations. The committee's original report included an endorsement of the "importation" of Chinese laborers, but that section was removed after objections were made from the floor. Yet, despite its endorsement for immigration, the report revealed that these southerners had not yet abandoned hope that their own native labor force, both white and black, could meet their needs. Noyes described southern laborers as "efficient, reliable, and better paid than any other class of agricultural labor in any country," and he concluded that they could be trained to used machinery and implements.[33]

The Louisville convention made clear that it placed a high priority on the needs of commercial agriculture. Benjamin Yancey, chairman of the Agriculture Committee, presented a summary that began with the statement that southern commercial prosperity depended upon agricultural prosperity. In the committee's opinion, the biggest threat to agricultural production was a widespread scarcity of labor, and it suggested that the Committee on Immigration report would propose the best solution for that problem. The Agriculture report also repeated the suggestion made at Memphis that federal property taxes imposed as wartime measures be abolished.[34]

The Committee on Immigration report was essentially the same as that of the Memphis convention resolution, a declaration of the South's need for European immigrants and a recommendation that various states should send forth immigration agents. In a departure from earlier views, this report included a statement that no action need be taken at that time to send immigration agents to Asia, as any "importation" of Chinese laborers could be handled by private actions. Because of the last item, the entire report generated heated debate, with most objection to it coming from the Texas delegation. Committee chairman James W. Massie acknowledged that there had also been disagreement within the committee as well on the question of Chinese labor, and that a special report would be forthcoming on that question. The delegates voted to adopt the committee's report, but it was obvious that there was a real difference of opinion on the subject.[35]

On the last day of the Louisville convention, the delegates considered two reports on the question of Chinese immigrants. The majority report favored encouragement of their immigration, and the minority report opposed it. Neither side disputed that the South needed more laborers, but opponents of Chinese immigration argued that the South had all the racial strife it could handle at the present without adding another complication. The delegate body preferred to avoid the question entirely, and it voted to table the discussion.[36] It was the last time that the subject would be brought before a commercial convention, and it was obvious from the way most of the delegates at Louisville reacted to the debate that the whole issue was seen more as an irritant than a serious proposal for public policy.

Southern press reports of the convention movement revival focused on the seriousness of the subject matter discussed rather than on petty disagreements, and they generally supported the movement's renewal. The host-city press was particularly supportive. The *Memphis Appeal* reminded its readers how influential delegates could do much to sway Congress to help the South. The paper asked Memphis residents to act so as to please their visitors: to be "open-hearted, liberal, candid, energetic, enterprising, and law-abiding." After the close of the meeting, while it was not at all pleased with the convention's preference for the Thirty-second Parallel transcontinental railroad route over the Thirty-fifth Parallel route, the paper concluded that overall the convention had been a positive experience. The New Orleans press was impressed with the caliber of the delegates, and the *Picayune* decided the New Orleans convention had been a good experience, if for no other reason than just to bring the men together. The local press was pleased with what had transpired at the Louisville meeting, and the *Courier-Journal* concluded that it had been comprised of "influential" men whose decisions should not be taken lightly by Congress, as the assembly represented every "important" commercial and business interest of the country.[37]

Each of the three conventions of 1869 received widespread coverage in major southern cities. Readers in Louisville, Richmond, Charleston, Atlanta, Mobile, New Orleans, and St. Louis were offered extensive reports on convention proceedings and editorials that endorsed the need for such concerted effort to revive the southern economy. The *Louisville Courier-Journal* hoped that the commercial conventions could serve to place the South's claims for a fair share of federal assistance in a position of "respect" with the American people. The *Richmond Enquirer* described the opening convention as an important event. Early on, the *Atlanta Constitution* joined the ranks of the movement's supporters by explaining that while politics were not "open for discussion" for the next few years, practical matters of business were. The newspaper even reprinted excerpts from editorials across the country praising the Louisville session. The *Charleston Courier* reported that the Memphis convention would help the South to diversify, to stimulate enterprise, to develop its resources, and to develop "practical and efficient" legislation. The *New Orleans Picayune* described the delegates at Louisville as men of great "influence and character," and it hoped that one result of the meeting might be federal aid for a southern Pacific railroad.[38]

Northern newspapers gave the conventions considerable attention, and for the most part they also gave them their support. News of the southern conventions was found in newspapers serving New York, Washington, Boston, Pittsburgh, Cincinnati, and Chicago. The *New York Times* was extremely positive about the conventions. For three days it provided its readers with summaries of the Memphis proceedings, and then it concluded with an editorial praising the meeting as a nonpartisan effort at economic reconstruction and evidence of an "improving spirit" in the South. Furthermore, the newspaper concluded that the composition of the delegations deserved "respectful attention." This same newspaper described the New Orleans convention in this manner: "Entirely harmonious and successful in its objects—composed entirely of the active members of the commercial, manufacturing, shipping, and agricultural interests." The *Times* referred to the Louisville convention as a "Peace Convention," and it offered the hope that, like the Memphis convention before it, this one would help bind the North and South as its delegates were men of experience and influence in commercial affairs. The *New York Tribune* showed enthusiasm for the Memphis convention's advocacy of a southern Pacific railroad route, but it did ridicule its discussion of a federal postal telegraph. The newspaper provided extensive coverage of the next two conventions as well. The *New York Commercial and Financial Chronicle* was impressed by the prominence of the businessmen in attendance at Louisville and by the national spirit of the gathering. Declaring that its recommendations, "as the mature thought of men of business," merited careful consideration, the paper seemed pleased that the convention had brought together men from all parts of the Union for an "exchange of ideas which cannot fail to be beneficial."[39]

Washington papers gave the movement prominent coverage, and the *Washington Chronicle's* reporter commented at the start of the Louisville convention that the meeting would show the people of the South that northerners, too, desired southern prosperity. While the space devoted to the conventions was smaller in Boston newspapers, all three sessions were noted. In the Midwest, the *Pittsburgh Commercial* and the *Cincinnati Commercial* used virtually the same Western Associated Press report for Memphis, which spoke of the session as "harmonious." The *Cincinnati Enquirer* welcomed the Louisville assembly as men "selected without regard to party—past or present." The *Chicago Tribune* was especially positive about the Memphis session, describing the delegations as including "many dignitaries and important businessmen." The New Orleans session drew favorable comment from the Midwest press as well. According to historian Peter Kolchin, this initial support might have been expected as the northern business press was generally supportive of efforts to revive trade between the North and the South.[40]

The Louisville convention, however, despite the positive reviews outside of the South described above, marked the start of a more negative analysis of the convention movement's southern demands upon the federal treasury. Some reports noted evidence of disharmony and delay in the proceedings, and the reporter for the *Cincinnati Commercial* finally concluded unhappily that the session was dominated by politicians, not businessmen, and that the southern delegates had held sway. The *Chicago Tribune* was particularly displeased by the demands for large sums of federal assistance, and implied that the northern delegates even considered leaving the session before its conclusion.[41]

Despite a few press suggestions to the contrary, the Southern Commercial Conventions of 1869 had been generally free of sectional hostility and partisan politics, albeit not free of other disagreements, and they had been united in pleading the case for infusion of northern capital into the South. On the one hand, they contended that such large internal improvement projects as clearing the Mississippi River, improving major southern harbors, maintaining the Ohio River canal at Louisville, and opening transit on the Tennessee River were of national interest, not of interest only to the South. So too, they insisted, was the cotton industry, and therefore it was in the best interest of the nation that levees be repaired. The other position they took was that the South promised a rich potential to investors, that railroads and shipping lines and textile manufactures and mining operations could realize profits. Both of these appeals were old, familiar tenets of the commercial convention movement. They were messages of optimism, and they came from men committed to expanding economic opportunity within the South without disrupting the basic components of the southern agricultural economy.

Theirs was not the only group effort to voice public opinion on matters of commercial policy in these years, but it was the only organized, bipartisan southern effort to present the needs of the South before national policy makers. The other trade association of the time that included representatives from both South and North, the National Board of Trade, had been organized the year before as a strictly national association, despite the fact that it too was intended to represent the business community on matters of commercial policy. Meeting each year in December during the same years of the commercial conventions, it included southerners among its participants: of the 159 officers and delegates at the annual meetings held in these three years, forty-seven represented southern cities. Among that group of southerners were nine who were sufficiently active in the Southern Commercial Convention movement to qualify as members of the Convention Elite. So, there was personnel crossover between the regional movement and the national association. However, the National Board of Trade differed in two key respects from the commercial conventions: its membership was composed of trade associations rather than individuals, and its meetings focused strictly on general trade issues rather than regional trade issues.[42]

While delegates to the National Board of Trade agreed with the Southern Commercial Conventions that Mississippi River navigation should be unrestricted, there were few other instances in these years when the National Board of Trade adopted policy statements on regional trade problems. As the secretary to the National Board of Trade, Hamilton A. Hill of Boston, explained to the delegates at the 1869 Richmond meeting, there was justification for the existence of both groups. The regional meetings were considered local in purpose and useful in directing attention to specific schemes of improvement rather than in focusing on national commercial policies. Looking back on the dual movements from a vantage point sixteen years later, Hill told the national group's Executive Council at its 1885 meeting that the main difference between their association and the regional commercial conventions was that men of influence in Washington, D.C., looked to the former more than to the latter as a recognized business authority.[43] The difference between the two groups is important to understand, as it made the commercial conventions even more important to those southerners anxious to promote the cause of southern economic reconciliation. While the National Board of Trade provided members of southern trade associations the opportunity to meet face-to-face with northern businessmen, it was not a forum in which they could address the needs of the South as distinct from the needs of other commercial interests.

As to politics, the conventions disavowed any political intent in their association. Yet, if the conventions had no outright partisan statements to make, they did provide evidence of the existence of a large body of men determined to do what was necessary to right the South economically from its state of disrepair. The political backgrounds of the southern delegates at the postwar conventions included a large number of former Whigs, and generally they represented the native southern white leadership rather than the Carpetbag leadership. In their speeches and resolutions, the delegates made frequent reference to their desire for national reconciliation and reunion, and they demonstrated a positive attitude toward President Grant. It seems their political message was targeted both toward encouraging moderation within the Republican party and toward bolstering the efforts of those southerners under the banner of Conservatives or Democrats, or united in fusion tickets with more moderate branches of the Republican party.

Speaking as representatives of the South meeting with supportive representatives from the North, the delegates at the Memphis convention used that occasion to make a united gesture of reconciliation. First, they secured a unanimous endorsement for former governor Patton's suggestion that the federal government grant tax amnesty to southern states who had not yet paid the federal property taxes that had been imposed in 1862 to finance the war effort, taxes which remained largely uncollected. Secondly, at the close of the convention, they made a joint statement about the process of sectional reconciliation. Basing their opinions on the belief that the vast majority of southerners wished for a "cordial and thorough restoration of fraternal relations," the delegates concluded that "the erroneous impressions upon the minds of the people of each section in regard to the other, so easily made and hard to remove, have been, and now are, the greatest obstacles in the way of a prompt and thorough adjustment of our political and social relations, which would restore peace, contentment and universal prosperity throughout the entire country." The Louisville convention appointed a special committee, whose membership included Patton and Henry Hilliard, to call on President Grant after the close of the session and to carry the thanks of the convention for his letter of support. They did so in November, 1869, and the president once again expressed his best wishes for their efforts.[44]

If, as this action suggests, one of the major goals of the 1869 commercial conventions had been to present conservative southern leadership as willing participants in the national economy, intent on cooperating with the parties in power to effect a return to economic prosperity for their homeland, the reaction outside of the South to their conventions should have by and large given them cause for hope. As indicated from the newspaper accounts referred to above, and as can be surmised from the positive comments made about the conventions by organizers of the National Board of Trade, it is not surprising that the Appleton's *Cyclopaedia* for 1869 devoted a special section to enthusiastic reports of the proceedings at the three commercial conventions held during that year.

This New York publication concluded that at all these conventions, there had been displays of good feeling, that "harmony pervaded the discussions, and measures having an important bearing upon the commercial interests of the country were adopted with unanimity."[45]

Thus, at the close of the first year during which Southern Commercial Conventions had made their reappearance, the movement had demonstrated that many southern businessmen and politicians carried high hopes for economic reconciliation. They used the conventions as forums for counseling moderation in political policy and as opportunities to seek the same federal largesse for the South that northern states had already enjoyed. However, the antisouthern rumblings in the press stories about the Louisville convention might have given southern delegates pause. As they faced crossing the Ohio River for the fourth postwar session, they could still take heart from the spirit of the three sessions of 1869, but they might also have had a sense of foreboding about the prospects for success of their mission.

10
The Window Closes
1870–1872

During the course of three commercial conventions in 1869, southerners had taken the opportunity to present a list of projects deemed critical for postwar southern economic well-being. The economic agenda proposed was true to a historic commercial convention vision of the South as a region whose prosperity derived from agriculture. Northerners who attended the sessions or who became otherwise familiar with the meetings must have concluded that the vanquished were ready to start to rebuild their economy, but that they did not consider themselves equipped to do so unassisted. The conventions were not, however, simply a one-way thoroughfare for communication, South to North. They also provided opportunities for northerners to present their own economic plans to the South, plans which revolved around expanding northern access to southern consumers.

The two Ohio River trading centers of Louisville and Cincinnati were keen rivals for the southern trade, and as of 1869 the city of Louisville enjoyed a decided advantage via the lines of the Louisville and Nashville Railroad. Cincinnati merchants who shipped through Louisville were often subjected to rate and schedule discriminations, while those who bypassed Louisville had to rely solely on roundabout access, westward by means of the Ohio River or eastward to Baltimore and then down the Atlantic Coast. Citizens of Cincinnati decided to build their own rail connection into the South, and they secured enabling legislation from the state in 1869, whereupon residents of the city voted approval of appointment of a board of trustees and ten million dollars in bond issues to construct the Cincinnati Southern Railroad. Two months after the close of the Louisville commercial convention, the Kentucky General Assembly convened, and Cincinnati sent representatives of the proposed railroad to lobby for a charter to cover the Kentucky segment of the line. Proponents of the Cincinnati Southern were simultaneously pursuing the same objective with the Tennessee legislature for that part of the road to run between Kentucky and Chattanooga. While the proponents succeeded in Tennessee, they failed in Kentucky against lobbying efforts of both Louisville boosters and agents of the Louisville and Nashville Railroad.[1]

Not ready to give up, the Cincinnati forces sought help from their congressmen, who introduced bills for federal charters for the road. By March of 1870, those efforts had also failed, and the Cincinnati Southern proponents returned to the task of securing a Kentucky charter. In that effort they found support in eastern Kentucky counties, where many welcomed the prospect of improved rail access to Chattanooga and the southern markets beyond. During 1870, representatives from the Cincinnati Southern Railroad held rallies throughout the state, including a large one in Lexington just before the October meeting of the Cincinnati commercial convention. By the time of the convention, civic leaders in both Cincinnati and Louisville saw the upcoming assembly as an opportunity to promote their respective causes.

The convention held at Cincinnati was not called by the Cincinnati Southern Railroad Company, but it was organized by a group of local civic leaders who supported that effort. That one of the trustees of the railroad, Richard Bishop, was the first speaker on the opening day of the convention was probably no coincidence. If these Ohioans sought to make an impression as efficient business operators, the convention unfolded in a manner that must have boosted that image. From the first day through the last, the assembly was a smooth operation, as civic leaders of the town worked to present a well-organized and businesslike commercial convention. The man placed in charge of proceedings was further proof of the serious, commercial purpose of the group: John Work Garrett, president of the Baltimore and Ohio Railroad.

From the start, the northern hosts offered their support for national reconciliation. George F. Davis, president of the Cincinnati Board of Aldermen, welcomed the delegates to the opportunity to seek acquaintance with each other and to thereby come to know the needs of each section. The featured speaker on opening day was George H. Pendleton, who had been the Democratic nominee for vice-president in 1864, and who had made a strong bid for the presidential nomination in 1868 but lost out as many judged him too much a wartime Peace Democrat. He directed them to the main objective of the meeting: consideration of the needs of the entire Mississippi Valley unhampered by feelings of sectionalism or localism. Among those needs, as he saw it, were people, but people of a special kind. They would be "active, enterprising, self-reliant, audacious people," who would require uninterrupted access to the Gulf and to the Chesapeake, to the canals of New York and to the Great Lakes. Their railroads would connect them to the Pacific, to Norfolk, and to Charleston and Savannah. Protected by levees, and freed from the constraints of artificial trade barriers, they would maintain the Union that insured their free government. He charged the delegates with the job of setting this transformation in motion. Lest they doubt its possibility, he reminded them of other signs of progress in their time: the ocean telegraph, the Union Pacific Railroad, the Suez canal, and all the modern machinery that allowed man to control the "mysterious forces which fill the earth, and sea, and air."[2]

The Committee of Arrangements orchestrated each step in a brisk, orderly fashion. It announced a list of twenty topics for consideration, ruled that the Louisville standing committees would be asked to report to this convention and would have representation on the new committees as well, and directed that each state delegation should select their representatives for the three general administrative committees. General Nathaniel Banks of Massachusetts, a Republican congressman serving at the convention as a member of the Credentials Committee, reported that 350 delegates had presented their credentials, representing twenty-five states and seventy-five principal cities. The records indicate that 231 of the participants resided in southern states. Among the better-known southerners appointed to various committees were manufacturer Joseph Anderson, banker Thomas Branch, lawyer Jeremiah Watkins Clapp, engineer Caleb Forshey, flour mill owner and lieutenant governor of Missouri Edwin Stanard, and railroad promoters Edwin Cole, E. A. James, Clinton Fisk, and James Throckmorton. Those northern delegates with national reputations included Republicans Benjamin Eggleston and Stanley Matthews of Ohio; Republican John Dravo, who was president of the Pittsburgh Coal Exchange; and Clement Vallandigham, the somewhat notorious Peace Democrat from Ohio.[3]

President Garrett spoke to these wartime veterans of reconciliation. They cheered him when he said the convention marked the first occasion since the war that representatives from all southern states had assembled on the soil of a northern state and been welcomed in such a way as to feel "that the Union is truly restored and that cordiality and fraternity again exist between the North and the South." This successful railroad entrepreneur evidently did not consider the postwar national political party conventions in the same light as this assembly. Garrett stated his conviction that restoration of the material prosperity of the South would benefit the whole nation, and that "harmony and cooperation" would be essential, along with federal expenditures for river and harbor improvements and a southern Pacific railroad. He paid homage to the war heroes of the South who had remained in their homeland to assist in rebuilding efforts. He gave special praise to General Robert E. Lee for his dual role as educator and railroad administrator, a mention not altogether altruistic, as Garrett's company had purchased majority ownership of Lee's Valley Railroad in an effort to ward off competition from the Pennsylvania Railroad. The subjects he considered important for the session to discuss included increasing the South's direct trade and cotton textile manufacturing, removing artificial trade barriers of all kinds, and bringing "speedy" restoration of constitutional rights to the South.[4]

Over the course of the three days of debate that followed, the conventioneers spent the majority of their time discussing proposals related to transportation improvements, giving equal attention to navigational projects and railroads. In regard to the first, navigation, the delegates placed responsibility with the federal government to fund work at the South's major harbors and to clear channels and fund construction of canals along the Mississippi, Ohio, and Tennessee rivers. The assembly voted in favor of federal control of levee construction along the Mississippi and federal action to remedy an access problem at the mouth of the Mississippi, which was judged to be so severe that it threatened the "best means of securing the prosperity of the whole country, promoting the happiness of the people, insuring peace, concord and unity at home, and respect and renown abroad." To this standard list of navigational requirements were added a canal across Florida, a canal system connecting intracoastal waterways between New Orleans and Florida, and another connecting the Mississippi River and the Rio Grande.[5]

The Cincinnati session included a positive summary of what federal assistance had been granted by Congress to these and other navigational projects, and it gave the convention movement credit for having secured two million dollars in recent appropriations. Ending in an upbeat mode, the River Navigation Committee recommended that more aid be earmarked for completion of the projects affected by the current federal appropriation. The assembly of delegates, though, were not in total agreement about the extent of progress to date. A Kentucky delegate insisted that the vote on the report be taken by states, and, while the report was adopted, five states, including Kentucky, Maryland, and North Carolina, voted against it.[6]

These businessmen considered other trade matters related to river commerce, matters which fell under the category of trade regulation. A special committee was created to report on problems associated with bridge construction, and its report calling for federal regulation to prevent navigation impediments was adopted. Another committee recommended disallowance of all tolls on rivers where federal funds had been spent for improvements. The report from a third committee generated a heated debate prior to its passage, as it suggested that municipal wharfage rates were unreasonably high, that the Constitution prohibited states and thereby cities from imposing tonnage taxes, and that Congress should consider enacting legislation against those rates that amounted to a virtual tonnage tax.[7]

Much of the discussion at Cincinnati centered around a subject long of interest to commercial conventions—increased levels of direct trade with Europe and South America. One benefit, it was presumed, from trade expansion would be increased numbers of European immigrants into the South, and the Committee on Direct Trade also served as the Committee on Immigration. The resolutions presented to the delegates focused on ways to make the trade more feasible for shippers. They called upon Congress to grant bounties to American shipbuilders, to allow for duty-free warehousing of naval supplies, to enact apprentice laws, and to award mail contracts to direct-service shipping lines. Until such time as these measures could be implemented and a sizable group of American ships be built, the resolutions favored allowing American shippers to purchase foreign ships. All were endorsed by the delegates.[8]

The railroad projects of interest to this convention were generally those located east of the Mississippi River. However, as had long been the case, this assembly endorsed a southern Pacific railroad, and it specified that it run along the Thirty-second Parallel and that there be branches connecting the trunk line with Memphis, Vicksburg, and New Orleans. As to federal aid, the report concluded that this road deserved the same degree of assistance that had been given to the Central Pacific and Union Pacific railroads. A special committee was assigned to deliver the report to President Grant and Congress, and that committee included General Banks as well as James Throckmorton, attorney for Tom Scott of the Texas Pacific Railroad, which was pursuing congressional incorporation. By the time that the convention met, the southern transcontinental project was under consideration in Congress. In June of 1870, the Senate had passed a bill providing federal assistance for a line along the Thirty-second Parallel, with five branches and specifications of a southern-style gauge. The bill still needed House approval, and the convention's message was surely intended for that congressional audience. These southerners continued to wage the battle for federal assistance to a southern transcontinental, a battle which would end in congressional compromise and far less aid to the southern railroad than had been awarded to the northern transcontinentals.[9]

If one of the major goals of promoters of the Cincinnati session was to secure public endorsement for rail access between the Queen City and the South, they succeeded. A special committee was named to report on railroad facilities between the Ohio River and the central South, and its chairman was E. A. James of Tennessee, described by the *Cincinnati Enquirer* as "a warm friend of the Southern Railroad." Predictably, the committee report endorsed two railroad projects designed to provide the southern linkage, the Cincinnati Southern Railroad and the Cumberland and Ohio Railroad, and it even included a section that called on the Kentucky General Assembly to approve the charter request of the first road. If that was not enough of a defeat of the Louisville forces, the committee endorsed the principle of federal charters for multistate railroad lines by supporting such an endeavor planned to run between Norfolk and St. Louis. This was asking the delegates to vote in favor of the same proposal that the Cincinnati Southern forces had taken to Congress earlier that year after having been rebuked by the Kentucky legislators. The Kentucky delegation objected to that section of the committee report, and it was tabled after a "lengthy and sectional" debate. When the report was resubmitted on the final day of the convention, it passed despite efforts of Louisville delegates to prevent its adoption.[10]

Attendants of the Cincinnati convention recommended aid for other railroads as well. Caleb Forshey's Committee on Trans-latitudinal Railroads presented a long list of north-south lines deserving federal aid, and it singled out the Atlantic and Pacific Railroad, represented at the convention by General Clinton Fisk of Missouri, for special federal assistance. The positive attitude about railroad growth should not be taken as an uncritical toleration of railroad business tactics, however, as the Cincinnati convention also spent considerable time discussing reform of railroad abuses. A committee designated to look into charges on passengers and freight traffic gave particular attention to short-haul rate discrimination, and it called upon both the federal government and state governments to enact legislation against the abuse. The report of the General Committee on Railroads was presented by Edwin Cole of the Nashville, Chattanooga and St. Louis Railroad, and it took the perspective of looking at southern railroads as components of a system. Cole's committee advocated gauge uniformity, cooperation among railroad managers, connection of track between roads, and federal assistance for roads located within the South and for a southern transcontinental road.[11]

Discussions of matters of federal fiscal and tax policies produced no consensus. The National Bank Currency Act of July, 1870, had settled the debate over distribution of national bank currency in a compromise, albeit one that did not provide the South and West with what they considered to be sufficient levels of available capital. However, still at issue was national policy on the tariff and other taxation, and the committee assigned to study finance and taxation split among itself on appropriate recommendations. The majority opinion, presented by banker Thomas Branch as a preliminary report, incorporated traditional Democratic opposition to protective tariffs, and it called for abolition of the income tax as well, with the implementation of a luxury tax in its place. The minority dissent, announced by Republican Daniel T. Jewett of Missouri, was not actually presented, but Jewett indicated that his faction on the committee disagreed with the majority position. In light of the split within the committee, the delegates decided to defer discussion until a final report could be presented. However, there was no final report from this committee, and no attempt was made during the remainder of the session to solicit such a report.[12]

Other actions taken at Cincinnati further testify to the commercial perspective of the assembly. Following the lead of the National Board of Trade, this 1870 convention endorsed the idea of creation of a federal Department of Commerce. On the basis that American commercial activities in Europe were being disrupted by the Franco-Prussian war, the convention called on President Grant to offer his good offices to restore peace. The convention took a surprisingly antibusiness position when it adopted a resolution condemning proposed changes in federal land policies, changes later enacted in 1876, which freed the way for corporations to purchase southern timberland for speculation. However, the convention's resolution on this matter argued that public grants of alternative land sections should continue to be made for internal improvement projects, as long as appropriate antispeculation restrictions were maintained; in that respect, the resolution was not as antibusiness as it seemed.[13]

The 1870 Cincinnati convention was unusual in that it did not designate a committee on the subject of manufacturing or mining, but there were several references to the importance of each. President Garrett called attention to the benefits of locating cotton textiles in the fields in his opening-day speech. The report on improvements to be made along the Tennessee River spoke of how the iron industry of that region was operating under capacity because of transportation problems. That must have struck a responsive chord, as, judged from the number of southern delegates who listed an iron-manufacturing company along with their names on the roster, the iron industry was well represented at Cincinnati. In its recommendations for harbor improvements, the convention emphasized the transportation needs of the commercial fertilizer and lumber industries, as well as those of agriculture. The resolution calling for construction of an inland canal system between the Gulf and the Atlantic presented a vision of a South that included extensive manufacturing and mining operations, which would in turn generate vastly increased volumes of traffic for interior railroads.[14]

Those present at the 1870 convention seemed to consider the event not just an opportunity for important commercial discussion, but also an occasion for offering gestures of political reconciliation as well. John Garrett had opened the meeting with a call for harmony and for recognition that a policy seeking economic restoration of the South was a policy that would advance the best interests of the whole country. In that spirit, Garrett advocated a specific, political recommendation: restoration of all constitutional rights in the South.[15] He referred to white males who were prevented from voting and holding office because of their participation in the Confederate government bodies. While many southerners had been granted amnesty, long lists of individuals requesting removal of prohibitions were still being submitted to Congress at the time of the Cincinnati convention. Once Garrett had introduced the issue, it must not have been too surprising that the convention body addressed the policy as a part of their official business, and in so doing took a significant departure from the deliberately nonpolitical agendas set by the first three postwar commercial conventions.

William Hastie of South Carolina, who had been appointed sheriff of Charleston after the Civil War, offered the first resolution on the subject of general amnesty. His words were evidently not strong enough for many. As soon as Hastie finished reading his proposal, James S. Gibbons of Philadelphia called for consideration of a resolution favoring not only general amnesty, but also abolition of all test oaths and removal of all political disabilities. In response, Henry M. Cheever of Detroit proclaimed they met as citizens who would "hail with pleasure the time when all political disabilities shall be removed by the Government." The convention body accepted a resolution that called for complete restoration of political privileges by voting "unanimously, heartily and cordially in the affirmative," whereupon the floor delegates broke into "prolonged and general applause."[16]

The delegate rosters at Cincinnati included men from both national political parties, and for the most part their attention had been devoted to matters of southern economic policy rather than partisan politics. In the closing moments of the assembly, they heard from two of the most prominent participants, Nathaniel Banks and John Garrett. Both men closed their speeches on a note of warning to the national political parties that reconciliation was proceeding, regardless of whether or not the parties were willing to acknowledge the fact. Banks stated it this way: just as the war itself had been initiated "outside of party," so too reconciliation would come outside of political organizations. Garrett assured them that such a meeting, involving veterans from both opposing armies, evidencing "cordiality and earnestness and fraternity" and still speaking "free from every political excitement," would move the whole country to accept the event as an expression of the real wishes of the American people.[17]

In that spirit of reconciliation, the convention voted to change the name of their association, from the Southern Commercial Convention to the National Commercial Convention. The idea had been proposed on the first day of the meeting, but at that time the delegates were evidently undecided on the question, and the matter was held for discussion until the last day. Even then, it generated debate prior to acceptance, but in the end it was adopted unanimously. The fact that the convention adopted a name change drew little comment from the southern press. As had the previous meetings, this one received widespread newspaper attention in the South. Most papers carried several days of reports, and there were no separate editorial comments. Even the *Louisville Courier-Journal* gave it straight news coverage. When these papers took notice of the name change of the organization, it was done without editorial comment. Northern newspapers also provided reports of the convention to their readers, but these reports were on the whole shorter than had been accorded to the 1869 conventions.[18]

The final commercial convention included in this study group met on September 25, 1871, at the Masonic Temple in Baltimore, Maryland. Under the name of the National Commercial Convention, it drew 280 delegates representing twenty-three states. For the first time in the history of the movement, there were more northern delegates present than southern; convention reports listed 136 southerners, making the southern share 49 percent. Information about these southern delegates suggests this group matched the characteristics of delegates at the preceding postwar conventions: commerce-oriented, longtime southerners, with antebellum political affiliations that were in line with the general southern population, and postwar representation in both major political parties. Their leaders, like those at all earlier conventions, were distinguished from the other southern delegates by their office-holding experience. In contrast to the leadership at the other postwar meetings, the southern leadership group at Baltimore included a higher proportion of men under age forty and a comparatively lower proportion of men who attended more than one commercial convention.

Among the most prominent public figures in the southern convention leadership, Democrats or Conservatives were in the majority: Elbert English of Arkansas; Thomas Bocock, General Robert Lilley, and Robert Ould of Virginia; Thomas A. R. Nelson and Robertson Topp of Tennessee; and John Garrett and Reverdy Johnson of the host state, Maryland. Only the Missouri contingent was led by Republicans, namely former governor Thomas C. Fletcher and Lieutenant Governor Edwin Stanard. Northerners who played a high-profile role at the convention were more notable for their business achievements than their politics: Richard Bishop of the Cincinnati Southern Railroad, who served as president; fellow Ohioan Hugh Jewett, Democrat and railroad promoter; Pennsylvanian John Dravo of the Pittsburgh Coal Exchange; and fellow Pittsburgh Republican business leader General James Moorhead, who was president of the Western Union company. Interestingly, Senator Henry Wilson, a Republican from Massachusetts, attended the meeting and was placed in a position of honor at the front of the meetingroom on opening day.[19]

In keeping with the association's new name, both the decorations of American eagles and flags and the speeches presented on the first day resounded with themes of Union and reconciliation. John Garrett, welcoming the visitors on behalf of his city, paid homage to soldiers from both sides of the Civil War battlefield. He spoke of the progress made toward reunion at the last meeting of the convention and of his hopes that this session would move the country further in that direction. In Cincinnati, Garrett reminded his audience, those men who had fought against each other in the war out of "honest conviction and stern principle" had gotten to know each other better and showed by their actions that they were dedicated to burying old hostilities. Northern convention delegates had voted in favor of both liberal federal aid for southern internal improvements and restoration of political rights in the South, and in response the southern delegates had advanced proposals for improvement projects outside of the South. The mayor of Baltimore, Robert T. Banks, went so far as to suggest that had representatives from all sections met together in that same manner before the war, the bloodshed might have been avoided. The featured orator, a longtime Democrat who would soon sit in the governor's office and then in the United States Senate, William Pinkney Whyte, praised the bravery and devotion of soldiers on both sides, and explained the southern defeat as coming without dishonor at the hands of a colossal foe.[20]

Judged from the topics assigned to the committees, this convention had a stronger interest in trade issues than in internal improvements. Although a Railroad Committee and one on interior lines of water transportation were created, conspicuously lacking were the usual committees dedicated to large yet specific projects, such as the southern Pacific railroad or obstructions at the mouth of the Mississippi River. By contrast committees were named on domestic commerce, foreign commerce, finance and taxation, tariffs, state inspections, public lands and immigration, and mineral and mining interests. Taken as a whole, the floor proposals assigned to committee consideration fell into one of two categories: matters having to do with commerce that merited congressional attention, or statements of political policy aimed at restoration of home rule in the South. Of the fifteen proposals on trade sent to committee, fourteen targeted federal government action.[21]

The recommendations having to do with federal policy toward the South gave the convention the opportunity to express support for President Grant, while at the same time urging a more lenient policy in the South. First, a Prussian-born carpetbag Republican and state senator serving in the South Carolina delegation, Frank Arnin, introduced a resolution calling on the government to allow residents of that state to settle their own problems caused by Ku Klux Klan violence. By summer of 1871, the Klan had become increasingly active in South Carolina, and President Grant was under pressure to declare martial law, against the wishes of the Republican state government. He would, in fact, do so within a month's time of the convention. The convention rejected Arnin's resolution, in effect casting a vote of no confidence in the state Republican administration. Shortly thereafter, a Georgia delegate presented a resolution in favor of general amnesty and restoration of full political rights in the South. This time, the convention accepted the subject as a fit one for action by the convention, but it sent the proposal to a committee for further consideration rather than act on it at that point as the sponsor had requested. Evidently, the message being sent was that the convention sought reconciliation, but under terms acceptable to moderate elements in the country.[22]

The Railroad Committee report centered on national policies rather than specific lines, and it took a procompany position. The committee supported uniform gauge, and it asked states to cooperate with each other in granting multistate charters. Although it suggested the appropriateness of some concessions by companies in the face of charges of long-haul versus short-haul rate discrimination, the report drew criticism from a reformist element among the delegates for not coming out strongly enough against that railroad abuse. In a statement that surely pleased President Bishop, the committee endorsed the Cincinnati Southern Railroad, and as a bow to the southern delegates in the audience, it called for completion of a southern Pacific railroad. The report from the committee concerned with waterway transportation, by contrast, followed the pattern set at previous conventions and listed those projects deserving of federal aid: a canal at Fort St. Philip around obstructions at the mouth of the Mississippi River; a Chesapeake and Delaware canal; canals in Wisconsin, at Louisville, and on the Tennessee River; and renovation of the Erie canal to make it more accessible to steam navigation.[23]

The Baltimore session endorsed the sentiment of previous conventions: that it was critical to the expansion of American commerce that a national shipbuilding industry grow, and that much of the responsibility for accomplishing that lay with the federal government. The delegates supported administration efforts to promote domestic building of iron steamers, called for increased federal assistance toward establishment of an efficient merchant marine, and rejected an anti-administration proposal to change navigation laws to allow Americans to purchase foreign ships for use in coastal trade. While the convention targeted the federal government for solutions, it did not place the blame for American shipping decline there, but rather laid that on American shipbuilders themselves for not keeping up with emerging technology. These businessmen seemed receptive to an extension of federal regulatory powers into logistical aspects of maritime traffic, such as quarantine reviews and harbor master and harbor pilot fees. The convention called for increased federal efforts to secure reciprocal trade agreements with South America and for federal reform of custom-house operations. The government was also urged to consider purchasing all existing telegraph lines and to become more involved in development of an American mining industry through funding of federal mineral surveys.[24]

The fiscal policy preferred by the Baltimore convention was that promoted by the growing liberal movement within the Republican party. The Finance Committee endorsed a contractionist currency policy that would return the country to specie payments, protection of federal bondholders by reducing the national debt gradually rather than precipitously, revenue tariffs that were not prohibitory, and abolition of the income tax. This general program was not acceptable to all of the delegates, and the report was voted on item by item at the insistence of its opponents, who lost out to the majority.[25]

Only a few of the measures considered at this convention could be viewed as southern issues. A proposal that southern state governments continue their efforts to attract European immigrants was accepted without dissention, and the delegate body endorsed a call for European nations to regulate the process more closely in order to better protect the departing voyagers. Another proposal, however, caused considerable commotion. Democrat Elbert English, a delegate from Arkansas, called for convention endorsement of refund of the money collected under the federal Cotton Tax. In support of the idea, Robertson Topp of Tennessee explained that southerners were pursuing the matter through the court process, but he expected that the only way they would see an actual return of the money would be through congressional action. A representative from Pennsylvania, General James S. Negley, jumped to his feet to object, claiming the convention might as well call for an end to federal taxes on the oil industry. A second Pennsylvanian, David Kirk of Pittsburgh, added the coal and iron industry to Negley's suggestion. The convention was forced to take a thirty-minute recess in light of the spirited debate which ensued. Upon reassembling, the floor delegates launched into a second round of disagreement. Finally, the vote was taken and the southern proponents prevailed. The *Baltimore Sun* reported that the vote brought cheers from the southerners. In contrast to the emotionalism of that exchange, a committee report in favor of a federal policy of general amnesty evidently passed without discussion. This policy, to be enacted in 1872, would, according to the report, remove the "last remaining cause of dissatisfaction and discord."[26]

The Baltimore convention was followed in daily reports carried by major newspapers across the South. They did so generally without editorial comment. The *Missouri Democrat*, however, even prior to the convention's choosing St. Louis for its next meeting site, issued a glowing opinion of the value of the organization, important "for encouragement of financial, commercial and material progress throughout the country." Those northern papers which had followed the previous conventions did so with the Baltimore session, but several expressed surprise at the length of topics the convention planners brought forward for consideration by the delegates. And, as had been true for consideration of the Cincinnati session, the northern reports of the Baltimore meeting were generally briefer and less prominently positioned on the page than had been the case for coverage of the first three postwar conventions.[27]

The delegates who attended the 1871 convention had been treated to a full schedule of sight-seeing in and around Baltimore, designed primarily to convince the visitors of the commercial accomplishments of the city. Sponsored by the Corn and Flour Exchange, the Baltimore and Ohio Railroad, and the local Arrangements Committee, these social outings had no doubt given the delegates and their guests ample opportunity to be together in a relaxed atmosphere. They had one last occasion to do that at a banquet, hosted by the local boosters, held at the Maryland Institute on Friday, after the conclusion of the proceedings. The local newspaper account of the festivities proclaimed that the speakers at the dinner presented sentiments "patriotic and eloquent," which "could have only been inspired by a truly national spirit and occasion."[28]

The history of the commercial convention movement had come full circle. In 1852, at the same Maryland Institute, there had been another banquet for delegates to a commercial convention. Then, as in 1871, a mood of festivity prevailed and the speakers rose to offer one toast after another, each more optimistic than the last about the future of the South. John Breckinridge, James Orr, Thomas Clingman, Solomon Downs, and William Dawson were among the dignitaries seated at the head table that December evening in 1852, and they celebrated the opportunities on the horizon for a people willing to commit to a pro-gram of market expansion and internal improvements for the South. Earlier in the afternoon, the assembly had agreed to meet again the following year, westward across the South at Memphis.[29] That 1852 decision marked the start of the recurring Southern Commercial Con-vention. Now, in 1871, the banquet that followed the Baltimore conven-tion marked the end of the movement.

Those present at the 1871 Baltimore session called for the next year's session to meet in St. Louis. There, on December 11, 1872, under the banner of the National Commercial Convention, a group of fewer than one hundred men deliberated for three days on issues such as river and harbor improvement projects, a southern transcontinental railroad, and regulation of fire and marine insurance carriers and of weights and measures standards. Dominated by Missourians and Ohioans, they spent a significant portion of their time together arguing whether the organization should continue its separate existence or merge with the National Board of Trade. In the end, the assembly voted to remain an independent group and to hold their next meeting in Pittsburgh the following September.[30]

The 1872 proceedings received scant press attention outside of St. Louis, and both southern and northern newspapers gave it only limited space, usually positioned in the telegraph news column.[31] No evidence has been located indicating that the 1873 Pittsburgh session was ever held. Certainly, the month of September, 1873, was not propitious for business in general, and it may well have been that the meeting of the convention was canceled in the wake of the panic that hit the financial markets that fall. Also, the outcome of the financial disaster would have made very difficult any further effort to rally northerners in support of federal expenditures to benefit the South.

By 1872 the commercial convention movement seemed to have lost the support of the large group of southerners who had been active participants during the years 1869, 1870, and 1871. One can only speculate as to why that change occurred, since the situation was not directly discussed at the 1872 convention, in the pages of the southern newspapers, or in the private records of members of the Convention Elite that have been examined for this study. However, several facts suggest why southern conservative leaders might no longer have sought to influence policy change through this particular association. These developments had more to do with politics than with economics.

The proponents of the postwar convention movement indicated that they supported the association as a nonpartisan vehicle to effect economic reconciliation between the defeated South and the rest of the Union. For many southern conservatives, the years of Congressional Reconstruction meant that regular political avenues provided them little access to policy making. Thus, they gathered under the auspices of this long-standing southern institution, with its reputation of legitimacy and its place of honor, and modified it to include not only southern representatives but also northerners and westerners. This expansion of the membership was more than merely symbolic; it was a recognition on the part of many southern leaders that they would need the cooperation of the other sections for the South to regain her economic vitality.

The message that came through time and again at the sessions was that southerners were not so very different from their northern counterparts who sat beside them. Like the North, they too saw benefit from transcontinental railroads, from regional railroad network expansion, and from river and harbor improvements. Carefully, the delegates voted in favor of projects located both within the South and outside the South. Those southerners who presented the case for federal assistance to levee repair reminded their northern audience that textile manufacturers would benefit too, as would all consumers of sugar. The South sought expanded direct trade with foreign consumers, but the southerners at the conventions proved willing to vote in favor of tariff relief to American shipbuilders, as the administration preferred that tactic to changing federal navigational laws. Southern delegates joined with midwesterners in asking for interior ports of entry. Finally, if immigration had proved so valuable to the North, it now could do the same for the South.

Just as the convention sessions included representatives from all sections, they also attracted members of both major national political parties, and yet they eschewed politics. They honored the war sacrifices of both the Union and the Confederacy, and included northern and southern military heroes and officeholders among their leadership. Notably, however, the association did not often put into positions of prominence members of southern state Radical Republican parties, and it did not count among its leadership many carpetbag Republicans. The political message was aimed at those southerners, northerners, and westerners who advocated moderation and reconciliation, and the association extended numerous gestures of support for President Grant in expectation that its message would fall on receptive ears in Washington. The delegates carefully made no overt attack on existing southern Republican officeholders or on the policy of black suffrage, but they pushed the association, and, they hoped, public opinion, toward favoring removal of proscriptions on southern white male voters.

By 1872, when the Southern Commercial Convention movement faded into history, there were signals that economic assistance was not going to materialize under the existing political framework, and there were also signs that new political avenues might be opening. Taken together, to many southern conservative leaders, these two realities might have served to undermine the usefulness of the type of association that the conventions provided. When Grant ran for the presidency the second time, the national Republican party was split by emergence of the Liberal Republican movement. Originating in a series of coalition party victories against Regular Republican administrations in Missouri, Tennessee, and Virginia, and calling for reconciliation and removal of all voter disabilities, this reformist faction provoked an antireconciliationist stance from the Grant camp. The election campaign saw the Republican party loyalists waving the "bloody shirt" of wartime sacrifices. Throughout the South, Conservatives and Democrats weighed the option of supporting the Liberal Republican ticket of Horace Greeley against that of boycotting the election. In the end, the Greeley ticket failed, and to a large extent that failure resulted from a significant number of white Democrats choosing the second option, to boycott the contest. The dismal showing of the combined efforts of Republican dissidents and Democratic party regulars caused many southern Democrats to reassess the entire strategy of reconciliation and a New Departure policy that had at its base acceptance of the past and an emphasis on the future. This same futuristic outlook ran through the speeches and resolutions of the commercial convention leaders, and to that extent the 1872 election results might have dampened the hopes of those who had so expectantly traveled to the postwar conventions. For many of them, the heavy Republican wins throughout the North must have signaled that hopes for leniency toward the South lay not in quiet demonstrations of conciliation, but only in the old pathway to power, Democratic party politics.[32]

The economic assistance requested by the commercial conventions had not been delivered by 1872, either by the national Republican administration or by the southern state Republican governments. Delegates at the five postwar conventions had made clear that they hoped their influence could be brought to bear to gain congressional approval for federal funding of major southern internal improvement projects. By the time of the last meeting, that had not come to pass, despite united efforts to secure such legislation on the part of southern congressmen. The conventions placed high priority on this extension of federal assistance to the South, and the fact that the funding had not been forthcoming must have dampened enthusiasm for seeking congressional action through a commercial association. Many of the programs that the conventions promoted—railroad expansion, river and harbor improvements, and levee control—had been undertaken by the southern state governments rather than by the federal government. These projects required massive state expenditures, and the cost had been multiplied in many instances by widespread corruption. The public had gained little in return except burdensome public debt. Despite feverish promotions, southern railroad expansion remained more hope than reality, and southern states saw their credit ratings plummet as railroad bonds flooded the financial markets.[33]

Given the lack of progress toward the economic objectives sought by the conventions, it might be reasonable to assume that by 1872 those who believed in the long-term viability of the southern economy opted to proceed toward implementing needed programs through new means. Whether it was through the Liberal Republican party, or through the Democrats, or through supporting fusion tickets, which called on voters from both parties to unite, many southerners shunned further attempts to seek assistance through the power of persuasion and comity, and they turned to the power of the ballot. In effect, the window of opportunity had closed for those who looked to the efficacy of nonpartisanship. That the Southern Commercial Convention association ceased to exist, for all intents and purposes, by 1872, perhaps serves as a significant indicator of the key importance of developments of that year in understanding how Reconstruction would come to an end within the next four years.

CONCLUSION
A Steadfast Vision

The *Chicago Tribune* seemed a bit suspicious of the commercial conventions that took place after the Civil War. While the midwestern newspaper gave each convention considerable coverage, what had begun in a positive vein in May of 1869 with the first convention turned critical by the time of the third convention. The story written about the first day's session at Louisville might have given those Chicago readers who had not yet put the war trauma entirely behind them cause for some concern. The reporter's description of the southern delegates at Louisville focused not so much on their words as on their demeanor and attitude. The southerners visiting that city for the session were "not carpetbaggers," but rather men with "plantation manners." In a summary of what made them unattractive to the Chicago observer, they were depicted as "not as thoroughly reconstructed as they ought to be."[1]

That particular northern reaction to the convention participants was in a sense reconfirmed by the description of the first day at the 1869 New Orleans convention reported to residents of Mobile by the local *Register.* In a story that ran across three columns of the front page, the newspaper printed a letter from one of Mobile's representatives who had attended the Memphis convention and had subsequently joined those delegates who traveled down to New Orleans for the succeeding session. He reported that when the group arriving from Memphis mingled with those who had already gathered where the opening-day processional march would begin, there was an air of festivity and "much greeting of old friends."[2]

These two reports, taken together, tell much about the convention movement. It attracted southerners who knew each other, and who had known each other for a long time. They were men who carried themselves in a manner that was distinctive, and perhaps not quite humble enough to suit many northerners, given the fact that the delegates had been the vanquished in the late struggle. What was apparent to these observers was also reflected in the biographical information about the convention participants. The identity of the postwar convention leadership was one of survivors from a time gone by who faced the future with the strength of resiliency rather than with the handicap of inflexibility. An imaginary mirror in front of which southern delegates to all of the commercial conventions might have passed would have, for the most part, reflected strikingly similar images during the twenty-six years of the movement: middle-aged white men, most of whom had been born in the South and had resided at several different locations within the South in the course of their lifetimes, yet representing as a group the major urban centers and commercial agriculture regions of the entire section. Their relatively substantial material holdings gave them a large stake in the well-being of their region's economy, and they were men who represented directly not so much the agriculturalist sector as the professional and commercial sectors, whose own prosperity was nevertheless directly tied to that of the region's commercial agriculture. The delegates were not always strangers to each other as they met together at the conventions, whether their knowledge of each other was derived from personal contact or from reputation. These men can best be described as leaders in their place and time, as men whose public activities stamped them with responsibilities beyond those of personal circumstance. This fact lends weight to the argument that leadership in the mid–nineteenth-century South can be described more by its persistence and continuity than by its discontinuity, despite a long-standing political divisiveness in the section that was sharply impacted by both glaring alteration of the political order and introduction of new economic relationships as a result of the Civil War.[3]

The historical continuity of the southern commercial conventions is derived, however, from more than the fact that participants demonstrated time and again a commonality in experience and background and a claim to leadership outside the sphere of the convention. What they said and did within the arena of the recurring sessions suggests a persistence of beliefs and values. That the same goals, ambitions, and dreams found expression on the floor of the assemblies time and again, through the flush years of the slave South into the uncertainty and tumult of the postwar South, says that the convention debates evidence another important dimension of southern cultural continuity, paralleling that revealed in the group portrait of the participants.

Much of the interest in tracing continuity in the history of the nineteenth-century South is due to the fact that the section so obviously underwent a radical change between the time of the firing on Fort Sumter at the start of the Civil War and the years of Reconstruction. The society of the antebellum South was based on slavery, with its distinct set of economic and social relationships that were in most ways in strong antipathy to the emerging industrial world. Yet, given the commercial nature of the agricultural base of the antebellum South and the expansion of that base in the wake of steam-powered transportation networks, which plied southern rivers and rolled across iron rails into previously insulated communities, the slave South was tied directly to a nonslave market economy. When the Confederacy went down to defeat and slavery was abolished, a region that defined prosperity, in part, in terms of expanding opportunities to market agricultural products faced circumstances that seemed to make that objective unlikely. Southerners who had prospered under slavery were unsure that free-labor conditions would bring predictability to the southern labor market, a predictability necessary in all enterprise but especially so in seasonal agricultural operations. Lacking the capital resources with which to repair and then resume expansion of a transportation infrastructure that had become to many a necessity and no longer an experiment, the South of the postwar years presented a substantially altered set of circumstances to those who had come to their adulthood in the slave South.

In many ways, it is not surprising that the commercial conventions resumed after the war. The antebellum conventions had attracted men who, despite their firm commitment to slavery, seemed willing to reach out to secure many of the benefits of a technologically modern economy. If any white males in the slave South could have been expected to remain optimistic during the transition to a free-labor economy and an economy with expanded ties to northern industrialism, it would have been men such as those. Their societal economic aspirations would have meshed well with those of northerners who had supported both an expanded economic role for government during the war years and the emergence of the new financial markets that brought large-scale investment opportunities to the private sector.

On an individual basis, evidence about the private aspirations of many of those active in the commercial convention movement points in the direction of change and attraction to middle-class enterprises. Among those delegates for whom information has been obtained about both antebellum occupation and postwar occupation, there was a marked tendency for involvement in law, commerce, and other professions after the Civil War. Many found in these middle-class professions after 1865 had been primarily engaged in agriculture before the war. Far more moved out of agriculture into law or commerce or a profession than left a non-agricultural occupation to go into agriculture.[4] Thus, they seem to have been anxious to seize whatever opportunities might exist in the new economic order on a private level as well as on a public level, and the convention association might have been seen as just such an opportunity. Providing a forum through which they might influence public attitudes in the South and in the North, the conventions gave such men access, not readily available otherwise, to large numbers of northern businessmen who presumably were linked to sources of northern investment capital.

The predisposition to accept economic change was paired with another characteristic that propelled them into a public forum. A great number of the men came from a tradition of involvement of concerned individuals in public affairs. Unlike as in the past, in 1869 few of them had an officeholding outlet for this inclination, and so to be selected to participate or even to self-nominate themselves to participate in a long-respected association probably presented a reasonable alternative. Schooled in a tradition of voluntary leadership, those who led the post-war commercial convention movement brought to its forum an optimism about the future. While this optimism would not have derived from their collective wartime experience, or even perhaps from their present personal circumstances so soon after the conflict had ended, it might have drawn on their earlier vision of a rich South whose agricultural bounties and market outlets promised prosperity.

Their activism in the postwar conventions marked a commitment on their part to work toward rebuilding the production and distribution edifices of southern commercial agriculture, though doing so without the control over labor that slavery had provided slaveholders. The creed of the postwar commercial conventions was not the New South creed so carefully described by historian Paul M. Gaston.[5] The commercial conventions held between 1869 and 1871 did not promote an economy balanced between diversified small farms on the one hand and urban-industrial combinations on the other. Rather, they were dedicated to taking up at the point where the Old South had been poised before the battle guns roared, reaping the benefits of modernizing the section's market access.

In that effort, it is not surprising that they turned to the federal government for the major part of the funding required for their transportation networks and levee repairs, for the commercial conventions held in the years before 1856 had witnessed the same attraction on the part of many of the delegates to that form of economic liberalism. If in 1869 they were naive in assuming that politicians in control of the federal purse strings would be willing to extend financial largesse to a vanquished South, that naivete was shared by many southern officeholders of the time as well as by many of the northerners mingling on the convention floor with the thousands of southern businessmen who traveled to the five sessions.

Clear also is that men active in the postwar conventions shared the same attitude toward the southern blacks that was evident among the leadership of the antebellum conventions. The convention spokesmen of the postwar years seemed shell-shocked by extension of the new rights to a race held in contempt by whites in a society defined by the hierarchical relationships of southern slavery. The power of the franchise had brought southern black males into a voter constituency long restricted to white males, and the reality of free-labor conditions meant that the landowner as employer no longer had absolute control over the terms of the economic relationship between farm worker and farm owner.

Their speeches and resolutions on the critical need to attract European immigrants to the South, and on the way that black voters had been beguiled by outsiders, give testimony to their perception of uncertainty about the future coexistence of former slaves and former slaveholders in the same world. That, too, should not be unexpected coming from a group whose representatives at the antebellum conventions had defiantly pressed forward with a proslavery crusade in the face of indications that the non-South was growing more and more intolerant of the political demands of slaveholders.

In yet another way the postwar leadership and the postwar convention ideology were linked to the antebellum experience. The sessions held after 1865 never repudiated the society that had existed in the Old South. They did not renounce the racism that underlaid slavery, they did not single out those who had led the secessionist movement for rebuke, and they did not cast aspersion on those who had supported the Confederacy. In fact, they took great care to glorify those who had come to the battlefield. That the absence of criticism of the old ways was due entirely to the fact that they were facing forward, looking to the future rather than lingering in the past, does not seem logical. Instead, an unspoken but deliberate choice was involved: to move forward by stepping back on a familiar pathway rather than by burning their bridges behind them. They chose to face the future without denying their history, buoyed by a persistent belief that the South offered great promise and that much was possible if reasonable men united to work for progress. To some extent, they exemplified important facets of Victorianism in their faith in technology, their sense of moral urgency in their mission, their commercial cosmopolitanism, and their optimistic expectations for the future.[6]

In many respects, the proponents of the program advocated at the long series of sixteen commercial conventions spanning both the two decades that preceded the Civil War and the first decade after the war resembled those who have been depicted as leading the South down a "Prussian road" of conservative industrialization, with the needs of diversified industry subordinated to those of commercial agriculture. Such men as Jonathan Wiener's Alabama planters, Lewis N. Wynne's Georgia planters, the North Carolina industrialists discussed by Dwight Billings, and the "graybeard" Redeemers studied by Laurence Shore sought to channel economic change so as to protect their own power.[7] Certainly, the commercial convention leadership had no intention of nominating themselves for retirement from influence wielding. Nor did they seem to be bent on fomenting economic revolution or abandoning the old racism. Yet, the commercial convention leaders were drawn generally from the commercial or professional ranks rather than from the planter ranks, and they were drawn also from the cities and towns of the South. This market orientation had given them an exposure to the modern economic world perhaps not as thoroughly internalized by others in their society, an orientation that seems to have served them well once the Civil War defeat thrust change upon their region. As it did for most southerners, the postwar experience brought a huge transition to the lives of these men. However, for the men of the commercial convention movement, the transition was not as sharp and not nearly as painful as it was for others. They saw opportunity in reconciliation. Either on the floors of the five conventions held between 1869 and 1871 or through other avenues, a great many of them took up the challenge to do what they could to salvage the South of their dreams.

Perhaps the story of the men who sustained the commercial convention movement can help explain the process of change in the South. As a group, they consistently exhibited an attraction to the values that C. Vann Woodward has described as integral to the New South: a "leaning to business, wealth, and commercial sympathies."[8] Furthermore, they shared these "leanings" for decades, as evidenced in their speeches, resolutions, and pronouncements at the sixteen conventions held between 1845 and 1871. Yet they had also shared a conviction that it was agriculture that provided the mainstay of the southern economy, and their commitment to the preeminence of agriculture remained strong, before and after the Civil War. On both counts, then, their commercial values and their agricultural priorities, their tenacity speaks to the question of degree of continuity in the history of the South. Still, information about their occupations suggests that their personal linkage to agriculture had frequently been balanced by links to nonagricultural economic endeavors. These men had, as a group, apparently always included those who were facilitators of commerce in the South. That their postwar business outlook became increasingly more urban, more focused on the problems and the opportunities for commercial expansion in the South, speaks to the degree of change in the history of the South.

The story of the commercial conventions is one of change, and one of continuity. It is an instance where both of these historical forces were played out in the lifetime of a movement, in a particular historical setting. The commercial conventions offered a vision that was a blend of mutually dependent commerce and agriculture. Steadfast and optimistic, this vision weighs heavily in the story, as does the manner in which the men of the movement clearly faced forward toward the future rather than backward toward the past. Receptive to opportunity, resilient in the face of social upheaval, they stayed their watch at the helm, steering their ship on that course which seemed to them to be the best choice at the time.

APPENDIX 1
Biographical Sources

Sources Consulted for All Delegates

These basic compendiums were used to discover officeholding histories and biographical information about the officeholders: *Biographical Directory of the American Congress, 1774–1971*; Robert Sobel, ed., *Biographical Directory of the United States Executive Branch, 1774–1971* (Westport, Conn., 1971); Jon L. Wakelyn, *Biographical Dictionary of the Confederacy*; Thomas B. Alexander and Richard E. Beringer, *The Anatomy of the Confederate Congress: A Study of the Influences of Member Characteristics on Legislative Voting Behavior, 1861–1865*; Robert Sobel and John Raimo, eds., *Biographical Directory of the Governors of the United States, 1789–1978*, 4 Vols. (Westport, Conn., 1978); Joseph E. Kallenbach and Jessamine S. Kallenbach, *American State Governors, 1776–1976*, 3 Vols.; W. Buck Yearns, ed., *The Confederate Governors*. Extensive records of southern state officeholders and wealthy property holders were generously made available to me by Ralph A. Wooster at Lamar State College of Technology in Beaumont, Texas. Wooster's unpublished records provide manuscript census data for the following state officeholders: Alabama legislators and sheriffs in 1850 and 1860, and Secession Convention delegates; Arkansas legislators in 1850 and 1860, county judges in 1860, and Secession Convention delegates; Florida legislators in 1850 and 1860, sheriffs in 1860, county commissioners in 1850 and 1860, and Secession Convention delegates; Georgia Secession Convention delegates; Kentucky legislators in 1850 and 1860; Maryland legislators in 1850 and 1860, and justices of the peace in 1850; Mississippi legislators in 1850 and 1860, county commissioners in 1860 and sheriffs in 1850, and Secession Convention delegates; Missouri legislators in 1850 and 1860, members of the county courts in 1850, and Secession Convention delegates; North Carolina legislators in 1850 and 1860, justices of the peace in 1850, and Secession Convention delegates; South Carolina legislators in 1850 and 1860, county officers in 1856, sheriffs in 1850 and 1860, and Secession Convention delegates; Tennessee legislators in 1850 and 1860; Texas legislators in 1850 and 1860, sheriffs in 1850, county commissioners in 1856–1860, and Secession Convention delegates; and Virginia legislators in 1850 and 1860, justices of the peace in 1850, and Secession Convention delegates. Wooster's files also include manuscript census data for those individuals reporting estates valued over $100,000 in 1860 within the states of Alabama, Georgia, Louisiana, Maryland, Mississippi, Missouri, Tennessee, and South Carolina. Confederate military personnel among the delegates were ascertained from Ezra J. Warner, ed., *Generals in Gray: Lives of the Confederate Commanders* (Baton Rouge, 1959).

Additional Sources Consulted for the Convention Elite

Manuscript sources included those listed in the Bibliography, as well as individual pardon requests sent to President Andrew Johnson, located in the Amnesty Papers, Records of the Adjutant General's Office, Record Group 94, Microfilm, National Archives, which provided a wealth of biographical information for the 129 members of the Elite whose records are included in that group.

General biographical sources of national scope consulted were Allen Johnson and Dumas Malone, eds., *Dictionary of American Biography*, 20 Vols., and *The National Cyclopaedia of American Biography*, 46 Vols. (New York, 1898–1936). General biographical sources of regional scope were Henry Stuart Foote, *The Bench and Bar of the South and Southwest* (St. Louis, 1876); Weston Arthur Goodspeed, ed., *The Province and the States: A History of the Province of Louisiana Under France and Spain, and of the Territories and States of the United States formed Therefrom*, 7 Vols. (Madison, 1904); William B. Hesseltine, *Confederate Leaders in the New South*; Robert Manson Myers, ed., *The Children of Pride: A True Story of Georgia and the Civil War* (New Haven, Conn., 1972).

Census data was obtained from microfilm copies of the Seventh Census of the United States, 1850, Population Schedules and the Eighth Census of the United States, 1860, Population Schedules, located at the St. Louis Public Library. The search for manuscript census data was confined to individuals whose state census records have been indexed by one of the following sources (in alphabetical order by state): Ronald Vern Jackson et al., eds., *Alabama 1860 Census Index* (Bountiful, Utah, 1985); Kathryn Rose Bonner, indexer, *Arkansas 1860 U.S. Census Index* (Marianna, Ark., 1984); Ronald Vern Jackson and

Gary Ronald Teeples, eds., *District of Columbia 1850 Census Index* (Bountiful, Utah, 1977); Arlis Acord, et al., comps., *An Index For the 1860 Federal Census of Georgia* (LaGrange, Ga., 1986); Ronald Vern Jackson, ed., *Kentucky 1860 East* (N. Salt Lake City, Utah, 1988), *Kentucky 1860 West* (N. Salt Lake City, Utah, 1987); Ronald Vern Jackson et al., eds., *Louisiana 1860 Census Index* (N. Salt Lake City, Utah, 1985); Ronald Vern Jackson and Gary Ronald Teeples, eds., *Maryland 1850 Census Index* (Bountiful, Utah, 1976); Kathryn Rose Bonner, indexer, *Mississippi 1860 U.S. Census Index*, 3 Vols. (Marianna, Ark., 1983); Ronald Vern Jackson, ed., *Missouri, 1860*, 2 Vols. (N. Salt Lake City, Utah, 1986); St. Louis Genealogical Society, *St. Louis and St. Louis County, Missouri, Index to 1860 Federal Census* (St. Louis, 1984); Ronald Vern Jackson et al., eds., *North Carolina 1850 Census Index* (Bountiful, Utah, 1976); Byron Sistler and Barbara Sistler, eds., *1860 Census—Tennessee*, 5 Vols. (Nashville, 1981); Ronald Vern Jackson, ed., *Texas 1860 Census Index* (Bountiful, Utah, 1985); and Ronald Vern Jackson et al., eds., *Virginia 1850 Census Index* (Bountiful, Utah, 1976). The following sources also provided census data in addition to information about party affiliations and officeholding: data collected and generously shared by William McKinley Cash for "Alabama Republicans During Reconstruction: Personal Characteristics, Motivations, and Political Activity of Party Activists, 1867–1880" (Ph.D. diss., University of Alabama, 1973); data collected and generously shared by David N. Young for "The Mississippi Whigs, 1834–1860," (Ph.D. diss., University of Alabama, 1968). Catherine S. Silverman, "Of Wealth, Virtue, and Intelligence: The Redeemers and Their Triumph in Virginia and North Carolina, 1865–1877"; and data collected and generously shared by Frank Mitchell Lowrey, II, for "Tennessee Voters During the Second Two-Party System, 1836–1860: A Study in Voter Constancy and in Socio-Economic and Demographic Distinctions" (Ph.D. diss., University of Alabama, 1973).

Additional information on federal officeholders was found in Frederick W. Moore, "Representation in the National Congress from the Seceding States, 1861–1865," *American Historical Review* 2 (January, April 1897): 279–93, 461–71; in *List of Post Offices in the United States with the Names of Postmasters Annexed* (Washington, D.C., 1862); and in data collected and generously shared by Johanna Nicol Shields for "The Making of American Congressional Mavericks: A Contrasting of the Cultural Attributes of Mavericks and Conformists in the United States House of Representatives, 1836–1840" (Ph.D. diss., University of Alabama, 1972). Rosters for members of individual state legislatures were located in Willis Brewer, *Alabama: Her History, Resources, War Record, and Public Men* (Montgomery, 1872); Dunbar Rowland, *History of Mississippi: The Heart of the South*, 2 Vols. (Chicago, 1925); Walter B. Edgar, ed.,

Biographical Directory of the South Carolina House of Representatives, 3 Vols. (Columbia, S.C., 1974); Emily Bellinger Reynolds and Joan Reynolds Faunt, comps., Biographical Directory of the Senate of South Carolina, 1776–1964 (Columbia, S.C., 1964); Robert M. McBride and Daniel M. Robison, eds., Biographical Directory of the Tennessee General Assembly, Vol. 1 (Nashville, 1975); Texas House of Representatives, Biographical Directory of the Texan Conventions and Congresses, 1832–1845 (Huntsville, Texas, 1942). Additional sources for discovering state officeholders were Dallas T. Herndon, Outline of Executive and Legislative History of Arkansas (n.p., 1922); J. Thomas Scharf, History of Baltimore City and County, 2 Vols. (Philadelphia, 1881); William B. Hesseltine and Larry Gara, "Mississippi's Confederate Leaders after the War," Journal of Mississippi History 13 (1951): 88–100; Dunbar Rowland, Courts, Judges, and Lawyers of Mississippi, 1798–1935 (Jackson, 1935); Lloyd A. Hunter, "Missouri's Confederate Leaders after the War," Missouri Historical Review 67 (April 1973): 371–96; Kemp B. Battle, "The Secession Convention of 1861," North Carolina Booklet 15 (April 1916): 177–202; Elizabeth G. Crabtree, North Carolina Governors, 1585–1968: Brief Sketches (Raleigh, 1968); John G. McCormick, Personnel of the [North Carolina] Convention of 1861 (Chapel Hill, 1900); written reports of Secession Convention candidate lists from county sheriffs to the Tennessee Secretary of State, supplied by Mrs. Cleo A. Hughes, State Archivist, Tennessee State Library and Archives, to Jerry Oldshue, May 6, 1968, and generously loaned to me by Mr. Oldshue; J. E. Ericson, "The Delegates to the [Texas] Convention of 1875: A Reappraisal," Southwestern Historical Quarterly 67 (July 1963): 22–27; William H. Gaines, Jr., Biographical Register of Members, Virginia State Convention of 1861, First Session (Richmond, 1969); Richard G. Lowe, "Virginia's Reconstruction Convention: General Schofield Rates the Delegates," Virginia Magazine of History and Biography 80 (July 1972): 341–60.

The following national and regional sources contained useful information for assignment of party or secession position: Proceedings of the First Three Republican National Conventions of 1856, 1860 and 1864 Including Proceedings of the Antecedent National Convention Held at Pittsburgh, in February, 1856, as Reported By Horace Greeley (Minneapolis, 1893); Official Proceedings of the National Republican Conventions of 1868, 1872, 1876 and 1880 (Minneapolis, 1903); Liberal Republican Party, National Convention 1872 (n.p., n.d.); the roster of delegates to the 1866 National Union convention in Earlene Williams Collier, "Response of Southern Editors and Political Leaders to the National Union Convention Movement of 1866" (Master's thesis, University of Alabama, 1963); Richard L. Hume, "The Black and Tan Constitutional Conventions of 1867–1869 in Ten Former Confederate States: A Study of Their Membership"; Daniel M. Robison, "The Whigs in the Politics of the Confederacy," *The East Tennessee Historical Society's Publications* 11 (1939): 3–10.

In addition to the state histories listed in the Bibliography, the following state studies provided biographical information: Clarence Phillips Denman, *The Secession Movement in Alabama* (Montgomery, 1933); Lewy Dorman, *Party Politics in Alabama From 1850 Through 1860* (Wetumpka, Ala., 1935); William Garrett, *Reminiscences of Public Men in Alabama, for Thirty Years* (Atlanta, 1872); *Memorial Record of Alabama*, 2 Vols. (Madison, Wis., 1893); Albert Burton Moore, *History of Alabama* (Tuscaloosa, 1934); Thomas McAdory Owen, *History of Alabama and Dictionary of Alabama Biography*, 4 Vols.; *Biographical and Historical Memoirs of Southern Arkansas* (Chicago, 1890); *Biographical and Historical Memoirs of Western Arkansas* (Chicago, 1891); *Centennial History of Arkansas* (Chicago, 1922); Fay Hempstead, *A Pictorial History of Arkansas, From Earliest Times to the Year 1890* (St. Louis, 1890); William T. Cash, *History of the Democratic Party in Florida, Including Biographical Sketches of Prominent Florida Democrats* (Tallahassee, 1936); Francis P. Fleming, ed., *Memoirs of Florida by Ronald H. Rerick*, 2 Vols. (Atlanta, 1902); Isaac Wheeler Avery, *The History of the State of Georgia from 1850 to 1881* (New York, 1881); Warren Grice, *The Georgia Bench and Bar* (Macon, 1931); Clark Howell, *History of Georgia*, 4 Vols. (Chicago, 1926); Augustus Longstreet Hull, *Annals of Athens, Georgia, 1801–1901* (Athens, 1906); Lucian Lamar Knight, *Reminiscences of Famous Georgians*, 2 Vols. (Atlanta, 1907–1908); Elizabeth Studley Nathans, *Losing the Peace: Georgia Republicans and Reconstruction, 1865–1871* (Baton Rouge, 1968); William J. Northen, ed., *Men of Mark in Georgia*, 6 Vols. (Atlanta, 1907–1912); Olive Hall Shadgett, *The Republican Party in Georgia: From Reconstruction Through 1900* (Athens, 1964); *The Biographical Encyclopedia of Kentucky of the Dead and Living Men of the Nineteenth Century* (Cincinnati, 1878); Lewis Collins, *History of Kentucky*, 2 Vols. (Covington, 1882); Clement A. Evans, ed., *Confederate Military History. Vol. 9, Kentucky* (Atlanta, 1899); Josiah Stoddard Johnston, ed., *Memorial History of Louisville from Its First Settlement to the Year 1896*, 2 Vols. (Chicago, 1896); *Biographical and Historical Memoirs of Louisiana* (Chicago, 1892); *Cohen's New Orleans Directory for 1854, Biography* (New Orleans, 1854); Charles B. Dew, "The Long Lost Returns: The Candidates and Their Totals in Louisiana's Secession Election," *Louisiana History* 10 (Fall 1969): 353–69; *Edward's Annual Directory to the Inhabitants, Institutions, Incorporated Companies, Manufacturing Establishments, Businesses, Business Firms, Etc., Etc., In the City of New Orleans for 1870* (New Orleans, 1869); Alceé Fortier, ed., *Louisiana: Comprising Sketches of Parishes, Towns, Events, Institutions, and Persons, Arranged in Cyclopedic Form*, 3 Vols. (n.p., 1914); *Gardner's New Orleans Directory for 1867* (New Orleans, 1867); Edwin L. Jewell, ed., *Crescent*

City Illustrated (New Orleans, 1873); Mary Lilla McLure, Louisiana Leaders, 1830–1860 (Shreveport, 1935); Joseph Karl Menn, The Large Slaveholders of Louisiana, 1860 (New Orleans, 1964); Clayton Rand, Stars in Their Eyes: Dreamers and Builders in Louisiana (Gulfport, 1953); Robert C. Reinders, End of An Era: New Orleans, 1850–1860 (New Orleans, 1964); George A. Simms, ed., Notable Men of New Orleans, 1905 (New Orleans, n.d.); Leon Cyprian Soulé, The Know Nothing Party in New Orleans: A Reappraisal (Baton Rouge, 1961); Philip D. Uzee, "The Beginnings of the Louisiana Republican Party," Louisiana History 11 (Summer 1971): 197–211; The Biographical Cyclopedia of Representative Men of Maryland and District of Columbia (Baltimore, 1879); John Francis Hamtramck Claiborne, Mississippi, as a Province, Territory and State, with Biographical Notices of Eminent Citizens, 2 Vols. (Jackson, 1880); Reuben Davis, Recollections of Mississippi and Mississippians (Boston, 1889); John W. Green, [Mississippi] Laws and Lawyers (Jackson, 1950); David Gaffney Sansing, "The Role of the Scalawag in Mississippi Reconstruction" (Ph.D. diss., University of Southern Mississippi, 1969); William V. N. Bay, Reminiscences of the Bench and Bar of Missouri (St. Louis, 1878); William Hyde and Howard L. Conard, eds., Encyclopedia of the History of St. Louis, 4 Vols. (St. Louis, 1899); Ernest D. Kargau, Mercantile, Industrial and Professional Saint Louis (St. Louis, n.d.); The Saint Louis Directory for the Years 1854–55 (St. Louis, 1854); J. Thomas Scharf, History of St. Louis City and County, 2 Vols. (Philadelphia, 1883); Walter B. Stevens, Centennial History of Missouri (The Center State): One Hundred Years of the Union, 1820–1921, 4 Vols. (St. Louis, 1921); A. J. D. Stewart, ed., The History of the Bench and Bar of Missouri, 2 Vols. (St. Louis, 1898); Samuel A'Court Ashe, et al., eds., History of North Carolina: From Colonial Times to the Present, 8 Vols. (Greensboro, 1905–1917); Robert Diggs Wimberly Connor, et al., History of North Carolina, 5 Vols. (Chicago, 1919); Cyclopedia of Eminent and Representative Men of the Carolinas of the Nineteenth Century, 2 Vols. (Madison, 1892); Jerome Dowd, Sketches of Prominent Living North Carolinians (Raleigh, 1888); W. McKee Evans, Ballots and Fence Rails: Reconstruction on the Lower Cape Fear (Chapel Hill, 1966); William A. Graham, "The North Carolina Union Men of 1861," North Carolina Booklet 11 (July 1911): 3–16; Archibald Henderson, et al., North Carolina: The Old North State and the New, 5 Vols. (Chicago, 1941); Max R. Williams, "The Foundations of the Whig Party in North Carolina (1830s)," North Carolina Historical Review 47 (Spring 1970): 115–29; John Hill Wheeler, Historical Sketches of North Carolina from 1584 to 1851, 2 Vols. (Philadelphia, 1851); Ulysses Robert Brooks, South Carolina Bench and Bar (Columbia, 1908); William J. Cooper, Jr., The Conservative Regime: South Carolina, 1877–1890 (Baltimore, 1968); J. C. Garlington, Men of the Time: Sketches of Living Notables. A Biographical Encyclopedia of Contempo-

raneous South Carolina Leaders (Spartanburg, 1902); John Belton O'Neall, *Biographical Sketches of the Bench and Bar of South Carolina*, 2 Vols. (Charleston, 1859); David Duncan Wallace, *The History of South Carolina*, 4 Vols. (New York, 1934); Joshua W. Caldwell, *Sketches of the Bench and Bar of Tennessee* (Knoxville, 1898); Stanley J. Folmsbee, Robert E. Corlew, Enoch L. Mitchell, *Tennessee: A Short History* (Knoxville, 1969); *History of Tennessee From the Earliest Time to the Present* (Nashville, 1886); Gary Kornell, "Reconstruction in Nashville, 1867–1869," *Tennessee Historical Quarterly* 30 (Fall 1971): 277–87; John Trotwood Moore and Austin P. Foster, *Tennessee: The Volunteer State, 1769–1923*, 4 Vols. (Chicago, 1923); Oliver Perry Temple, *Notable Men of Tennessee From 1833 to 1875: Their Times and Their Contemporaries* (New York, 1912); James Alexander Baggett, "Origins of Early Texas Republican Party Leadership," *Journal of Southern History* 40 (August 1974): 441–54; Randolph Campbell, "The Whig Party of Texas in Elections of 1848 and 1852," *Southwestern Historical Quarterly* 73 (July 1969): 17–34; Paul D. Casdorph, *A History of the Republican Party in Texas, 1865–1965* (Austin, 1965); Frank W. Johnson, *A History of Texas and Texans*, 5 Vols. (Chicago, 1914); James Daniel Lynch, *The Bench and Bar of Texas* (St. Louis, 1885); W. C. Nunn, *Texas Under the Carpetbaggers* (Austin, 1962); Walter Prescott Webb and H. Bailey Carroll, eds., *The Handbook of Texas*, 2 Vols. (Austin, 1952); Philip Alexander Bruce, et al., *History of Virginia*, 6 Vols. (Chicago, 1924); Henry T. Shanks, *The Secession Movement in Virginia, 1847–1861* (Richmond, 1934); Lyon Gardiner Tyler, ed., *Encyclopedia of Virginia Biography*, 5 Vols. (New York, 1915).

Sources for biographical data on those active in specific industries included Maury Klein, "Southern Rail Road Leaders, 1865–1893: Identities and Ideologies," *Business History Review* 42 (No. 3, 1968): 288–310; E. H. Talbott and H. R. Hobart, eds., *The Biographical Directory of the Railway Officials of America* (Chicago, 1885); James F. Doster, "The Georgia Railroad and Banking Company in the Reconstruction Era," *Georgia Historical Quarterly* 48 (March 1964): 1–32; James Neal Primm, "Yankee Merchants in a Border City: A Look at St. Louis Businessmen in the 1850s," *Missouri Historical Review* 78 (July 1984): 375–86; Richard W. Griffin, "Reconstruction of the North Carolina Textile Industry, 1865–1885," *North Carolina Historical Review* 41 (January 1964): 34–53; J. Carlyle Sitterson, *Business Leaders in Post-Civil War North Carolina, 1865–1900* (Chapel Hill, 1957); William Kauffman Scarborough, *The Overseer: Plantation Management in the Old South* (Baton Rouge, 1966).

The following biographical studies, along with those listed in the Bibliography, proved useful: William Ernest Smith, *The Francis Preston Blair Family in Politics*, 2 Vols. (New York, 1933); William C. Davis, *Breckinridge: Statesman, Soldier, Symbol* (Baton Rouge, 1974); Marc W. Kruman, "Thomas L. Clingman and the Whig Party: A Reconsideration," *North Carolina Historical Review* 64 (January 1987): 1–18; Robert F. Durden, "J.D.B. De Bow: Convolutions of a Slavery Expansionist," *Journal of Southern History* 17 (November 1951): 441–61; Willis Duke Weatherford, *James Dunwoody Brownson De Bow* (Charlottesville, 1935); Minnie M. Ruffin, "General Solomon Weathersbee Downs: Democratic Leader of North Louisiana, 1840–1852," *Louisiana Historical Quarterly* 17 (January 1934): 5–47; Robert James Rayback, *Millard Fillmore: Biography of a President* (Buffalo, 1959); J. Harvey Mathes, *General Forrest* (New York, 1902); Fletcher M. Green, "Duff Green: Industrial Promoter," *Journal of Southern History* 2 (February 1936): 29–42; Nathaniel C. Hughes, Jr., *General William Joseph Hardee, Old Reliable* (Baton Rouge, 1965); Bernard Christian Steiner, *Life of Reverdy Johnson* (Baltimore, 1914); Edward Younger, *John A. Kasson: Politics and Diplomacy from Lincoln to McKinley* (Iowa City, 1955); Lillian Adele Kibler, *Benjamin F. Perry: South Carolina Unionist* (Durham, 1946); William Mecklenburg Polk, *Leonidus Polk: Bishop and General*, 2 Vols. (New York, 1893); Avery O. Craven, *Edmund Ruffin Southerner: A Study in Secession* (Baton Rouge, 1966); Florence L. Dorsey, *Master of the Mississippi* [Henry Shreve] (Boston, 1941); Rudolph R. Von Abele, *Alexander H. Stephens: A Biography* (New York, 1946); Nancy L. Priest, "Joseph Rogers Underwood: Nineteenth Century Kentucky Orator," *Register of the Kentucky Historical Society* 65 (October 1977): 286–303; Lynwood M. Holland, *Pierce M. B. Young: The Warwick of the South* (Athens, Ga., 1964).

APPENDIX 2
Occupation Categories

The eight major categories of occupations used in the study comprise these various occupations and combination occupations:

1. Lawyer: Lawyer, Lawyer-Editor, Lawyer-Medical Doctor, Lawyer-Educator.
2. Agriculturalist: Planter, Farmer, Planter-Medical Doctor, Planter-Editor, Planter-Educator, Planter-Engineer, Planter-Editor-Medical Doctor, Planter-Educator-Minister.
3. Commercialist: Merchant, Banker, Railroad Promoter or other Transportation Industry, Insurance Industry Representative, Manufacturer, Lawyer-Merchant, Lawyer-Banker, Lawyer-Transportation Industry, Lawyer-Manufacturer, Lawyer-Editor-Banker, Merchant-Manufacturer, Lawyer-Editor-Banker-Manufacturer, Banker-Merchant, Banker-Manufacturer, Merchant-Editor, Banker-Educator, Banker-Editor, Banker-Medical Doctor, Merchant-Steamboat Captain.
4. Professional: Editor, Educator, Minister, Medical Doctor, Editor-Educator, Engineer, Steamboat Captain, Career Military.
5. Planter-Lawyer
6. Planter-Commerce: Planter-Merchant, Planter-Banker, Planter-Transportation Industry, Planter-Manufacturer, Planter-Merchant-Banker, Planter-Banker, Planter-Merchant-Manufacturer, Planter-Merchant-Manufacturer-Banker.
7. Lawyer-Planter-Commerce: Lawyer-Planter-Merchant, Lawyer-Planter-Banker, Lawyer-Planter-Editor, Lawyer-Planter-Merchant-Banker.
8. Miscellaneous: Slave trader, Planter and Slave trader, Clerk, Student, Machinist.

NOTES

Notes to Introduction

1. The largest collective biographies of individuals from this same time period and region are those by Ralph A. Wooster, *The People in Power: Courthouse and Statehouse in the Lower South, 1850-1860, Politicians, Planters, and Plain Folk: Courthouse and Statehouse in the Upper South, 1850-1860*, and *The Secession Conventions of the South*. Other group biographies of southern regional scope include Thomas B. Alexander and Richard E. Beringer, *The Anatomy of the Confederate Congress: A Study of the Influences of Member Characteristics on Legislative Voting Behavior, 1861-1865*, 13-34; James Alexander Baggett, "Origins of Upper South Scalawag Leadership," 53-73; Don H. Doyle, *New Men, New Cities, New South: Atlanta, Nashville, Charleston, Mobile, 1860-1910*, 87-135; Richard L. Hume, "The Black and Tan Constitutional Conventions of 1867-1869 Ten Former Confederate States: A Study of Their Membership," 655-75; Terry L. Seip, *The South Returns to Congress: Men, Economic Measures, and Intersectional Relationships, 1868-1879*, 10-43; Jon L. Wakelyn, *Biographical Dictionary of the Confederacy*, 14-60.

2. Wilbur J. Cash, *The Mind of the South*, 210; Thomas B. Alexander, "Persistent Whiggery in the Confederate South, 1860-1877," 305, and "The Dimensions of Continuity across the Civil War," 84; Jona569than M. Wiener, *Social Origins of the New South: Alabama, 1860-1885*, 8-28; Dwight B. Billings, Jr., *Planters and the Making of a "New South": Class, Politics, and Development in North Carolina, 1865-1900*, 73-109; A. Jane Townes, "The Effect of Emancipation on Large Landholdings, Nelson and Goochland Counties, Virginia," 408-9; Randolph B. Campbell, "Population Persistence and Social Change in Nineteenth-Century Texas: Harrison County, 1850-1880," 193, 197-203; Michael Wayne, *The Reshaping of Plantation Society: The Natchez District, 1860-1880*, 86-91; Gail Williams O'Brien, *The Legal Fraternity and the Making of a New South Community, 1848-1882*, 56-57, 63-69, 74-75. These studies, taken as a whole, criticize the suggestion made by C. Vann Woodward, *Origins of the New South, 1877-1913*, 140-41, 154, that the lead-

ership origins of the New South lay not with the old establishment but rather with a newly empowered middle class. Modifying his assessment of the sharpness of the break in personnel in a more recent publication, he still suggested that power groups of the postwar South resided in a class no longer identifiable as planter class (*Thinking Back: The Perils of Writing History*, 74).

3. Gavin Wright, *The Political Economy of the Cotton South: Households, Markets, and Wealth in the Nineteenth Century*, 89; Robert William Fogel, *Without Consent or Contract: The Rise and Fall of American Slavery*, 87, 95, 106, 110; Fogel and Stanley L. Engerman, *Time on the Cross: The Economics of American Negro Slavery*, 1:247–57.

4. The evidence of merger with the planters at the 1854 Charleston convention is found in "The Great Southern Convention in Charleston," (July–November 1854) 491 (Commercial Convention Proceedings are listed by host city in the Bibliography). The merger is discussed in Weymouth T. Jordan, *Rebels in the Making: Planters' Conventions and Southern Propaganda*, 91, 99. Eugene D. Genovese's *The Political Economy of Slavery: Studies in the Economy and Society of the Slave South*, 180–208, stands out as one of the strongest presentations of the power of the planter hegemony in the Old South.

5. Doyle, *New Men*, xiv, 17–19, 138. Doyle, however, in my opinion, gave insufficient credit to the prominence and policy-influencing role of antebellum business associations. For other major work on the linkage between the antebellum and postwar urban South, see David R. Goldfield, *Cotton Fields and Skyscrapers: Southern City and Region, 1607–1980*, 11, 36–43, and "Pursuing the American Urban Dream: Cities in the Old South," 63, 91; Howard N. Rabinowitz, "Continuity and Change: Southern Urban Development, 1860–1900," 92. Leonard P. Curry was among the first to draw attention to the urban character of the antebellum South in "Urbanization and Urbanism in the Old South: A Comparative View."

6. "The Great Southern Convention in Charleston," (June 1854) 635.

7. James Charles Cobb argued persuasively that the relationship between planter and industrialist was complex, and that they shared a central set of policies and thus worked together rather than in conflict ("Beyond Planters and Industrialists: A New Perspective on the New South," 55–57).

8. Recent studies address the extent of modern economic relationships and ideological attraction to modernism among southern leaders. Laurence Shore, in *Southern Capitalists: The Ideological Leadership of an Elite, 1832–1885*, 13, 117, 151–52, 156–57, traced how leaders adopted basic tenets of modernism in the years before the Civil War and adapted them to meet changed circumstances after 1865. Shore gave insufficient credit, however, to the commercial conventions for fostering this perspective, as he focused primarily on only the last four antebellum conventions and ignored altogether the postwar meetings. Dan T. Carter, in *When the War Was Over: The Failure of Self-Reconstruction in the*

South, 1865–1867, 104–45, argued that proponents of modernization had existed before the war, spoke out in favor of change after the war, but ultimately rejected the basic values of plantation society. For work tracing the critical role of community leaders in implementing modern economic change, see Lacy K. Ford, Jr., *Origins of Southern Radicalism: The South Carolina Upcountry, 1800–1860,* 253–54, 276–77, and "Rednecks and Merchants: Economic Development and Social Tensions in the South Carolina Upcountry, 1865–1900," 302–3; John C. Inscoe, *Mountain Masters, Slavery, and the Sectional Crisis in Western North Carolina,* 7–8, 52, 263.

9. For a summary of the thesis of each work, see William W. Davis, "Ante-Bellum Southern Commercial Conventions," 153, 201; Robert Royal Russel, *Economic Aspects of Southern Sectionalism, 1840–1861,* 149–50; John G. Van Deusen, *The Ante-Bellum Southern Commercial Conventions,* 13–14, 108–11; Herbert Wender, *Southern Commercial Conventions, 1837–1859,* 236. For studies of individual conventions, see James H. Easterby, "The Charleston Commercial Convention of 1854"; Herbert Wender, "The Southern Commercial Convention at Savannah, 1856"; Jere W. Roberson, "The Memphis Commercial Convention of 1853: Southern Dreams and 'Young America,'" and "To Build a Pacific Railroad: Congress, Texas, and the Charleston Convention of 1854."

10. Ulrich B. Phillips, "The Central Theme of Southern History," 35; Avery O. Craven, *The Growth of Southern Nationalism, 1848–1861,* 278; David M. Potter, *The Impending Crisis, 1848–1861,* 467; Charles S. Sydnor, *The Development of Southern Sectionalism, 1819–1848,* 254; Clement Eaton, *The Freedom-Of-Thought Struggle in the Old South,* 345; Genovese, *Political Economy,* 126; Harold D. Woodman, *King Cotton and His Retainers: Financing and Marketing the Cotton Crop of the South, 1800–1925,* 143; Carl N. Degler, *Place Over Time: The Continuity of Southern Distinctiveness,* 52; Fred Bateman and Thomas Weiss, *A Deplorable Scarcity: The Failure of Industrialization in the Slave Economy,* 132; Richard N. Current, *Northernizing the South,* 43–44; John McCardell, *The Idea of a Southern Nation: Southern Nationalists and Southern Nationalism, 1830–1860,* 91–140.

11. Ronald T. Takaki, *A Pro-Slavery Crusade: The Agitation to Reopen the African Slave Trade,* 148–56; Shore, *Southern Capitalists,* 53; Wright, *Political Economy,* 152.

12. E. Merton Coulter, *The South During Reconstruction, 1865–1877,* 233–34. Mention is made of the conventions in two books on other subjects: Leonard P. Curry, *Rail Routes South: Louisville's Fight for the Southern Market 1865–1872,* 98; Lucy M. Cohen, *Chinese in the Post–Civil War South: A People Without a History,* 25, 63, 72. The postwar conventions receive no mention in the recently published addition to the New American Nation Series, Eric Foner, *Reconstruction: America's Unfinished Revolution, 1863–1877.*

Notes to Chapter One

1. *Journal of the Proceedings of the South-Western Convention, Began and Held At the City of Memphis, On the 12th November, 1845,* 7–14.

2. *Memphis Appeal,* May 19, 1869.

3. Dearing's address is reprinted in Wender, *Commercial Conventions,* 11. Biographical information on Dearing is in John F. Stover, *Iron Road to the West: American Railroads in the 1850s,* 73. Activities of the Augusta conventions can be traced through the *Columbus Enquirer,* April 12, June 14, August 23, October 31, 1838. De Bow reprinted the resolutions passed at the 1839 Charleston convention in an 1852 publication, "Southern Commercial Conventions." For further discussion of the Direct Trade Conventions, see Wender, *Commercial Conventions,* 11–48; Van Deusen, *Commercial Conventions,* 14; Davis, "Commercial Conventions," 154; Sydnor, *Southern Sectionalism,* 254; Russel, *Southern Sectionalism,* 15–32.

4. These early commercial conventions drew their audiences primarily from the southeast Atlantic coast; the most states ever represented at a single convention were eight, and over 75 percent of the delegates at the last convention came from the host state, South Carolina (Wender, *Commercial Conventions,* 30). De Bow harked back to the direct trade conventions whenever he traced the history of the commercial convention movement. See De Bow, "Direct Trade of Southern States with Europe," 208–9; "Commercial Independence of the South," 477–93; "Great Southern Convention in Charleston," (July–November 1854) 96; "Southern Convention at Savannah, Georgia," 551.

5. Sydnor, *Southern Sectionalism,* 264; Merl E. Reed, "Government Investment and Economic Growth: Louisiana's Ante-Bellum Railroads," 189; John Niven, *John C. Calhoun and the Price of Union: A Biography,* 294; Charles M. Wiltse, *John C. Calhoun: Secessionist, 1840–1850,* 235–46. The Chicago session was held in July, 1847; St. Louis and Memphis hosted conventions in October, 1849, and New Orleans in January and June of 1851. See "The Chicago and Memphis Conventions"; "Chicago Internal Improvements Convention, 1847." Van Deusen, in *Commercial Conventions,* 24–31, discussed this series of 1845–1851 conventions.

6. The first issue of *De Bow's Review* carried a report of the 1845 Memphis convention, "Convention of Southern and Western States." On De Bow's role in the founding of the commercial convention movement, see Ottis Clark Skipper, *J. D. B. De Bow: Magazinist of the Old South,* 15–30. De Bow attended more conventions than any delegate and was honored with the presidency of the 1857 session at Knoxville.

7. De Bow, "Cause of the South," 107, includes his 1851 appeal for a large convention. For published reports of the 1852 New Orleans convention, see *Proceedings of the South-Western Rail Road Convention Held in New Orleans in January, 1852* and *New Orleans Picayune,* January 5–10, 1852. A brief history of the entire southwestern railroad convention movement is in De Bow, "Address to the Peo-

ple of the Southern and Western States," which includes his own address to the 1852 convention. De Bow reprinted his appeal for an ongoing organization in his introduction to the reports of the 1853 convention, "The Memphis Convention," 255–56. For a discussion of De Bow's involvement in the 1851–1852 New Orleans conventions, see Davis, "Commercial Conventions," 175.

8. *De Bow's Review* 13 (September 1852): 320; *Baltimore Southern and Western Commercial Convention, Held in Baltimore, December 18th, 1852, Under the Auspices of the Board of Trade*, 1–13; *Baltimore Sun*, December 20, 1852; "The Baltimore Southern Commercial Convention."

9. The 1859 session issued a call to meet again in November of 1860 following the national elections, but such a session was never held. A small group of 203 delegates, including De Bow, assembled in Macon on October 14, 1861, and held a Southern Commercial Convention in conjunction with a Cotton Planter's Convention. Debates revolved around the problems of bankers and importers in the face of wartime restrictions. A full report of the convention's proceedings can be found in the *Charleston Mercury*, October 16–18, 1861. The Macon convention is not included in the series discussed in this collective biography.

10. *Richmond Enquirer*, October 15, 1868; Nelson Morehouse Blake, *William Mahone of Virginia: Soldier and Political Insurgent*, 89–90; *New York Times*, October 20, 28, 1868.

11. *Minutes of the Proceedings of the Commercial Convention Held in the City of Memphis, Tennessee, May 1869*, 1–150; *Memphis Appeal*, May 18, 20–22, 1869. The decision to use the word *Southern* in the convention name was mildly debated but finally insisted on by a delegate from Cincinnati, who argued that the purpose of the meeting was to consider matters of vital interest to the South. A brief sketch of all conventions held in 1869 can be found in "Commercial Conventions," [*Appleton's*] *Annual American Cyclopaedia and Register of Important Events of the Year 1869*, 114–18.

12. General Bussey was open with the delegates about the deliberate timing of the New Orleans convention (*Memphis Appeal*, May 20, 1869).

13. *Proceedings of the Commercial Convention Held in New Orleans, May 24th, 26th, 27th, and 28th, 1869*; *New Orleans Picayune*, May 25–29, 1869. Vandever's speech was printed in the issue of May 25, 1869, and also appeared in "An Abstract of the Most Important Documents Published by the New Orleans Commercial Convention, May 1869." The invitation to Louisville was issued by the Kentucky delegates (*New Orleans Picayune*, May 29, 1869). In the same story it was reported that the New Orleans session also recommended that another convention be held on the subject of commerce and trade within the Mississippi valley, and the delegates approved a resolution calling for a meeting in August at Davenport, Iowa. General Vandever did preside over a subsequent Mississippi valley commercial convention held in Keokuk, Iowa, on September 7, 1869. See "Commercial Conventions," [*Appleton's*] *Annual Cyclopaedia of 1869*, 116–17, and *New York Times*, September 9–10, 1869.

14. Coverage of the Louisville convention is found in *Louisville Courier-Journal*, October 12–18, 1869. See *Louisville Courier-Journal*, October 13, 1869, for Fillmore's opening speech. Information about the Cincinnati convention is taken from *Proceedings of the Southern Commercial Convention at its Annual Session at Cincinnati Ohio, October 1870.* The exact number of southern delegates was 230, and the number of northern was 120.

15. The best coverage of the Baltimore convention can be found in the *Baltimore Sun*, September 25–30, 1871. The official report of the convention, *Proceedings of the National Commercial Convention Held at Baltimore, September 25–29, 1871*, is less detailed. For the St. Louis convention, see *Proceedings of the National Commercial Convention Held At St. Louis, December 11th, 12th and 13th, 1872* and *Missouri Democrat*, December 12–14, 1872. The session received only limited coverage in the *New York Times*, December 14, 1872.

16. Only delegates from southern states have been included in this collective biography. The 5,716 delegate set is composed of those who attended the following sixteen conventions: the 1845 convention held in Memphis, the 1852 New Orleans railroad convention, all nine sessions held between 1852 and 1859, and all five held between 1869 and 1871. Lists of southern representatives and senators are found in the *Biographical Directory of the American Congress 1776–1971* and include the twenty-ninth through forty-first Congresses. The number of delegates to the Secession Conventions is from Wooster, *Secession Conventions*, 4; Confederate congressmen profiles are found in Alexander and Beringer, *Confederate Congress*, 354–89.

17. The Upper South region comprises the District of Columbia and the states of Virginia, Maryland, North Carolina, Kentucky, Tennessee, Arkansas, and Missouri. The Lower South region comprises South Carolina, Florida, Georgia, Alabama, Mississippi, Louisiana, and Texas. In an east-west division, the South Atlantic region comprises the District of Columbia and the states of Maryland, Virginia, North Carolina, South Carolina, Florida, and Georgia. The South Central region comprises Kentucky, Tennessee, Alabama, Mississippi, Louisiana, Texas, Arkansas, and Missouri. The total number of delegates to prewar conventions for whom southern state of residency is known is 4,124. The total number for the postwar conventions is 1,661.

18. The remaining delegates were Michigan and Iowa with eight; Kansas and New Jersey with five; Wisconsin with four; Rhode Island with two; and one each from Connecticut, Massachusetts, Vermont, Minnesota, Montgomery, Nevada, and California. None of the northern delegates are included in the collective biography set.

19. Even De Bow had a schedule conflict that prevented him from attending the 1854 session; he accepted a committee assignment, however, and duly reported to the next session (Skipper, *De Bow*, 86). John A. Quitman missed two sessions due to schedule conflicts, and he missed a third for reasons of ill health (Robert E. May, *John A. Quitman: Old South Crusader*, 101, 290, 330–31). Albert Pike was invited by the Arkansas legislature to attend the 1853 Mem-

phis convention, but he could not go; he subsequently attended three sessions, but he refused to attend the 1857 session for political reasons (Frederick W. Allsopp, *The Life Story of Albert Pike*, 45, 62). Edmund Ruffin was prevented from attending the 1857 session due to a death in his family (Betty L. Mitchell, *Edmund Ruffin: A Biography*, 102). Ruffin missed the 1859 convention due to a hand injury (William Kauffman Scarborough, ed., *The Diary of Edmund Ruffin*, Vol. 1, *Toward Independence, October 1856–April 1861*, 304). Duff Green attended the Louisville session but missed the Cincinnati meeting due to ill health (Duff Green to President Southern Commercial Convention, n.d., Duff Green Papers, Southern Historical Collection, University of North Carolina, Chapel Hill).

20. In the Internal Improvement subset, 16 percent attended more than one convention. In the Mid-1850s subset, the count is 433 out of 3,218, or 13 percent. The count for the Montgomery-Vicksburg subset is highest at 46 out of 153, or 30 percent, but very few delegates were at those sessions. The Postwar subset count is 289 out of 1,677, or 17 percent.

21. For notices of local Arrangement Committee meetings, see *Charleston Courier*, April 3, 1854; *New Orleans Picayune*, January 8, 1855; *Brownlow's Knoxville Whig*, July 18, 1857. Albert Pike criticized the New Orleans City Council for its failure to send letters soliciting delegate appointments from state governors (*Proceedings of the Southern Commercial Convention Held in the City of New Orleans*, 22). De Bow, along with other delegates attending the Richmond session, blamed bad weather for the sparse turnout in 1856; however, he also alluded to a delay in advance notification ("Southern Convention at Richmond," 340). For subsequent convention planning, see "Southern Convention at Savannah," 102; *Official Report of the Debates and Proceedings of the Southern Commercial Convention, Assembled at Knoxville, Tennessee, August 9th, 1857*, 93; "The Southern Convention at Knoxville," 320; "Late Southern Convention at Montgomery," 606. In 1869 the Memphis Chamber of Commerce formed three committees to organize and secure funding for the session and raised over four thousand dollars to cover the convention costs; the Memphis City Council agreed to cover any deficits (*Memphis Appeal*, May 14, 17, 1869). The local committee in Baltimore raised thirty thousand dollars to fund their convention (*Baltimore Sun*, September 25, 1871).

22. For samples of convention circulars, see *De Bow's Review* 14 (May 1853): 424–28; *De Bow's Review* 21 (November 1856): 550–53; *New York Times*, October 23, 1856; *Brownlow's Knoxville Whig*, July 18, 1857; *Natchez Mississippi Free Trader*, May 3, 1858; invitation to the 1857 Knoxville convention, Campbell Family Papers, Perkins Library, Duke University, Durham. The circular mailed out prior to the 1869 Memphis convention, reprinted in *Minutes of the . . . Commercial Convention in Memphis, 1869*, 7–8, was sent two months in advance to state governors; mayors; boards of trade; chambers of commerce; private railroad, manufacturing, and insurance companies; steamship and steamboat lines; and prominent merchants, bankers, and agriculturalists. For

examples of government appointments, see *Memphis Appeal*, May 17, 1853; *Charleston Courier*, April 4, 1854; *Richmond Enquirer*, January 18, 1856; Leroy P. Graf and Ralph W. Haskins, eds., *The Papers of Andrew Johnson*, 2:229; letter of David Campbell to William B. Campbell, April 10, 1854, Campbell Family Papers; letter of James Lyons to Henry A. Wise, April 23, 1858, James Lyons Papers, Perkins Library, Duke University. For reports of public meetings to elect delegates, see *Richmond Whig and Public Advertiser*, December 17, 1852; *Memphis Appeal*, May 30, 1853; *Charleston Courier*, April 7, 1854; *Richmond Enquirer*, January 24, 1856.

23. Gavin Wright, *Old South, New South: Revolutions in the Southern Economy since the Civil War*, 34–49.

24. *Minutes of the . . . Commercial Convention in Memphis, 1869*, 8; *Baltimore Sun*, September 25, 1871; *Louisville Courier-Journal*, October 12, 1869; *Proceedings of the . . . Commercial Convention at Cincinnati, 1870*, 14.

25. *Proceedings of the Southern and Western Commercial Convention, At Memphis, Tennessee, In June, 1853*, 23–24; *Proceedings of the Southern Commercial Convention in New Orleans*, 8; Henry Washington Hilliard, *Politics and Pen Pictures: At Home and Abroad*, 256; *Chicago Tribune*, October 14, 1869. For other evidence of women in the audiences, see *Baltimore . . . Commercial Convention, 1852*, 13; *Charleston Courier*, April 10, 1854; *Memphis Appeal*, May 19, 1869; *Louisville Courier-Journal*, October 13, 1869; *Proceedings of the . . . Commercial Convention at Cincinnati, 1870*, 125.

26. For evidence of complimentary railroad passage, see *Richmond Enquirer*, April 16, 1854; "Southern Convention at Savannah," 96; "Southern Convention at Knoxville," 320; *New Orleans Picayune*, May 29, 1869; *Proceedings of the . . . Commercial Convention at Cincinnati, 1870*, 119. According to the *Memphis Appeal*, May 13, 21, 1869, those delegates at Memphis who accepted the invitation of the New Orleans convention rode down for free. Governor Rufus Bullock of Georgia chartered a special train on which that state's delegates made the trip to Louisville; the *Atlanta Constitution*, October 11, 1869, was critical of this expenditure. For accounts of entertainment, see *Baltimore Sun*, December 20, 1852; *Charleston Courier*, April 3, 1854; *New Orleans Picayune*, May 25, 27, 1869; *Louisville Courier-Journal*, October 15, 1869; *Baltimore Sun*, September 25, 1871. A copy of the program from the Louisville banquet is found in the Benjamin Cudworth Yancey Papers, Southern Historical Collection, University of North Carolina Library, Chapel Hill.

27. *Journal of the . . . South-Western Convention At Memphis, 1845*, 14; "Southern Convention at Savannah," 85; *Proceedings of the Commercial Convention Held in New Orleans, 1869*, 21; *Louisville Courier-Journal*, October 14, 1869.

28. *Journal of the . . . South-Western Convention At Memphis, 1845*, 5–6, 16–21, 22–24. De Bow, in "Convention of the Southern and Western States," 12, noted that extraneous subjects were deliberately excluded.

29. "Southern Convention at Knoxville," 313, 319; "Late Southern Conven-

tion at Montgomery," 578–99; "The Late Southern Convention [Vicksburg]," 96; "Editorial Miscellany [Vicksburg]," 713. My conclusions about the business-like operations of the majority of conventions counter those of Russel, *Southern Sectionalism*, 144–47, and Owen Peterson, "Speaking in the Southern Commercial Conventions, 1837–1859," 214–16.

30. "Memphis Convention," 256.

Notes to Chapter Two

1. C. Wright Mills, *The Power Elite*; Floyd Hunter, *Community Power Structure*; Robert A. Dahl, *Who Governs?*. Susan B. Hansen's "Elite Informants and Theoretical Guidance in Policy Analysis" is a more recent study that supports the use of information obtained from members of an elite in understanding the decision making involved in public policy formation. Another work that has helped shape the methodology used in this study is Peter Morriss's "Power in New Haven: A Reassessment of 'Who Governs?,'" 459, for emphasis on the important role played by those who acquiesce in the decision-making process. Peter Bachrach's definition is found in *The Theory of Democratic Elitism: A Critique*, 77. On page 52 he contended that democratic elites must share a general consensus about the "public interest" in order to rule well and remain in power. Later, in *Political Elites in a Democracy*, page 6, he added that political elites can make decisions by preventing others from having the opportunity to make a decision on particular issues. Some have even insisted that a ruling elite must be powerful in nonpolitical areas to qualify as a true elite: Robert A. Dahl, "A Critique of the Ruling Elite Model," 465; Dankwart A. Rustow, "The Study of Elites: Who's Who, When, and How," 711.

2. These historians have stressed the importance of reputation in elite status: Allan G. Bogue, "Some Dimensions of Power in the Thirty-Seventh Senate," 287; Burton W. Folsom II, "The Politics of Elites: Prominence and Party in Davidson County, Tennessee, 1835–1861," 362; Shore, *Southern Capitalists*, 13. O'Brien, in *Legal Fraternity*, 20, used social-science theory to arrive at a definition of power used in selecting which characteristics she would study about North Carolina lawyers—"the capacity of an individual to affect the lives of others." I find O'Brien's definition too broad. By contrast, a strictly institutional approach to identifying members of southern urban elites is used in Doyle, *New Men*, 332 n. 3. For sources on the importance of a shared social background, see Robert Perrucci and Marc Pilisuk, "Leaders and Ruling Elites: The Interorganizational Bases of Community Power," 1056; Samuel P. Hays, "New Possibilities for American Political History: The Social Analysis of Political Life," 201; Herbert G. Gutman, "Work, Culture, and Society in Industrializing America, 1815–1919," 542.

3. The sources consulted for biographical information are discussed in Appendix 1.

4. Lawrence Stone's "Prosopography," 57–65, presents a thought-provoking essay on the advantages and the pitfalls of the collective biography method, and many of his comments apply to my presentation. This biography of the convention delegates clearly falls into the elitist school of the prosopography method, in that it is concerned with a restricted number of individuals from a carefully selected group. Findings are limited by the quantity of data discovered about the convention membership and by the fact that conclusions are not based on a sampling technique. So, it is not argued that the findings of the collective biography describe the entire universe of participants in the commercial convention movement, but rather that the findings apply to those for whom information was obtained. The fact that men of a particular type attended in such numbers is, however, in and of itself important.

5. Information for members of the Confederate Congress comes from Alexander and Beringer, *Confederate Congress*; information for members of the secession bodies is from Wooster, *Secession Conventions*; statistics on planters and farmers residing in counties producing high levels of cotton are taken from Wright, *Political Economy*. Wright's data derives from a sample of 5,229 farms or plantations found in the manuscript census of 1860 in 413 counties producing at least one thousand bales of cotton each. The actual sample is the Parker-Gallman sample collected under the supervision of Robert Gallman and William N. Parker as supported by the National Science Foundation. The sample is described more fully by Wright in his second chapter.

6. In determining how to classify the occupation of an individual delegate, the general rule applied was that the occupation an individual gained primary income or reputation from, as could best be determined, would be used. The eight major categories of occupation, including their particular combinations, are found in Appendix 2.

7. The low percentage of manufacturers among commercial convention delegates closely matches the low percentage of manufacturers found among southern planters by Bateman and Weiss, *Deplorable Scarcity*, 121, 163.

8. The number of Elite delegates for whom wealthholding information in each measurement was found are as follows: 1850 Estate Value, 83 delegates; 1860 Personal Estate Value, 174 delegates; 1860 Real Estate Value, 175 delegates; 1860 Total Estate Value, 188 delegates; 1850 Slaveholding, 29 delegates; 1860 Slaveholding, 105 delegates. The comparative number of Delegate Rank members is: 1850 Estate Value, 78 delegates; 1860 Personal Estate Value, 267 delegates; 1860 Real Estate Value, 260 delegates; 1860 Total Estate Value, 276 delegates; 1850 Slaveholding, 54 delegates; 1860 Slaveholding, 227 delegates. There were also forty-two individuals who applied for a presidential pardon in 1865 because they had estates valued at over $20,000 in 1860. The 1850 median estate value for the Convention Elite was $14,600, yet 82 percent are ranked in the top quartile ranging between $29,000 and $1,000,000. The Delegate Ranks showed a median value of $14,786 and a similar top quartile profile.

9. Aggregate census data is taken from *Statistics of the United States in 1860*,

295. Of those delegates for whom both occupation and estate value have been obtained, 208 were engaged in agriculture, and 30 percent of that group had estate values over $200,000. That compares to 19 percent out of 124 commercialists and 15 percent out of 152 lawyers. There were a total of 244 delegates in this group with estate values over $100,000. Of those, 135 had ties to agriculture, 67 practiced law, and 64 were engaged in commerce.

10. The findings that wealth was concentrated are in line with findings about other study groups. However, the degree of concentration is not as sharp as that found among residents of Charleston, South Carolina, where over one-half of the wealth in 1860 was held by only 3 percent of the study group (Michael P. Johnson, "Wealth and Class in Charleston in 1860," 66). Wiener, in *Social Origins*, 16, saw the same pattern: increases of wealth in Alabama among the upper–middle class and decreases in the share owned by those at the top during the decade prior to 1860. Similar wealth concentrations were found in northern cities by Edward Pessen, "How Different from Each Other Were the Antebellum North and South?," 1133.

11. The average value cited for the Cotton South is that held by slaveholders within the study group. The average held by nonslaveholders was even lower, at $1,781. The study of lawyers in Guilford County, North Carolina, found that the average value of 1860 real estates held by those in the highest powerholder class was $10,850, and the average personal estate value of the same group was $26,055 (O'Brien, *Legal Fraternity*, 62). Members of the Delegate Ranks held 1860 real-estate levels close to those of the planters studied by Wiener, *Social Origins*, 13, who had a median real-estate value of $48,700 in 1860, slightly above that held by members of the Delegate Ranks.

12. Aggregate figures on slaveholding in 1860 are drawn from the federal census returns in Joseph C. G. Kennedy, comp., *Agriculture of the United States in 1860*, 247. The number of delegates for whom 1850 slaveholding data has been obtained is seventy-six, too small to be of realistic use in drawing conclusions. However, their ownership levels demonstrate the general increase between 1850 and 1860 in the importance of slave property as a part of total wealth.

13. Among the comparison groups, only the slaveholders within the Cotton South had a higher proportion at the twenty-slave or more level.

14. Wooster, *People in Power*, 117, and *Politicians, Planters, and Plain Folk*, 127–29.

15. Bertram Wyatt-Brown, in *Southern Honor: Ethics and Behavior in the Old South*, 192–94, labeled the state of southern education "primitive," and he also found no real consensus among planters as to the value of education. Clement Eaton, in *Freedom-of-Thought*, 71, concluded that the academy system met the needs of the southern upper class fairly well. Data on church seating capacity was reported in the 1860 census, and listings for each state are found in *Statistics of the United States in 1860*, 497–501. Samuel S. Hill, Jr., ed., in *Encyclopedia of Religion in the South*, 199, acknowledged the social influence of members of the South's Presbyterian and Episcopalian churches.

16. Mobility statistics on Confederate congressmen are taken from Wakelyn, *Biographical Dictionary*, 17. The same pattern applied to southern state legislators and officers (Wooster, *Politicians, Planters, and Plain Folk*, 29–31, and *People in Power*, 27, 54).

17. Election data is taken from W. Dean Burnham, *Presidential Ballots, 1836–1892*, 246–47.

18. Evidence about party affiliation questions the conclusion by Roberson, "Memphis Commercial Convention," 284, that Democrats were in the bare majority at the 1853 Memphis convention.

19. For information on the presidential election, see Potter, *Impending Crisis*, 443.

20. Information on secession position is known for thirty-six members of the 1858–1859 subset. Those who could be considered Immediate Secessionists numbered fourteen, or 39 percent. Votes in the 1860 election are known for twenty-two members of that subset; Breckinridge garnered the votes of nine members, or 41 percent, of the total. For those historians who agree on the disunionist nature of the late antebellum conventions, see Russel, *Southern Sectionalism*, 142–43; Wender, *Commercial Conventions*, 207; Craven, *Growth of Southern Nationalism*, 278; Takaki, *Pro-Slavery Crusade*, 149–50. McCardell's contention in *Idea of a Southern Nation*, 138, that at the Vicksburg 1859 session "only the most hardened secessionists bothered to attend" is incorrect, as is Van Deusen's description in *Commercial Conventions*, 67, of the Vicksburg session as composed almost entirely of radicals.

21. Positions on parties of 1866 are known for forty-eight individuals, twenty-seven of whom were in the Elite. Positions on the 1868 election were measured for sixty men, thirty-two of whom were in the Elite. Positions on the 1872 election were tallied for thirty-six delegates, split equally between the two groups. Positions on the 1876 election are known for thirty-six men, twenty-four of whom came from the Elite. Among the ninety-nine for whom a national postwar party affiliation is known, sixty-five came from the Elite. And among the sixty-five for whom state-level affiliations were gathered, thirty belonged to the Elite.

Notes to Chapter Three

1. Alexander and Beringer, in *Confederate Congress*, 26, maintained that overall, officeholding experiences of members of the Confederate Congress were similar to those of former federal legislators and that secession did not usher in a new body of leaders. Wooster did not collect information on prior officeholding for his study of Secession Convention delegates. Wakelyn, in *Biographical Dictionary*, 21, 27, 60, agreed with Alexander and Beringer about Confederate congressmen, but he contended that most other Confederate leaders represented a new leadership class, a class first emerging in the 1850s and not continuing in power after the war.

2. Biographical information for all members of congress discussed in this chapter is taken primarily from *Biographical Directory of the American Congress,* supplemented where so noted by additional sources. All references to estate values are derived from data taken from the federal manuscript census returns. Information about Clay is also taken from Frank L. Owsley, "The Clays in Early Alabama History," and from C. C. Clay to Andrew Johnson, November 20, 1865, Amnesty Papers, Alabama, Records of the Adjutant General's Office, Record Group 94, National Archives.

3. Alexandre Mouton to James D. B. De Bow, n.d., James Dunwoody Brownson De Bow Papers, Perkins Library, Duke University; for a brief biography of Mouton, see Joseph E. Kallenbach and Jessamine S. Kallenbach, *American State Governors, 1776–1976,* 2:374–75; Harry Howard Evans, "James Robb: Banker and Pioneer Railroad Builder of Antebellum Louisiana." A biography of Robb is found in Allen Johnson and Dumas Malone, eds., *Dictionary of American Biography,* 15:644.

4. Albert Pike to Andrew Johnson, June 24, 1865, Amnesty Papers, Arkansas. For biographies, see Allsopp, *Albert Pike;* Johnson and Malone, eds., *Dictionary American Biography,* 14:593.

5. For information on Dawson, see Josephine Mellichamp, *Senators from Georgia,* 127–30. For a sketch of Lyons, see Ezra J. Warner and W. Buck Yearns, eds., *Biographical Register of the Confederate Congress,* 155–56; James Lyons to Andrew Johnson, July 17, 1865; James Lyons to Andrew Johnson, September 18, 1865, Amnesty Papers, Virginia. The president of the 1855 Southern Commercial Convention, Mirabeau Buonaparte Lamar, had presided over the Republic of Texas prior to his distinction at New Orleans.

6. Ray Gregg Osborne, "Political Career of James Chamberlain Jones, 1840–1857"; Eli Evans, *Judah P. Benjamin: The Jewish Confederate;* Robert Douthat Meade, *Judah P. Benjamin: Confederate Statesman;* Benjamin Kaplan, "Judah P. Benjamin."

7. For Maury's speech at the Charleston convention, see "Great Southern Convention in Charleston," (July–November 1854) 260. For biographical information about Maury, see Peter C. Thomas, "Matthew Fontaine Maury and the Problem of Virginia's Identity, 1865–1873"; Jaquelin Ambler Caskie, *Life and Letters of M. F. Maury;* Wakelyn, *Biographical Dictionary,* 317.

8. The thoughts of John Bell on the value of economic diversification are included in his senate speech, *Protection to American Industry. Views of Hon. John Bell.*

9. A biography of Tilghman can be found in Johnson and Malone, eds., *Dictionary American Biography,* 8:545; see also a biography in the Tench Tilghman Diary, Southern Historical Collection.

10. A biography of Calhoun is in Thomas McAdory Owen, *History of Alabama and Dictionary of Alabama Biography,* 3:285. Information on Clark comes from Kallenbach, *American Governors,* 2:567–68; Charles Clark to Andrew

Johnson, September 12, 1865, Amnesty Papers, Mississippi; and Robert W. Dubay, "Mississippi," 127–29.

11. For a more complete biography of Yancey, see John Witherspoon DuBose, *The Life and Times of William Lowndes Yancey*. For a biography of Pryor, see Robert S. Holzman, *Adapt or Perish: The Life of General Roger A. Pryor, C.S.A.*; and for his own summary of his Confederate experience, see Roger A. Pryor to Andrew Johnson, June 1, 1865, Amnesty Papers, Virginia.

12. William H. Perrin, J. H. Battle, and G. C. Kniffin, *Kentucky: Genealogy and Biography*, 4:142–46; Kallenbach, *American Governors*, 3:216; Charles Anderson, "The Cause of the War: Who Brought It On, and For What Purpose?" 6–8. Chauncey I. Filley, in *Some More Republican History of Missouri*, 83, included his autobiography as a part of his history of the Missouri Republicans. For a biography of Garrett, see Johnson and Malone, eds., *Dictionary American Biography*, 7:163; for a summary of his role in guiding the Baltimore and Ohio Railroad, see John F. Stover, *History of the Baltimore and Ohio Railroad*, 80, 95, 104, 161; for reference to his usefulness to the Democrats, see William Jefferson Buchanan to Frank P. Blair, Jr., November 20, 1871, The Papers of the Blair Family, Library of Congress. Like Anderson, Bishop had been born in Kentucky but settled permanently on the north side of the Ohio River (Kallenbach, *American Governors*, 3:220).

13. Information on Clayton is found in Graf and Haskins, eds., *Papers of Andrew Johnson*, 2:247. Hardeman conveys his life history in Thomas Hardeman to Andrew Johnson, July 17, 1865, Amnesty Papers, Georgia. Hilton recounts his reactions to secession in Robert B. Hilton to Andrew Johnson, July 3, 1865, Amnesty Papers, Florida.

14. Brief biographies of Patton can be found in Kallenbach, *American Governors*, 2:10–11; Marjorie Howell Cook, "Restoration and Innovation: Alabamians Adjust to Defeat, 1865–1867," 38. Patton recounts his political history in Robert M. Patton to Andrew Johnson, July 1, 1865, Amnesty Papers, Alabama. Information about Patton's involvement with railroads and industry is summarized in Carter, *When the War Was Over*, 47. For Patton's remarks to the Memphis Convention, see *Memphis Appeal*, May 19, 1869. His postwar enthusiasm for economic diversification is expressed in Patton, "The New Era of Southern Manufactures."

15. Henry S. Foote to Andrew Johnson, June 30, 1866, Amnesty Papers, Tennessee. For more information about Foote, see John Edmond Gonzales, "Henry Stuart Foote: Confederate Congressman and Exile" and "Henry Stuart Foote: A Republican Appointee in Louisiana."

16. For information on Topp, see Graf and Haskins, eds., *Papers of Andrew Johnson*, 2:317n. Topp's attendance at the National Board of Trade meeting is recorded in *Proceedings of the Third Annual Meeting of the National Board of Trade, Held in Buffalo, December, 1870*, 4.

17. See Graf and Haskins, eds., *Papers of Andrew Johnson*, 1:367n, for a sketch of Brown. Hilliard, *Politics and Pen Pictures*, 255; Henry W. Hilliard to Andrew

Johnson, July 1, 1865, Amnesty Papers, Georgia. For a comment on his political life, see Carlton Jackson, "Alabama's Hilliard: A Nationalistic Rebel of the Old South," 183–205.

18. James L. Alcorn to Andrew Johnson, July 26, 1865, Amnesty Papers, Mississippi. See Lillian A. Pereyra, *James Lusk Alcorn: Persistent Whig* for a full biography.

19. Francis H. Pierpont to Andrew Johnson, September 16, 1865, Amnesty Papers, Virginia. For his biography, see Charles B. Dew, *Ironmaker to the Confederacy: Joseph Reid Anderson and the Tredegar Iron Works.*

20. Jeremiah Watkins Clapp to Andrew Johnson, September 11, 1866, Amnesty Papers, Mississippi; Clapp, *Address Delivered At The University of Mississippi, on Behalf of the Board of Trustees, on Commencement Day, June 29, 1866, by Hon. J. W. Clapp, A Member of the Board,* 5,11.

Notes to Chapter Four

1. *New Orleans Picayune,* November 18, 1845. The correspondent was aboard the *Maria.*

2. Genovese, *Political Economy,* 13, 269–70, and *The World the Slaveholders Made: Two Essays in Interpretation,* 101; William L. Barney, *The Secessionist Impulse: Alabama and Mississippi in 1860,* 26–27; Randolph B. Campbell, "Planters and Plain Folk: Harrison County, Texas, as a Test Case, 1850–1860," 389; William J. Cooper, Jr., *The South and the Politics of Slavery, 1828–1856,* 59–64, 370–71; Degler, *Place Over Time,* 70; James Oakes, *The Ruling Race: A History of American Slaveholders,* 68; Wayne, *Reshaping of Plantation Society,* 14; Wooster, *People in Power,* 54, 117, and *Politicians, Planters, and Plain Folk,* 127.

3. Fogel, *Without Consent,* 87–88, 90, 95, 110; Fogel and Engerman, *Time on the Cross,* 1:247–57; John Hebron Moore, *The Emergence of the Cotton Kingdom in the Old Southwest: Mississippi, 1770–1860,* 289–92; Wright, *Political Economy,* 88, 106, 126, 141–47.

4. Shore, *Southern Capitalists,* 32, 37, 188–90.

5. Woodman, *King Cotton,* 142–43. My view is contrary to that of McCardell in *Idea of a Southern Nation,* 92, who claimed that the conventions held after 1852 fell under the control of those who gloried in the South's economic distinctiveness from the industrial North.

6. Steven Hahn, "The Yeomanry of the Nonplantation South: Upper Piedmont Georgia, 1850–1860," 42. His findings are challenged in a review essay by George M. Fredrickson, "Down on the Farm," 39.

7. J. Mills Thornton III, *Politics and Power in a Slave Society: Alabama, 1800–1860,* 436; Inscoe, *Mountain Masters,* 152–54; Paul D. Escott, *Many Excellent People: Power and Privilege in North Carolina, 1850–1900,* 4–5; Ford, *Southern Radicalism,* 276–77.

8. Ford, *Southern Radicalism,* 233.

9. *Journal of the . . . South-Western Convention At Memphis*, 1845, 7; *Proceedings of the . . . Rail Road Convention in New Orleans*, 1852, 1, 4; "Southern and Western Rail-Road Convention [New Orleans]," 305, 308. De Bow presented a brief biographical sketch of White in "Pioneers of the Southwest: Maunsel [sic] White of Louisiana."

10. *Proceedings of the . . . Rail Road Convention in New Orleans*, 1852, Appendix, 94; *Baltimore . . . Commercial Convention*, 1852, 1, 12; "Memphis Convention," 255, 257. In an editorial of June 6, 1853, the *Memphis Appeal* claimed that the South looked to the conventions for practical guides on how to improve her cities, schools, and railroads.

11. The *Charleston Mercury*, April 5, 1854, hoped that the convention would not be political as it certainly had enough regular business to keep it busy. On April 11, 1854, the *Richmond Whig and Public Advertiser* exhorted the promoters to keep the movement from degenerating into political bickering.

12. "Great Southern Convention in Charleston," (July–November 1854) 95; *Richmond Enquirer*, April 20, 1854; *Missouri Democrat*, April 28, 1854. *Proceedings of the Southern Commercial Convention in New Orleans*, 4; "Southern Commercial Convention at New Orleans," 356–57. The report carried by *De Bow's Review* matches that in *The Journal of Proceedings of the Commercial Convention of the Southern and Western States, Held In the City of Charleston, South-Carolina, During the Week Commencing on Monday, 10th April, 1854.*

13. *Richmond Dispatch*, January 31, 1856; "Southern Convention at Richmond," 343–44; *Richmond Dispatch*, February 1, 1856.

14. "Southern Convention at Savannah," 86–87. Van Deusen, in *Commercial Conventions*, 57, marked the change of the movement from the Savannah session, where political issues were brought out into open debate.

15. *Official Report of the . . . Commercial Convention At Knoxville*, 1857, 11–16; "Southern Convention at Montgomery, Alabama," 425. De Bow later printed his speech separately as "The Rights, Duties, and Remedies of the South," 225–38.

16. "Late Southern Convention [Vicksburg]," 94; *Jackson Mississippian*, May 13, 1859. Davis, in "Commercial Conventions," 186–87, considered the last two conventions to be purely political expressions, not valid commercial conventions.

17. *Journal of the . . . South-Western Convention At Memphis*, 1845, 22; James Proctor Screven to John Screven, June 9, 1853, Arnold and Screven Family Papers, Southern Historical Collection; "Southern Commercial Convention at New Orleans," 626; *Memphis Appeal*, June 10, 1853; *Richmond Whig and Public Advertiser*, June 24, 1853; *New Orleans Picayune*, June 10, 1853; *Charleston Mercury*, April 11, 17, 1854. The sessions at Baltimore in 1852 and at Richmond in 1856 attracted a higher than usual number of political officeholders, 37 percent and 20 percent respectively, due to the proximity of Washington, D.C., in the first case and hence the short travel distance for congressmen, and in the second case due to the fact that the convention invited the Virginia

legislature to attend since turnout of regular convention participants was so low. The percentage of political officeholders at Charleston, Savannah, and Knoxville—13 percent, 12 percent, and 11 percent respectively—was in line with that of earlier sessions. This evidence contests McCardell's *Idea of a Southern Nation*, 131–33, which marks the Charleston convention of 1854 as the start of the takeover of the movement by politicians.

18. "Southern Convention at Savannah," 96. William N. Parker, in "The South in the National Economy, 1865–1970," 1024–27, 1045, concluded that the South's choice to concentrate on cotton production was a logical one, given the crop's long-standing place in the region's economy and the fact that as a very labor intensive process the cotton culture used production methods readily available; he claimed that for the South to have changed, the entire national economy would have needed to change on a basis as massive as the New Deal. Gilbert C. Fite, in *Cotton Fields No More: Southern Agriculture, 1865–1980*, 31, 49, admitted the dominance of agriculture but criticized southern overdependence on cotton.

19. "Great Southern Convention in Charleston," (July–November 1854) 491; "Southern Convention at Savannah," 99. Jordan, in *Rebels in the Making*, 82, 91, cited evidence of a continuation of the merger until 1856, but official reports of the conventions made no reference to any such combination.

20. *Official Report of the . . . Commercial Convention At Knoxville, 1857*, 11–16; De Bow, "Rights, Duties, and Remedies of the South," 225–38, and "Importance of an Industrial Revolution in the South"; *Proceedings of the . . . Rail Road Convention in New Orleans, 1852*, 80–87.

Notes to Chapter Five

1. Similarly, Marc W. Kruman, in *Parties and Politics in North Carolina, 1836–1865*, 64, 142, found a general consensus between the two major political parties in North Carolina between 1840 and 1860 supporting government action in the economy; Peter Wallenstein, in *From Slave South to New South: Public Policy in Nineteenth-Century Georgia*, 24, suggested that in Georgia one of the basic strategies behind public investment was to seek economic growth. By contrast, Thornton, in *Politics and Power*, 98–116, argued that the public policy of Alabama legislators was based on a determination to avoid government assistance to private enterprise.

2. *Journal of the . . . South-Western Convention At Memphis, 1845*, 11, 25–26; *Proceedings of the . . . Commercial Convention At Memphis, 1853*, 17, 12–13; "Memphis Convention," 268–69, 264–65. Whig newspapers were surprised at Calhoun's advocacy, but they praised the convention stand favoring federal action. See *Richmond Whig and Public Advertiser*, December 2, 1845; *New Orleans Picayune*, November 20, 1845. The *New York Times*, June 10, 1853, said

that the resolution on federal aid to the Mississippi River was one of the most important acts of the convention.

3. "Great Southern Convention in Charleston," (July–November 1854) 92, 96, 260–61, 400–404. Likewise, a proposal that the federal government appropriate funds to improve the Louisville and Portland canal was withdrawn (ibid., 507).

4. "Southern Commercial Convention at New Orleans," 628, 749–50; *Proceedings of the Southern Commercial Convention in New Orleans*, 16, 21–22; *Official Report of the . . . Commercial Convention At Knoxville, 1857*, 39–40; "Southern Convention at Knoxville," 306–7; "Late Southern Convention [Vicksburg]," 100–101; *Jackson Mississippian*, May 17, 1859.

5. *Journal of the . . . South-Western Convention At Memphis, 1845*, 26; *Proceedings of the . . . Commercial Convention At Memphis, 1853*, 5; "Great Southern Convention in Charleston," (July–November 1854) 508. Fite, in *Cotton Fields No More*, 31, pointed out that poor roads and limited mail service served to further isolate the southern farm population.

6. Stover, *Iron Road*, 60–63, 89–92.

7. Other prominent railroad men attended as delegates: Edmund Fontaine of the Virginia Central; Henry W. Conner and John Caldwell of the South Carolina; Isaac Scott of the Macon and Western; Louisiana's John Calhoun of the New Orleans, Jackson and Great Northern; Walter Goodman of the Mississippi Central; Vernon K. Stevenson of the Nashville and Chattanooga; and Levin L. Shreve, Albert Fink, and James Guthrie of the Louisville and Nashville. Romulus M. Saunders, eminent jurist and legislator from North Carolina, who had recently returned from service as United States minister to Spain, regretted his inability to attend the upcoming 1852 New Orleans convention, but he urged the promoters to feel confident as they had invited men of intelligence who possessed real managerial experience with railroad operations (*Proceedings of the . . . Rail Road Convention in New Orleans, 1852*, 50).

8. Milton S. Heath, in "Public Railroad Construction and the Development of Private Enterprise in the South Before 1861," 42–47, found that the majority of funding for initial construction and development of railroads came from public sources rather than private ones.

9. *Journal of the . . . South-Western Convention At Memphis, 1845*, 9; *Proceedings of the . . . Rail Road Convention in New Orleans, 1852*, 6, 11, Appendix 82–83; "Southern and Western Rail-Road Convention [New Orleans]," 311, 315; *Baltimore . . . Commerical Convention, 1852*, 2; *Baltimore Sun*, December 20, 1852; "Southern Commercial Convention at New Orleans," 759; *Proceedings of the Southern Commercial Convention in New Orleans*, 26; "Southern Convention at Savannah," 93, 99. The same point made by De Bow was made by Alfred D. Chandler, Jr., ed. and comp., *The Railroads: The Nation's First Big Business. Sources and Readings*, 7–9, 22. Van Deusen, in *Commercial Conventions*, 35, credited the 1852 convention for much of the railroad growth of the

mid-1850s. For more on the Baltimore success, see Stover, *Baltimore and Ohio Railroad*, 71.

10. *Proceedings of the . . . Rail Road Convention in New Orleans, 1852*, 12, Appendix 89–90; *Proceedings of the . . . Commercial Convention At Memphis, 1853*, 16, 19–20; "Memphis Convention," 267, 270–71; "Southern Commercial Convention at New Orleans," 751; "Southern Convention at Savannah," 99; *Official Report of the . . . Commercial Convention At Knoxville, 1857*, 86, 92. In 1858, a federal postal contract was awarded to the road and the company broke ground, but by 1859 the company had run into troubles and lost the contract (Robert Royal Russel, *Improvement of Communication with the Pacific Coast as an Issue in American Politics, 1783–1864*, 237–43). For a summary of Benjamin's involvement with the project, see Eli Evans, *Judah P. Benjamin*, 44–45, 93.

11. *Proceedings of the . . . Rail Road Convention in New Orleans, 1852*, Appendix 76 and 90, 6; "Great Southern Convention in Charleston," (June 1854) 638. Robb wrote to Governor Robert C. Wickliffe of Louisiana on the subject of railroad promotion, and these series of letters were published as James Robb, *Internal Improvements; a Series of Letters by James Robb, esq.*

12. *Journal of the . . . South-Western Convention At Memphis, 1845*, 27; *Proceedings of the . . . Rail Road Convention in New Orleans, 1852*, 10; "Southern and Western Rail-Road Convention [New Orleans]," 314; *Proceedings of the . . . Commercial Convention At Memphis, 1853*, 22; "Memphis Convention," 273; "Great Southern Convention in Charleston," (July–November 1854) 258–60, 637; "Southern Commercial Convention at New Orleans," 751–52; *Proceedings of the Southern Commercial Convention in New Orleans*, 22; "Southern Convention at Richmond," 350; "Southern Convention at Savannah," 99. Speaking from personal experience, James Robb admitted the unwillingness of southerners to invest in the South as long as states continued to repudiate debt. He blamed low levels of southern railroad investments on that, rather than on any lack of capital in the South (*Proceedings of the . . . Rail Road Convention in New Orleans, 1852*, Appendix 74).

13. Robert Royal Russel, "The Pacific Railway Issue in Politics Prior to the Civil War," 189–90.

14. *Proceedings of the . . . Rail Road Convention in New Orleans, 1852*, 11; "Southern and Western Rail-Road Convention [New Orleans]," 315; *Baltimore . . . Commercial Convention, 1852*, 9–13; *Baltimore Sun*, December 20, 1852; Frank Heywood Hodder, "The Railroad Background of the Kansas-Nebraska Act," 12–15; S. G. Reed, *A History of the Texas Railroads*, 97; *Memphis Appeal*, May 14, 1853. Both the Vicksburg and El Paso Railroad and the Texas Western Railroad charters would become merged under the Atlantic and Pacific's efforts to form the Southern Pacific Railroad in 1856. See *First Annual Report to the Board of Directors of the Southern Pacific Railroad Company Chartered by the State of Texas*, 5–7; *The Texas Almanac for 1858*, 119.

15. *Proceedings of the . . . Commercial Convention At Memphis, 1853,* 18–19, 61. The *New York Times,* June 10, 1853, followed this debate with interest, and reprinted the Pacific railroad resolutions in their entirety.

16. Van Deusen, in *Commercial Conventions,* 96, concluded that the way the conventions promoted a southern route for the Pacific railroad did more than anything else to brand the delegates as visionaries to many of their contemporaries.

17. Merl E. Reed, *New Orleans and the Railroads: The Struggle for Commercial Empire, 1830–1860,* 100, 122; Hodder, "Railroad Background of the Kansas-Nebraska Act," 16–17; Russel, *Communication with the Pacific Coast,* 188; Stover, *Iron Road,* 107–9; J. Fred Rippy, *The United States and Mexico,* 148; *Charleston Mercury,* April 13, 1854. See also Roberson, "To Build a Pacific Railroad," 118–21, for a discussion of the convention's debate over the road.

18. "Great Southern Convention in Charleston," (July–November 1854) 97, 205–12. For a brief description of Pike's activities on behalf of the Pacific railroad, see Allsopp, *Albert Pike,* 62.

19. "Great Southern Convention in Charleston," (July–November 1854) 408–9, 494–506; "Great Southern Convention in Charleston," (June 1854) 636–37. Russel, in *Communication with the Pacific Coast,* 188–90, argued that most of Pike's success at the convention could be attributed to southern disappointment over congressional action on this issue.

20. *Richmond Enquirer,* April 21, 1854; *Charleston Mercury,* April 12–13, 1854; *New Orleans Picayune,* April 22, 1854; *New York Times,* April 14, 18, 1854; *New York Tribune,* April 19, 1854.

21. Thomas B. Alexander, *Sectional Stress and Party Strength: A Study of Roll-Call Voting Patterns in the United States House of Representatives, 1836–1860,* 91.

22. *Proceedings of the Southern Commercial Convention in New Orleans,* 10; "Southern Commercial Convention at New Orleans," 524. See Hinton Rowan Helper, *The Impending Crisis of the South: How To Meet It,* 22–23; Shore, *Southern Capitalists,* 61.

23. "Southern Commercial Convention at New Orleans," 520–21, 635; *Richmond Whig and Public Advertiser,* January 16, 1855; *Richmond Enquirer,* January 16, 1855; *Charleston Mercury,* January 12, 15, 1855; Russel, *Communication with the Pacific Coast,* 191–97; Hodder, "Railroad Background of the Kansas-Nebraska Act," 17–18; *American Railroad Journal* 29 (January 5, 1856): 8. Roberson, in "To Build a Pacific Railroad," 138, claimed that Pike's company was never organized. However, both Merl Reed, in *New Orleans and the Railroads,* 78, and Allsopp, in *Albert Pike,* 62, maintained that Pike appeared before the Louisiana legislature and obtained a charter for a Southern Pacific Railroad.

24. *Richmond Daily Dispatch,* February 4, 1856. For information on Green's involvement with the road, see Roberson, "To Build a Pacific Railroad," 134. For the history of the Southern Pacific Railroad Company, see *First Annual Report of the Southern Pacific,* 5–8, 12; *Texas Almanac for 1858,* 121; S. G. Reed, *History of the Texas Railroads,* 101; *American Railroad Journal* 29 (March 22, 1856): 187–88; ibid. (June 13, 1856): 377; ibid. 30 (October 11, 1856): 649; *De*

Bow's Review 21 (September 1856): 282–83. The report of the House Special Committee was reprinted in *American Railroad Journal* 29 (August 16, 1856): 513–14. The Republican party had promoted a plank calling for the central route, and the American party under Fillmore had no Pacific railroad plank, but Fillmore was a pro–Pacific railroad man (Russel, *Communication with the Pacific Coast*, 220).

25. "Southern Convention at Savannah," 99, 309–12.

26. Russel, *Communication with the Pacific Coast*, 226–28; *American Railroad Journal* 30 (March 7, 1857): 157; *Texas Almanac for 1858*, 121; *Official Report of the . . . Commercial Convention At Knoxville, 1857*, 15, 23, 30–31, 87–88.

27. "Late Southern Convention [Vicksburg]," 101; *Jackson Mississippian*, May 17, 1859. The Southern Pacific Railroad Company underwent reorganization, but its president, J. Edgar Thompson of the Pennsylvania Railroad, was unable to secure federal assistance for the road and resigned in August, 1860. The road continued in operation through the Civil War, and it was extended after the war as the Texas Pacific Railroad. In 1872, under the presidency of Thomas Scott, the railroad was granted a congressional charter to build the Southern Pacific. Scott, however, sold the road to Jay Gould, who in turn granted the transcontinental right to Collis P. Huntington's Southern Pacific Railroad. The Vicksburg, Shreveport and Texas road was forced to turn operations over to its contractors, who continued to run the road until 1861. See *The Texas Almanac for 1859*, 222; *New Orleans Picayune*, May 11, 16, 1859; *The Texas Almanac for 1860*, 220; Merl Reed, *New Orleans and the Railroads*, 79, 124; Russel, *Communication with the Pacific Coast*, 269–70; Walter Prichard, ed., "A Forgotten Engineer: G. W. R. Bayley and His 'History of the Railroads of Louisiana,'" 1187; Emilia Gay Means, "East Texas and the Transcontinental Railroad," 54–57. For more on railroad politics in 1859, see Maury Klein, *Union Pacific: Birth of a Railroad, 1862–1893*, 12; Russel, *Communication with the Pacific Coast*, 227–32.

28. Russel, in *Communication with the Pacific Coast*, 272, believed that Texas railroad building was on the verge of a great burst of activity in 1860, and that had the war not come it might well have resulted in completion of the first railroad to the Pacific. Roberson, in "To Build a Pacific Railroad," 138–39, felt that Pike's plan offered the last real chance the South had to build a southern road as the activities of the Atlantic and Pacific Railroad dimmed enthusiasm in Texas for the transcontinental project. For an overview of southern railroads as of 1860, see Stover, *Railroads of the South*, 11. Certainly the success of Georgia's state-financed Western and Atlantic Railroad gave the delegates reason to support state involvement in railroad building (Wallenstein, *From Slave South to New South*, 59).

29. Woodman, in *King Cotton*, 158–59, contended that southern planters were better off using northern suppliers as they could thereby obtain better credit rates than would have been available from southern wholesalers, who would have themselves had to use northern suppliers, and whose involvement

in supplying the southern market would have only increased the final cost to the consumer.

30. *Baltimore . . . Commercial Convention, 1852,* 6–9; *Baltimore Sun,* December 20, 1852; *Proceedings of the . . . Commercial Convention At Memphis, 1853,* 16; "Memphis Convention," 268; "Great Convention in Charleston," (July–November 1854) 202, 405; "Southern Commercial Convention at New Orleans," 750; *Proceedings of the Southern Commercial Convention in New Orleans,* 21. The *New York Times,* June 10, 1853, felt the direct trade sentiments of the Memphis convention were foolish. The *Boston Evening Transcript,* June 13, 1853, on the other hand, commended the convention for showing energy on this issue.

31. *Richmond Daily Dispatch,* February 4, 1856; "Southern Convention at Savannah," 96–98; *Official Report of the . . . Commercial Convention At Knoxville, 1857,* 71–78; "Southern Convention at Knoxville," 311; "Late Southern Convention [Vicksburg]," 100–101; *Jackson Mississippian,* May 17, 1859. Ex-governor of Virginia David Campbell was generally critical of the conventions as being too visionary, but he considered Mann's idea practical (David Campbell to William B. Campbell, December 18, 1856, Campbell Family Papers). Mann's company issued stock but never built a ship (Russel, *Southern Sectionalism,* 119–20).

32. *Baltimore . . . Commercial Convention, 1852,* 6–8; *Proceedings of the . . . Commercial Convention At Memphis, 1853,* 12, 16; "Memphis Convention," 264, 268; "Great Southern Convention in Charleston," (July–November 1854) 201, 260; "Southern Convention at Savannah," 97. Maury was supported in this effort by Bishop James Otey of Maury County, Tennessee, whose 1853 speech in favor of expanded Amazon trade was printed as an appendix to the proceedings (*Proceedings of the . . . Commercial Convention At Memphis, 1853,* 24–29). Roberson, in "Memphis Commercial Convention," 295, cited support for Maury as evidence of the convention's support for the platforms of "Young America." Van Deusen, in *Commercial Conventions,* 92, concluded that the conventions were attracted to South America as a potential market for cotton exports.

33. "Great Southern Convention in Charleston," (July–November 1854) 203–4; "Great Southern Convention in Charleston," (June 1854) 641; "Southern Convention at Savannah," 92–93.

34. *Official Report of the . . . Commercial Convention At Knoxville, 1857,* 30, 67–70, 79–86; "Southern Convention at Knoxville," 305, 313–15; "Late Southern Convention [Vicksburg]," 101; *Jackson Mississippian,* May 17, 1859.

35. "Southern Commercial Convention at New Orleans," 632; *Proceedings of the Southern Commercial Convention in New Orleans,* 18; *Official Report of the . . . Commercial Convention At Knoxville, 1857,* 86, 92.

36. *Richmond Whig and Public Advertiser,* December 23, 1852; *Richmond Enquirer,* June 17, 1853, and January 28, 1856; *Mississippi Free Trader,* May 31, 1858; *New Orleans Picayune,* May 20, 1858.

37. Larry Schweikart, *Banking in the American South from the Age of Jackson to Reconstruction*, 250–54; Bateman and Weiss, *Deplorable Scarcity*, 163.

38. Unlike northern farm production, southern farm staple-crop production, especially cotton, did not require a range of industrial activities for support (Parker, "South in the National Economy," 1043). The position of the commercial convention on industrial diversification supports the contention of Raimondo Luraghi's *The Rise and Fall of the Plantation South*, 108, that southern planters supported only those industries of immediate interest to them. For evidence of planter support for state legislation favoring industry, see Stephen J. Goldfarb, "A Note on Limits to the Growth of the Cotton-Textile Industry in the Old South," 548.

39. *Proceedings of the . . . Rail Road Convention in New Orleans, 1852*, 49; *Baltimore . . . Commercial Convention, 1852*, 17; *Proceedings of the . . . Commercial Convention At Memphis, 1853*, 6, 23, 17; "Memphis Convention," 258, 273, 268; *Memphis Appeal*, June 10, 1853. Bruce W. Collins, in "Governor Joseph E. Brown, Economic Issues, and Georgia's Road to Secession, 1857–1859," 221, argued that Brown exemplified a secessionist who was also a modernist in his approval of state aid to railroads, a combination that is distinctly different from the kind of antimodernist secessionist described by Thornton.

40. "Great Southern Convention in Charleston," (July–November 1854) 200, 255–58, 405, 508; "Great Southern Convention in Charleston," (June 1854) 635–36, "Southern Convention at Savannah," 92, 98; *Official Report of the . . . Commercial Convention At Knoxville, 1857*, 67; "Southern Convention at Knoxville," 310; "Late Southern Convention [Vicksburg]," 102. For more on cotton textile representatives at the 1854 convention, see Ernest M. Lander, Jr., "Charleston: Manufacturing Center of the Old South," 349.

41. Claudia Dale Goldin, *Urban Slavery in the American South, 1820–1860: A Quantitative History*, 125–26; Fred Bateman, James Foust, and Thomas Weiss, "The Participation of Planters in Manufacturing in the Antebellum South," 287; "Late Southern Convention [Vicksburg]," 102; *Jackson Mississippian*, May 17, 1859.

42. Wender, *Commercial Conventions*, 236.

Notes to Chapter Six

1. *Memphis Appeal*, June 10, 1853. Oakes, in *Ruling Race*, 127–30, argued that a gospel of prosperity and the defense of slavery were inseparable in the minds of most slaveholders, although he used the term *prosperity* to describe asperations for individual gain rather than for regional status as I use it here.

2. Elizabeth Fox-Genovese, *Within the Plantation Household: Black and White Women of the Old South*, 55; see pages 53–57 for her expanded discussion. See also Genovese, *Political Economy*, 19–23, and *World the Slaveholders Made*, 121–28; and Fox-Genovese and Genovese, *Fruits of Merchant Capital: Slavery*

and Bourgeois Property in the Rise and Expansion of Capitalism, 5, 18. James Oakes, *Slavery and Freedom: An Interpretation of the Old South,* 52–56, focused on the tension between capitalism and slavery in the South.

3. William W. Freehling, *The Road to Disunion,* Vol. 1, *Secessionists at Bay, 1776–1854,* 121–22.

4. *Journal of the . . . South-Western Convention At Memphis, 1845,* 22; *Proceedings of the . . . Rail Road Convention in New Orleans, 1852,* 8, Supplement 75; "Southern and Western Rail-Road Convention [New Orleans]," 312; De Bow, "Importance of an Industrial Revolution," 81–82.

5. *Baltimore . . . Commercial Convention, 1852,* 3, 10, 15; *Baltimore Sun,* December 20, 1852; *Richmond Whig and Public Advertiser,* December 23, 1852; *New York Times,* December 22, 1852.

6. *Proceedings of the . . . Commercial Convention At Memphis, 1853,* 4, 18, 22–23, 14–15, 17; "Memphis Convention," 257, 269, 273, 266, 268; *Memphis Appeal,* June 10, 1853; *New York Times,* June 10, 1853. For more about Quitman and Thrasher, see May, *John A. Quitman,* 272–73; Roberson, "Memphis Commercial Convention," 291–92. Eaton, in *Freedom-of-Thought,* 228–32, referred to the home-education movement as one designed to isolate southern learning institutions from antislavery ideas. Current, in *Northernizing the South,* 43–44, saw it as an effort to balance the "yankeeism" of the economic program. For more on the movement, see also Craven, *Growth of Southern Nationalism,* 254–57.

7. "Great Southern Convention in Charleston," (July–November 1854) 95.

8. Ibid., 98, 399–400, 204, 507. For more on Tift, see William Warren Rogers, ed., "Nelson Tift Applies for a Pardon, 1865," 230–32; Nelson Tift Diary (1835–1851), Southern Historical Collection.

9. "Great Southern Convention in Charleston," (July–November 1854) 93, 509.

10. *Charleston Mercury,* April 17, 1854; *Richmond Enquirer,* April 20, 1854; *Missouri Democrat,* April 28, 1854; *New York Tribune,* April 19, 1854.

11. *Proceedings of the Southern Commercial Convention in New Orleans,* 4–5, 11; "Southern Convention at New Orleans," 356–57, 525–26.

12. *Proceedings of the Southern Commercial Convention in New Orleans,* 17, 13; "Southern Convention at New Orleans," 628–29; *Charleston Mercury,* January 15, 1855; *Missouri Democrat,* January 24, 1855; *Richmond Enquirer,* January 16, 17, 1855; *Richmond Whig and Public Advertiser,* January 16, 1855; *New York Times,* January 17, 1855.

13. "Southern Convention at Richmond," 343; *Richmond Dispatch,* February 1, 1856.

14. "Southern Convention at Richmond," 344, 346–47; *Richmond Dispatch,* February 2, 1856.

15. A full report of the dinner was carried in the *Richmond Dispatch,* February 2, 1856. De Bow's coverage of the dinner did not include all of the toasts. The *Richmond Enquirer,* February 4, 1856, made special note of the pro-South

speeches at the banquet. Other newspapers made no comment other than to report commercial topics discussed at the convention sessions. See *New York Times*, February 6, 1856; *Richmond Whig and Advertiser*, February 5, 1856; *Charleston Mercury*, February 6, 1856; *Missouri Democrat*, February 2, 1856.

16. "Southern Convention at Richmond," 351; *Richmond Dispatch*, February 4, 1856; "Southern Convention at Savannah," 551–53.

17. "Southern Convention at Savannah," 551–53.

18. Drew Gilpin Faust elaborated the way that the proslavery argument had evolved to this point by the 1850s, and the way that proslavery proponents showed a high degree of conformity on the basic elements of the argument (*The Ideology of Slavery: Proslavery Thought in the Antebellum South, 1830–1860*, 10). Genovese, in *World the Slaveholders Made*, 99, saw the positive-good proslavery argument as a decisive turning point in the history of southern slaveholders. While he did not place a date on that turning point, he saw George Fitzhugh's books published in 1854 and 1857 as representing the "final formulation" of that worldview. Barney, in *The Secessionist Impulse*, 184, described the proslavery argument as a reaffirmation of the essential goodness of southern institutions. David Donald, in "The Pro-Slavery Argument Reconsidered," 12–16, argued that the extreme proslavery proponents came from the periphery of their society and looked back to an older South with nostalgia, an argument not supported by the history of the commercial conventions.

19. See Takaki, *Pro-Slavery Crusade*, 23–72, for arguments made by proponents, and 103–28 for those made by opponents; Freehling, *Road to Disunion*, 137.

20. Takaki, *Pro-Slavery Crusade*, 9–21; Barney, *Secessionist Impulse*, 5–8; Thornton, *Politics and Power*, 320; Shore, *Southern Capitalists*, 53.

21. Shore, *Southern Capitalists*, 49–52.

22. "Southern Convention at Savannah," 86–87.

23. Ibid., 89, 91.

24. Ibid., 92, 94.

25. Ibid., 216–17, 221–22, 224.

26. Ibid., 217–18, 222. Scott's fear of European immigrants supports the observation of the same fear among southern planters by Ira Berlin and Herbert G. Gutman, "Natives and Immigrants, Free Men and Slaves: Urban Workingmen in the Antebellum American South," 1178, 1197–98.

27. "Southern Convention at Savannah," 223.

28. Ibid., 219–20.

29. *Charleston Mercury*, December 12, 1856; *Missouri Democrat*, December 13, 1856; *Richmond Whig and Public Advertiser*, December 13, 1856; *Richmond Enquirer*, December 16, 1856; *Savannah Daily Morning News*, December 16, 1856; *Charleston Courier*, December 11–13, 1856; *New Orleans Picayune*, December 17, 1856; *New York Times*, December 12, 15, 1856. In a postconvention editorial on December 26, 1856, the *Richmond Whig* claimed that no one in Christendom could condone the slave trade.

30. "Southern Convention at Savannah," 224. In a speech made that same year to a different audience, another who had attended the Savannah session argued that as long as slavery was kept profitable, it had no fear from enemies within the South (David Flavel Jamison, *Annual Address Before The State Agricultural Society of South Carolina; Proceedings of the State Agricultural Society*, 353–55). Jamison favored secession after the 1860 Democratic convention, but he feared the rest of the South would not leave (David Flavel Jamison to John Jenkins, June 8, 1860, David Flavel Jamison Papers, Perkins Library, Duke University). Jamison would later serve as president of the South Carolina Secession Convention.

31. "Southern Convention at Savannah," 219–21, 223–24.

32. Ibid., 94, 101.

33. Ibid., 94, 102; Brownlow's *Knoxville Whig*, July 18, 1857. The other committee members were William Graham Swan, a former Democrat then American party nonslaveholder; John Cochran of Alabama, who had argued against reopening the trade; a Virginia planter, Williams Boulware; and the wealthy South Carolina lawyer Mitchell King.

34. *Official Report of the . . . Commercial Convention At Knoxville, 1857*, 15; De Bow, "Rights, Duties, and Remedies of the South," 228, 238.

35. *Official Report of the . . . Commercial Convention At Knoxville, 1857*, 16–19.

36. Ibid., 23–28; "Southern Convention at Knoxville," 303–5.

37. *Official Report of the . . . Commercial Convention At Knoxville, 1857*, 19, 30; "Southern Convention at Knoxville," 305. The Virginia delegate was a Mr. Campbell, first name not identified, and his speech is found only in the official report.

38. De Bow's coverage of the reopening debate is extremely abbreviated, whereas the official report included a full transcript. See *Official Report of the . . . Commercial Convention At Knoxville, 1857*, 35–39, 43–55.

39. Ibid., 55–59.

40. Ibid., 63–65.

41. Ibid., 67, 71.

42. Ibid., 79, 87–92, 96; "Southern Convention at Knoxville," 313, 316–19, 440. The ruling from De Bow was reported in his *Review*, but not in the official report. William Yancey's biographer, DuBose, in *William Lowndes Yancey*, 1:367, claimed Yancey was made a member of the committee without prior consultation. According to May, *John A. Quitman*, 330–31, the senator had been appointed a delegate to the Knoxville convention, considered attending, but chose instead to travel to Hot Springs, Arkansas, for health reasons.

43. *Official Report of the . . . Commercial Convention At Knoxville, 1857*, 43–44, 51, 62–63.

44. *Richmond Whig and Public Advertiser*, August 21, 1857; *Richmond Enquirer*, August 18, 1857; *Missouri Democrat*, August 19, 1857; *Charleston Courier*, August 15, 17, 19, 1857; *Charleston Mercury*, August 17, 19, 1857; *New*

York Tribune, August 14, 15, 1857; *Boston Evening Transcript,* August 15, 1857;
New York Times, August 19, 1857.
   45. *Official Report of the . . . Commercial Convention At Knoxville, 1857,* 95.

Notes to Chapter Seven

   1. "Southern Convention at Montgomery, Alabama," 424–28. Privately,
Lyons warned his brother-in-law, Governor Henry A. Wise of Virginia, not to
engage in a public dispute with the committee (James Lyons to Henry A. Wise,
April 23, 1858, James Lyons Papers).
   2. "Southern Convention at Montgomery," 427.
   3. *Mississippi Free Trader,* May 3, 1858. De Bow's biographer felt that by 1858
De Bow was a confirmed secessionist (Skipper, *De Bow,* 120).
   4. Alexander, *Sectional Stress and Party Strength,* 97–98; Degler, *Place Over
Time,* 115–16; Potter, *Impending Crisis,* 315–26; Craven, *Growth of Southern
Nationalism,* 288–95.
   5. "Southern Convention at Montgomery," 574–76. According to Yancey,
no official report of the convention was ever printed despite there being a contract for the job (DuBose, *William Lowndes Yancey,* 1:366).
   6. "Southern Convention at Montgomery," 577–78.
   7. Ibid., 579–82.
   8. Ibid., 582. Pryor soon thereafter wrote of his speech to James Johnston
Pettigrew of South Carolina, who had authored his legislature's minority
report in opposition to Governor Adams's proposal. Pryor requested that Pettigrew forward his legislative report for publication in *The South* (Roger A.
Pryor to James Johnston Pettigrew, May 29, 1858, Pettigrew Family Papers,
North Carolina Department of Archives and History, Raleigh). For more information about Pettigrew's report, see Shore, *Southern Capitalists,* 54–55.
   9. "Southern Convention at Montgomery," 583–86.
   10. The passage from Yancey's correspondence is quoted in DuBose, *William
Lowndes Yancey,* 367. The analysis of his strategy in the state election contest is
taken from Thornton, *Politics and Power,* 373–78.
   11. "Southern Convention at Montgomery," 587–88, 591–93.
   12. Ibid., 594–98. The term *fogies* was used frequently by youthful members
of the fire-eater movement in an effort to repudiate conservatism (Thornton,
Politics and Power, 365). Yancey at the time of his speech in Montgomery was
forty-four years old.
   13. "Southern Convention at Montgomery," 585, 587, 580–81, 596.
   14. Ibid., 599–603.
   15. Scarborough, *Diary of Edmund Ruffin,* 1:188, 191; Hilliard, *Politics and
Pen Pictures,* 256.
   16. "Southern Convention at Montgomery," 579, 603–4. For more information on Walker's activities, see Robert E. May, *The Southern Dream of a Carib-*

bean Empire, 1854–1861, 79–133. For more information on Percy Walker's political defection, see Thornton, *Politics and Power*, 359.

17. *Charleston Mercury*, May 19, 15, 1858; *Richmond Whig and Public Advertiser*, May 21, 1858; *Richmond Enquirer*, May 19–24, 1858; *Missouri Democrat*, May 13–14, 1858; *Mississippi Free Trader*, May 31, 1858; *New Orleans Picayune*, May 20, 1858.

18. *New York Times*, May 14, 20, 1858; *New York Tribune*, May 15, 22, 1858.

19. *Jackson Mississippian*, May 13, 1859, listed eighty-one delegates. "Late Southern Convention [Vicksburg]" did not include a delegate roster but mentioned the names of sixty-two delegates in its reprint of the proceedings. I used De Bow's report for the official delegate count. John Quitman had also been named to the committee, but he had died in 1858. De Bow personally urged Ruffin to attend (J. D. B. De Bow to Edmund Ruffin, April 13, 1859, Edmund Ruffin Papers, Southern Historical Collection). Ruffin was prevented from attending due to a medical problem, and he noted afterward that the convention had been thinly attended, an indication to him of less than former interest in the meetings (Scarborough, *Diary of Edmund Ruffin*, 1:301, 304–5).

20. "Late Southern Convention [Vicksburg]," 94–97; *Jackson Mississippian*, May 13, 1859. The membership of the central committee was published in "Editorial Miscellany [Vicksburg]," 713. McRae arrived at the convention on the fourth day.

21. "Late Southern Convention [Vicksburg]," 97; "Southern Convention at Vicksburg," 208–11, 218–20.

22. "Late Southern Convention [Vicksburg]," 469–70, 360–62, 364–65. Farrow corresponded with Pettigrew after the session to inform him of his personal stand at the convention, to forward his remarks for publication in the *Charleston Courier*, and to lodge a complaint against Spratt for not representing his faction's viewpoint adequately (James Farrow to James Johnston Pettigrew, May 13, 1859, and May 23, 1859, Pettigrew Family Papers).

23. "Late Southern Convention [Vicksburg]," 99–101. The report of Henry Hughes was published separately as *A Report on the African Apprentice System, Read at the Southern Commercial Convention* [1859]. His more famous work, *Treatise on Sociology: Theoretical and Practical*, had been published a few years earlier, in 1854. For a brief biography of Hughes and a reprint of that 1854 work, see Faust, "Henry Hughes: Treatise on Sociology," in *Ideology of Slavery*, 239–71.

24. "Southern Convention at Vicksburg," 470–71; *Jackson Mississippian*, May 17, 1859.

25. "Late Southern Convention [Vicksburg]," 99–101. Clark's speech was reported in the *Jackson Mississippian*, May 17, 1859.

26. "Editorial Miscellany [Vicksburg]," 713; *Jackson Mississippian*, May 13, 17, 1859; *Natchez Courier*, May 17, 1859.

27. *Richmond Enquirer*, May 14, 1859; *Charleston Mercury*, May 27, 1859;

New Orleans Picayune, May 11–13, 1859; Lynchburg Daily Virginian, May 23, 1859; New York Times, May 19, 1859.
28. Shore, Southern Capitalists, 59.
29. Genovese, World the Slaveholders Made, 134–35; Oakes, Ruling Race, 227.
30. Russel, Southern Sectionalism, 142–43; Craven, Growth of Southern Nationalism, 278; McCardell, Idea of a Southern Nation, 138; Van Deusen, Commercial Conventions, 69, 62; Wender, Commercial Conventions, 228, 207; Davis, "Commercial Conventions," 187; Thomas, "Matthew Fontaine Maury," 217.

Notes to Introduction to Part III

1. Beringer et al., Why the South Lost the Civil War, 9, 56–57, 216–17, 433–34; Stanley Lebergott, "Why the South Lost: Commercial Purpose in the Confederacy, 1861–1865," 58–67; Luraghi, Rise and Fall, 113, 123–37, 151.

Notes to Chapter Eight

1. The procedure of viewing the history of the postwar period in terms of a series of choices has been suggested by Harold D. Woodman in "Sequel to Slavery: The New History Views the Postbellum South," 554. He stressed the importance of the ideological legacy of slavery and the way that this legacy hindered southern efforts to build a society in tune with the culture of the modern world.
2. Carter, When the War Was Over, 23, 102–3, 143, 216–18; Foner, Reconstruction, 124–26, 132–40. For descriptions of devastation in the individual states, see Escott, Many Excellent People, 86, 103; Wayne, Reshaping of Plantation Society, 34–36; William C. Harris, Presidential Reconstruction in Mississippi, 18–36; James Douglas Smith, "Virginia During Reconstruction, 1865–1870—A Political, Economic, and Social Study," 173–92; Joe Gray Taylor, Louisiana Reconstructed, 1863–1877, 64–65; Francis Butler Simkins and Robert Hilliard Woody, South Carolina During Reconstruction, 3–10; Cook, "Restoration and Innovation," 77–88; Alexander, Political Reconstruction in Tennessee, 51–52. On railroad conditions, see John F. Stover, The Railroads of the South, 1865–1900, 50–52. On landowner concerns about labor, see James L. Roark, Masters Without Slaves: Southern Planters in the Civil War and Reconstruction, 131–41; Wayne, Reshaping of Plantation Society, 60.
3. James L. Alcorn to Andrew Johnson, July 26, 1865, Amnesty Papers, Mississippi; John L. Morehead to Andrew Johnson, July 24, 1865, Amnesty Papers, North Carolina; H. L. Hart to Andrew Johnson, June 28, 1865, Amnesty Papers, Florida; William S. Hastie to Andrew Johnson, October 24, 1865, and George W. Williams to Andrew Johnson, August 23, 1865, Amnesty Papers, South Carolina; William M. Byrd to Andrew Johnson, July 26, 1865, David P.

Lewis to Andrew Johnson, August 9, 1865, and William Miller to Andrew Johnson, August 3, 1865, Amnesty Papers, Alabama; Robert D. Lilley to Andrew Johnson, June 20, 1865, Amnesty Papers, Virginia; Winfield S. Featherston to Andrew Johnson, June 10, 1865, Amnesty Papers, Mississippi; Harry T. Hays to Andrew Johnson, June 21, 1865, Amnesty Papers, Louisiana.

4. Joseph R. Anderson to Dilworth Porter and Company, July 15, 1865, and Thomas Branch to Andrew Johnson, July 28, 1865, Amnesty Papers, Virginia; William J. Hardee to William T. Sherman, February 9, 1866, Amnesty Papers, Alabama; Nathan B. Forrest to Andrew Johnson, July 1, 1865, Amnesty Papers, Tennessee; Elbert H. English to Andrew Johnson, June 14, 1865, and J. J. Reynolds to Andrew Johnson, August 4, 1865, Amnesty Papers, Arkansas.

5. Morris Emanuel to Andrew Johnson, September 8, 1865, Amnesty Papers, Mississippi; Samuel Tate to Andrew Johnson, May 24, 1865, Amnesty Papers, Tennessee; Petitioners to Andrew Johnson, June 30, 1865, Amnesty Papers, Alabama; William B. Johnston to Andrew Johnson, July 8, 1865, and Thomas Hardeman to Andrew Johnson, July 17, 1865, Amnesty Papers, Georgia.

6. Henry W. Hilliard to Andrew Johnson, July 1, 1865, Amnesty Papers, Georgia; Charles K. Marshall to Andrew Johnson, August 14, 1865, Amnesty Papers, Mississippi.

7. Robert M. Patton to Andrew Johnson, July 1, 1865, Amnesty Papers, Alabama; Harvey W. Walter to Andrew Johnson, August 12, 1865, Amnesty Papers, Mississippi; Benjamin C. Yancey to Andrew Johnson, August 2, 1865, Amnesty Papers, Georgia.

8. A recent analysis of the southern reaction to defeat proposes that many southerners offset a sense of shame with some comfort that they had behaved honorably in choosing to support the Confederacy (Beringer et al., *Why the South Lost*, 405–12).

9. Alexander, "Persistent Whiggery in the Confederate South," passim, and "The Dimensions of Continuity across the Civil War," 84–85; Carter, *When the War Was Over*, 65–68, 230; Michael Perman, *Reunion Without Compromise: The South and Reconstruction, 1865–1868*, 65, 342, and "The Whigs: Fulcrum of Faction and Party," in *The Road to Redemption: Southern Politics, 1869–1879*, 87–107.

10. Jeremiah W. Clapp to Andrew Johnson, July 26, 1865, Amnesty Papers, Mississippi; Clapp, *Address Delivered At The University of Mississippi*, 4–16. This speech includes many of the postwar themes traced by historian Gaines M. Foster in *Ghosts of the Confederacy: Defeat, the Lost Cause, and the Emergence of the New South, 1865 to 1913*, 22–29, 37–43.

11. Jeremiah W. Clapp to Andrew Johnson, September 11, 1866, Amnesty Papers, Mississippi.

12. The overview of southern politics as presented here is taken in large part from Perman, "The Politics of Convergence: Reconstruction, 1869–1873," in *Road to Redemption*, 3–107. The states of Missouri, Kentucky, Delaware, Maryland, West Virginia, and Tennessee were not subjected to congressional

Reconstruction, but they were part of the larger contest between Republicans and Democrats or Conservatives.

13. For information on sugar production, see Taylor, *Louisiana Reconstructed*, 316–19, 365–68; for descriptions of changes in the rice industry, see Simkins and Woody, *South Carolina During Reconstruction*, 236–61. The description of the three main systems that evolved in the cotton industry is taken from Woodman, "The Reconstruction of the Cotton Plantation in the New South," 114–16; Woodman, "Postbellum Social Change and Its Effects on Marketing the South's Cotton Crop," 225–30; Wiener, *Social Origins*, 66–73; Wiener, "Class Structure and Economic Development in the American South, 1865–1955," 975–76, 986; and Roark, *Masters Without Slaves*, 142–43.

14. Foner, *Reconstruction*, 166–75; Michael W. Fitzgerald, "'To Give Our Votes to the Party': Black Political Agitation and Agricultural Change in Alabama, 1865–1870," 501–5; Roark, *Masters Without Slaves*, 198–99; Wayne, *Reshaping of Plantation Society*, 125, 147.

15. Foner, *Reconstruction*, 372–74; Wiener, *Social Origins*, 67.

16. On cotton expansion, see Wright, *Political Economy*, 180–84; Fite, *Cotton Fields No More*, 6–7; Harris, *Presidential Reconstruction*, 227; Cook, "Restoration and Innovation," 112. On the new role of southern landowners, see Wright, *Old South, New South*, 49; Barbara Jeanne Fields, "The Advent of Capitalist Agriculture: The New South in a Bourgeois World," 81.

17. Harris, *Presidential Reconstruction*, 214–16; Charles Lewis Price, "Railroads and Reconstruction in North Carolina, 1865–1871," 356–57; Wallenstein, *From Slave South to New South*, 171; Carter, *When the War Was Over*, 124–25; Foner, *Reconstruction*, 211; Stover, *Railroads of the South*, 29; Cook, "Restoration and Innovation," 121–23.

18. Foner, *Reconstruction*, 379–81; William C. Harris, *The Day of the Carpetbagger: Republican Reconstruction in Mississippi*, 162–64, 541; Wiener, *Social Origins*, 148–52; Billings, *Planters and the "New South,"* 91–95; Mark W. Summers, *Railroads, Reconstruction, and the Gospel of Prosperity: Aid Under the Radical Republicans, 1865–1877*, 36, 48, 83–84; Wallenstein, *From Slave South to New South*, 181; Price, "Railroads and Reconstruction in North Carolina," 365–66; William E. Parrish, *Missouri Under Radical Rule, 1865–1870*, 198–202, 209; Pereyra, *James Lusk Alcorn*, 110–12; Alexander, *Reconstruction in Tennessee*, 168–70; Perman, *Road to Redemption*, 33–34, 44–45, 68–72.

19. Schweikart, *Banking in the South*, 309–11; Woodman, *King Cotton*, 250; Carter, *When the War Was Over*, 137–38, 99; Taylor, *Louisiana Reconstructed*, 347; Foner, *Reconstruction*, 381; Patrick J. Hearden, *Independence and Empire: The New South's Cotton Mill Campaign, 1865–1901*, 27–34; George Ruble Woolfolk, *The Cotton Regency: The Northern Merchants and Reconstruction, 1865–1880*, 46, 82.

20. *Minutes of the . . . Commercial Convention in Memphis, 1869*, 7–8, 48.

21. *Washington Chronicle*, October 15, 1869.

22. For similar findings of a shift into commercial and professional occupations after the war, see William B. Hesseltine, *Confederate Leaders in the New
South*, 21–22; Wakelyn, *Biographical Dictionary*, 50.
23. Data on 1870 estate valuations was obtained for too few individuals to
provide a basis from which to draw conclusions.
24. Wiener, *Social Origins*, 8, 22; Sarah Woolfolk Wiggins, *The Scalawag in
Alabama Politics, 1865–1881*, 130–31; Billings, *Planters and the "New South,"*
101; O'Brien, *Legal Fraternity*, 74–75; John J. Beck, "Building the New South:
A Revolution from Above in a Piedmont County," 452–53; Townes, "Effect of
Emancipation on Large Landholdings," 408–9; Catherine S. Silverman, "Of
Wealth, Virtue, and Intelligence: The Redeemers and Their Triumph in Virginia and North Carolina, 1865–1877," 42; Wayne, *Reshaping of Plantation
Society*, 86–99.
25. Foner, *Reconstruction*, 399–400; Woodman, "Sequel to Slavery,"
552–54; Wright, *Old South, New South*, 48–49.

Notes to Chapter Nine

1. *Memphis Appeal*, May 19, 1869. Clapp spoke at a later convention, held in
Memphis in November, 1875, in support of a southern Pacific railroad. See C.
Vann Woodward, *Reunion and Reaction: The Compromise of 1877 and the End of
Reconstruction*, 85.
2. *Memphis Appeal*, May 19, 1869. Hesseltine, in *Confederate Leaders*, 27–41,
concluded that Robert E. Lee, rather than Jefferson Davis, symbolized acceptance of the new order in the postwar South.
3. *Memphis Appeal*, May 22, 1869.
4. *Proceedings of the Commercial Convention Held in New Orleans*, 1869, 50,
66. The St. Louis delegate was A. W. Slayback.
5. Woodman, "Sequel to Slavery," 551. For a general discussion of the efforts
to attract immigrants, see Rowland T. Berthoff, "Southern Attitudes Toward
Immigration, 1865–1914," 328–33, 336–38, 342. For discussions of efforts in
individual states, see Robert F. Futrell, "Efforts of Mississippians to Encourage
Immigration, 1865–1880," 67–68, 73–74; Vernon Lane Wharton, *The Negro in
Mississippi, 1865–1890*, 101–4; Harris, *Day of the Carpetbagger*, 498–505; Simkins and Woody, *South Carolina During Reconstruction*, 243–47; Taylor, *Louisiana Reconstructed*, 388–92; Jack P. Maddex, Jr., *The Virginia Conservatives,
1867–1879: A Study in Reconstruction Politics*, 178–82; Parrish, *Missouri Under
Radical Rule*, 179–86. On southern efforts to import Chinese laborers, see
Cohen, *Chinese*, 49–101.
6. *Memphis Appeal*, May 22, 1869.
7. *Proceedings of the Commercial Convention Held in New Orleans*, 1869,
49–51.
8. Seip, *South Returns to Congress*, 267–68; Richard H. Abbott, *The

Republican Party and the South, 1855–1877: The First Southern Strategy, 227; Richard Franklin Bensel, *Yankee Leviathan: The Origins of Central State Authority in America, 1859–1877,* 300–301, 344–45. These findings challenge Woodward's suggestion in *Reunion and Reaction,* 55–67, that the South lagged two decades behind the West in pressing for federal aid to internal improvements, with the southern effort occurring after 1876, rather than during Reconstruction.

9. Woolfolk, *Cotton Regency,* 129–41, 194–95.

10. *New Orleans Picayune,* May 25, 1869; *New York Tribune,* May 25, 1869; *Washington Chronicle,* May 25, 1869; *Mobile Register,* May 25, 1869.

11. *Proceedings of the Commercial Convention Held in New Orleans, 1869,* 8–11. Parrish, in *Missouri Under Radical Rule,* 188–90, wrote of the way St. Louis civic leaders fought for revitalization of river traffic in the late 1860s as they realized that much of the western trade was bypassing the river and going by rail through Chicago.

12. *Proceedings of the Commercial Convention Held in New Orleans, 1869,* 12–13, 15–18, 19–20. For information on Walker, see Johnson and Malone, *Dictionary of American Biography,* 19:337.

13. *Louisville Courier-Journal,* October 13, 12, 1869. The convention was promoted by the paper, and its editor, Henry Watterson, was in charge of delegate seating.

14. *Louisville Courier-Journal,* October 12, 13, 1869. The *Cincinnati Enquirer,* October 13, 1869, noted that President Grant's telegram was "loudly applauded."

15. *Memphis Appeal,* May 22, 1869.

16. For a report of the floor debate, see *Louisville Courier-Journal,* October 16, 1869; for the report itself, see ibid., Supplement; Seip, *South Returns to Congress,* 147–84; Bensel, *Yankee Leviathan,* 289–95, 321–29. Bensel has argued that the net impact of the 1870 currency legislation was to release only a relatively small amount of new currency, four million dollars.

17. Coulter, in *South During Reconstruction,* 249, suggested that federal delays in clearing war-related obstructions from the eastern harbors might have been deliberate efforts to prevent direct trade with Europe. The conventions made no such accusation or insinuation. Coulter's work on Reconstruction was published in 1947, and his biased perspective on the process of Reconstruction led him to be suspicious of northern intentions toward the South.

18. *Memphis Appeal,* May 22, 1869. From 1867 to 1870, Alcorn served as president of the Mississippi state Liquidating Levee Board. His biographer believed that one of the reasons Alcorn was attracted to the Republican party was that he believed only the party in power could bring Mississippi the internal improvements it so desperately needed (Pereyra, *James Lusk Alcorn,* 75–77, 98). For an example of his effort to seek federal support for levee construction, see Alcorn, *Mississippi River Levees; Speech of the Hon. James L. Alcorn, of Mississippi, In the Senate of the United States, January 21, 1873.* Perhaps Erastus

Wells was remembering his time at the Memphis convention when he spoke in support of federal aid to internal improvements and opened his remarks with a reference to the demands of commercial bodies for such assistance (Wells, *Cheap Transportation of the Products of the West; Speech of Hon. Erastus Wells, of Missouri, in the House of Representatives, January 31, 1874*, 3).

19. *Proceedings of the Commercial Convention Held in New Orleans, 1869*, 86, 74, 57, 39–45, 60, 77–81. In the two years preceding the convention meeting, several companies had been chartered to dig a ship channel between the Mississippi and the Gulf, but their efforts had failed (Taylor, *Louisiana Reconstructed*, 187–89).

20. *Louisville Courier-Journal*, October 17, 1869.

21. For a brief overview of these transcontinental railroad projects, see Oscar Osburn Winther, *The Transportation Frontier: Trans-Mississippi West, 1865–1890*, 99–103, and Stover, *American Railroads*, 67–82. For a more detailed discussion of the Atlantic and Pacific Railroad, see H. Craig Miner, *The St. Louis–San Francisco Transcontinental Railroad: The Thirty-fifth Parallel Project, 1853–1890*, 17–58.

22. *Memphis Appeal*, May 21, 1869. This convention resolution would have supported the efforts of two Texas railroads, the Southern Pacific Railroad and the Memphis, El Paso and Pacific. For information on the Southern Pacific Railroad operating in Texas, see Means, "East Texas and the Transcontinental Railroad," 52–56. For information about the Memphis, El Paso and Pacific Railroad, see Woodward, *Reunion and Reaction*, 70–73.

23. *Proceedings of the Commercial Convention Held in New Orleans, 1869*, 49–51, 59–70, 89. The Texas delegation supported a second line, which later became the International and Great Northern Railroad after it merged with the Houston and Great Northern. See S. G. Reed, *History of Texas Railroads*, 150–51. Forshey was a civil engineer later hired by the New Orleans Chamber of Commerce to testify in opposition to James B. Eads's plan to build jetties at the mouth of the Mississippi River (Caleb Goldsmith Forshey, *Fort St. Philip Canal and Jetties at the Mouths of the Mississippi River; Remarks before the Senate Committee on Transportation and the House Committee on Railroads and Canals*).

24. See *Louisville Courier-Journal*, October 16, 1869, for the debate; ibid., Supplement, for the reports; *Washington Chronicle*, October 19, 1869.

25. Woodward, *Reunion and Reaction*, 70–73.

26. *Memphis Appeal*, May 22, 1869; *Louisville Courier-Journal*, October 16, 1869, Supplement.

27. *Louisville Courier-Journal*, October 15, 1869; ibid., October 16, 1869, Supplement.

28. *Proceedings of the Commercial Convention Held in New Orleans, 1869*, 24–26, 42–44, 74–76; *Louisville Courier-Journal*, October 16, 1869. The *Cincinnati Enquirer*, October 18, 1869, took special note of the levee report, as it reminded its readers what an important consumer market those producers along the river were.

29. *Memphis Appeal,* May 22, 1869; *Proceedings of the Commercial Convention Held in New Orleans, 1869,* 81–85; *Louisville Courier-Journal,* October 16, 1869, Supplement.

30. *Memphis Appeal,* May 22, 1869. For more on Maury's report, see Thomas, "Matthew Fontaine Maury," 223–25. For the debate about membership on the Immigration Committee, see *Memphis Appeal,* May 20, 1869. The controversial debate was not reported in the official proceedings.

31. *Memphis Appeal,* May 22, 21, 1869.

32. *Memphis Appeal,* May 25, 1869. As a member of the Constitutional Union movement in Mississippi, Yerger had vigorously opposed black suffrage (Harris, *Presidential Reconstruction,* 243).

33. See *Proceedings of the Commercial Convention Held in New Orleans, 1869,* 71–72, for the report; see *New Orleans Picayune,* May 28, 29, 1869, for the report and the discussions.

34. *Louisville Courier-Journal,* October 16, 1869, Supplement.

35. *Louisville Courier-Journal,* October 15, 1869. The *Cincinnati Enquirer,* October 15, 1869, noted the use of the word *importation* in reference to Oriental laborers, and the *Chicago Tribune,* October 16, 1869, carried an editorial condemning the convention for its racist immigration report.

36. *Louisville Courier-Journal,* October 17–18, 1869. For a brief discussion of the Chinese immigration debate at the commercial conventions of 1869, see Cohen, *Chinese,* 63, 72.

37. *Memphis Appeal,* May 11, 21–23, 1869; *New Orleans Picayune,* May 30, 1869; *Louisville Courier-Journal,* October 17–18, 1869.

38. *Louisville Courier-Journal,* May 9–10, 1869; *Richmond Enquirer and Examiner,* May 22, 1869; *Atlanta Constitution,* May 22 and October 26, 1869; *Charleston Courier,* May 22, 1869; *New Orleans Picayune,* October 19, 1869. For other southern newspaper coverage of the conventions, see *Louisville Courier-Journal,* May 15, 19–22, 29, 30–31, 1869; *Richmond Enquirer and Examiner,* May 18–22, 24, 27, 30, 1869; *Atlanta Constitution,* May 21–22, 25, 28–29, June 1, and October 11, 14–16, 19, 21–22, 1869; *Charleston Courier,* May 22, 24–25, 28–29, and October 12–13, 15, 1869; *Mobile Register,* May 25–28, and October 13, 16, 1869; *Missouri Democrat,* May 18–22, 24–25, 27–29, June 1, and October 11–14, 18, 1869; *Memphis Appeal,* May 20, 25, 27, and October 13–17, 1869.

39. *New York Times,* May 24, 29, and October 4, 1869; extended coverage also ran in issues of May 20–22, 25–27, September 4, and October 9, 12–15, 1869. *New York Tribune,* May 1, 24, 1869; for additional coverage, see May 20–22, 25, 27–29, and October 15, 18, 1869; "The Louisville Convention," *New York Commercial and Financial Chronicle,* October 23, 1869, 519–21.

40. *Washington Chronicle,* October 14, 1869; for more coverage, see ibid., May 20–22, 25, 28, 1869; *Washington National Intelligencer,* May 18, 20, 28–29, and October 12–13, 15, 18, 1869; *Boston Evening Transcript,* May 22, 1869; *Boston Post,* May 17–18, 20, 22, 25, 27, 29, and October 14–15, 18, 1869; *Pitts-*

burgh Commercial, May 19–22, 25, 27, 1869; *Cincinnati Commercial,* May 18–22, 25, 28, 1869; *Cincinnati Enquirer,* October 11, 1869; *Chicago Tribune,* May 20, 1869; for other coverage, see ibid., May 21, 22, 24–25, 27, 28, 1869. Peter Kolchin, "The Business Press and Reconstruction, 1865–1868," 187–88.

41. *Cincinnati Enquirer,* October 14, 16, 1869; *Pittsburgh Commercial,* October 14, 1869; *Cincinnati Commercial,* October 13, 1869; *Chicago Tribune,* October 14, 1869.

42. At each annual meeting there was a report from the Executive Council summarizing the annual meeting of the previous year as well as results of lobbying efforts during the time between annual meetings. For summaries of the proposals discussed at the first four meetings, see *Proceedings of the First Annual Meeting of the National Board of Trade, Held in Cincinnati, December, 1868,* 4–7; *Proceedings of the Second Annual Meeting of the National Board of Trade, Held in Richmond, December, 1869,* 2–9; *Third Annual Meeting of the National Board of Trade, Buffalo, 1870,* 6–13; *Proceedings of the Fourth Annual Meeting of the National Board of Trade, Held in St. Louis, December, 1871,* 1–25. The membership lists were taken from these same reports.

43. *Second Annual Meeting National Board of Trade, Richmond, 1869,* 5–6; Hamilton Andrews Hill, *Commercial Conventions and the National Board of Trade, An Address, Chicago, April 28, 1885,* 22.

44. *Memphis Appeal,* May 21–22, 1869; *Louisville Courier-Journal,* October 16, 17–18, and November 4, 1869; *New York Times,* November 4, 1869. For more information about the federal tax, see Carter, *When the War Was Over,* 98–99.

45. "Commercial Conventions," [Appleton's] *Annual Cyclopaedia of the Year 1869,* 118.

Notes to Chapter Ten

1. A detailed discussion of the rivalry between the Louisville faction and the Cincinnati Southern Railroad promoters is found in Curry, *Rail Routes South,* 65–102; a more condensed discussion is in Stover, *Railroads of the South,* 212–14.

2. *Proceedings of the . . . Commercial Convention at Cincinnati, 1870,* 6–9. The convention proceedings were reported by the local press, but not in as much detail. See *Cincinnati Enquirer,* October 4–8, 1870. For information on Pendleton's role in the national Democratic party, see Edward L. Gambill, *Conservative Ordeal: Northern Democrats and Reconstruction, 1865–1868,* 98, 123–42.

3. *Proceedings of the . . . Commercial Convention at Cincinnati, 1870,* 11–21, 30–36.

4. Ibid., 23–25. The *Richmond Dispatch,* October 8, 1870, took editorial note of how Garrett's praise for Lee had drawn cheers from the audience. For information on the Baltimore and Ohio Railroad and the Valley Railroad of Virginia,

see Stover, *Railroads of the South*, 65–66. Lee died eight days after Garrett's speech.

5. *Proceedings of the . . . Commercial Convention at Cincinnati, 1870*, 87–96, 101–8, 63–65, 108–14.

6. Ibid., 53–63. The other states that voted against the report were Michigan and New York, along with a minority from the Tennessee delegation. According to Bensel, *Yankee Leviathan*, 344, the 1870 appropriations earmarked just 5 percent of total expenditures for the South, and most of that was to fund improvements at the mouth of the Mississippi River.

7. *Proceedings of the . . . Commercial Convention at Cincinnati, 1870*, 79–83, 74–75.

8. Ibid., 50–52.

9. Ibid., 52–53, 100, 117–18. For more information about the progress of the Southern Pacific bill in Congress, see Seip, *South Returns to Congress*, 239–43, and Summers, *Railroads, Reconstruction, and Prosperity*, 168–72. For more on Tom Scott, see Woodward, *Reunion and Reaction*, 70–73.

10. *Proceedings of the . . . Commercial Convention at Cincinnati, 1870*, 75–77, 124; *Cincinnati Enquirer*, October 4, 1870. An Alabama delegate later remarked that Kentucky was foolish not to assist the Cincinnati Southern as the trade demand was strong (*Speech of Col. William J. Sykes at Elyton, Alabama, March 6th, 1871*, 2–4).

11. *Proceedings of the . . . Commercial Convention at Cincinnati, 1870*, 119–22, 69, 115–16. Another vote supported the efforts of the Atlantic and Pacific Railroad (ibid., 72). For more on Fisk's role with the Atlantic and Pacific, see Miner, *St. Louis-San Francisco Transcontinental Railroad*, 58–72.

12. *Proceedings of the . . . Commercial Convention at Cincinnati, 1870*, 67–68. On the Currency Act, see Seip, *South Returns to Congress*, 183–84.

13. *Proceedings of the . . . Commercial Convention at Cincinnati, 1870*, 49, 47, 73–74. Woodward, in *Reunion and Reaction*, 53–54, argued that southern businessmen generally opposed restrictions against speculation, as they wanted to attract northern investment to the region. In Mississippi, restrictions were not effective, and served only as a paper barrier to speculation in the timberlands (Harris, *Day of the Carpetbagger*, 523).

14. *Proceedings of the . . . Commercial Convention at Cincinnati, 1870*, 25, 59, 88–89, 112–13.

15. Ibid., 25.

16. Ibid., 96–97. For a discussion of Grant's conversion to support general amnesty by the close of 1871, see Abbott, *Republican Party and the South*, 215–17.

17. *Proceedings of the . . . Commercial Convention at Cincinnati, 1870*, 123, 127.

18. Ibid., 28, 118. *Louisville Courier-Journal*, October 5–8, 1870; *Richmond Dispatch*, October 6–8, 10, 1870; *Atlanta Constitution*, October 6–9, 1870; *Charleston Courier*, October 7–8, 10, 12, 1870; *New Orleans Picayune*, October

5–8, 1870; *Mobile Register,* October 5, 7–8, 12, 1870; *Missouri Democrat,* October 4, 7–8, 1870; *Baltimore Sun,* October 5, 7–8, 1870; *New York Times,* October 5–7, 1870; *New York Tribune,* October 6–7, 1870; *Washington Chronicle,* October 6–9, 1870; *Boston Evening Transcript,* October 5, 1870; *Boston Post,* October 6–8, 1870; *Pittsburgh Commercial,* October 5–8, 1870; *Chicago Tribune,* October 5, 8, 1870.

19. *Baltimore Sun,* September 26, 1871. The newspaper reports have more detail than the official report.

20. Ibid.

21. Ibid., September 27, 1871.

22. Ibid. For information about the Klan problem, see Simkins and Woody, *South Carolina During Reconstruction,* 462–63; Perman, *Road to Redemption,* 34–35.

23. *Baltimore Sun,* September 29–30, 1871.

24. Ibid., September 30, 1871.

25. Ibid. On fiscal policy among liberal Republicans, see Foner, *Reconstruction,* 489.

26. *Baltimore Sun,* September 29–30, 1871. Efforts to seek refund of the Cotton Tax were defeated by northern Republicans in 1873. Abbott, *Republican Party and the South,* 224.

27. *Richmond Enquirer and Examiner,* September 27–30, and October 2, 1871; *Charleston Courier,* September 26–30, and October 2, 1871; *Memphis Appeal,* September 26–28, 30, 1871; *Atlanta Constitution,* September 26, 28–30, 1871; *New Orleans Picayune,* September 26–29, 1871; *Mobile Register,* September 27, 29–30, 1871; *Louisville Courier-Journal,* September 26–27, 29–30, 1871; *Missouri Democrat,* September 27, 29–30, 1871; *New York Times,* September 26–27, 29, 1871; *New York Tribune,* September 26–27, 1871; *Washington Chronicle,* September 27–28, 1871; *Boston Evening Transcript,* September 26, 28, 1871; *Boston Post,* September 26–27, 29, 1871; *Pittsburgh Commercial,* September 27–29, 1871; *Cincinnati Enquirer,* September 19, 26–28, 30, 1871; *Chicago Tribune,* September 26, 28–30, and October 2, 1871.

28. *Baltimore Sun,* September 30, 1871.

29. Ibid., December 20, 1852.

30. *Commercial Convention at St. Louis, 1872,* passim; *Missouri Democrat,* December 12–14, 1872.

31. *Louisville Courier-Journal,* December 13–14, 1872; *Atlanta Constitution,* December 10–11, 14, 1872; *Baltimore Sun,* December 12–14, 1872; *New York Times,* December 14, 1872; *Washington Chronicle,* December 13–14, 1872; *Pittsburgh Commercial,* December 12–14, 1872; *Cincinnati Commercial,* December 12–13, 1872; *Chicago Tribune,* December 12–14, 1872.

32. This assessment of the impact of the 1872 election is drawn from the following sources: Earle Dudley Ross, *The Liberal Republican Movement,* 150–92; Perman, "The Climax of Convergence: The Election of 1872," in *Road to Redemption,* 108–31; Foner, *Reconstruction,* 499–511.

33. Abbott, *Republican Party and the South*, 223–24; Seip, *South Returns to Congress*, 220–27, 266–68; Foner, *Reconstruction*, 379–84, 390–92; Summers, *Railroads, Reconstruction, and Prosperity*, 209, 249–50; Thornton, "Fiscal Policy and the Failure of Radical Reconstruction in the Lower South," 351, 378, 382–83. For descriptions of economic policy failures in various states, see George H. Thompson, *Arkansas and Reconstruction: The Influence of Geography, Economics, and Personality*, 5, 232–35; Alexander, *Reconstruction in Tennessee*, 241; Escott, *Many Excellent People*, 161–62; Harris, *Day of the Carpetbagger*, 296–98, 372–75; Taylor, *Louisiana Reconstructed*, 187–201; Maddex, *Virginia Conservatives*, 276–82; Wallenstein, *From Slave South to New South*, 176–81.

Notes to Conclusion

1. *Chicago Tribune*, October 14, 1869.
2. *Mobile Register*, May 28, 1869.
3. For another view of how the Civil War was less a dividing line in American politics than has been supposed, see Joel H. Silbey, "Conclusion," 130–31.
4. Occupations in both historical time periods could be determined for 249 delegates, 160 of whom were members of the Convention Elite. The same general percentages of occupation persistence and change applied equally to Elite and non-Elite. Among antebellum lawyers, 76 percent remained lawyers after the war, 13 percent became commercialists, and only 5 percent became farmers. Among antebellum commercialists, 79 percent were in the same occupation after the war, 10 percent became lawyers, and only 8 percent became farmers. Among those who had combined farming with either law or commerce or both prior to the war, 27 percent continued to do so after the war, 43 percent became lawyers, 19 percent went into commerce, and only 8 percent went exclusively into farming. While 67 percent of those exclusively engaged in agriculture in the antebellum period remained so after the war, 17 percent became commercialists, 11 percent professionals, and 5 percent lawyers. Admittedly, this information undercounts instances of involvement in mixed enterprise, as it is more likely that only the predominant occupations would have been recorded in the historical record sources.
5. Paul M. Gaston, *The New South Creed: A Study in Southern Mythmaking*, 63–71.
6. Victorianism among southerners has been discussed in Ford, *Origins of Southern Radicalism*, 233; Richard D. Brown, "Modernization: A Victorian Climax," 545–48; Daniel Walker Howe, "American Victorianism as a Culture," 519–26. Laurence Shore, in *Southern Capitalists*, 110–12, 170–75, also found that many southern leaders who espoused a pragmatic conservatism after the war did so without denigrating the past. By contrast, Wiener, in *Social Origins*,

186–89, found that proponents of the New South made a conscious effort to provoke disdain for the old order.

7. Wiener, *Social Origins*, 137–56, and "Class Structure and Economic Development," 986; Lewis Nicholas Wynne, *The Continuity of Cotton: Planter Politics in Georgia, 1865–1892*, 66, 101; Billings, *Planters and the "New South,"* 77, 101–9; Shore, *Southern Capitalists*, 109.

8. Woodward, *Thinking Back*, 94.

BIBLIOGRAPHY

Primary Sources

Manuscript Sources

Manuscript Division, Library of Congress, Washington, D.C.: The Papers of the Blair Family

North Carolina Department of Archives and History, Raleigh, North Carolina: Pettigrew Family Papers.

William R. Perkins Library, Duke University, Durham, North Carolina: John C. Breckinridge Papers, Campbell Family Papers, Jefferson Davis Papers, James Dunwoody Brownson De Bow Papers, David Flavel Jamison Papers, James Lyons Papers, Matthew Fontaine Maury Papers, Benjamin Cudworth Yancey Papers.

Southern Historical Collection, University of North Carolina Library, Chapel Hill, North Carolina: James Lusk Alcorn Papers, Richard Dennis Arnold Papers, Arnold and Screven Family Papers, David Franklin Caldwell Papers, John Francis Hamtramck Claiborne Papers, Clingman and Puryear Family Papers, De Rosset Family Papers, Platt K. Dickinson Letters, Simpson Fouché Papers, Duff Green Papers, Thomas Jefferson Green Papers, Mitchell King Papers, Alexander Robert Lawton Papers, Edward McCrady L'Engle Papers, Maury Family Papers, Christopher Gustavus Memminger Papers, William Porcher Miles Papers, Nisbet Family Papers, Orr and Patterson Family Papers, James Hervey Otey Papers, John Perkins Papers, Benjamin Franklin Perry Papers, Leonidus Polk Papers, Polk and Yeatman Family Papers, Quitman Family Papers, Edmund Ruffin Papers, Nelson Tift Diary, Tench Tilghman Diary, Maunsell White Papers, Benjamin Cudworth Yancey Papers.

Government Documents

Amnesty Papers. Records of the Adjutant General's Office. Record Group 94. Microfilm. National Archives.

Bureau of the Census. Seventh Census of the United States, 1850. Population Schedules. Microfilm of National Archives manuscript copies. St. Louis Public Library.

Bureau of the Census. Eighth Census of the United States, 1860. Population Schedules. Microfilm of National Archives manuscript copies. St. Louis Public Library.

Newspapers and Periodicals

American Railroad Journal
Atlanta Constitution
Baltimore American
Baltimore Sun
Boston Evening-Transcript
Boston Post
Charleston Courier
Charleston Mercury
Chicago Tribune
Cincinnati Commercial
Cincinnati Enquirer
Columbus Enquirer
De Bow's Review
Jackson Mississippian
Brownlow's *Knoxville Whig*
Louisville Courier-Journal
Lynchburg Virginian
Memphis Appeal
Mobile Register
Nashville Republican Banner
Natchez Courier
Natchez Mississippi Free Trader
New Orleans Picayune
New York Times
New York Tribune
Pittsburgh Commercial

Raleigh Register
Richmond Dispatch
Richmond Enquirer and Examiner
Richmond Whig and Public Advertiser
St. Louis Missouri Democrat
Savannah Morning News
Washington Chronicle
Washington Evening Star
Washington National Intelligencer

Commercial Convention Proceedings

Baltimore

Baltimore Southern and Western Commercial Convention, Held in Baltimore, December 18th, 1852, Under the Auspices of the Board of Trade. Baltimore, 1852. Baker Library, Harvard University.
"The Baltimore Southern Commercial Convention." *De Bow's Review* 14 (April 1853): 373–79.
Proceedings of the National Commercial Convention Held at Baltimore, September 25–29, 1871. Baltimore, 1871. Library of Congress.

Charleston

"The Great Southern Convention in Charleston." *De Bow's Review* 16 (June 1854): 632–41.
"The Great Southern Convention in Charleston." *De Bow's Review* 17 (July–November 1854): 91–99, 200–213, 250–61, 325–26, 398–410, 491–510.
Journal of Proceedings of the Commercial Convention of the Southern and Western States, Held In the City of Charleston, South-Carolina, During the Week Commencing on Monday, 10th April, 1854. Charleston, 1854. Library of Congress.

Cincinnati

Proceedings of the Southern Commercial Convention at its Annual Session at Cincinnati Ohio, October 1870. Cincinnati, 1871. Chicago University.

Knoxville

Official Report of the Debates and Proceedings of the Southern Commercial Convention, Assembled At Knoxville, Tennessee, August 9th, 1857. Knoxville, 1857. Tennessee State Library and Archives.
De Bow, James Dunwoody Brownson. "The Rights, Duties, and Remedies of the South." De Bow's Review 23 (September 1857): 235.
"The Southern Convention at Knoxville." De Bow's Review 23 (September 1857): 298–321.

Memphis

"Convention of Southern and Western States." Commercial Review of the South and West [De Bow's Review] 1 (January 1846): 7–21.
Journal of the Proceedings of the South-Western Convention, Began and Held At the City of Memphis, On the 12th November, 1845. Memphis, 1845. State Historical Society of Missouri.
"The Memphis Convention." De Bow's Review 15 (September 1853): 254–74.
Proceedings of the Southern and Western Commercial Convention, At Memphis, Tennessee, In June, 1853. Memphis, 1854. The Library Company of Philadelphia.
Minutes of the Proceedings of the Commercial Convention Held in the City of Memphis, Tennessee, May 1869. Memphis, 1869. St. Louis Mercantile Library.

Montgomery

"Late Southern Convention at Montgomery." De Bow's Review 24 (June 1858): 574–606.
"Southern Convention at Montgomery, Alabama." De Bow's Review 24 (May 1858): 424–28.

New Orleans

De Bow, James Dunwoody Brownson. "Importance of an Industrial Revolution in the South." De Bow's Review 12 (May 1852): 554–62.
Proceedings of the South-Western Rail Road Convention Held in New Orleans in January, 1852. New Orleans, 1852. Historic New Orleans Collection.
"Southern and Western Rail-Road Convention." De Bow's Review 12 (March 1852): 305–18.

Proceedings of the Southern Commercial Convention Held in the City of New Orleans. New Orleans, 1855. Special Collections Division, Tulane University Library.
"Southern Commercial Convention at New Orleans." *De Bow's Review* 18 (March–June 1855): 353–60, 520–28, 623–35, 749–60.
"An Abstract of the Most Important Documents Published by the New Orleans Commercial Convention, May 1869." *De Bow's Review,* After the War Series 7 (August 1869): 688–95.
Proceedings of the Commercial Convention Held in New Orleans, May 24th, 26th, 27th, and 28th, 1869. New Orleans, 1869. LSU Special Collections, Hill Memorial Library, Louisiana State University.

Richmond

"Southern Convention at Richmond." *De Bow's Review* 20 (March 1856): 340–54.

St. Louis

Proceedings of the National Commercial Convention Held At St. Louis, December 11th, 12th and 13th, 1872. St. Louis, 1873. St. Louis Mercantile Library.

Savannah

"Southern Convention at Savannah, Georgia." *De Bow's Review* 21 (November 1856): 550–53.
"Southern Convention at Savannah." *De Bow's Review* 22 (January–March 1857): 81–105, 216–24, 307–18.

Vicksburg

"Editorial Miscellany." *De Bow's Review* 26 (June 1859): 713.
"The Late Southern Convention." *De Bow's Review* 27 (July 1859): 94–103.
"Recent Southern Convention at Vicksburg." *De Bow's Review* 27 (September 1859): 360–65.
"Southern Convention at Vicksburg." *De Bow's Review* 27 (August, October 1859): 205–20, 468–71.

Published Letters, Speeches, Pamphlets, and Miscellaneous Documents

Alcorn, James Lusk. *Mississippi River Levees; Speech of the Hon. James L. Alcorn, of Mississippi, In The Senate of the United States, January 21, 1873.* Washington, D.C., 1873.

Anderson, Charles. "The Cause of the War: Who Brought It On, and For What Purpose?" *Loyal Publication Society, No. 17.* New York, 1863.

Bell, John. *Protection to American Industry. Views of Hon. John Bell.* Washington, D.C., 1858.

Boucher, Chauncey Samuel, and Robert P. Brooks, eds. *Correspondence Addressed to John C. Calhoun, 1837–1849. Annual Report of the American Historical Association for the Year 1929.* Washington, D.C.: Government Printing Office, 1930.

"The Chicago and Memphis Conventions." *Commercial Review of the South and West [De Bow's Review]* 4 (September 1847): 122–27.

"Chicago Internal Improvements Convention, 1847." *Industrial Resources, etc., of the Southern and Western States* 1 (1852): 254–56.

Clapp, Jeremiah W. *Address Delivered At The University of Mississippi, on Behalf of the Board of Trustees, on Commencement Day, June 29, 1866, by Hon. J. W. Clapp, A Member of the Board.* Memphis, 1866.

"Commercial Conventions." *[Appleton's] Annual American Cyclopaedia and Register of Important Events of the Year 1869.* New York, 1870.

"Commercial Independence of the South." *De Bow's Review* 13 (November 1852): 477–93.

De Bow, James Dunwoody Brownson. "Address to the People of the Southern and Western States." *Industrial Resources, etc., of the Southern and Western States* 2 (1852): 434–56.

———. "Cause of the South." *De Bow's Review* 10 (January 1851): 106–11.

———. "Direct Trade of Southern States with Europe." *Commercial Review of the South and West [De Bow's Review]* 4 (October 1847): 208–25.

Filley, Chauncey I. *Some More Republican History of Missouri.* St. Louis, 1902.

First Annual Report to the Board of Directors of the Southern Pacific Railroad Company Chartered by the State of Texas. New York, 1856. St. Louis Mercantile Library.

Forshey, Caleb Goldsmith. *Fort St. Philip Canal and Jetties at the Mouths of the Mississippi River; Remarks before the Senate Committee on Transportation and the House Committee on Railroads and Canals.* Washington, D.C., 1874.

Graf, Leroy P., and Ralph W. Haskins, eds. *The Papers of Andrew Johnson.* Vol. 1,

1822–1851. Vol. 2, *1852–1857*. Knoxville: University of Tennessee Press, 1967–1970.

Helper, Hinton Rowan. *The Impending Crisis of the South: How To Meet It*. Edited by George M. Fredrickson. Cambridge: Harvard University Press, 1968.

Hill, Hamilton Andrews. *Commercial Conventions and the National Board of Trade, An Address, Chicago, April 28, 1885*. Boston, 1885.

Hilliard, Henry Washington. *Politics and Pen Pictures: At Home and Abroad*. New York, 1892.

Hughes, Henry. *A Report on the African Apprentice System, Read at the Southern Commercial Convention* [1859]. N.p., n.d. Mississippi Department of Archives and History.

Jamison, David F. *Annual Address Before the State Agricultural Society of South Carolina; Proceedings of the State Agricultural Society*. N.p., 1856.

Kennedy, Joseph C. G., comp. *Agriculture of the United States in 1860*. Washington, D.C., 1864.

Patton, Robert M. "The New Era of Southern Manufactures." *De Bow's Review*, After the War Series 3 (July–August 1867): 56–68.

"Pioneers of the Southwest: Maunsel [sic] White of Louisiana." *De Bow's Review* 25 (October 1858): 480–82.

Proceedings of the First Annual Meeting of the National Board of Trade, Held in Cincinnati, December, 1868. Boston, 1869.

Proceedings of the Fourth Annual Meeting of the National Board of Trade, Held in St. Louis, December, 1871. Boston, 1872.

Proceedings of the Second Annual Meeting of the National Board of Trade, Held in Richmond, December, 1869. Boston, 1870.

Proceedings of the Third Annual Meeting of the National Board of Trade, Held in Buffalo, December, 1870. Boston, 1871.

Robb, James. *Internal Improvements; a Series of Letters by James Robb, esq. Addressed to Gov. Robert C. Wickliffe and dated February 1 to 12, 1856*. New Orleans, 1856.

Scarborough, William Kauffman, ed. *The Diary of Edmund Ruffin*. Vol. 1, *Toward Independence, October 1856–April 1861*. Baton Rouge: Louisiana State University Press, 1972.

"Southern Commercial Convention [Richmond]." *Hunt's Merchants' Magazine* 34 (March 1856): 392–93.

"Southern Commercial Conventions." *Industrial Resources, etc., of the Southern and Western States* 3 (1852): 92–117.

Statistics of the United States in 1860. Washington, D.C., 1866.

Sykes, William J. *Speech of Col. William J. Sykes at Elyton, Alabama, March 6th,*

1871. Decatur, Ala., 1871. Pamphlet in the Library of Congress Rare Book Room.

The Texas Almanac for 1858. Galveston, 1857.

The Texas Almanac for 1859. Galveston, 1858.

The Texas Almanac for 1860. Galveston, 1859.

Wells, Erastus. *Cheap Transportation of the Products of the West; Speech of Hon. Erastus Wells, of Missouri, in the House of Representatives, January 31, 1874.* Washington, D.C., 1874.

Secondary Sources

Abbott, Richard H. *The Republican Party and the South, 1855–1877: The First Southern Strategy.* Chapel Hill: University of North Carolina Press, 1986.

Alexander, Thomas B. "The Dimensions of Continuity across the Civil War." In *The Old South in the Crucible of War,* edited by Harry P. Owens and James J. Cooke, 81–97. Jackson: University Press of Mississippi, 1983.

———. "Persistent Whiggery in the Confederate South, 1860–1877." *Journal of Southern History* 27 (August 1961): 305–29.

———. *Political Reconstruction in Tennessee.* Nashville: Vanderbilt University Press, 1950.

———. *Sectional Stress and Party Strength: A Study of Roll-Call Voting Patterns in the United States House of Representatives, 1836–1860.* Nashville: Vanderbilt University Press, 1967.

Alexander, Thomas B., and Richard E. Beringer. *The Anatomy of the Confederate Congress: A Study of the Influences of Member Characteristics on Legislative Voting Behavior, 1861–1865.* Nashville: Vanderbilt University Press, 1972.

Allsopp, Frederick W. *The Life Story of Albert Pike.* Little Rock: Parke-Harper News Service, 1920.

Bachrach, Peter. *Political Elites in a Democracy.* New York: Atherton Press, 1971.

———. *The Theory of Democratic Elitism: A Critique.* Boston: Little, Brown and Co., 1967.

Baggett, James Alexander. "Origins of Upper South Scalawag Leadership." *Civil War History* 29 (March 1983): 53–73.

Barney, William L. *The Secessionist Impulse: Alabama and Mississippi in 1860.* Princeton: Princeton University Press, 1974.

Bateman, Fred, and Thomas Weiss. *A Deplorable Scarcity: The Failure of Industrialization in the Slave Economy.* Chapel Hill: University of North Carolina Press, 1981.

Bateman, Fred, James Foust, and Thomas Weiss. "The Participation of Planters in Manufacturing in the Antebellum South." *Agricultural History* 47 (April 1974): 277–97.

Beck, John J. "Building the New South: A Revolution from Above in a Piedmont County." *Journal of Southern History* 53 (August 1987): 441–70.

Bensel, Richard Franklin. *Yankee Leviathan: The Origins of Central State Authority in America, 1859–1877.* Cambridge: Cambridge University Press, 1990.

Beringer, Richard E., Herman Hattaway, Archer Jones, and William N. Still, Jr. *Why the South Lost the Civil War.* Athens: University of Georgia Press, 1986.

Berlin, Ira, and Herbert G. Gutman. "Natives and Immigrants, Free Men and Slaves: Urban Workingmen in the Antebellum American South." *American Historical Review* 88 (December 1983): 1175–1200.

Berthoff, Rowland T. "Southern Attitudes Toward Immigration, 1865–1914." *Journal of Southern History* 17 (August 1951): 328–50.

Billings, Dwight B., Jr. *Planters and the Making of a "New South": Class, Politics, and Development in North Carolina, 1865–1900.* Chapel Hill: University of North Carolina Press, 1979.

Biographical Directory of the American Congress, 1774–1971. Washington, D.C.: Government Printing Office, 1971.

Blake, Nelson Morehouse. *William Mahone of Virginia: Soldier and Political Insurgent.* Richmond: Garrett & Massie, 1935.

Bogue, Allan G. "Some Dimensions of Power in the Thirty-Seventh Senate." In *Dimensions of Quantitative Research in History,* edited by William O. Aydelotte, Allan G. Bogue, and Robert William Fogel, 285–318. Princeton: Princeton University Press, 1972.

Brown, Richard D. "Modernization: A Victorian Climax." *American Quarterly* 27 (December 1975): 533–48.

Burnham, W. Dean. *Presidential Ballots, 1836–1892.* Baltimore: The Johns Hopkins Press, 1955.

Campbell, Randolph B. "Planters and Plain Folk: Harrison County, Texas, as a Test Case, 1850–1860." *Journal of Southern History* 40 (August 1974): 369–98.

———. "Population Persistence and Social Change in Nineteenth-Century Texas: Harrison County, 1850–1880." *Journal of Southern History* 48 (May 1982): 185–204.

Carter, Dan T. *When the War Was Over: The Failure of Self-Reconstruction in the South, 1865–1867.* Baton Rouge: Louisiana State University Press, 1985.

Cash, Wilbur J. *The Mind of the South.* New York: Alfred A. Knopf, 1941.

Caskie, Jaquelin Ambler. *Life and Letters of M. F. Maury.* Richmond: Richmond Press, 1928.

Chandler, Alfred D., Jr., ed. and comp. *The Railroads: The Nation's First Big Business. Sources and Readings.* The Forces in American Economic Growth Series, edited by Alfred D. Chandler, Jr. New York: Harcourt, Brace & World, 1965.

Cobb, James Charles. "Beyond Planters and Industrialists: A New Perspective on the New South." *Journal of Southern History* 54 (February 1988): 45–68.

Cohen, Lucy M. *Chinese in the Post–Civil War South: A People Without a History.* Baton Rouge: Louisiana State University Press, 1984.

Collins, Bruce W. "Governor Joseph E. Brown, Economic Issues, and Georgia's Road to Secession, 1857–1859." *Georgia Historical Quarterly* 71 (Summer 1987): 189–225.

Cook, Marjorie Howell. "Restoration and Innovation: Alabamians Adjust to Defeat, 1865–1867." Ph.D. diss., University of Alabama, 1968.

Cooper, William J., Jr. *The South and the Politics of Slavery, 1828–1856.* Baton Rouge: Louisiana State University Press, 1978.

Coulter, E. Merton. *The South During Reconstruction, 1865–1877.* Baton Rouge: Louisiana State University Press, 1947.

Craven, Avery O. *The Growth of Southern Nationalism, 1848–1861.* Baton Rouge: Louisiana State University Press, 1953.

Current, Richard N. *Northernizing the South.* Mercer University Lamar Memorial Lectures, no. 26. Athens: University of Georgia Press, 1983.

Curry, Leonard P. *Rail Routes South: Louisville's Fight for the Southern Market, 1865–1872.* Lexington: University of Kentucky Press, 1969.

————. "Urbanization and Urbanism in the Old South: A Comparative View." *Journal of Southern History* 40 (February 1974): 43–60.

Dahl, Robert A. "A Critique of the Ruling Elite Model." *American Political Science Review* 52 (June 1958): 463–69.

————. *Who Governs?* New Haven: Yale University Press, 1961.

Davis, William W. "Ante-Bellum Southern Commercial Conventions." *Alabama Historical Society Transactions* 5 (1904): 153–202.

Degler, Carl N. *Place Over Time: The Continuity of Southern Distinctiveness.* Baton Rouge: Louisiana State University Press, 1977.

Dew, Charles B. *Ironmaker to the Confederacy: Joseph Reid Anderson and the Tredegar Iron Works.* New Haven: Yale University Press, 1966.

Donald, David. "The Pro-Slavery Argument Reconsidered." *Journal of Southern History* 38 (February 1971): 3–18.

Doyle, Don H. *New Men, New Cities, New South: Atlanta, Nashville, Charleston, Mobile, 1860–1910.* Chapel Hill: University of North Carolina Press, 1990.

Dubay, Robert W. "Mississippi." In *The Confederate Governors*, edited by W. Buck Yearns, 108–29. Athens, Ga.: University of Georgia Press, 1985.

DuBose, John Witherspoon. *The Life and Times of William Lowndes Yancey*. 2 vols. New York: Peter Smith, 1942.

Easterby, James H. "The Charleston Commercial Convention of 1854." *South Atlantic Quarterly* 25 (April 1926): 181–97.

Eaton, Clement. *The Freedom-of-Thought Struggle in the Old South*. New York: Harper & Row, 1964.

Escott, Paul D. *Many Excellent People: Power and Privilege in North Carolina, 1850–1900*. Chapel Hill: University of North Carolina Press, 1985.

Evans, Eli. *Judah P. Benjamin: The Jewish Confederate*. New York: The Free Press, 1987.

Evans, Harry Howard. "James Robb: Banker and Pioneer Railroad Builder of Antebellum Louisiana." *Louisiana Historical Quarterly* 23 (January 1940): 170–258.

Faust, Drew Gilpin, ed. *The Ideology of Slavery: Proslavery Thought in the Antebellum South, 1830–1860*. Baton Rouge: Louisiana State University Press, 1981.

Fields, Barbara Jeanne. "The Advent of Capitalist Agriculture: The New South in a Bourgeois World." In *Essays on the Postbellum Southern Economy*, edited by Thavolia Glymph and John J. Kushma, 73–94. The Walter Prescott Webb Memorial Lectures, no. 18. College Station: Texas A & M University Press for the University of Texas at Arlington, 1985.

Fite, Gilbert C. *Cotton Fields No More: Southern Agriculture, 1865–1980*. Lexington: University Press of Kentucky, 1984.

Fitzgerald, Michael W. "'To Give Our Votes to the Party': Black Political Agitation and Agricultural Change in Alabama, 1865–1870." *Journal of American History* 76 (September 1989): 489–505.

Fogel, Robert William. *Without Consent or Contract: The Rise and Fall of American Slavery*. New York: W. W. Norton, 1989.

Fogel, Robert William and Stanley L. Engerman. *Time on the Cross: The Economics of American Negro Slavery*. 2 vols. Boston: Little, Brown and Co., 1974.

Folsom, Burton W., II. "The Politics of Elites: Prominence and Party in Davidson County, Tennessee, 1835–1861." *Journal of Southern History* 39 (August 1973): 359–78.

Foner, Eric. *Reconstruction: America's Unfinished Revolution, 1863–1877*. The New American Nation Series, edited by Henry Steele Commager and Richard B. Morris. New York: Harper & Row, 1988.

Ford, Lacy K., Jr. *Origins of Southern Radicalism: The South Carolina Upcountry, 1800–1860.* New York: Oxford University Press, 1988.

———. "Rednecks and Merchants: Economic Development and Social Tensions in the South Carolina Upcountry, 1865–1900." *Journal of American History* 71 (September 1984): 294–318.

Foster, Gaines M. *Ghosts of the Confederacy: Defeat, the Lost Cause, and the Emergence of the New South, 1865 to 1913.* New York: Oxford University Press, 1987.

Fox-Genovese, Elizabeth. *Within the Plantation Household: Black and White Women of the Old South.* Chapel Hill: University of North Carolina Press, 1988.

Fox-Genovese, Elizabeth, and Eugene D. Genovese. *Fruits of Merchant Capital: Slavery and Bourgeois Property in the Rise and Expansion of Capitalism.* New York: Oxford University Press, 1983.

Fredrickson, George M. "Down on the Farm." *New York Review of Books* 34 (April 23, 1987): 37–39.

Freehling, William W. *The Road to Disunion.* Vol. 1, *Secessionists at Bay, 1776–1854.* New York: Oxford University Press, 1990.

Futrell, Robert F. "Efforts of Mississippians to Encourage Immigration, 1865–1880." *Journal of Mississippi History* 20 (April 1958): 59–76.

Gambill, Edward L. *Conservative Ordeal: Northern Democrats and Reconstruction, 1865–1868.* Ames: Iowa State University Press, 1981.

Gaston, Paul M. *The New South Creed: A Study in Southern Mythmaking.* New York: Alfred A. Knopf, 1970; Vintage Books, 1973.

Genovese, Eugene D. *The Political Economy of Slavery: Studies in the Economy and Society of the Slave South.* New York: Pantheon, 1965; Vintage Books, 1965.

———. *The World the Slaveholders Made: Two Essays in Interpretation.* New York: Pantheon, 1969; Vintage Books, 1971.

Goldfarb, Stephen J. "A Note on Limits to the Growth of the Cotton-Textile Industry in the Old South." *Journal of Southern History* 48 (November 1982): 545–58.

Goldfield, David R. *Cotton Fields and Skyscrapers: Southern City and Region, 1607–1980.* Baton Rouge: Louisiana State University Press, 1982.

———. "Pursuing the American Urban Dream: Cities in the Old South." In *The City in Southern History: The Growth of Urban Civilization in the South,* edited by Blaine A. Brownell and David R. Goldfield, 52–91. Port Washington, N.Y.: Kennikat Press, 1977.

Goldin, Claudia Dale. *Urban Slavery in the American South, 1820–1860: A Quantitative History.* Chicago: University of Chicago Press, 1976.

Gonzales, John Edmond. "Henry Stuart Foote: A Republican Appointee in Louisiana." *Louisiana History* 1 (Spring 1960): 137–46.

———. "Henry Stuart Foote: Confederate Congressman and Exile." *Civil War History* 11 (December 1965): 384–95.

Gutman, Herbert G. "Work, Culture, and Society in Industrializing America, 1815–1919." *American Historical Review* 88 (June 1973): 531–87.

Hahn, Steven. "The Yeomanry of the Nonplantation South: Upper Piedmont Georgia, 1850–1860." In *Class, Conflict, and Consensus: Antebellum Southern Community Studies*, edited by Orville Vernon Burton and Robert C. McMath, Jr., 29–56. Westport, Conn.: Greenwood Press, 1982.

Hansen, Susan B. "Elite Informants and Theoretical Guidance in Policy Analysis." In *Handbook of Political Theory and Policy Science*, edited by Edward Bryan Portis and Michael B. Levy, 199–211. Westport, Conn.: Greenwood Press, 1988.

Harris, William C. *The Day of the Carpetbagger: Republican Reconstruction in Mississippi*. Baton Rouge: Louisiana State University Press, 1979.

———. *Presidential Reconstruction in Mississippi*. Baton Rouge: Louisiana State University Press, 1967.

Hays, Samuel P. "New Possibilities for American Political History: The Social Analysis of Political Life." In *Sociology and History: Methods*, edited by Seymour M. Lipset and Richard Hofstadter, 181–227. New York: Basic Books, 1968.

Hearden, Patrick J. *Independence and Empire: The New South's Cotton Mill Campaign, 1865–1901*. De Kalb: Northern Illinois University Press, 1982.

Heath, Milton S. "Public Railroad Construction and the Development of Private Enterprise in the South Before 1861." *Journal of Economic History*, Supplement to 10 (1950): 40–67.

Hesseltine, William B. *Confederate Leaders in the New South*. Baton Rouge: Louisiana State University Press, 1950.

Hesseltine, William B., and Larry Gara. "Mississippi's Confederate Leaders After the War." *Journal of Mississippi History* 13 (1951): 88–100.

Hill, Samuel S., Jr., ed. *Encyclopedia of Religion in the South*. Macon, Ga.: Mercer University Press, 1984.

Hodder, Frank Heywood. "The Railroad Background of the Kansas-Nebraska Act." *Mississippi Valley Historical Review* 12 (June 1925): 3–22.

Holzman, Robert S. *Adapt or Perish: The Life of General Roger A. Pryor, C.S.A.* Hamden, Conn.: Archon Books, 1976.

Howe, Daniel Walker. "American Victorianism as a Culture." *American Quarterly* 27 (December 1975): 507–32.

Hume, Richard L. "The Black and Tan Constitutional Conventions of 1867–

1869 in Ten Former Confederate States: A Study of Their Membership."
Ph.D. diss., University of Washington, 1969.

Hunter, Floyd. *Community Power Structure.* Chapel Hill: University of North
Carolina Press, 1953.

Inscoe, John C. *Mountain Masters, Slavery, and the Sectional Crisis in Western
North Carolina.* Knoxville: University of Tennessee Press, 1989.

Jackson, Carlton. "Alabama's Hilliard: A Nationalistic Rebel of the Old
South." *Alabama Historical Quarterly* 31 (Fall and Winter, 1969): 183–205.

Johnson, Allen, and Dumas Malone, eds. *Dictionary of American Biography.* 20
vols. New York: Charles Scribner's Sons, 1928–1937.

Johnson, Michael P. "Wealth and Class in Charleston in 1860." In *From the
Old South to the New: Essays on the Transitional South,* edited by Walter J.
Fraser, Jr., and Winfred B. Moore, Jr., 65–80. Westport, Conn.: Greenwood
Press, 1981.

Jordan, Weymouth T. *Rebels in the Making: Planters' Conventions and Southern
Propaganda.* Tuscaloosa: Confederate Publishing Co., 1958.

Kallenbach, Joseph E., and Jessamine S. Kallenbach. *American State Governors,
1776–1976.* 3 vols. Dobbs Ferry, N.Y.: Oceana Publications, 1977–1982.

Kaplan, Benjamin. "Judah P. Benjamin." In *Jews in the South,* edited by
Leonard Dinnerstein and Mary Dale Palsson, 75–88. Baton Rouge: Louisiana State University Press, 1973.

Klein, Maury. *Union Pacific: Birth of a Railroad, 1862–1893.* Garden City, N.Y.:
Doubleday & Co., 1987.

Kolchin, Peter. "The Business Press and Reconstruction, 1865–1868." *Journal
of Southern History* 33 (May 1967): 183–96.

Kruman, Marc W. *Parties and Politics in North Carolina, 1836–1865.* Baton
Rouge: Louisiana State University Press, 1983.

Lander, Ernest M., Jr. "Charleston: Manufacturing Center of the Old South."
Journal of Southern History 26 (August 1960): 330–51.

Lebergott, Stanley. "Why the South Lost: Commercial Purpose in the Confederacy, 1861–1865." *Journal of American History* 70 (June 1983): 58–74.

Luraghi, Raimondo. *The Rise and Fall of the Plantation South.* New York: New
Viewpoints, 1978.

McCardell, John. *The Idea of a Southern Nation: Southern Nationalists and Southern Nationalism, 1830–1860.* New York: W. W. Norton, 1979.

Maddex, Jack P., Jr. *The Virginia Conservatives, 1867–1879: A Study in Reconstruction Politics.* Chapel Hill: University of North Carolina Press, 1970.

May, Robert E. *John A. Quitman: Old South Crusader.* Baton Rouge: Louisiana
State University Press, 1985.

————. *The Southern Dream of a Caribbean Empire, 1854–1861.* Baton Rouge: Louisiana State University Press, 1973.

Meade, Robert Douthat. *Judah P. Benjamin: Confederate Statesman.* New York: Oxford University Press, 1943.

Means, Emilia Gay. "East Texas and the Transcontinental Railroad." *East Texas Historical Journal* 25 (1987): 49–59.

Mellichamp, Josephine. *Senators from Georgia.* Huntsville: The Strode Publishers, 1976.

Mills, C. Wright. *The Power Elite.* New York: Oxford University Press, 1956.

Miner, H. Craig. *The St. Louis-San Francisco Transcontinental Railroad: The Thirty-fifth Parallel Project, 1853–1890.* Lawrence: University Press of Kansas, 1972.

Mitchell, Betty L. *Edmund Ruffin: A Biography.* Bloomington: Indiana University Press, 1981.

Moore, John Hebron. *The Emergence of the Cotton Kingdom in the Old Southwest: Mississippi, 1770–1860.* Baton Rouge: Louisiana State University Press, 1988.

Morriss, Peter. "Power in New Haven: A Reassessment of 'Who Governs?'" *British Journal of Political Science* 2 (October 1972): 457–65.

Niven, John. *John C. Calhoun and the Price of Union: A Biography.* Baton Rouge: Louisiana State University Press, 1988.

Oakes, James. *The Ruling Race: A History of American Slaveholders.* New York: Alfred A. Knopf, 1982.

————. *Slavery and Freedom: An Interpretation of the Old South.* New York: Alfred A. Knopf, 1990.

O'Brien, Gail Williams. *The Legal Fraternity and the Making of a New South Community, 1848–1882.* Athens, Ga.: University of Georgia Press, 1986.

Osborne, Ray Gregg. "Political Career of James Chamberlain Jones, 1840–1857." *Tennessee Historical Quarterly* 12 (September–December 1948): 195–228, 322–34.

Owen, Thomas McAdory. *History of Alabama and Dictionary of Alabama Biography.* 4 vols. Chicago: S. J. Clarke, 1921.

Owsley, Frank L. "The Clays in Early Alabama History." *Alabama Review* 2 (October 1949): 243–68.

Parker, William N. "The South in the National Economy, 1865–1970." *Southern Economic Journal* 46 (April 1980): 1019–48.

Parrish, William E. *Missouri Under Radical Rule, 1865–1870.* Columbia: University of Missouri Press, 1965.

Pereyra, Lillian A. *James Lusk Alcorn: Persistent Whig.* Baton Rouge: Louisiana State University Press, 1966.

Perman, Michael. *Reunion Without Compromise: The South and Reconstruction, 1865–1868.* Cambridge: Cambridge University Press, 1973.

———. *The Road to Redemption: Southern Politics, 1869–1879.* Chapel Hill: University of North Carolina Press, 1984.

Perrin, William H., J. H. Battle, and G. C. Kniffin. *Kentucky: Genealogy and Biography.* 7 vols. 1885. Reprint. Owensboro, Ky.: Genealogical Reference Co., 1972.

Perrucci, Robert, and Marc Pilisuk. "Leaders and Ruling Elites: The Interorganizational Bases of Community Power." *American Sociological Review* 35 (December 1970): 1040–57.

Pessen, Edward. "How Different from Each Other Were the Antebellum North and South?" *American Historical Review* 85 (December 1980): 1119–49.

Peterson, Owen. "Speaking in the Southern Commercial Conventions, 1837–1859." In *Oratory in the Old South, 1828–1860,* edited by Waldo W. Braden, 190–217. Baton Rouge: Louisiana State University Press, 1970.

Phillips, Ulrich B. "The Central Theme of Southern History." *American Historical Review* 34 (October 1928): 30–43.

Potter, David M. *The Impending Crisis, 1848–1860.* New York: Harper & Row, 1976

Price, Charles Lewis. "Railroads and Reconstruction in North Carolina, 1865–1871." Ph.D. diss., University of North Carolina, 1959.

Prichard, Walter, ed. "A Forgotten Engineer: G. W. R. Bayley and His 'History of the Railroads of Louisiana.'" *Louisiana Historical Quarterly* 30 (October 1947): 1065–1325.

Rabinowitz, Howard N. "Continuity and Change: Southern Urban Development, 1860–1900." In *The City in Southern History: The Growth of Urban Civilization in the South,* edited by Blaine A. Brownell and David R. Goldfield, 92–122. Port Washington, N.Y.: Kennikat Press, 1977.

Reed, Merl E. "Government Investment and Economic Growth: Louisiana's Ante-Bellum Railroads." *Journal of Southern History* 28 (May 1962): 183–201.

———. *New Orleans and the Railroads: The Struggle for Commercial Empire, 1830–1860.* Baton Rouge: Louisiana State University Press for the Louisiana Historical Association, 1966.

Reed, S. G. *A History of the Texas Railroads.* Houston: The St. Clair Publishing Co., 1941.

Rippy, J. Fred. *The United States and Mexico.* New York: F. S. Crofts & Co., 1931.

Roark, James L. *Masters Without Slaves: Southern Planters in the Civil War and Reconstruction.* New York: W. W. Norton, 1977.

Roberson, Jere W. "The Memphis Commercial Convention of 1853: Southern Dreams and 'Young America.'" *Tennessee Historical Quarterly* 33 (Fall 1974): 279–96.

———. "To Build a Pacific Railroad: Congress, Texas, and the Charleston Convention of 1854." *Southwestern Historical Quarterly* 78 (October 1974): 117–39.

Rogers, William Warren, ed. "Nelson Tift Applies for a Pardon, 1865." *Georgia Historical Quarterly* 51 (June 1967): 230–32.

Ross, Earle Dudley. *The Liberal Republican Movement.* New York: Cornell University, 1919.

Russel, Robert Royal. *Economic Aspects of Southern Sectionalism, 1840–1861.* Urbana: University of Illinois Press, 1924.

———. *Improvement of Communication with the Pacific Coast as an Issue in American Politics, 1783–1864.* Cedar Rapids: The Torch Press, 1948.

———. "The Pacific Railway Issue in Politics Prior to the Civil War." *Mississippi Valley Historical Review* 12 (June 1925): 187–201.

Rustow, Dankwart A. "The Study of Elites: Who's Who, When, and How." *World Politics* 18 (1966): 690–717.

Schweikart, Larry. *Banking in the American South from the Age of Jackson to Reconstruction.* Baton Rouge: Louisiana State University Press, 1987.

Seip, Terry L. *The South Returns to Congress: Men, Economic Measures, and Intersectional Relationships, 1868–1879.* Baton Rouge: Louisiana State University Press, 1983.

Shore, Laurence. *Southern Capitalists: The Ideological Leadership of an Elite, 1832–1885.* Chapel Hill: University of North Carolina Press, 1986.

Silbey, Joel H. "Conclusion." In *A Crisis of Republicanism: American Politics in the Civil War Era,* edited by Lloyd E. Ambrosius, 129–31. Lincoln: University of Nebraska Press, 1990.

Silverman, Catherine S. "Of Wealth, Virtue, and Intelligence: The Redeemers and Their Triumph in Virginia and North Carolina, 1865–1877." Ph.D. diss., City University of New York, 1972.

Simkins, Francis Butler, and Robert Hilliard Woody. *South Carolina During Reconstruction.* Chapel Hill: University of North Carolina Press, 1932.

Skipper, Otis Clark. *J. D. B. De Bow: Magazinist of the Old South.* Athens: University of Georgia Press, 1958.

Smith, James Douglas. "Virginia During Reconstruction, 1865–1870—A Political, Economic, and Social Study." Ph.D. diss., University of Virginia, 1960.

Stone, Lawrence. "Prosopography." *Daedalus* (Winter 1971): 46–79.

Stover, John F. *American Railroads.* Chicago: University of Chicago Press, 1961.

————. *History of the Baltimore and Ohio Railroad*. West Lafayette: Purdue University Press, 1987.

————. *Iron Road to the West: American Railroads in the 1850s*. New York: Columbia University Press, 1978.

————. *The Railroads of the South, 1865–1900*. Chapel Hill: University of North Carolina Press, 1955.

Sturges, Kenneth M. *American Chambers of Commerce*. New York: Moffatt, Yard and Co., 1915.

Summers, Mark W. *Railroads, Reconstruction, and the Gospel of Prosperity: Aid Under the Radical Republicans, 1865–1877*. Princeton: Princeton University Press, 1984.

Sydnor, Charles S. *The Development of Southern Sectionalism, 1819–1848*. Baton Rouge: Louisiana State University Press, 1948.

Takaki, Ronald T. *A Pro-Slavery Crusade: The Agitation to Reopen the African Slave Trade*. New York: The Free Press, 1971.

Taylor, Joe Gray. *Louisiana Reconstructed, 1863–1877*. Baton Rouge: Louisiana State University Press, 1974.

Thomas, Peter C. "Matthew Fontaine Maury and the Problem of Virginia's Identity, 1865–1873." *Virginia Magazine of History and Biography* 90 (April 1982): 213–37.

Thompson, George H. *Arkansas and Reconstruction: The Influence of Geography, Economics, and Personality*. Port Washington, N.Y.: National University Publications, Kennikat Press, 1976.

Thornton, J. Mills, III. "Fiscal Policy and the Failure of Radical Reconstruction in the Lower South." In *Race, Region, and Reconstruction: Essays in Honor of C. Vann Woodward*, edited by J. Morgan Kousser and James M. McPherson, 349–94. New York: Oxford University Press, 1982.

————. *Politics and Power in a Slave Society: Alabama, 1800–1860*. Baton Rouge: Louisiana State University Press, 1978.

Townes, A. Jane. "The Effect of Emancipation on Large Landholdings, Nelson and Goochland Counties, Virginia." *Journal of Southern History* 45 (August 1979): 403–12.

Van Deusen, John G. *The Ante-Bellum Southern Commercial Conventions*. Durham: Duke University Press, 1926.

Wakelyn, Jon L. *Biographical Dictionary of the Confederacy*. Westport, Conn.: Greenwood Press, 1977.

Wallenstein, Peter. *From Slave South to New South: Public Policy in Nineteenth-Century Georgia*. Chapel Hill: University of North Carolina Press, 1987.

Warner, Ezra J., and W. Buck Yearns, eds. *Biographical Register of the Confederate Congress*. Baton Rouge: Louisiana State University Press, 1975.

Wayne, Michael. *The Reshaping of Plantation Society: The Natchez District, 1860–1880*. Baton Rouge: Louisiana State University Press, 1983.

Wender, Herbert. "The Southern Commercial Convention at Savannah, 1856." *Georgia Historical Quarterly* 15 (June 1931): 173–91.

———. *Southern Commercial Conventions, 1837–1859*. Baltimore: The Johns Hopkins Press, 1930.

Wharton, Vernon Lane. *The Negro in Mississippi, 1865–1890*. Chapel Hill: University of North Carolina Press, 1947; New York: Harper & Row, 1965.

Wiener, Jonathan M. "Class Structure and Economic Development in the American South, 1865–1955." *American Historical Review* 84 (October 1979): 970–92.

———. *Social Origins of the New South: Alabama, 1860–1885*. Baton Rouge: Louisiana State University Press, 1978.

Wiggins, Sarah Woolfolk. *The Scalawag in Alabama Politics, 1865–1881*. University: University of Alabama Press, 1977.

Wiltse, Charles M. *John C. Calhoun: Secessionist, 1840–1850*. Indianapolis: The Bobbs-Merrill Company, 1951.

Winther, Oscar Osburn. *The Transportation Frontier: Trans-Mississippi West, 1865–1890*. Histories of the American Frontier, edited by Ray Allen Billington. New York: Holt, Rinehart and Winston, 1964.

Woodman, Harold D. *King Cotton and His Retainers: Financing and Marketing the Cotton Crop of the South, 1800–1925*. Lexington: University Press of Kentucky, 1968.

———. "Postbellum Social Change and Its Effects on Marketing the South's Cotton Crop." *Agricultural History* 56 (January 1982): 215–30.

———. "The Reconstruction of the Cotton Plantation in the New South." In *Essays on the Postbellum Southern Economy*, edited by Thavolia Glymph and John J. Kushma, 95–119. The Walter Prescott Webb Memorial Lectures, no. 18. College Station: Texas A & M University Press for the University of Texas at Arlington, 1985.

———. "Sequel to Slavery: The New History Views the Postbellum South." *Journal of Southern History* 43 (November 1977): 523–54.

Woodward, C. Vann. *Origins of the New South, 1877–1913*. Baton Rouge: Louisiana State University Press, 1951.

———. *Reunion and Reaction: The Compromise of 1877 and the End of Reconstruction*. Boston: Little, Brown and Co., 1951.

————. *Thinking Back: The Perils of Writing History.* Baton Rouge: Louisiana State University Press, 1986.

Woolfolk, George Ruble. *The Cotton Regency: The Northern Merchants and Reconstruction, 1865–1880.* New York: Bookman Associates, 1958.

Wooster, Ralph A. *The People in Power: Courthouse and Statehouse in the Lower South, 1850–1860.* Knoxville: University of Tennessee Press, 1969.

————. *Politicians, Planters, and Plain Folk: Courthouse and Statehouse in the Upper South, 1850–1860.* Knoxville: University of Tennessee Press, 1975.

————. *The Secession Conventions of the South.* Princeton: Princeton University Press, 1962.

Wright, Gavin. *Old South, New South: Revolutions in the Southern Economy since the Civil War.* New York: Basic Books, 1986.

————. *The Political Economy of the Cotton South: Households, Markets, and Wealth in the Nineteenth Century.* New York: W. W. Norton, 1978.

Wyatt-Brown, Bertram. *Southern Honor: Ethics and Behavior in the Old South.* New York: Oxford University Press, 1982.

Wynne, Lewis Nicholas. *The Continuity of Cotton: Planter Politics in Georgia, 1865–1892.* Macon, Ga.: Mercer University Press, 1986.

INDEX

Abbott, Richard H., 197
Accommodationists: convention delegates as, 7–8; among Convention Elite, 78–83
Adams, James H., 134, 135, 137
African apprentice system, 155, 157
Age: of convention delegates, 47–48, 161, 189–90
Agricultural Association of Slave-holding States, 97
Agriculture: importance of, 5, 6, 7–8, 88, 89, 97, 192, 217, 221, 242, 245, 246; reform of, 97; importance of to South, 169, 181–83
Alcorn, James L.: biography of, 81; requests amnesty, 81, 174; on levee repairs, 205; mentioned, 40, 185, 198
Alexander, Thomas B.: on leadership persistence, 4, 177, 191; on Confederate congressmen, 62–63, 268n5
Allen, Thomas, 40, 126
Amazon River valley, 172
Amnesty, general political: debated, 229–30, 235
Amnesty, presidential: requests for, 71, 75, 79, 81, 82, 174–80
Anderson, Charles: biography of, 76; mentioned, 77, 185, 202, 207
Anderson, Joseph Reid: biography of, 81–82; requests amnesty, 82, 175; mentioned, 40, 106, 169, 185, 223
Appleton's Cyclopedia, 219–20
Arnin, Frank, 233
Ashe, William S., 169
Atchison, Topeka and Santa Fe Railroad, 206
Atlanta Constitution, 215
Atlanta 1881 International Cotton Exposition, 90
Atlantic and Ohio Telegraph Company (Western Union), 186, 231
Atlantic and Pacific Railroad, 109, 206, 227
Attica, Greece, 131

Bachrach, Peter, 41–42
Baker, R. B., 138

Baldwin, John Brown, 20
Baltimore and Ohio Railroad, 77, 104, 222, 235
Baltimore 1852 commercial convention: purpose of, 19, 93; on railroads, 105; on southern Pacific railroad, 108; on direct trade, 116, 117; sectionalism of, 126; social activities of, 236
Baltimore 1871 commercial convention: delegate description, 231; opening day, 232; on reconciliation, 233, 235; on railroads, 233; on river and harbor improvements, 233; on shipbuilding, 234; on commerce regulation, 234; on fiscal policies, 234; on immigration, 234; social activities of, 236; mentioned, 22
Baltimore Sun, 235
Banking: in postwar South, 184; federal policies debated, postwar, 203–4
Banks, Nathaniel P., 186, 223, 226, 230
Banks, Robert T., 232
Barksdale, Ethelbert, 158
Barney, William L., 89, 134
Bateman, Fred, 9–10, 119
Bates, Edward, 93
Beck, John J., 191
Bell, John: biography of, 73; mentioned, 40, 61, 109, 120, 123
Benjamin, Judah P.: biography of, 72–73; mentioned, 40, 71, 106, 169
Bennett, Hendley S., 154
Bensel, Richard F., 197
Benton, Thomas Hart, 151
Beringer, Richard E., 62–63, 268n5
Bethea, Tristam B., 73, 146
Bible, 131
Billings, Dwight B., 4, 191, 246–47
Birthplaces: of convention delegates, 58–59, 187
Bishop, Richard M.: biography of, 77; mentioned, 22, 186, 222, 231, 233
Black codes, 179, 182
Black southerners: none present at conventions, 187
Black suffrage, 180